DATE DUE

JA __ '94			
SE 23 '94			
DE 22 '95			
JL 10 09			

Twentieth-Century France

Twentieth-Century France

Politics and Society 1898–1991

James F. McMillan
Senior Lecturer in History, University of York

Edward Arnold
A division of Hodder & Stoughton
LONDON NEW YORK MELBOURNE AUCKLAND

© 1985 and 1992 James F. McMillan

First published in Great Britain as *Dreyfus to de Gaulle* 1985
Published as *Twentieth-Century France*
(with revisions and additional chapters) 1992

Distributed in the USA by Routledge, Chapman and Hall, Inc.
29 West 35th Street, New York, NY 10001

British Library Cataloguing-in-Publication Data
McMillan, James F.
  Twentieth-century France: Politics and society in
  France 1898–1991.
  I. Title
  944.08

  ISBN 0-340-52239-9

Library of Congress Cataloging in Publication Data
McMillan. James F., 1948–
    [Dreyfus to de Gaulle]
    Twentieth/century France: politics and society in France.
  1898–1991/James F. McMillan.
      p. cm.
    'Chapters 1–18 first published in Great Britain as Dreyfus to
  de Gaulle, 1985'–
    Includes bibliographical references and index.
    ISBN 0-340-52239-9: $15.95
    1. France – Politics and government – 20th century. 2. Political
  stability – France – History – 20th century. 3. Social movements –
  France – History – 20th century. 4. Politics and war. I. Title.
  DC369.M36   1992
  944.081–dc20   91-30407
                                                               CIP

Typeset in 10/11 pt Linotron Times Roman by Rowland Phototypesetting Limited,
Bury St Edmunds, Suffolk. Printed and bound in Great Britain for Edward Arnold,
a division of Hodder and Stoughton Limited, Mill Road, Dunton Green, Sevenoaks,
Kent TN13 2YA by Biddles Limited, Guildford and King's Lynn.

To the memory of my cousin, John William McMillan, 1941–83
and of my friend Ian Silcock, 1945–1988

Contents

Preface

The present work is a revised and enlarged edition of *Dreyfus to de Gaulle: Politics and Society in France 1898–1969*, published in 1985. Encouraged by the generally favourable reception accorded to the first edition, I have sought to act on the suggestion made by a number of reviewers that I bring the story right up to date. Hence the addition of two substantial new chapters dealing with the period after the departure of de Gaulle in April 1969 to the appointment of Edith Cresson as France's first woman prime minister in May 1991. I have profited, too, from the opportunity to correct a number of errors in the original text as well as to incorporate new material based on the latest research, the extent of which is reflected in the considerable extensions to the bibliography. In a new 'Afterword' I have attempted to pull together some of the more important elements in the narrative. As before, the focus is on national political life, which inevitably does scant justice to themes such as regional diversity and cultural expression. I hope, however, that the book at least succeeds in placing politics within a larger social and economic context and in rendering intelligible a complicated but always fascinating, and ultimately inspiring, history.

James F. McMillan
June 1991
York

I

1898–1914 *The* Belle Époque

1
France and the Dreyfus Affair

Before the Affair

In 1898 the Third Republic had been in existence for 28 years. Born accidentally in 1870 as a direct consequence of the military disasters sustained by the Second Empire in the Franco-Prussian War, it had already lasted longer than any previous regime since the French Revolution. Its continuing survival, however, was not something its rulers took for granted, since its early years were spent in establishing and consolidating its authority against challenges from both Left and Right.

The first challenge came from the Left, in the shape of the Paris Commune, a patriotic and revolutionary uprising of the Parisian working classes. The leaders of the new Republic, headed by Adolphe Thiers, suppressed the shortlived revolution in May 1871 with a ferocity worthy of the Tsars, thereby serving notice from the outset of the Republic's commitment to the defence of order and property. But true conservatives still hankered after a monarchical restoration: and, having won a majority in the National Assembly elected in February 1871, they had the opportunity of effecting one. In the end they failed, partly because of internal differences in the monarchist camp, more because of the absence of genuine monarchist sentiment in the country at large. By the end of the 1870s it was clear that the Republicans had been successful in their endeavours to convince the great mass of Frenchmen – which meant, above all, the peasantry – that the Republic was the best guarantee of firm, stable and moderate government. Two electoral victories testified eloquently to the Republican ascendancy. In 1877 they thwarted President MacMahon's attempt to reverse their victory at the polls in 1876 by his dissolution of the Chamber of Deputies on 16 May and ordering of fresh elections, which, despite all the pressure brought to bear by the administration on behalf of 'official' candidates, the Republicans still won. Then in 1879 they secured a majority in the second chamber, the Senate. When, the same year, Jules Grévy took over from MacMahon as President of the Republic, the moderate or 'Opportunist' Republicans were masters in their own house. They were still in power 20 years later.

The Republican ideology derived from a particular reading of French history. At its core was an unequivocal acceptance of the Revolution of 1789, understood as the fountain and origin of the principle of popular sovereignty. The true ends of political struggle were the establishment and defence of a democratic Republic against the forces of reaction and privilege, represented by Royalists, Bonapartists, and, not least, the Catholic Church. Rationalists, often subscribers to positivism and fascinated by science, the new generation of Republican leaders – men such as Léon Gambetta and Jules Ferry – believed in progress and had a boundless faith in what could be accomplished by education. In the early 1880s they carried through a series of 'laic laws', in the teeth of clerical and conservative opposition, to establish a system of free, compulsory and secular State education at the primary level. For them, the great matters of politics were the safety of the Republic, the inculcation of patriotism, the laicity of the State – not the 'social question' or the politics of class struggle, whose very existence they denied. Such an ideology struck responsive chords among the great mass of the French people. Ostensibly democratic, Republicans could count on the support of all shades of 'progressive' opinion in a crisis. At the same time, the regime did not neglect the material interests of important sections of the French population – notably those of the peasants and small, independent producers – as we shall have occasion to see. The 'Freycinet Plan' of 1878, by which the State set up a massive investment programme to develop the country's communications networks (especially the railways), did much to win the business community over to the Republic.

Not that the regime was without its critics. As will be explained in chapter 2, 'Radical' Republicans considered that the moderation of the Opportunists was excessive. By the 1890s the far Left was once again a force to be reckoned with, resuscitated and reorganized after the crushing of the Commune and bent on making class the central issue in politics. On the extreme Right, no form of Republicanism was acceptable to either diehard monarchists or the nascent 'revolutionary' Right, which preached the doctrines that came to be known as 'integral nationalism'. Republicans, therefore, were ever fearful for the safety and continuing survival of their regime, their paranoia heightened by episodes such as the Boulangist campaign of the late 1880s, when a protest movement spearheaded by General Boulanger briefly united the discontents of both Left and Right and came close to toppling the Republic in 1889. The regime also laid itself open to attack by its enemies through the venality of some of its leaders, which came to light in scandals such as the Daniel Wilson Affair of 1887 and the Panama Scandal of 1892.

To a degree, the Republic's own constitution enhanced the impression of vulnerability. The executive power was deliberately kept weak, so that the President was frequently an ineffective and insignificant figure. Real power in the political system lay with the Chamber of Deputies, which asserted its right to bring down ministries with monotonous regularity (the Third Republic had 60 governments between 1870 and 1914). The second chamber, the Senate, was elected by indirect suffrage and, staffed largely by superannuated professional politicians and civil servants, over-represented rural, conservative France, thus acting as a further brake on any tendency towards radical political initiatives. Nevertheless, in reality, the Republic was far from being the shaky edifice its critics made it out to be. Presidents did have powers (to appoint the prime minister, to sign treaties with foreign governments) if they cared to use them: much depended on the man and the circumstances in which he held office. Ministerial instability was to some extent an optical illusion, since it was more often than not the same faces that reappeared in reshuffled cabinets. Aristide Briand, for instance, of whom much more will be heard, was a minister in 25 governments and in all held office for some

16½ years. On the whole, however, the political system added up to a fairly negative conception of government and took a rather complacent view of the social and political order, saving always its eternal vigilance against threats from 'reactionaries' and 'clericals'.

By the 1890s the moderate Republicans appeared more securely installed than ever. Not only had they survived all the best efforts of their enemies to overthrow them, but, from 1892, it became evident that Pope Leo XIII wished French Catholics and royalists to abandon their futile machinations against the regime and to work within the existing institutions. Moderate Republican leaders welcomed this *Ralliement*, or rallying of French Catholics to the Republic. Politically, they hoped that it would produce a broadening of the base of the regime to include former opponents on the Right along with the further isolation of the Left. The condemnation for treason of an obscure army captain, Dreyfus, had no immediate repercussions on the *Ralliement*, which continued to be promoted by both Catholic and Republican politicians under the Méline government of 1896–8. Whether the *Ralliement* would have succeeded had the Dreyfus Case not become the Dreyfus Affair may well be doubted, since the 'new spirit' did not reach down to grass-roots supporters of either the Church or the Republic. But what is not in doubt is that the emergence of the affair not only killed the *Ralliement*, but confronted the Third Republic with a crisis which rocked the regime to its foundations.

The Development of the Affair

In September 1894 the French counter-espionage service discovered that military secrets were being passed to Germany. The evidence came from the now infamous *bordereau*, a list containing military information, allegedly recovered from the waste-paper basket of the German military attaché in Paris. French Intelligence identified the handwriting on the *bordereau* as that of Captain Alfred Dreyfus, an Alsatian Jewish officer on the General Staff. Protesting his innocence in vain, Dreyfus was convicted of treason by a military court in December 1894 and banished to life imprisonment on Devil's Island.

There matters might well have rested, but for the Dreyfus family's refusal to accept the army's verdict. By dint of patient enquiries they eventually discovered that, after all, it was not the *bordereau* which formed the principal evidence against Dreyfus, but a secret dossier prepared by Colonel du Paty de Clam and withheld from the defence on the authority of the Minister of War, General Mercier. In order to publicize their findings, the Dreyfus family enlisted the support of Bernard Lazare, a Jewish intellectual, who in 1896 issued a pamphlet entitled *Une erreur judiciaire*, calling for a retrial on the grounds that Dreyfus had been irregularly condemned. Some newspapers began to discuss the matter, mostly unsympathetically, but press speculation at least rekindled public interest in the Dreyfus case, and more important, began to bring to light the evidence adduced at the trial. On 10 November 1896 *Le Matin* published the *bordereau* itself.

In the meantime, and quite independently, the new head of Military Intelligence, Colonel Picquart, had also come to the conclusion that Dreyfus might be innocent. He became aware that, even with Dreyfus safely incarcerated on Devil's Island, military secrets were still being leaked to Germany, and from an intercepted letter in March 1896 (the *petit bleu*) he deduced that the German military attaché's contact was Commandant Esterhazy, a man of highly dubious reputation. Even more disturbingly, Picquart identified Esterhazy's handwriting as matching that on the *bordereau*. On informing his superiors of his investigations, however, Picquart was shocked first by their flat refusal to reopen the Dreyfus case and then by his own transfer to Tunisia. His replacement in Paris was Colonel Henry, the officer originally charged with handling the *bordereau,* who now began to doctor the files with forged evidence of Dreyfus's guilt.

But, even as the army chiefs set about their cover-up, they came under increasing pressure to consider revision. Unwittingly, by feeding evidence to the nationalist and anti-Semitic press, they furnished the Dreyfusards with material which pointed ultimately to the culpability of Esterhazy rather than of Dreyfus. Demands for more information were expressed not only in the press but also in parliament, notably by the prestigious senator Scheurer-Kestner. His doubts, aroused by the Dreyfus family, were exacerbated when he learned about the fate of Picquart. The army was forced to investigate Esterhazy but, in a farcical trial which lasted all of three minutes, completely exonerated him. Picquart, on the other hand, was condemned for contravening the regulations on secrecy and discharged.

The acquittal of Esterhazy soon proved to be a pyrrhic victory. Incensed by the blatant contempt for justice revealed by the military hierarchy, the famous novelist Émile Zola published a sensational open letter – the celebrated *J'accuse* – to the President of the Republic in Clemenceau's newspaper *L'Aurore*. Ridiculing the whitewashing of Esterhazy and singling out certain officers by name (such as Mercier and du Paty de Clam) Zola denounced the army's crime against Dreyfus and warned against a conspiracy to subvert the Republic itself. Overnight, on 13 January 1898, the Dreyfus case ceased to be a judicial matter and emerged as a political question of the first magnitude. Whatever Premier Méline might have said as recently as December 1897, there now very definitely was a Dreyfus 'Affair'.

For the whiff of scandal would not blow away. Zola himself was sentenced for defamation and fled to England. His trial gave rise to further talk about secret documents which, though clearly establishing the guilt of Dreyfus, could not be revealed without implicating the Kaiser and possibly damaging Franco-German relations to the point of unleashing war. Méline's successors in office continued to assert that the army had given them irrefutable evidence of Dreyfus's guilt. Cavaignac, the new Minister of War, unwisely cited some of these 'proofs' in a speech to parliament, which gave the Dreyfusard camp the opportunity to expose them as forgeries, perpetrated by Henry. Acknowledging his crime, the latter committed suicide in August 1898 and Cavaignac resigned. Still the army would not consent to a retrial. This came only under a new President of the Republic (Loubet replaced Félix Faure after the latter expired through over-exerting himself while entertaining his mistress in the Elysée Palace) and a new prime minister (Waldeck-Rousseau succeeded Dupuy in June 1899). In August 1899 the broken victim was brought back from Devil's Island to stand trial at Rennes. Once again, the intransigent military judges found him guilty though this time only by a majority of five to two and 'with extenuating circumstances' – a ludicrous verdict, since Dreyfus was either a traitor or he was not. Convinced that the army would never admit to any judicial error and anxious to liquidate the affair as quickly as possible, Waldeck arranged for Dreyfus to receive a presidential pardon. It was 1906 before the Appeal Court quashed the Rennes verdict. Dreyfus was reinstated in the army, and awarded the Legion of Honour. Picquart, too, was reintegrated into the service, and rose to be a general and minister of war.

Dimensions of the Affair

The full truth about the Dreyfus Affair is still not known, and probably never will be. Theories abound as to who the real traitor was. Historians, like contemporaries, cannot agree on the affair's ultimate significance. Some hold that its importance has been wildly exaggerated in Republican historiography, and that the great mass of the French people was left cold by the whole saga. The affair, in this view, excited Parisians rather than provincials, and never became a major electoral issue, either in 1898 or in 1902. The idea that the country was split into two hostile camps, Dreyfusard and anti-Dreyfusard, should be regarded as a myth manufactured in the press by self-seeking politicians and self-important intellectuals. Others have seen in the Dreyfus Affair a kind of bloodless civil war, an event of greater significance in French history than even the First World War. On balance, it seems clear enough that the affair's true dimensions are to be seized from its capacity to generate passion rather than indifference.

Thus, it was not indifference which lay behind the attempts on the part of the ruling Opportunist politicians to stifle the affair by denying its existence. Rather, they recognized a potentially disruptive threat to the brand of political stability which they had carefully cultivated since 1879 and which left them free to enjoy the benefits of power and property. As Méline well understood, all the agitation and adverse publicity alarmed the business community, particularly as France was due to host the World's Fair exhibition in 1900. Faced with the prospect of political upheaval and a slump in trade, moderate Republicans had every incentive to appeal for domestic tranquillity. Likewise, if the Guesdist socialists dismissed the affair as a 'bourgeois' quarrel, of no relevance to the French working classes, this should not be written off as indifference, but viewed in the context of their short- and long-term strategy for bringing their Marxist version of socialism to power. Socialists were obliged to take up a position on the affair, even a negative one, since the movement was divided in its response to Dreyfus. Jaurès was the chief spokesman for those who saw an opportunity to make socialists the champions of justice and argued powerfully that in order to remain a socialist one was not required to put oneself outside humanity.

It is true enough that genuine partisans of Dreyfus – those whose paramount aim was to see justice done to an innocent man – were always a tiny minority. These *dreyfusistes* can be distinguished from the majority of *dreyfusards*, who saw Dreyfus as a symbol or a cause to be exploited for political advantage. No doubt, there were those who, like Jaurès, contended that justice for Dreyfus was inseparable from the resolution of the political problems bequeathed to France by the French Revolution. Nevertheless, true *dreyfusistes* like Charles Péguy never lost sight of the legal, human and moral dimensions of the case and were disillusioned by its development into a political scandal. Some of these, indeed, resented the decision of Dreyfus and his family to acccpt the Presidential pardon rather than to fight on for a complete vindication. Most *dreyfusards*, however, suffered from no such qualms, since for them the fate of Dreyfus the man was only of secondary importance. For Radical politicians, Dreyfus mattered because he could be used to demonstrate the existence of a reactionary plot against the Republic. Here was a fine opportunity to displace the moderate Republicans in power by breaking up the *Ralliement* and returning to the happy ways of Republican 'concentration' against the 'clerical–militarist threat'. At the same time, to shift the political focus onto Dreyfus had the merit, in the eyes of many Radicals, of diverting attention away from the 'social question' and the issues raised by the socialists. The cry of 'no enemies to the Left' and calls for Republican vigilance could be emotive slogans designed to mask political ambition and social conservatism.

But the affair remains much more than an episode in political intrigue or a fuss created by a handful of intellectuals. The intensity of feeling which it engendered was, if anything, more apparent on the anti-Dreyfusard side. The irrational, intransigent stance adopted by the military chiefs defies any easy explanation. Confronted with Picquart's evidence, they had ample opportunities to reconsider the case against Dreyfus, yet they always rigidly set their faces against revision. Partly, this was a question of human fallibility – they were touchy individuals who resented any challenging of their competence. More fundamentally, perhaps, their mentality was coloured by the ambiguous position in which the French army was placed after 1870.

On the one hand, as inheritors of Jacobin patriotism, Republicans proclaimed that a strong army was essential if France were ever to recover Alsace-Lorraine. Serious, if not wholly successful, attempts to reform the army were made in 1873 and 1889, the aim being to replace the old professional army with genuine universal conscription. Ostensibly, at least, the army enjoyed considerable prestige in most Republican and democratic circles. On the other hand, the Right had come to regard the army as the true respository of the interests of the nation. In contrast to the corrupt parliamentary regime, it embodied the principle of hierarchy and, it was believed, could act as an instrument for the moral reform of society. This was increasingly the view of the officer corps itself. But the army was not without its critics. Conscription had introduced members of the educated middle classes to the discomforts and harsh discipline of military life. Their disagreeable experience was portrayed in a crop of literary works by writers such as Courteline, Lucien Descaves and Georges Darien. The spread of socialism was accompanied by a growth in anti-militarism, which affected even the primary schoolteachers upon whom the Republic's founding fathers had counted so much to be the lay apostles of patriotism.

Such attacks could only compound the uncertainties and rivalries within the army itself: the lack of promotion prospects in peacetime and the tedium of garrison life were not conducive to high morale. At the same time, military leaders were obsessed with French security and the possibility of having to fight a war launched by Germany to break up the recently signed alliance with Russia. War-scares, spy-mania and xenophobia were rife in the 1890s. The counter-espionage service which unmasked the traitor Dreyfus had contingency plans for the mass arrests of aliens and subversives in the event of war. Perhaps it was this almost paranoid belief in its role as the unique guarantor of national security that made the army contest so bitterly what it deemed to be partisan and politically motivated attacks on its honour on the part of the *dreyfusards*.

Whatever its motives, the army clearly conspired to thwart the course of justice. In that sense there was a 'militarist' plot. Whether there was a 'clerical – militarist' plot is another matter. Certainly, the Jesuits were famous for their success in preparing candidates for the military training schools and the well-known Jesuit Father du Lac had close links with military circles, even if he never wielded the fantastic powers of manipulation attributed to him. Most Catholics, of course, like the rest of the population, had no reason, initially, to doubt Dreyfus's guilt. They had confidence in the integrity of the army, believed what successive ministers of war affirmed and noted that the most vociferous champions of Dreyfus were not infrequently sworn enemies of the Church.

On the whole, churchmen preferred not to get involved in the affair. Pope Leo XIII entertained doubts about Dreyfus's guilt but was reluctant to be seen meddling in French domestic politics. Likewise, the French bishops asserted that the matter was an entirely judicial one, and that it was not for them to intervene. Priests were among the contributors to the fund opened by the anti-Semitic newspaper *La Libre Parole* for the widow of Colonel Henry, but the majority maintained a prudent silence. A leading layman, the deputy Albert de Mun, was solicited by the Dreyfus family to take up his case but he refused. On the other hand, a heterogeneous collection of Catholics, which included the veteran politician Louis Buffet, Paul Viollet, a founder member of the League of the Rights of Man, and the Abbé Brugerette, spoke up for Dreyfus. Thus, though generally unsympathetic, French Catholics usually stayed out of the affair. The exceptions were members of the recently founded Assumptionist Order, who through their daily newspaper *La Croix* thundered against Dreyfus and defended the army against what they called a 'Judeo-Masonic conspiracy'. It was above all their violent and anti-Semitic polemics which allowed *dreyfusards* to detect and denounce clerical aggression in the affair. It was they, too, who ensured that, once the *dreyfusards* triumphed, the Church would be a target for retribution.

Among the supporters of Dreyfus, it was the intellectuals who provided the intensity and moral fervour which marked the *dreyfusard* campaign. Their entry was precipitated by Zola's *J'accuse*, which was followed by a *Manifesto of the Intellectuals*, signed by prominent academics, scientists and writers, among them Anatole France, André Gide and Marcel Proust. The prestigious ecole Normale Supérieure at the rue d'Ulm was a hotbed of *dreyfusard* sentiment, thanks largely to the activity of its socialist librarian Lucien Herr. Reluctant as some were (Daniel Halévy was one), French intellectuals felt themselves called to take a political stand and to act as the conscience of the nation. For them, what was at stake was nothing less than the rights of the individual in a democratic society when confronted by bureaucratic tyranny and arguments of *raison d'état*. Imbued with an almost mystical faith in Republican justice (perhaps best recaptured in Péguy's *Notre Jeunesse*) they opposed a conception of the social order which accorded primacy to authority, hierarchy and blind obedience to whatever the military might decree to be in the public interest. That the cause of the individual needed defending was evident from the widespread support for the army not just among outright anti-Republicans such as Charles Maurras and his associates in the *Action Française* but also among conservative Republican nationalists who joined the *Ligue de la Patrie Française*, founded at the beginning of 1899 by François Coppée and Jules Lemaître, and rapidly able to recruit up to 200,000 members.

It is true that perhaps some of the Republican intellectuals acted from a mixture of motives, sometimes as much concerned to distinguish themselves as an educated élite capable of leadership in the age of the masses as preoccupied with the merits of the Dreyfus case. It is true also that their intervention contributed much to the resurrection of the ideological battles associated with the French Revolution and its legacy, which may well have diverted the country from tackling other problems. Certainly, they ensured that anti-clericalism would be the foremost political issue in the immediate aftermath of the affair. Not all of the friends of liberty and the rights of man were averse to persecution, provided that the victim was the Catholic Church. In the end, however, Republican intellectuals upheld and vindicated a tradition of justice which stretched back to the Enlightenment. In the circumstances of the 1890s that was no small achievement.

If the affair generated passion outside the world of intellectuals and politicians, this had much to do with the spread of literacy and the availability of a popular press. Some historians, indeed, have seen the affair principally as a manifestation of the new power of the Fourth Estate. If the affair was a defeat for the army, the Church, even the State itself, it was a triumphant victory for the press. In reality, the role of the press in the affair was much more complicated and ambiguous. Without the newspapers, of course, the Dreyfus case would never have escaped from the army's *chose jugée*. On the other hand, it was press reports that convinced the public of Dreyfus's guilt back in 1894 and even in 1898 the majority of the newspapers still sided with the anti-*dreyfusards*. For much of the time between 1894 and 1898 the press had little to say about Dreyfus: it assumed a determining role only at the peak of the affair, when it was clear that there really was a mystery and rumours were rampant about spies and the possibility of war. After the Presidential pardon, the newspapers quickly lost interest in Dreyfus again. Dreyfus the man was not news. It would appear, therefore, to be something of an exaggeration to represent the affair as an assertion of the power of the press over established institutions.

The affair's repercussions were felt more by city dwellers than by rural communities. Rural France, as represented, say, by the peasants of the Dauphiné, took little part in the debate over the rights of man and nationalism which the affair provoked among Parisians and the more educated inhabitants of urban areas, such as Grenoble. That is not to say that the affair lacked a truly popular dimension. On the contrary, its popular impact is to be sought not in the press, or electoral politics, or intellectual debate, but in widespread demonstrations of anti-Semitic feeling.

Anti-Semitism may not have been at the root of the affair – there is no decisive evidence that the army chiefs decided to victimize Dreyfus on account of his race and Picquart, the staunch advocate of revision, was a notorious anti-Semite – but it became a central issue because of the way it was invoked by the anti-*dreyfusards*. That Dreyfus was a Jew was cited as evidence of his undoubted guilt and the campaign to rehabilitate him was represented as a conspiracy hatched by a powerful Jewish 'syndicate'. The ravings of the professional anti-Semites like Drumont enjoyed considerable success precisely because anti-Semitism permeated practically every layer of French society and held special appeal for discontented elements in the population, be they aristocratic Catholics, small traders or urban artisans. Anti-Semitism in late nineteenth-century France was a myth with enormous potential for mobilizing popular support.

Thus, it mattered little that the fantasies of *La Libre Parole* bore little relation to the real-life situation of the French Jewish community. Drumont, publication of whose *La France Juive* in 1886 turned him into the prophet of French anti-Semitism, insisted that the country was being swamped by Jews, whereas in the late 1890s the Jewish population amounted only to about 80,000, most of them resident in Paris. Many were recent immigrants from Alsace or from eastern Europe, working as sweated labour in the Paris garment industry. Though hardly plutocrats, it is true enough that they could be represented as an alien presence and threat to the French way of life. The older, native, highly assimilated French Jews, like the Halévys, not infrequently shared the general prejudice against the newcomers and were most reluctant to commit themselves to the cause of Dreyfus for fear of feeding anti-Semitic legends about the power of the 'syndicate'.

No matter. The anti-Semitic mentality was ready to blame the Jews for any social or political ill. The Left itself had set the example by identifying Jews with a ruling plutocracy, personified by the Rothschilds. Catholics, displaced from political and administrative power, found new reasons for hating Jews, who seemed to do so well in the world of politics and State education, to add to their traditional, religious, anti-Semitism, which condemned the Jews for the execution of Christ. Struggling shopkeepers and artisans, hit by economic change, had no difficulty in blaming Jewish finance for their plight, and were encouraged to do so by Catholic social reformers like the *abbés démocrates*. Impoverished female workers in the clothing industry contributed to the Henry fund, apparently because they considered Jews to be harsh employers. Likewise peasants, still coping with the aftermath of the phylloxera disaster, might attribute their ruin to the Jews, even if there was no Jewish presence in their areas. Among local notables, anti-Semitism might be paraded as a badge advertising their refusal to accept the social and political values of the Republic. In regions where a Jewish community either was or had been strong, anti-Semitism was endemic, as in Algeria (with 44,000 Jews) and in eastern France, for so long the area with the largest Jewish population in France, and responsible for a disproportionately high share of contributions to the Henry fund. By June 1897, when the French Anti-Semitic League was founded, the country was ripe for populist anti-Semitic agitation. The Dreyfus Affair seemed to offer just the right opportunity for the creation of a new mass-based movement of the Right, held together by anti-Semitism.

The full force of anti-Semitic feeling was revealed in January–February 1898, at the very height of the affair, following upon the acquittal of Esterhazy and Zola's *J'accuse*. In Algeria, in particular, anti-Semitism took the form of an explosion of rioting, amounting to a virtual pogrom. In metropolitan France, disturbances were reported in at least 55 places, mainly in the parts of the east and west dominated by the Right. A number of these incidents were serious enough to require troops to be sent to quell the rioting. Significantly, the most frequent manifestations of violence were attacks on Jewish shops and business premises, which suggest that the riots were some kind of popular protest. Dreyfus, evidently, was a symbol not only for intellectuals and politicians. In giving free reign to anti-Semitic prejudice, the affair laid bare some of the deepest tensions and anxieties agitating the French population at the turn of the century. In raising the spectre of a new right-wing challenge to the Republic, based on a broad anti-Semitic alliance, it posed the question of the survival of the regime itself, and made possible the reformation of the French Left around the banner of Republican defence. In short, the affair was a moral, political and social crisis of the first magnitude, a key episode for acquiring any understanding of twentieth-century French history.

2
The Republic of the Radicals

Although it did not become fully evident until after the elections of 1902, one of the main results of the agitation over Dreyfus was to make the Radicals the decisive force on the French political scene. Between 1898 and 1906, with the support of the French Left generally, Radicals were able to enact a programme of anti-clerical legislation which, in their own eyes, represented the fulfilment of an historical mission. Thereafter, while remaining at the centre of the stage and retaining widespread support in the country, their credibility as a party of the Left was openly and bitterly questioned by their Socialist allies of the era of the *Bloc des Gauches*. As early as 1906, they were experiencing a crisis of identity and acquiring a reputation for political ambivalence. To understand the nature of Radicalism is therefore a necessary preliminary to any wider appreciation of the apparent confusion and contradictions of French politics under the Third Republic.

Radical France

'Radical France' existed long before the Radical party was formally constituted in l901. As a doctrine, Radicalism was fundamentally a militant commitment to Republicanism, deriving ultimately from a quasi-mystical attachment to the French Revolution, understood and accepted as a *bloc*. It emerged as a distinct political tendency under the July Monarchy, when it formed the extreme Republican opposition to the regime of Louis-Philippe. Its first flowering came with the revolution of 1848, by which time it was committed to two main goals: the establishment of manhood suffrage and the enactment of some degree of social reform. The experience of the short-lived Second Republic was also important for the organizational side of the movement. Resistance first to Louis Napoleon's *coup d'état* of 1851 and then to the Second Empire itself turned Radicalism into the intransigent opposition to Napoleon III. By 1869 its aspirations were expressed in Gambetta's Belleville programme, which renewed the commitment to democracy and social reform but also stressed the paramount importance of the laicity of the State.

After 1870 the aim of Radical Republicans was the regeneration of France through the creation of a strong, secular republic. They could rejoice that at least part of their programme was carried out by the laic laws of 1879–84 and the establishment of a genuinely compulsory military service in 1889. On the other hand, the full anti-clerical programme of separation of Church and State was still a long way from realization, as was any significant advance in social legislation. Equally, their dream of revenge against Germany derived little encouragement from the foreign and imperial policies of the moderate Republicans. Indeed, the brief flirtation of the Radicals with the adventurer General Boulanger and the involvement of some of their leading lights (notably Georges Clemenceau) in the Panama scandal, consolidated the hold on power of the moderates and condemned the Radicals to the political wilderness for most of the 1890s. (Léon Bourgeois's Radical-dominated cabinet of 1895–6 lasted a mere six months.) It is against this somewhat chequered background that the resurgence of the Radicals has to be appreciated.

Even when Radical politicians were out of office, Radicalism itself retained deep roots in French political culture. First and foremost Radicalism was an attitude of mind, an outlook shaped by a sense of participation in a long and arduous struggle against reaction, and it was nourished by networks of individuals committed to preserving the traditions which radicalism embodied. One organization which cultivated the Radical historical sensibility was Freemasonry. The attractions of the lodges were both ideological and social. They had converted from deism to Republicanism, positivism and anti-clericalism under the Second Empire and they also served to make good business and political contacts through their clientele of schoolteachers, petty bureaucrats, lawyers, doctors, artisans and shopkeepers – precisely the sort of people from the petty and professional bourgeoisie who looked to the Republic to further their interests. Freemasonry was by no means a mass movement in the early twentieth century: membership was around the 30,000 mark. Nor was its influence as great as hysterical right-wing propaganda made out. Yet the lodges were more than social clubs or gathering places for those with a taste for ritual without religion. Their organizational skills and sensitivity to local affairs were of immense value in mobilizing support for Radical politicians at election times. It was no accident that the short-lived Bourgeois cabinet contained eight Freemasons and that all the members of the Combes ministry of 1902 had Masonic connexions. The Grand Orient – headquarters of the most influential group of Masons – did not dictate Radical party policy but it did bring together men motivated by common interests and aspirations at both regional and national level.

Other organizations to form and define the Radical mentality were the League of the Rights of Man and Free Thought. The former was originally founded in 1888 to counter the Boulangist threat, and was reconstituted in 1898 at the height of the Dreyfus Affair in order to safeguard the principles of 1789 against the apparent militarist threat to the Republic. Although in theory free from the sectarian views of Masonry on the subject of religion – one of the founder members was the Catholic *dreyfusard* of the École des Chartes, Paul Viollet – it quickly established itself as the champion of Republican justice against priests as well as generals. Its prestige owed much to the prominent role played by well-known figures, including Anatole France, but it also recruited among the tiny Protestant community. Francis de Pressensé, son of a distinguished Protestant pastor, became president of the society in 1903. Free Thought appealed to an even wider, more popular, audience, including workers and small peasant proprietors. Militantly secular, celebrating civil baptisms, marriages and festivals, it increasingly won recruits from socialism rather than Radicalism.

Within areas of Radical strength, organization was supplied essentially by local committees, whose main preoccupation was to see that the right candidates got elected as deputies. It was to 'make' the elections of 1902 that the party was founded in 1901 by a congress of national and local politicians, Freemasons, journalists and representatives of local committees. Radicalism had strong regional bases. Its adherents were most numerous in the Midi, where the influential newspaper *La Dépêche de Toulouse* provided a platform for the expression of Radical views and allowed southern Radicalism to appear as something more than just a winegrowers' pressure group. Support was also strong in central France (in the Lot, Cantal and Corrèze), in some departments of the centre–east (Jura, Saône-et-Loire) and around Paris (Seine-et-Marne, Loiret). What is interesting is that by 1900 'Radical France' was by no means identical with the regions that had sided with the Second Republic in 1849 and 1851. In areas with a tradition of voting to the Left – the Mediterranean region, the Rhone Valley – Radicalism had begun to make way for socialism.

Even as a united party Radicals retained a decentralized structure which left power still essentially in the hands of local committees. Party discipline was virtually non-existent. Many a candidate ran under the Radical label at election time only to repudiate party policy (as laid down by the annual conference) in the Chamber. Such a party, we shall see, was singularly ill-equipped to tackle the problems of government.

The *Bloc des Gauches*

It was the formation of the Waldeck-Rousseau cabinet of 'Republican defence' in June 1899 which inaugurated what, in retrospect, came to be seen as the 'golden age' of Radicalism; but that was not immediately apparent. The general agitation over Dreyfus, culminating with an abortive attempt by the nationalist Paul Déroulède to stage a *coup d'état* on the occasion of President Faure's funeral, and an assault on President Loubet at the Auteil races, created a sense of crisis among the Republic's political leaders, who feared for the survival of the regime. In the event, however, it was not the Radicals who emerged as the chief guardians of the Republican citadel, but the moderates, headed by the new premier René Waldeck-Rousseau.

Cold, aloof, and marked by a pessimism which contrasted sharply with the optimism of Gambetta's generation of Republicans, Waldeck was a wealthy barrister who favoured firm government and disliked extremism of all kinds. The part played by the Assumptionists during the Dreyfus Affair convinced him that the religious orders must be brought to heel (the Napoleonic Concordat provided only for relations between the State and the secular clergy, while Rome had never recognized the Organic Articles by which governments had sought to control the orders). Waldeck had no intention of fulfilling the Radical programme of separation of Church and State, but, inevitably, by making anti-clericalism government policy, he ensured that the Radicals would support his ministry. The Assumptionists were declared to be an illegal association and dissolved in 1900. Waldeck introduced legislation requiring all religious orders to seek authorization, which he intended should be granted by the Council of State. When his bill became law in 1901, however, the more virulently anti-clerical Radical deputies had been able to modify it so that parliament, rather than the Council of State, should be the authorizing body. The nominal author of the law was little pleased by this outcome, but the

Radicals were delighted. Their hope was that the Law of Associations might be only the beginning of a full-scale anti-clerical onslaught.

To this end, in June 1901, Radicals constituted themselves into the Radical and Radical-Socialist party, in readiness for the elections of 1902. 'Clerical-ism' and the question of who should control the State were once again the principal issues, just as in the 1870s and 1880s. The results were a famous victory for the Left, with the Republican *bloc* winning about 370 seats in a Chamber of 588. Radicals and Radical-Socialists alone accounted for 219 deputies. For the essentially moderate Waldeck-Rousseau, this was an excess-ive majority. Rather than face a parliament full of rabid anti-clericals, he resigned. His successor was Emile Combes, who was able to put together what (with the exception of the short-lived cabinet of Léon Bourgeois in 1896) was effectively the first Radical ministry of the Third Republic.

Combes was the personification of anti-clericalism and small-town Radical-ism. Of humble parentage, he had originally been destined for the priesthood, until his seminary teachers decided that he lacked a vocation. After a spell of teaching in a Catholic school, he had studied medicine and settled as a country doctor in the Charente-Inférieure. Having been initiated into Free-masonry he entered local politics and was elected senator for his department in 1885. A good constituency parliamentarian, he also enjoyed a reputation as a political operator in the corridors of power. Though not an atheist – he adhered to spiritualism and believed in the immortality of the soul – he was animated by a profound hatred of the Church which had once rejected him. His interpretation of the 1902 election results was that he had been given a mandate to wage war on the religious orders.

Guaranteed an unassailable position in parliament and with the active sup-port of Jaurès and other Socialists co-operating through the parliamentary *délégation des gauches*, Combes saw to it that the vast majority of France's 3,216 religious congregations were denied authorization. By a law of 7 July 1904 his government prohibited even authorized orders from teaching, thus closing about a third of the Catholic schools in the country. Combes also wanted ex-members of religious orders to be denied the right to teach as private citizens, but even diehard anti-clericals like Clemenceau balked at such an infringement of individual liberty. Though passed by the Chamber, Combes's bill was rejected by the Senate.

The persecution of the congregations was only the beginning of a wider confrontation with the Church. Combes was soon at loggerheads with Rome over the question of episcopal appointments, and the chances of conciliation were not improved by the death of the aged Leo XIII in 1903. His successor, Pius X, was not prepared, like Leo, to go to virtually any lengths to salvage the Concordat. He and his new Secretary of State, Merry del Val, believed that the appeasement of the French Republicans had gone too far and that the time had come to fight for Catholic interests. When President Loubet and Foreign Minister Delcassé paid a State visit to Italy in April 1904 without calling also at the Vatican, the Pope and his Secretary of State were quick to see an affront to papal prestige and endorsement of the papacy's loss of its temporal power. A note of protest, drawn up by Merry del Val and couched in intemperate language, was leaked to the newspaper *Humanité* and the furore which followed its publication led to a rupture in diplomatic relations between France and the Holy See.

The clamour for separation now became louder, but, even so, Combes still hesitated, fearing to abandon all control over a completely independent Church in what, in many areas, he still regarded as a 'clerical' country. The pace, however, was dictated by the Socialists, upon whom the Radicals had come to depend for support in the Chamber. For the Socialist leader Jaurès, the time had arrived to settle the hoary problem of Church–State relations once and for all. Another Socialist, Francis de Pressensé, drafted the bill which formed the basis of the Separation Law. Combes delayed giving government backing to the bill for as long as possible, but his hand was forced by the *affaire des fiches* – a scandal resulting from the revelation that promotions in the army were being influenced by files on the religious behaviour of officers kept by the Freemasons with the connivance of the Minister of War, General André. In November 1904 Combes produced a government text which failed to satisfy the more militant anti-clericals, before being forced out of office in January 1905. The new premier, Rouvier, was a moderate, but as the price of left-wing support for his government he was obliged to let the separation go forward. Skilfully steered through the Chamber by Aristide Briand, still at this juncture regarded as a Socialist, the Separation Bill was voted by the deputies on 3 July 1905 by 314 votes to 233, and following its passage through the Senate, it became law on 11 December 1905.

Pius X was not slow in making known his outrage at the passing of the Separation Law. In the encyclical *Vehementer* of February 1906 he rejected the French State's right to repudiate unilaterally a treaty negotiated by his predecessor Pius VII and Napoleon. Whereas most of the French bishops and a number of prominent Catholic laymen believed that the Church could live with the Law's stipulation that it should constitute itself into *associations cultuelles* for the purpose of registering with the State, the Pope continued with his fulminations in the encyclical *Gravissimo* of August 1906. Obsessed, as ever, with the question of papal prestige, deeply suspicious of the proposed associations as being likely to undermine the hierarchical structure of the Church, and fearful at the spread of what he considered error not only in society at large but within the Church itself (in the shape of the so-called 'Modernist' movement), Pius X could see no advantages for the Church in coming to terms with the masters of the Third Republic.

It may be, too, that he was discouraged by the failure of Catholic France to rise in a movement of mass resistance to the Separation Law, at least at the ballot box, in the elections of May 1906. A certain number of ugly incidents did take place early in 1906 when, in conformity with the Law's requirements that an inventory of Church property should be carried out, the State's agents clashed with Catholics in the more intransigent areas (the Vendée, and parts of Flanders and the Pyrenees). The Rouvier government's inept handling of this situation precipitated its fall, and the new government of Sarrien, with Clemenceau as Minister of the Interior, suspended the taking of inventories rather than resort to force. Thus it was that in May 1906 the voters were able to go to the polls in an atmosphere of relative calm and their indifference to the fate of the Church was only too apparent in the results. Radicals and Radical–Socialists emerged with 247 deputies, the Socialists had 74, while the Catholic and nationalist groups could muster only about 175 deputies between them. Only with difficulty could it be argued that the anti-clerical legislation of the *Bloc des Gauches* had been foisted upon an unwilling

Catholic population. The Church might have done well to comply with the Law as best it could, but, prevented from doing so by papal intransigence, it suffered financially to the tune of 500 million francs.

From Clemenceau to Caillaux

In October 1906, to reflect the sweeping triumph of the Radicals in the recent elections, Georges Clemenceau replaced Sarrien as prime minister at the head of a new Radical-dominated cabinet. Now that the religious issue had been settled and the Radicals no longer needed Socialist support for a majority in the Chamber, the time had come to see what Radicalism had to offer other than anti-clericalism. In the 1890s some Radicals (most notably Léon Bourgeois) associated themselves with the fashionable doctrine of solidarism, an attempt to find a *via media* between extreme *laissez-faire* individualism on the one hand, and socialist collectivism on the other. Clemenceau announced an impressive package of legislation, which included the introduction of an income tax, the 10-hour working day, and old-age pensions. Yet, although by the Third Republic's standards, the Clemenceau ministry was comparatively long-lived, lasting until 1909, virtually none of the proposed reforms reached the statute book (the exceptions were the nationalization of the Western Railway and the establishment of a new Ministry of Labour), though it proved possible to rush through a bill raising the salaries of MPs from 9,000 to 15,000 francs. In the end, the Clemenceau government revealed the bankruptcy of Radicalism as a politically progressive force and made Clemenceau himself into a living symbol of the State's repression of organized labour.

Clemenceau, the implacable democrat, was not himself a son of the people. He was born in 1841 into an old bourgeois family which had a landed estate in the Vendée. From his father, a ferocious *bleu* who all his life opposed the predominant conservatism of the region, he inherited the purest and most militant brand of Republicanism. While a medical student in Paris under the Second Empire he earned a short spell in prison in 1862. In the Chamber of Deputies in the early days of the Third Republic, he acquired a reputation for extreme Radicalism. Nicknamed 'The Tiger', and feared equally for his skills as debater and as duellist, he was essentially combative and destructive by temperament. His position was best summed up by his phrase '*je suis contre*'. His real talent was for hating. Even his private life was filled with rancour. When his American wife sought consolation in the arms of others for his constant infidelities, he not only divorced her but had her deported from the country.

Clemenceau was 65 when he assumed office in 1906. His political career had almost been terminated by his associations with the shady financier Cornelius Herz, the man at the centre of the Panama scandal. Having lost his seat in the elections of 1893, he returned to parliament only in 1902, as a senator (despite his long-standing advocacy of a single chamber). The Dreyfus Affair gave him the opportunity to make a political comeback. Once installed in power, he discovered that the business of governing was not quite so simple as he had liked to make out in opposition. Radical colleagues who had united on the religious issue were not necessarily prepared to rally behind the government's programme of social reforms. Socialists who had supported the Separation expected a great deal more from Clemenceau than he was capable of delivering. The breach with the Left, however, would not have been nearly so bitter but for the premier's own savage methods of dealing with labour protest.

The first signs of his brutal treatment of trade unionists came when he was Minister of the Interior in the Sarrien government. Following the pit disaster at Courrières in March 1906, in which over 1,000 miners lost their lives, spontaneous strikes broke out all over the northern coalfields. Clemenceau's riposte was to send in 20,000 troops to occupy the area. When the *Confédération Générale du Travail* (CGT) tried to stage a general strike beginning on May Day 1906, he had several of their leaders arrested on trumped-up charges of conspiracy. In March 1907 troops were again drafted to take over from striking electricity workers in Paris (though in the event their services were not required). In bloody incidents in 1908 involving clashes between workers and the police, two workers were killed at Draveil and four were killed and some 50 injured at Villeneuve St Georges. Though in the former case the police fired upon unarmed men, Clemenceau defended their action in parliament. And, though much of the violence at Villeneuve St Georges could be attributed to the agitation of an *agent provocateur*, Clemenceau arrested prominent leaders of the CGT, and used as evidence against them violent language spoken by the *provocateur* in the pay of his own police force. Not for nothing was Clemenceau known as *le premier flic de France* – France's first cop.

Thus, as prime minister, Clemenceau was concerned more with the defence of the social order and upholding the authority of the French State than with social reforms. True, he was not one of those Radicals (of whom there were not a few) who would have preferred to see the CGT dissolved altogether. On the other hand, in the case of the State's own employees, he denied their right to belong to the union of their choice. In 1907 he made it plain to primary school teachers that there could be no question of allowing their organizations to affiliate to the CGT. In March 1909 he dismissed postal workers who went on strike. The more left-wing elements of the Radical party, well aware of the extent to which minor functionaries formed a crucial element in the party's electoral machine and clientele, objected to the government's failure to enact a promised statute regulating the pay and conditions of service of civil servants. They also complained about the government's recourse to repression in general. In May 1909 the executive committee of the party formally condemned the government which, according to the veteran Radical Camille Pelletan, had shown itself to be more oppressive than the Second Empire.

The Clemenceau regime revealed the severe limitations of Radicalism as a force for change. Its relationship with power was ambivalent, even contradictory. Evidently, its reforming impulse had been spent by the anti-clerical struggles of 1899–1905. Radicalism remained above all an outlook, an attitude of mind, rather than a coherent doctrine or, still less, a party programme. The Radical party itself remained a very broad church, ranging from near-socialists to Republican conservatives who identified readily with the emphasis on private property, the defence of the social order and financial orthodoxy which characterized the standpoint of the moderate Republicans of the *Alliance démocratique*. The party's leaders were only too well aware of the non-existence of any internal consensus on reform and, even more so, of the unpopularity of reforms which might hit the pockets of their property-owning electorate. For the Radical clientele, Radicalism existed to put men they could trust in high places in the expectation of receiving all the benefits State patronage could bestow. (Indeed one Radical complaint against Clemenceau was that he did not operate the spoils system effectively enough.)

At the same time, the Radicals were not at ease with power. Paradoxically, considering that they were the dominant political grouping on the French political scene between 1902 and 1936, they regarded government more from a negative than a positive viewpoint. For, if in their view it was necessary to take power in order to reward one's friends, it was even more vital in order to keep out one's enemies. As the Radical philosopher Alain explained, government was not about leadership and action but about the limitation and control of power. Clearly, such an outlook was not without its virtues, particularly in the face of the temptations of fascism in the 1920s and 30s. On the other hand, it was equally not without its drawbacks. For one thing, it made even modest reform difficult to effect and helped introduce a kind of sclerosis into political and social life. For another, it blurred the lines of political debate and obfuscated real political issues. By deploying the rhetoric of the revolutionary tradition and by donning the mantle of progress while remaining, at bottom, deeply conservative, the Radicals contributed to a general degredation of French political life.

Perhaps the politician most at home in this murky ambience was not a Radical (though he had many Radical admirers) but a renegade socialist, Aristide Briand. Briand succeeded Clemenceau as premier in July 1909. A Breton lawyer endowed with enormous charm (appreciated as much by women as by his fellow politicians), he had first risen to prominence in the 1890s as a man of the Left and advocate of the revolutionary general strike. Elected deputy in 1902, he immediately displayed his skills as a parliamentarian as *rapporteur* of the commission charged with preparing the Separation bill. Gradually, he severed all connexions with parties and ideologies, to emerge very much his own man and a man of government (he was in office almost continuously between 1909 and 1913 and in all was to be a minister some 25 times). Ironically, it was the former apostle of the general strike who adopted *clemenciste* methods to crush a strike of railwaymen in 1910: he arrested their leaders and mobilized the striking workers as army reservists. For Briand well understood that the first rule in the parliamentary game of retaining a 'republican majority' was to stand firm in the defence of the social order. Despite their strong representation in the Chamber of Deputies (Radicals, Radical-Socialists and Independent Socialists between them accounted for 47 per cent of the seats in parliament after the elections of 1910), Radicals could not be united behind a programme of reform. Briand was content, therefore, to work the system on an opportunist, day-to-day basis. To the extent that he and other moderate prime ministers of these years (such as Barthou and Poincaré) manifested any kind of ideological commitment, it was to nationalism.

By 1913, therefore, the Radical party was in some disarray. Torn by internal divisions, it was under increasing pressure from the socialist Left while being upstaged by the 'poincarism' of the moderate Republicans (the Barthou cabinet of 1913 included only 3 Radicals and unashamedly cultivated right-wing support). It was in these circumstances that Radicalism acquired a new and, ostensibly, implausible chief.

Joseph Caillaux was born into a conservative *grand bourgeois* family. His father had been a minister in the notorious '16 May' cabinet of MacMahon, and he himself began his career as a high official at the Ministry of Finance. Entering parliament in 1898, a year later, still aged only 36, he was made Minister of Finance by Waldeck-Rousseau. Reserved, arrogant and aloof, he had few personal or political friends but many contacts, high and low, in the world of finance. His name became associated with the campaign to introduce a progressive income tax, despite the fact that he boasted to his mistress that his real aim was to scupper the reform while appearing to support it. Clemenceau reappointed him to the Finance Ministry and in 1911 he himself became prime minister. By this time, he had begun to think of reviving the *Bloc des gauches*, though for the moment he was unable to secure Socialist support because of his refusal to reinstate railway workers dismissed after the 1910 strike. He was also much preoccupied with the threatening international climate – the Agadir incident was the major event of his premiership – and he intended to raise his voice against the rampant chauvinism of the Right. He therefore joined the Radical party and almost immediately found himself elected its leader. At the party congress in Paris in October 1913 he made a strong speech in which he called on the Radicals to unite on a programme of domestic reform (meaning the introduction of income tax) and repeal of the Three Year Law on military service, recently passed in August 1913.

Caillaux offered the Radicals the welcome prospect of a return to a dominating position in government. Again Minister of Finance in the cabinet formed by Doumergue in December 1913, he was seen as the real centre of its authority and a likely future prime minister. Speculation mounted that, after the elections of May 1914, it might be possible to form a Caillaux–Jaurès administration, if the Socialists could be persuaded to abandon their policy of non-participation in government. The consternation of the Right was great – so great that the editor of the conservative newspaper *Le Figaro* began to conduct a campaign of unparalleled vilification against the Radical leader, with the certain connivance of Briand and Barthou and the tacit approbation of the President of the Republic, Raymond Poincaré. Among other anti-Caillaux items, the paper had begun to publish compromising letters written by Caillaux to his second wife before they married and obtained from the first, divorced, Mme Caillaux. Whether out of a sense of outrage and loyalty to her husband, or whether because there were more startling revelations of either a personal or political kind still to come, on 16 March 1914 Mme Henriette Caillaux entered the offices of the *Figaro* and shot the editor, Gaston Calmette, dead in his chair.

For the time being the career of Joseph Caillaux was over, but the Radicals carried on his policy of fighting the elections of 1914 in alliance with the Socialists against the Three Year Law. Between them, the Left secured 50 per cent of the seats (for only 38 per cent of the votes), with the Radicals taking 172, and the Socialists 104, and Independent Socialists 24. It is, however, by no means clear that these results heralded a revival of the *Bloc des gauches*. Many Radicals were not opposed to the Three Year Law and when the renegade socialist Viviani became the new premier in June 1914 he skilfully put together a cabinet which, though dominated by Radicals, was not prepared to rescind the law. Once again, the government was able to find its parliamentary majority from the Centre rather than the Left. The fragmentation and ambiguities of Radicalism persisted and its disarray was completed by the advent of the First World War. Even in the 'golden years' the 'Radical Republic' was less a reality than an aspiration.

3
The Challenge of the Left

Following the repression of the Paris Commune in 1871, the French Left was crippled for almost a decade. Yet by 1914 the French socialist party had emerged as the second largest political party in France, while the CGT had a membership of 687,000. The more conservative parties increasingly expressed concern about the defence of order and the safety of property, which suggests that in the years before the First World War the French Left came to pose a considerable challenge to existing political and social structures. The precise nature of that challenge, however, needs to be defined.

The Road to Unity

Around 1900 perhaps the most characteristic of the French Left was its fragmentation. In the 1890s, the word 'socialism' had no very definite meaning, other than denoting the creed of those who favoured the reorganization of society on some kind of collectivist basis. 'Socialists' came in many shapes and forms (even the likes of Drumont and Clemenceau had claims to be socialists of some sort) and, far from being a united band of brothers dedicated to the overthrow of the capitalist system, socialists were bitterly divided among themselves over dogmas, strategies and personalities. The road to unification proved to be a singularly rocky one.

At least five main groups can be distinguished at the turn of the century. The *Parti Ouvrier Français* (POF) of Jules Guesde considered itself to be the authentic representative of Marxist socialism in France. Guesde, the son of a schoolteacher, had been first a follower of Gambetta, then an anarchist, before his conversion to Marxism while in exile after the Commune. In the POF, founded in 1880, he deliberately set out to create a class-based party which would unite all socialists on strictly Marxist terms. Initially, therefore, his stance was particularly sectarian and doctrinaire. Trade unions were to be subject to political control by the party. Elections were valued only as 'schools of socialism', that is as a means of educating the electorate rather than returning MPs. Social reforms were held to be a useless, even dangerous, palliative serving only to disguise the viciousness of the capitalist system and to stave off the day of its demise. Socialists who were prepared to compromise with the existing order were contemptuously written off as 'possibilists'. Over the course of the 1890s, however, Guesde relented somewhat and softened his hardline approach. His view on elections mollified after his own election as deputy for Roubaix in 1893 and in the Chamber he showed signs of a willingness to collaborate with other socialists on various questions of social reform, notably in the matter of regulating the hours and conditions of working women. In the 1890s it seemed that reformism rather than Marxism formed the likelier basis on which a united socialist party would be brought into being.

But the reformist camp was itself by no means united. The one thing all the different groups had in common was a belief that they were the heirs of an indigenous French revolutionary tradition and that their task was to complete the great enterprise begun in 1789. Theirs was a moral and republican socialism which sprang from French revolutionary ideals of justice rather than the inexorable laws of Marxist economics. The group associated with Dr Paul Brousse, another ex-anarchist and, by profession, a comfortably-off doctor, focused on practical, immediate problems, especially at the municipal level. It was their espousal of this 'gas and water' socialism that earned them Guesde's derisive label of 'possibilists', though they retaliated in kind by calling the Guesdists 'impossibilists'. A split, however, developed in the ranks of the possibilists around 1890, when Jean Allemane, a typographer and ex-*communard*, broke away to form a socialist group more overtly proletarian than radical – bourgeois in flavour. Allemane was probably as much an anarchist as a socialist and seems to have entertained hopes of marrying revolutionary socialism with revolutionary syndicalism. The *allemanistes* were strong in Paris where, above all, they envisaged themselves as maintaining the traditions of the *sans-culottes* and the *communards*.

Competing with the Allemanists for the distinction of representing the extreme wing of French revolutionary socialism were the Blanquists. After 1880 they had abandoned the old-style conspiratorial and *putsch*-type methods of Blanqui himself, in favour of more broad-based agitation among the working classes. Animated by impassioned spirits such as Louise Michel, the famed 'Red Virgin' of the Commune, and Henri Rochefort, the corrosive journalist of *L'Intransigeant*, they engaged in the politics of festival, employing rituals such as processions to the *Mur des féderés* in the Père Lachaise cemetery, where the *communards* had made their last stand, and funerals and commemorations of their leaders, to make an impact on their supporters. Before the Boulangist crisis, they tended to view elections in much the same light as the Marxists, valuing them for educative purposes only. Thereafter, following their chief Edouard Vaillant, most came to see the parliamentary regime, however imperfect, as preferable to 'caesarism'. Their ranks were reinforced in 1896 by some dissident Allemanists.

Finally, there was a group of socialists who, while acknowledging their indebtedness to the French revolutionary tradition, considered themselves to be 'independents'. One of the most prominent of these was Alexandre Millerand, an ambitious barrister, who was to become the first socialist to hold ministerial office. In a speech at St Mandé in 1896 he formulated a minimum programme of gradual nationalization, municipal socialism and the conquest of a parliamentary majority. Far and away the most outstanding figure among the independents, however, was Jean Jaurès, in his own lifetime a socialist legend, almost a socialist saint. The son of a less than successful businessman and small cultivator in the department of the Tarn, he had a brilliant academic career, first as a schoolboy and then as a student at the École Normale Supérieure. After a spell as a schoolmaster and professor of philosophy at the University of Toulouse, he entered politics as a supporter of Ferry and moderate Republicanism, but gradually (and untypically) evolved towards the Left. In the elections of 1893 he was returned as the socialist candidate of the miners of Carmaux.

Jaurès's socialism is not easy to define. Certainly, he is not to be classified simply as a reformist, as so many text books label him. He always claimed to be a revolutionary and his (extremely eclectic) ideas were constantly evolving. He accepted a number of Marxist doctrines, such as the labour theory of value, the centralization and concentration of capital and the inevitability of the downfall of the capitalist system. Yet he could not accept the Marxist view that economic forces alone determined the course of history. Other, human, elements were also important: the aesthetic sense, the search for ideals, the craving of the individual to establish community with others. He admired the earlier, utopian socialists for their moral emphasis, even if he rejected their solutions to the social question. Jaurès, ultimately, tried to elaborate a synthesis of materialism and idealism which would merge the ideas of Marx with those of Benoît Mâlon, the founder of the *Revue Socialiste*,who sought to make socialism as broad a church as possible. Jaurès was searching for a psychological revolution proceeding ineluctably from a social revolution, in order to set man free from spiritual as much as physical bondage. One of the greatest orators of his day, Jaurès was to be the chief architect of socialist unification.

Unification, however, seemed an elusive goal at the time of the Dreyfus Affair, which produced further splits in the socialist ranks. Guesde consistently held that the affair was a 'bourgeois' quarrel, of no concern to the exploited working class. Vaillant and the Blanquists eschewed such extremist rhetoric, but still preferred to view the issue from a purely tactical standpoint. Even Millerand, who was to join the Waldeck-Rousseau government of 'republican defence' in June 1899, resisted Radical pressure to join the *dreyfusard* camp, until after Henry's suicide. But Jaurès, who initially had expressed indignation that Dreyfus had escaped the firing squad, once convinced of his innocence, came to see in his condemnation a sinister reactionary plot against the Republic. After his defeat in the elections of 1898 he devoted himself to demonstrating Dreyfus's innocence in a series of newspaper articles entitled *Les preuves*, and in the process established himself as the foremost spokesman for socialism in France, a shining example to young intellectuals of the generation of Léon Blum who came to see socialism as the party of justice and humanitarianism.

For Jaurès, the implications of the affair demanded not only socialist but Republican unity, and for that reason he supported Millerand's presence in the Waldeck-Rousseau cabinet. The Blanquists would in all probability have accepted ministerial participation but for the inclusion in the cabinet of General Gallifet, the 'butcher' of the Commune, as Minister of War. Guesde was even more intransigent. Smarting at his defeat in the elections of 1898 and resentful of the ascendency which Jaurès had begun to exercise over the socialist movement, he gravitated back towards the hard-line faction in his party which had never been reconciled to his flirtation with reformism. Millerand was denounced as a traitor to the working class and his case referred to the Socialist International which, dominated by German Marxists who had little prospect of participating in the government of their own country, not surprisingly condemned ministerial participation at its Amsterdam Congress in 1904. Jaurès, placing the interests of socialist unification above all else, bowed to the International's decision and accepted that unity must be achieved on a Marxist, revolutionary basis. Vaillant, too, as leader of the Federation of the Seine, the largest of the party's cohorts, worked tirelessly for unity and increasingly associated himself with the approach of Jaurès. The way was thereby cleared for the creation of a French Section of the Workers' International, the SFIO, in April, 1905. Paradoxically, unity was finally achieved by repudiating the indigenous democratic socialist tradition which had attracted so many recruits to socialism in the first place – not least Jaurès himself.

The Impact of Socialism

After unification, the SFIO developed steadily until by July 1914 it had more than 90,000 members and 104 deputies in the Chamber. It is hard, however, to represent the growth of socialism in France as a success story. By comparison with the two million card-carrying members of the German SPD, the SFIO's membership was meagre. Moreover, the triumph of Guesde over Jaurès on the issue of '*Millerandisme*' left a baleful legacy. True enough, in practice Jaurès remained the outstanding figure in the French socialist movement, suffusing it with his own warmth and capacity for compromise. Nevertheless, the dogma of non-participation in so-called bourgeois cabinets banished French socialists to the political wilderness for 30 years. Jaurès, a potential prime minister, could only criticize from the sidelines. In any case, he tended to display a certain naïveté about the inevitability of socialist success – Clemenceau once remarked that you could always identify a speech by Jaurès by the number of verbs in the future tense.

Socialists claimed to speak for the exploited factory proletariat but they were by no means an exclusively workers' party. For one thing, as we shall see, industrial workers were not the typical representatives of the French working class, which itself was not the largest element in the French population. Perhaps surprisingly, in view of its commitment to collectivization of the land, socialism won a certain number of recruits in the countryside, notably in parts of the south of France and in the centre. The standard explanation for peasant socialism has been the influence of the revolutionary tradition, manifested as a predisposition in certain areas to side with the extreme Left whatever that happened to be – Radical, socialist, or later, communist. Thus it has been claimed, for instance, that the department of the Allier, Guesdism was a kind of latter-day Jacobinism, while in the Midi its impact was attributable to the activities of ex-Radicals and Freemasons, such as Dr Ferroul, the mayor of Narbonne.

Recent research, however, has suggested that, in Provence at least, support for socialism among peasants cannot be explained entirely by the invocation of the revolutionary tradition. It has been argued that peasants were genuinely converted to socialist ideology, which appeared to offer party-specific solutions to the special problems of the region. Hit by falling prices, the widespread destruction of vines by phylloxera and competition from the New World, French peasant farmers – especially wine growers – turned to the cooperative and collectivist remedies prescribed by socialists as their best hope for recovery and prosperity. Much of the case rests on assumptions about the determining influences of socio-economic geography and regional traditions on voting behaviour, and it is by no means proved. But the point remains that the existence of a relatively high rural sector in France was not necessarily the barrier to the advance of socialism that many have considered it to be.

It was in the north of France that the socialist claim to be the party of the workers was strongest. Guesdism took root among northern textile workers, in towns like Lille, Roubaix and Tourcoing. Yet it is not at all certain that it was the ideological appeal of Guesdism which attracted the workers. Other proletarians – for instance the textile workers of eastern France and the miners of the north – were highly resistant to Marxism. It seems more likely that Guesdist success in the Nord can be attributed to the party's organizational skills in the region, above all to its ability to penetrate the social and cultural life of the community. Outstandingly gifted propagandists were also crucial, such as Gustave Delory, a former textile worker who became mayor of Lille, and then its deputy. In so far as French workers of the artisan type – and, at the turn of the century, these were still the characteristic workers in the French labour force – looked to socialism, it was usually to a kind of 'trade' socialism rather than Guesdism. Confronted with threats to their wages, status and security by the spread of mechanization, they turned first to the co-operative movement and then to syndicalism rather than to Marxist socialism.

Revolutionary Syndicalism

If socialism in France failed to develop into a mass movement on the scale of German social democracy, one reason was that the socialists were not the only spokesmen for the oppressed proletariat. The syndicalist wing of the French labour movement explicitly rejected parliamentary socialism in favour of direct action. As set out in the CGT's Charter of Amiens of 1906, revolutionary syndicalism proclaimed the inevitability of class warfare but insisted that the salvation of the working class had to be sought through its own efforts, not by adherence to any political party. All political parties, socialists included, were fraudulent: democracy itself was a sham: and government merely the instrument of the ruling class. In the syndicalist view, the only solution was to destroy the whole edifice and start afresh, using the *syndicat*, or trade union, as the co-ordinating agency in a decentralized social and political system dominated by small producers. The means by which the present society would be transformed was direct action, meaning industrial action, the culmination of which would be the revolutionary general strike, the supreme act of class warfare which would usher in a new era of human social organization.

As a doctrine, revolutionary syndicalism clearly owed a great deal to anarchism, itself yet another, and important, variation on the collectivist theme in late-nineteenth-century France. Deriving initially from the theories of Pierre-Joseph Proudhon (1809–68), anarchism began as a rejection of the State and of large-scale private property, along with the advocacy of a philosophy of self-help for the working classes. In the 1880s and early 1890s, under the intellectual influences of Bakunin, Nechaev and Kropotkin, anarchism passed from Proudhonist mutualism to a phase of 'propaganda by the deed', characterized by recourse to terrorism and culminating in the assassination of the President of the Republic, Sadi Carnot, in 1894. The draconian repression of the movement which followed this outrage drove anarchism towards a new home in the trade unions and revolutionary syndicalism.

The French labour movement was attracted to revolutionary syndicalism rather than parliamentary socialism for a number of reasons. Trade unionists in France had a long tradition of independent action, stretching back to the Second Empire. The artisans and workers who rallied to the Commune were fired by Proudhonist rather than Marxist ideals. When trade unionism revived after the Commune, Guesdist attempts to subordinate the *syndicats* to the overall objectives of the party flew in the face of those traditions. For a time, Guesde did succeed in capturing control of the National Federation of French Trade Unions, but in 1895, when the newly formed CGT replaced the National Federation, trade unionists reverted to their traditional line, all the more willingly in that in 1892 they had already affirmed their faith in the revolutionary general strike.

Another factor in the shift towards revolutionary syndicalism was the role of a uniquely French labour institution, the *Bourse du Travail*. The *Bourse* was a kind of trades council which co-ordinated the action of all the different trade unions in a particular area and provided not just a political meeting place but a centre for a great variety of activities which made it the focal point for the social and cultural life of the working-class community. Originally intended to be a sort of labour exchange, the *Bourse* supplemented its assistance in job-finding with the creation of mutual-aid societies, strike funds, education courses, library facilities, and many other services. Paradoxically, the man who more than any other saw the revolutionary potential of the *Bourses*, Fernand Pelloutier, was not himself a worker but a bourgeois, disaffected by what he saw as the corruption of his own class and convinced that the workers held out the only hope for the creation of a better world. In the *Bourses du Travail* he envisaged a genuine proletarian alternative to decadent bourgeois society; and, on becoming secretary of the National Federation of *Bourses du Travail* in 1895, he threw himself into the work of developing their possibilities. Within five years, he had increased the number of *Bourses* from 34 to 55, and the number of associated *syndicats* from 606 to 1,065 – a fact all the more remarkable given that Pelloutier was already mortally ill with tuberculosis.

Paradoxically, revolutionary syndicalism reflected not just a predilection for militancy on the part of French trade unionists, but their weakness, both organizationally and in the face of particularly intransigent employers. Certain unions – the print workers for example – did have good organization. Other, potentially very powerful, groups of workers, such as the miners and the railwaymen, were divided into different unions and short of recruits. At its pre-war peak in 1912, the CGT could claim only 687,000 members out of an industrial workforce of over four million. Its financial resources were negligible (amounting, in 1910, to a mere 20,000 francs, or £800). Within the confederation smaller unions counted the same as larger ones for voting purposes, and, in their desperate financial and organizational straits, even Alphons Merrheim, secretary-general of the powerful and officially revolutionary Metal-Workers' Federation, became pessimistic about the workers' chances of toppling the capitalist system. Apart from the repressive capacity of the French State, he recognized that the employers themselves, especially in his own iron and steel industry, had become much more effectively organized in cartels. The union's advocacy of the general strike was therefore increasingly a reference to a weapon in the class war which was unlikely to be used. Proletarian revolution had been postponed indefinitely, and possibilities were opened up for collaboration with the Jaurèsian wing of the SFIO. It would, nevertheless, be a mistake to underestimate the originality and genuinely revolutionary side of French syndicalism. In the careers of men like Alfred Rosmer, a former anarchist who turned to syndicalism after 1908, and Pierre Monatte, founder of the newspaper *La Vie Ouvière* in 1909, can be seen a commitment to revolution and fidelity to the independence of the *syndicat*. Revolutionary syndicalism continued to offer an alternative to the frequently ineffective socialism of the Second International.

Equally, it is possible to exaggerate the gap which separated syndicalists and socialists. As far as Jaurès and Vaillant were concerned, they were two wings – one political, the other economic – of one great labour movement. On the syndicalist side, the fact that the Charter of Amiens prescribed neutrality for the unions did not preclude informal links with the SFIO on matters of common interest. During the strike-torn year of 1906 the SFIO consistently supported the CGT and striking workers. However much individual leaders of the CGT might denounce socialist politicians as class traitors and counsel abstention at elections, it is unlikely that ordinary trade unionists voted other than socialist.

Indeed, in the years immediately preceding the First World War, the CGT and the SFIO seemed to be drawing closer together. When Léon Jouhaux took over as secretary-general of the CGT in 1909 he pursued a flexible policy which, without abandoning the rhetoric of revolution, in practice steered the movement onto a more reformist path. At the same time, the prominence of Jaurès in the campaign against imperialism and the menace of war could not but impress the anti-militarist leaders of the CGT. It is true that the Socialist party did not speak with one voice on the question of war and the defence of the *patrie*. One faction headed by Gustave Hervé preached an extreme anti-militarism, denying the claims of nation over class and advocating a general strike to thwart conflict. The Guesdists maintained that to struggle against war was futile, since imperialism and war were inherent in the capitalist system and would be instrumental in its downfall. Jaurès, however, once again in agreement with Vaillant, distinguished carefully between imperialist wars and the legitimate defence of one's country. Aggressive wars were a supreme evil, to be combated by all the forces, parliamentary and extra-parliamentary, at the disposal of the French working class.

Precisely because he came to incarnate the socialist search for peace in an increasingly threatening international climate, Jaurès came to be identified by ultra-nationalists as their most deadly enemy. Not only did he raise the spectre of uniting the SFIO and the CGT, but equally alarmingly, he held out at least the possibility of effecting some kind of alliance with the Radicals under Caillaux. The prospect of a Caillaux–Jaurès collaboration provoked not only the smear campaign against the former which led to Madame Caillaux's assassination of the editor of *Le Figaro*, but it also unleashed the hysteria which nerved an unbalanced right-wing fanatic, Raoul Villain, to gun down Jaurès, on 31 July 1914. The man who had recently brought the socialists to the greatest electoral triumph of their history and who, even as war became more and more imminent, refused to accept its inevitability, was buried on 4 August, the day after Germany declared war on France. Abandoning their various anti-militarist stances, socialists and syndicalists, in their great majority, rallied to the defence of their country. War temporarily brought about that unity in the labour movement which had proved so elusive in peacetime, but the price to be paid later would be exhorbitantly high.

4
The Right and Nationalism

In the early years of the Third Republic's history, it was not the Left but the Right that Republicans considered to be the most serious threat to their regime. By 1900, however, they could congratulate themselves on a succession of famous victories over the forces of reaction and authoritarianism – the defeat of the monarchist challenge of the 1870s, the routing of Boulangism in the 1880s and, most recently, the containment of the noisy antirepublicanism which had accompanied the campaign against Dreyfus. The traditional Right – those who had opposed the Republic in the name of Legitimism, Orleanism of Bonapartism – seemed to be on the point of political extinction and the Republic more solidly established than ever.

But the right-wing challenge to democracy did not disappear in the years before the First World War. Rather, it appeared in a new guise. Favoured by an intellectual climate in which disillusionment with liberalism, rationalism and positivism – the credos which had fired the founding fathers of the Republic – was rife, another Right emerged which looked very different from the old-style reactionaries who hankered nostalgically after the golden days of the *Ancien Régime*, the Empire or even the July Monarchy. The new Right, whose dominant traits were aggressive nationalism, racialism and antiparliamentarism, had all the appearances of a revolutionary movement. It looked forward more to the fascism of the twentieth century than backwards to the conservatism of the nineteenth century. And even if, in its turn, the new Right, like the old, was to join the ranks of the vanquished of history, it was not before its activities both troubled the tranquillity of the republican order and left their mark on the political development of the regime.

The New Right and Integral Nationalism

The doctrines of what came to be called 'integral' nationalism had three main exponents in France. The first, Paul Déroulède (1846–1914), had founded the French League of Patriots in 1882. Initially a Radical Republican (his League earned the plaudits of such as Gambetta and Victor Hugo), Déroulède became disillusioned with the Republic's inability to satisfy the nation's need for revenge against Germany for the humiliation of 1870. Hence his support for General Boulanger in the 1880s and his attempted *coup d'état* on the occasion of President Faure's funeral in 1899. The latter episode was a fiasco, but Déroulède is not to be dismissed as an eccentric crank who struck no chords with sections of French public opinion. His own funeral attracted the biggest gathering of mourners seen since the burial of Victor Hugo.

The two other leading lights of integral nationalism in France were Maurice Barrès (1862–1923) and Charles Maurras (1868–1952). Famed as a novelist, Barrès seems to have exercised an ascendency over young French intellectuals which bears comparison with that of Châteaubriand or Lamartine earlier in the nineteenth century. Though claiming to be a Republican, he stipulated that he wanted a certain kind of Republic. 'I love the Republic', he said, 'but armed, glorious, organized'. Like Déroulède, Barrès was at heart an authoritarian with a complete contempt for parliament. One recent study views him as France's first national socialist. It was, however, Charles Maurras who did most to turn integral nationalism into a coherent doctrine, through his many publications and especially through the columns of the *Action Française*, the newspaper of his movement of the same name. A native of Provence and an advocate of the revival of the *langue d'oc*, Maurras may have derived his jaundiced view of existence from painful experiences in his childhood and adolescence: the death of his father, the onset of deafness and the loss of his religious faith. His politics amounted largely to the expression of his personal bitterness and hates, though they were no less influential for their poisoned origins.

Integral nationalism as preached by Déroulède, Barrès and Maurras bore little relation to the idealistic and romantic nationalism of the Republicans, except in so far as both coveted military glory for the *patrie*. But, as became all too evident in the course of the Dreyfus Affair, the new Right looked to the army as much to enforce order and discipline at home as to perform feats of arms in the field. For integral nationalists were at least as preoccupied with domestic as with foreign enemies: hence their intolerance and racialism, manifested in attempts to distinguish 'genuine' Frenchmen from 'alien' elements in the population – usually identified as Jews, Protestants, Free-masons and naturalized Frenchmen. According to Barrès, these were incapable of the total commitment to country that was the hallmark of the true nationalist. To him, nationalism was a psychological, almost a mystical, phenomenon, bred by a sense of communion with the national soil and the cult of one's ancestors. It required an unconditional acceptance of France as the paramount good. As Barrès put it, a nationalist was 'a Frenchman who was aware of his formation'.

Allied to the racialism of the integral nationalists was an utter repudiation of parliamentary democracy – especially since they considered the French system to be dominated by precisely those sections of the population they held in so much contempt as imperfectly formed Frenchmen. The Jewish, Protestant and Masonic masters of the corrupt bourgeois Republic could never, in their eyes, generate the heroic leadership essential for the recovery of the lost provinces and of France's rightful place as the greatest power in Europe. Maurras's alternative to the regime was a return to monarchical institutions, not out of any sense of fidelity to the Bourbons as such, but because monarchy consecrated a social order based on the principle of hierarchy. Similarly, without being himself a believer, let alone a practising Catholic, Maurras affirmed the claims of the Catholic Church to primacy in laying down the moral precepts by which men should live. He had a special hatred of intellectuals who dared to suggest that the rights of individuals should take precedence over the interests of society as a whole. In pursuit of his political objectives, he was ready to resort to violence and a *coup d'état*. For a brief period, indeed, royalists of the *Action Française* engaged in tentative collaboration with certain anarcho-syndicalists in a *politique du pire*. A joint nationalist – syndicalist study group, the *Cercle Proudhon* was established and several left-wing newspapers – notably Hervé's *Guerre Sociale* and Janvion's *Terre Libre* – were induced to aim anti-Semitic propaganda at the working class. These initiatives accomplished little in the way of practical results, but they nevertheless demonstrate the extent to which the new Right should be identified with the politics of violence and disorder, and with fascism rather than conservatism.

Maurras's *Action Française* provided not only the doctrine but also the drive and the organization of the radical Right in the years before the First World War. Founded in 1898 at the height of the Dreyfus Affair, it sought to mobilize the urban masses just as Boulangism had done in the 1880s. The movement attracted the support not just of *bien-pensant*, clerical and military circles but also of disaffected artisans and petty bourgeois – clerical workers, shop workers, primary teachers, commercial travellers and the like. Some of these, along with right-wing students from the faculties of Law and Medicine, found further scope for activism in the *camelots du roi*, a band of royalist thugs only too willing to practise as well as to preach the politics of violence. They were especially evident in the Latin Quarter of Paris, where a favourite pastime was disrupting the classes of 'left-wing' professors, but they were ready to engage in street brawls with any political opponents. Yet, in spite of its taste for activism and its professed antipathy to intellectuals, *Action Française* had plenty of admirers in the literary and intellectual world and among orthodox conservatives. In no small measure this could be attributed to the array of talent to be found among Maurras's collaborators – men such as the novelist Léon Daudet, the historian Jacques Bainville and the art historian Louis Dimier. Historians, indeed, were assigned a vital role by *Action Française* in that the movement actively promoted a view of the French past which challenged the glorification of the French Revolution and the Republican tradition in the 'orthodox' version of events taught by the University at every level of the educational system. The *Action Française* newspaper itself was considered necessary reading by many people who, like Marcel Proust, disliked its politics but admired its literary pages. At the very least, *Action Française* made anti-republicanism respectable, if not fashionable, in important sections of French public opinion.

The Traditional Right

Except perhaps for the most diehard Legitimists, the traditional Right could not but welcome the authoritarian challenge to the Republic posed by the new Right. The old élites still found it difficult to come to terms with their exclusion from political power and the success of the Republicans in projecting themselves as the most reliable defenders of the order and stability desired by a largely conservative and rural electorate. If the Boulangist episode had taught them that they could no longer aspire to complete control of the political system, they continued to find ways to express their alienation from the regime which they despised as *la gueuse* ('the slut').

The most important of these ways was through the politics of religion. The traditional Right dissociated itself from the Republican ideal of *laïcisme* and made the defence of the Catholic Church its chief political preoccupation. Combes's offensive against Catholic schools and the religious orders produced strong resistance among the Catholic aristocracy and bourgeoisie who had persistently refused to send their children to State schools (in 1899 43 per cent of all secondary schools were Catholic, and Jesuit establishments in particular were much appreciated, not merely for their snob value but for their sound education and excellent examination results). In June 1901 the two leading Catholic politicians of the *Ralliement*, Albert de Mun and Jacques Piou, grouped the right-wing deputies in the Chamber into a new organization called the *Action Libérale* in order to fight the Radicals and Socialists at the forthcoming elections of 1902. When they won only another 20 seats, mainly in traditionally right-wing areas such as the west, the north, the north-east and the south-west of France, Piou and de Mun founded a new political party, the *Action Libérale Populaire*, in May 1902 to build up a mass-based organization to resist *combisme*.

Led by de Mun in the Chamber and organized nationally by Piou (who had lost his seat in the 1902 elections) the ALP was fortified financially by 'laundered' funds from the dissolved religious orders and built up a network of 700 local committees and a membership of 160,000 by the end of 1904 (about five times as large as Socialist membership at this stage). Unlike most of the left-wing parties, the ALP did not underestimate the contribution women could make to the cause. As early as July 1902 the ALP organized a 10,000-strong 'March of Mothers', headed by Madame Piou and the Countess de Mun, to protest at Combes's treatment of the religious orders. In the Patriotic League of French Women, the party enjoyed the collaboration of a body which was nominally apolitical but in practice espoused the ALP programme of the defence of Catholic schools. Viewed by at least some of its leaders as a French equivalent of the English Primrose League (a Tory pressure group in which women played a prominent role), the League was much more successful than any of the feminist organizations or its royalist rival, the League of French Women, in attracting recruits, mainly from the world of the aristocracy and Catholic bourgeoisie. By 1914 it had 585,000 members, who engaged in all kinds of activities – lectures, the promotion of the cult of Joan of Arc, organizing pilgrimages and retreats, and, above all, diffusing Catholic newspapers (the League developed close ties with the Catholic daily, *La Croix*).

For all its propaganda and organizational efforts, the ALP won only 64 seats in the elections of 1906. Except in the most Catholic and conservative parts of the country, the electorate was not ready to rally to the banner of what was seen as a Catholic confessional party. Even the passing of the Separation Law and the disturbances that accompanied the inventories of Church property failed to mobilize support behind the Church. It had been the great hope of the ALP leaders that moderate Republicans would join them in an anti-collectivist alliance, as at the time of the *Ralliement* proper, but even these were reluctant to become too closely associated with a party which could so easily be branded as 'clerical'. The moderates were certainly hungry to regain office but, realizing that, with the Separation issue resolved, many Radicals were now ripe for wooing away from the Socialists, they felt no compelling need to ally with the ALP. By 1914 right-wing traditionalists had to accept that in the ALP they were doomed to permanent opposition.

Accordingly, some of the more intransigent members shifted their allegiance to the *Action Française*.

The limited political and social impact of the traditional 'clerical' Right derived in some measure from the reverses in the fortunes of the Church itself. 'Defence of the Church' was not a banner to which many Frenchmen were likely to flock in what was largely a 'dechristianized' society. Despite a number of spectacular conversions (involving mainly literary figures: Huysmans, Bourget and Claudel for instance) the Church's credibility with intellectuals was small, and probably diminishing. In the towns and cities of France the urban working classes usually grew up in isolation from the ministrations of official religion, though there are signs that elements of the bourgeoisie shed some of their anti-clericalism over the course of the nineteenth century and returned to the fold at least in terms of outward conformity. Certain parts of rural France – the diocese of Orleans for example – had long been notorious for their low levels of religious practice, though it may well be that, thanks to the pastoral and missionary zeal of the clergy in developing an 'ultramontane' brand of piety in tune with traditional popular religious beliefs and customs, the secular drought was not quite as desperate as is sometimes claimed. Nevertheless, it seems that barely 25 per cent of the adult population could be classified as practising Catholics, and the great majority of these were women – which did not help as far as votes were concerned.

Conventional political action was only one outlet for the expression of right-wing disenchantment with the Republic. Various forms of 'social' Catholicism also gave conservatives an opportunity to highlight the shortcomings of the regime in its treatment of the less fortunate members of the community. Just as it was Legitimists who took the lead in addressing the problems caused by the spread of industrialization under the July Monarchy, so in the *belle époque* diehard 'integral' Catholics could reject the liberal bourgeois state in the pursuit of a social order founded on the anti-liberal, anti-rational and anti-secular principles of Pius IX's *Syllabus of Errors*. Among less intransigent Catholics, Leo XIII's encyclical *Rerum Novarum* (1891) not only gave papal backing to laymen such as Albert de Mun and the northern textile manufacturer Léon Harmel who sought to promote social reform by non-collectivist means, but also inspired a new generation of young clerics to participate in the Catholic social movement. Since these priests (who included the *abbés* Lemire, Gayraud and Garnier) also accepted Leo XIII's exhortation to rally to the Republic, they became known as the *abbés démocrates* and were hailed as the harbingers of a second 'Christian democracy' (the first having been that associated with Buchez, Ozanam and the *Ere Nouvelle* group around 1848). Again, even more than in the political sphere, women assumed an important role within the whole array of Catholic charitable initiatives, particularly in organizations concerned with the welfare of women and children. Upper-class ladies such as Mme Chenu, Mlle Mercédès Le Fer de la Motte, Lucie Félix-Faure Goyau, Mlle Chaptal and others all endeavoured to translate their religious commitment into efforts to alleviate the suffering of the poor and to awaken the social conscience of the Catholic bourgeoisie.

The results were often disappointing. The traditionalist Catholic approach to social reform was narrowly paternalist. *Rerum Novarum* itself, often hailed as a landmark in the evolution of Catholic awareness of the 'social question', was inspired largely by alarm at the spread of socialism and vigorously defended the rights of private property. The Christian democratic movement foundered in part because of internal disputes but ultimately because Leo XIII, in his encyclical *Graves de communi* (1901), condemned what he saw as the movement's dangerous politicization. The boldest of Catholic social experiments in the years before 1914, the *Sillon*, incurred even greater papal displeasure. Founded by the dynamic and charismatic Marc Sangnier in 1899, the *Sillon* went far beyond the limited approach to social questions of the paternalists. From the outset, it accepted democracy, hoping originally to transform it in line with Christian principles but gradually coming to realize that the Church would have to accept a pluralistic society in which Christianity would be only one competing element among many within a democratic framework. Alarmed by its desire to free itself from any kind of clerical control, Pius X condemned the movement in 1910.

The institutional Church and the traditional Right may have done little enough to solve the 'social question' but, by directing attention towards it, they did raise one issue to which moderate Republicans were increasingly sensitive: anti-socialism. The 'Opportunist' or 'Progressive' Republicans who had ruled for 20 years after 1879 were split by the Dreyfus Affair. Some of their number, such as Poincaré and Barthou, were persuaded to back Waldeck-Rousseau in 1899 in his policy of 'Republican defence' and in 1901 they formed a new party, the *Alliance démocratique*, which was prepared to ally openly with the Radicals. Other moderate Republicans followed Méline into opposition beside the Catholic *ralliés* of the ALP and in 1903 they formed their own Republican Federation of France, with a view to defending the interests of the industrial and commercial bourgeoisie. Although schisms soon developed within the Republican Federation over matters of Republican orthodoxy and ideological purity (some 30 deputies broke away towards the *Alliance démocratique* in 1911 to protest against its 'soft' line on clericalism and its excessive bias to the Right) moderate Republicans of all shades shared the same vigorously anti-collectivist outlook on social questions. As Caillaux discovered in 1911–12, the price of the support of the *Alliance démocratique* was the shelving of his reform programmes, while Briand was tolerated precisely because he had no plans for reform.

Thus, the left-wing mystique of the Third Republic notwithstanding, by 1911 there developed a situation in which anti-socialism established a large area of common ground between conservatives of all hues, whether traditionalist or Republican. Moderate Republicans who denounced the ALP's 'clericalism' were sensitive to its insistence on the dangers from the Left and the need to defend the social order. The old Right remained in the political wilderness, and its more intransigent members continued to harbour undying hatred for the Republic on ideological grounds. They could, however, console themselves with the knowledge that at least their property rights were safe and that their staunch anti-socialism gave them a certain credibility.

Poincaré and the 'Nationalist Revival'

If anti-collectivism was the principal preoccupation of the Right, it was closely followed by a loudly proclaimed commitment to nationalism. The revolutionary Right, as we have seen, promoted its own brand of aggressive, 'integral', nationalism. The traditional Right distinguishing between the *pays légal* and the *pays réel* – the political structures of the country and their own conception of the real, eternal, France – favoured any measures that would exalt French prestige or military glory. From around 1910, conscious of the growing danger of war, conservative Republicans – such as Poincaré, Barthou and the ex-Socialist Millerand – also engaged in a campaign to engender a greater sense of national unity and pride in the *patrie*, the culmination of which was the passing of the Three Year Law on military service in August 1913.

The key figure in the politics of the so-called 'nationalist revival' was Raymond Poincaré, a successful lawyer from Lorraine. Cold, aloof and unemotional, Poincaré's overriding political concern was the maintenance and enhancement of France's prestige as a great power. As prime minister (1912) and then as President of the Republic (he succeeded Fallières in 1913) Poincaré quite deliberately set out to make nationalism the central political issue of the day. But it was not patriotism alone which made him place nationalism at the top of the political agenda. The 'nationalist revival' was in a real sense a political manoeuvre as much as a response to the deterioration of the international situation or a reflection of mounting chauvinism among the French people.

The nationalist revival affected only a tiny sector of the population – notably right-wing politicians and journalists and, inevitably, the military. Far from being borne to power on a tide of nationalist sentiment, Poincaré was troubled by what he saw as a general lack of patriotism – hence his mission to arouse a spirit of *fierté nationale*. To be sure, over the course of the late nineteenth and early twentieth centuries, it is possible to trace an enhanced sense of belonging to a wider French national community. The completion of the road and railway networks, the experience of military service, above all, perhaps, the spread of elementary education helped to make 'peasants into Frenchmen'. Nevertheless, regional diversity remained strong, even if regionalism was a negligible political force. Nor did the primary schoolteachers of France always succeed in instilling patriotism into their charges – indeed, a significant minority of the *instituteurs* themselves were won over to anti-militarism and revolutionary syndicalism. An older generation of historians who imagined that nationalism replaced religion as the creed of the French masses was mistaken about the nature and influence of both nationalism and Catholicism. The uneven elaboration of a national identity did not turn the French into a nation of patriots. The politicans, therefore, remained obsessed with the need to forge a united nation – always, of course, in their own image. The Radicals conceived of the nation as a product of the French Revolution. The extreme Right had its vision of a strong hierarchical state from which the traces of the revolutionary legacy had been expunged. Nationalism, in short, divided Frenchmen as much as it united them and was frequently a label attached to the promotion of sectional interests.

It is not altogether surprising, then, to discover that Poincaré and other apologists for the nationalist revival were playing their own political game, whose objective was to break up the Radical–Socialist political *bloc* and to recapture the political initiative for the Centre–Right. One way of accomplishing this was to make some overtures towards the Church and its political allies, as Briand did with his non-vindictive application of the Separation Law and by his defeat of the railwaymen's strike in 1910. Another plan adopted by the moderates to stir up dissension among the Left was to bring forward the issue of proportional representation, a measure favoured by the Socialists but bitterly opposed by the Radicals, chief beneficiaries of the existing system. A proportional representation bill was carried in the Chamber of Deputies, after months of debate, in July 1912.

The promotion of the Three Year Law must also, at least in part, be viewed within the context of the Centre-Right's bid to contain the Left. Poincaré and his military advisers were convinced of the necessity of adopting three-year service on purely military and strategic grounds, but the debate on the Law was not conducted on the merits of the military argument alone. Rather, it generated ideological conflict which served to emphasize the gap between Left and Right. All sections of the Right had no difficulty in identifying with a measure designed to strengthen French military power and prestige and rallied to a government which seemed to want to repair the damage inflicted upon the army by the Dreyfus Affair and its aftermath, the *affaire des fiches*. The High Command appreciated War Minister Millerand's exposition of their views in cabinet, while other palliatives such as the reintroduction of military parades were warmly welcomed. The Left, especially the leaders of the CGT and the SFIO, grew alarmed at the Republic's new-found reverence for professional soldiers and their values of hierarchy, discipline and obedience. Jaurès, deeply troubled by the menacing shadow of war after the Agadir crisis of 1911, wrote *L'Armée nouvelle*, a passionate defence of the concept of a citizen-army, which also furnished the opposition with much of its ammunition against the Three Year Bill. With a sufficient number of Radicals won over by the Centre and the Right, however, the bill became law.

The 'nationalist revival', therefore, in the end helped to forge links between the elements of the Right as a whole. By itself becoming a more conservative entity, the moderate Republic of Poincaré was able not only to meet the challenge of the Left but also to contain, and even absorb, the threat posed by extremists of the Right.

5
The Road to War

For the diplomats and politicians charged with the conduct of French foreign policy, the essential task was plain enough: how to preserve and promote the interests of France as a great power. After the war of 1870–1 it was evident that, alone, France could not match the formidible military might of the newly created German Empire. To guarantee her security, let alone fight any putative war of *revanche* for the recovery of the provinces of Alsace and Lorraine ceded to Germany in 1871, France was obliged to try to put together a system of alliances. Only with the signing of the Military Convention with Russia on 17 August 1892, ratified on 4 January 1894, did France finally break out of the diplomatic isolation in which the manoeuvres of Bismarck had maintained her after 1871: only then did her policy-makers begin to act with the confidence and assurance that France was, once again, truly a great power. In the interim, however, at least some Frenchmen, notably the Opportunist statesman Jules Ferry, drew consolation and hope for the future out of the creation of a French colonial empire.

France and Empire

The first step towards the establishment of a new French colonial empire had been taken in 1830, with the military invasion of Algiers. Subsequently, under the Second Empire, Cambodia and the Middle East experienced French penetration, while in the 1880s Tunisia (1881) and Madagascar (1885) both became protectorates. The Tonkin expedition of 1885, an attempt to consolidate the French position in Indo-China, however, resulted in failure and revealed that the cause of empire was far from popular. Nationalists of both the Jacobin and integral variety bayed for Jules Ferry's blood, alleging that his policy of overseas expansion was a diversion from the central problem: Germany. Ferry resigned from office, subsequently complaining bitterly that the only aspect of the empire of any interest to the French public was the belly dance.

Yet colonial expansion continued. The prime movers were the armed forces. Vast tracts of west and central Africa were acquired by French army and navy officers acting independently of – indeed sometimes contrary to – government policy in the 1880s and early 1890s. A rising in Madagascar in 1895 provided the pretext for savage military repression and outright annexation in 1896. Imperial engagements allowed French officers to see action and win medals and promotion: for many they were a welcome escape from the tedium of life in the barracks. Of course Marshal Lyautey and other apologists for the military, such as the philosopher-soldier Ernest Psichari, justified their depredations in terms of services rendered to the French State and the carrying out of a 'civilizing mission' towards inferior peoples: though, paradoxically, those who went to administer the colonies were rarely enlightened idealists but often failures from the mother country who had frequently been unable to obtain the *baccalauréat*. Catholic missionaries also baptized the ideal of empire, in their efforts to claim Africa and Indo-China not just for France but for the Church. Social darwinist notions of race struggle and racial supremacy were widely diffused through pulp novels and travel literature in the 1890s, glamourizing the imperial idea and no doubt increasing its popularity.

The most vociferous and active partisans of empire were, naturally, the members of the colonial lobby itself, the so-called *parti colonial*. Formed around the deputy Eugène Étienne, this consisted of professional men – journalists, writers, academics, civil servants, politicians – but also hard-headed businessmen who formed a number of extremely effective pressure groups both inside and outside parliament. For Étienne, as for Ferry, colonies were necessary to demonstrate that, after 1870, France was not finished as a great power. Though small – in 1914 it numbered at most 10,000 and more likely less than 5,000 members – the colonial lobby exercised considerable influence on French policy-making, partly because of the notorious ministerial and parliamentary indifference to colonial affairs, partly because the new Foreign Minister, Théophile Delcassé, shared their vision of French imperial greatness and made the cause of empire an essential element in his foreign policy.

French imperialism was not confined to the establishment and exploitation of a colonial empire. On the contrary, French financial imperialism was carried on largely outside the colonies, which received only about 9 per cent of all French overseas investments. The French were a thrifty people, and for a century had enjoyed the benefits of financial stability. Accordingly, they had amassed savings of the order of 300 milliard francs by 1914. Investors, reluctant to invest in industry at home and not attracted by the very low interest rates offered by French banks, frequently invested abroad. Roughly 10 million Frenchmen held foreign shares. In 1914 some 45 milliard francs were tied up in investments abroad, either in state bonds or in private enterprise.

Thus, while monopoly capitalism in the Marxist sense was still relatively weak in France (that is, the fusion of finance and industrial capital to form 'monopoly' capital), the French State was by no means insensitive to the political advantages conferred by the investment of French funds overseas. Some politicians, like the banker Rouvier, explicitly argued the case for practising economic imperialism by using French financial power to bring political and economic pressure to bear on other states. The classic example was that of the Ottoman Empire, two thirds of whose public debt was owed to French creditors and whose administration was in the hands of French officials. In the years immediately preceding the First World War, lobbied by French industrialists, governments tried to force the banks to link loans to overseas customers with exports of French goods, notably war *matériel*.

In the colonies financial imperialism was sometimes totally absent, notably in Black Africa and Madagascar, but in other parts of the empire it was very much in evidence. Morocco is perhaps the most obvious example, where powerful interests such as the Schneider Company and the Banque de Paris et des Pays-Bas (Paribas) were involved. Indo-China is another example, exploited by bankers and traders for its rubber but also, in the dreams of at least some businessmen, potentially a door to the allegedly fabulous markets of the Chinese interior.

To determine the precise influence of imperialistic considerations on the making of French foreign policy is virtually impossible: but it would be naïve to assume that they were not of major importance. At the same time, France remained very much a European power, conscious that if outside Europe her great rival was Britain, within Europe the main threat to her security was Germany.

Foreign Policy 1898–1911

The making of foreign policy was the preserve of a tiny handful of Frenchmen. Among the politicians, the two most important figures were the Foreign Minister and the President of the Republic, though how much influence each exercised depended largely on the characters of the individuals concerned. During Delcassé's tenure of the Quai d'Orsay (1898–1905) the Foreign Minister's role was decisive, not least because he was prepared to make use of various agents who operated outwith the normal diplomatic channels. After his resignation, the permanent officials at the Quai – invariably members of an upper-middle-class élite and not infrequently part of an old-boy network based on the École Libre des Sciences Politiques – enjoyed considerable independence until Poincaré, first as Foreign Minister and then as President, reasserted political control. Ambassadors such as the Cambon brothers in Berlin and London and Camille Barrère in Rome liked to initiate, rather than implement, policy, and were prone to evading or exceeding their instructions. The *cabinet noir*, the Foreign Office department which specialized in intercepting and decoding diplomatic communications, also contributed to the making of policy. Such were the people who spoke in the name of 'France' and defined French interests.

The dominance of the few in the making of French foreign policy was consolidated by the absence of any effective parliamentary control and the lack of real public interest in foreign affairs. Deputies, normally so willing and eager to establish their reputations by interpellating a minister on his policies, refrained from meting out their standard treatment to Foreign Ministers. This was partly because they were ill-informed – Albert de Mun complained with some justification that deputies in the German Reichstag knew more about French policy than those in the Chamber in Paris. Partly, too, deputies preferred to concentrate on local, party, or sectional interests, rather than on national policy. In this respect they merely reflected the outlook of most of their electorate, who travelled little and had rarely any more than a passing interest in, or knowledge of, other countries or peoples.

Traditionally, England, not Germany, was France's principal enemy. Plans for war with Britain, predicated on German neutrality, were abandoned only in 1907, three years after the signing of the *Entente Cordiale*. After 1870, however, Germany was perceived to be the main threat to France's position as a major power. Given the chauvinistic belligerence of the right-wing press, policy-makers seem to have assumed that there could be no genuine *rapprochement* with Germany. That is not to say, however, that outside of nationalist and revanchist circles, France and Germany were deemed to be implacable enemies, destined once again to contest the verdict of 1870–1. By 1900 popular enthusiasm for the cause of the lost provinces had waned, and practically no one could be found who was ready to fight for their return. On the contrary, after 1870, many Frenchmen, while deploring Prussian militarism, expressed nothing but admiration for the achievements of German education and culture. Wagner played to full and enthusiastic audiences at the Paris Opera House.

Furthermore, French financial and business links with Germany were strong, especially in heavy industry. After 1906 Michelin and Renault acquired German subsidiaries, while AEG took over a number of French firms. German steel-makers had interests in French Lorraine and Normandy, while Schneider and Saint-Gobain held shares in the coal industry of the Ruhr and German Lorraine. German exports to France increased by 35 per cent between 1905 and 1909. The joint agreement signed between France and Germany in 1909 for the commercial exploitation of Morocco was prepared by preliminary deals struck by French and German financiers and businessmen. Many prosperous Frenchmen welcomed the attempts of Joseph Caillaux to reach an understanding with Germany rather than risk war, defeat and – most terrifying prospect of all – another Commune. If Germany came to be identified as the 'hereditary enemy' it was not entirely because of 1870, but on account of, on the one hand, Germany's policy of *Weltpolitik* especially in its manifestations after 1905, and, on the other hand, the image of Germany fashioned by the paranoid and xenophobic authors of French policy, obsessed by the relative demographic and economic decline of France when compared with the German juggernaut.

Delcassé, who became Foreign Minister in 1898, was a notorious Germano-phobe. His immediate preoccupation, however, was with Britain. His predecessor at the Quai, Gabriel Hanotaux, under pressure from the 'colonial lobby', had initiated a policy of imperial expansion in Africa, with a view to forcing Britain to reach a negotiated settlement over Egypt (the French had never accepted the British occupation of 1881) and to linking up France's colonies in north Africa with those in east Africa. But when in July 1898 Colonel Marchand, after a magnificent march, reached Fashoda on the Upper Nile, his small band of French troops was confronted by the army of General Kitchener. War between France and Britain threatened until, bowing to *force majeure*, Marchand withdrew. The nationalist press in France vented its ire at this 'humiliation' and Delcassé himself flirted briefly with the idea of cultivating Germany in order to try to coerce Britain into leaving Egypt. Anglo-French relations deteriorated even further as a result of the Boer War, which produced strongly pro-Boer sentiments in the French press.

Only in 1903 did Delcassé recognize Germany as the decisive enemy. Earlier however, the colonial lobby had concluded that it was in French interests to come to terms with Britain if France were ever to build a 'Greater France' along the shores of the Mediterranean. They eventually persuaded Delcassé to try to barter acknowledgement of British claims in Egypt for recognition of the primacy of the French presence in Morocco. Italian support for the French design was secured in 1900 by a deal that balanced acknowledgement of French pre-eminence in Morocco by recognition of Italian ambitions in Tripoli. Moreover, though Italy remained a member of the Triple Alliance between Germany, Austria and Italy, in 1902 France negotiated a secret commitment from Italy not to join in any aggressive act against France. British support was not purchased so easily, given her longstanding strategic interest in Morocco as a safeguard for the security of Gibraltar and access to the Suez Canal via the Mediterranean. But British policy-makers were conscious that the days of 'splendid isolation' were numbered and a closer involvement in European affairs inevitable. In 1904, following overtures from French ambassador Paul Cambon in London and reciprocal state visits by Edward VII and President Loubet, an *entente cordiale* was agreed which resolved the outstanding colonial disputes between France and Britain, leaving Delcassé free to pursue the 'forward policy' in Morocco favoured by the *parti colonial*.

The first step was to reduce Morocco to financial servitude by gaining control of the Moroccan public debt and then to proceed to establish a protectorate virtually by stealth, as in Tunisia in 1881. The very speed and success of the French strategy, however, provoked German intervention in the form of the Kaiser's landing at Tangier in March 1905. Germany, he announced, demanded recognition both of the independence of the Sultan and of legitimate German interests in Morocco: and an international conference should arbitrate on the future of the 'Moroccan Question'. Delcassé wanted France to stand firm against what he and the nationalist press had no difficulty in representing as German aggression and intimidation. The French Chamber of Deputies, however (in which Delcassé was an isolated and unpopular figure), refused to back the Foreign Minister and premier Rouvier felt he had no alternative but to sack him if he were to reach a negotiated settlement with Germany. Once again the nationalists were quick to sense a French humiliation. In reality, the international conference convoked at Algeciras in 1906 thwarted German ambitions more than French. Morocco was placed under an international guarantee, but in practice French influence remained preponderant. Delcassé had to go, and France did not get her protectorate, but the crisis had not broken up the Anglo-French *entente*, as Holstein and Bülow had hoped. If anything, it emerged more solid than before and suspicion of German ambitions was intensified.

Even so, France and Germany were still not sworn enemies. The new ambassador in Berlin, Jules Cambon, appointed in January 1907, worked hard to effect a *rapprochement* despite the attempts of fanatically Germanophobe officials at the Quai d'Orsay to sabotage his efforts. The Franco-German agreement on Morocco of February 1909, by which Germany recognized the primacy of French interests in the country but gained the right to a share in its economic exploitation, appeared to hold out hope for a brighter future. That Morocco continued to be a centre of crisis and international tension was due more to French than to German action. From the second half of 1910, flouting the arrangements of 1906 and 1909, French policy (formulated more by the permanent officials than by the weak Foreign Ministers Pichon and Cruppi) opted for a military takeover of Morocco. Under the spurious pretext of restoring order after a revolt against the Sultan (who had not, as the French claimed, called for French assistance) French troops marched on Fez and proceeded to penetrate further into the interior. The riposte of the German

Foreign Minister Kiderlen-Wächter was to send the gunboat *Panther* to Agadir to back German demands for 'compensation' in the French Congo, a solution first suggested to him by French Finance Minister Caillaux, in secret exchanges behind the backs of the Foreign Minister and the officials at the Quai.

Here, for French nationalists, was yet another example of intolerable German provocation. The danger of war was real, all the more so in that Britain, to judge by Chancellor of the Exchequer Lloyd George's speech at the Mansion House on 21 July 1911, appeared not only to share the French interpretation of German action but to be ready to support France in a fight. Fortunately, however, in both France and Germany there were people who preferred negotiation to war. The new French premier, Joseph Caillaux, was one of these, particularly once he discovered that the French army could not be certain of winning a war and that Russia, France's ally, did not recognize the Moroccan crisis as a case for activating the alliance. Still negotiating behind the back of the weak Foreign Minister, Justin de Selves, Caillaux signalled that he was ready to cede part of the French Congo and to guarantee German economic interests in Morocco in return for German agreement to the establishment of a French protectorate. Once news of the proposed deal became public nationalists expressed their outrage both inside and outside parliament. The Chamber voted the Franco-German Convention of November 1911 but the Senate, dissatisfied more by Caillaux's methods than by his policy, forced his resignation in January 1912. Once again, after France had done as much as any power to push Europe to the brink of war, a major conflict was averted by horse-trading over colonial possessions. Whether a clash could be avoided in the future was another matter. From 1911 many people began to doubt it, among them the new French premier Raymond Poincaré.

From Agadir to Armageddon

Poincaré's mission was to affirm the primacy of international affairs before a public opinion that, outside nationalist circles, was much more preoccupied with domestic affairs. As already related, the politics of the nationalist revival were partly the product of an internal power struggle. In Poincaré's own mind, however, especially after Agadir, international issues took precedence. Alarmed not simply by the aggressive posture of Germany, but also, possibly more so, by the unwillingness of Russia to back France over Morocco, he resolved to stiffen the Russian alliance, which he never ceased to regard as the cornerstone of French security.

Poincaré was no war-monger. He had no plans to launch a war of revenge in order to recover Alsace and his own native Lorraine. After Agadir, though, he seems to have been increasingly pessimistic about the prospects for peace in Europe. He did not want war, but if war had to come, he aimed to ensure that France would not be unprepared, either diplomatically or militarily. His night-mare was that, in the hour of crisis, France might stand alone against the might of Germany: hence his almost slavish attachment to the Russian alliance and his strenuous opposition to any attempts to break down the rigid barriers erected between the Triple Entente of France, Russia and Britain and the Triple Alliance of Germany, Austria-Hungary and Italy. Having restored ministerial authority at the Quai d'Orsay, he proceeded to curb the initiatives of independent-minded ambassadors such as Barrère and Jules Cambon, who were looking for ways to ease tensions with Italy and Germany respectively. Alerted by the British ambassador to France, Sir Francis Bertie, he became greatly alarmed at the possibility of a *rapprochement* between Germany and Britain as a result of the Haldane Mission in 1912. With regard to Russia, he feared both her flirtations with Italy, and, much worse, her detachment and re-alignment with Austria-Hungary, possibly opening the way to a resurrection of the old *Dreikaiserbund* established by Bismarck. In 1912 he went in person to St Petersburg to pledge French commitment to the Franco-Russian alliance. It was no part of his plan to give Russia a blank cheque – indeed, he did what he could to exercise a restraining hand upon her – but undoubtedly his conception of obtaining a favourable balance of power maintained through an armed peace made Europe a more dangerous place and brought the continent to the brink of war.

On the military front, Poincaré fully accepted the strategy of the all-out offensive adopted by the French High Command under its new Chief, General Joffre, in their Plan 17 of August 1911. He also fully supported the military arguments for a return to three years' military service, despite the fact that the two-year system had been in operation only since 1905. The law of 1905 demanded high-calibre reservists, but by about 1912 the High Command was convinced that the quality of the troops – conscript NCOs in particular – was not adequate to the task. In February and March of 1913, even before the German army once again raised its numbers, French army chiefs received the backing of premier Briand and President Poincaré for three-year service. Moreover, in the event of war, Plan 17 envisaged a strike against Germany through Alsace-Lorraine. (Joffre, in fact, would have preferred to attack via Belgium, but violation of Belgian neutrality was acceptable neither to the French political leadership nor the British government.) The full strategic and geo-political reasons for the adoption of the law for extended service could not, of course, be divulged in the course of public debate – both to conceal French plans from the enemy and to prevent Republican sensitivities from being disturbed at the prospect of offensive war waged by France. Arguments tended, therefore, to rage along ideological lines, as we have seen.

Few Frenchmen either wanted or expected war in 1914. Indeed, at the beginning of the year a few signs pointed to a slight improvement in Franco-German relations. In January Poincaré accepted an invitation to dine at the German Embassy, while in February agreement was reached on the joint Franco-German financing of the Constantinople–Baghdad railway. During most of the month of July French public opinion was concentrated not on the events set in train by the assassination of the Austrian Archduke Francis Ferdinand and his wife at Sarajevo on 28 June, but by the trial of Madame Caillaux. On 15 July Poincaré and Prime Minister Viviani went ahead with a pre-arranged visit to Russia and Scandinavia, which suggests they did not anticipate the outbreak of war, let alone plan it.

War came because of Austrian and Russian intransigence over Serbia, combined with Germany's reckless determination to exploit the crisis to force a decisive readjustment of the balance of power in her favour – an adjustment acceptable neither to France nor to Britain. The fact that German military plans required the destruction of France and the violation of Belgian neutrality allowed the French to represent their participation in the war as legitimate self defence in the face of outrageous German aggression. France, however, played her full share in ensuring that the war would be a general one. In the final crisis, neither ambassador Paléologue in Moscow nor President Poincaré (the real arbiter of French policy given the incapacity of Viviani) sought to deter Russia from making Serbia an occasion for war or the implementation of the alliance. Their inflexible commitment to the political and strategic imperatives of the Russian alliance, the Three Year Law and Plan 17 shows that France fully subscribed to the notions of prestige, power politics and empire over which the war was fought. If the 'Old Diplomacy' was largely to blame for the outbreak of war, no country was more wedded to the concept than France.

6
A *Belle Époque?*

In the troubled years after the First World War at least some Frenchmen looked back to what they fondly imagined was a lost golden age, a world of financial stability, material progress and glittering artistic achievements. The French, in this view, were a happy, tranquil people, little perturbed by the political agitation that went on both inside and outside parliament, confident in the greatness of the French State and justly proud of the achievements of a civilization that could produce Cézanne and Matisse in painting, Debussy in music, Proust in literature, Bergson in philosophy, the Curies in physics and Henri Poincaré in mathematics – to name but the most outstanding geniuses of the age. In reality, of course, as we have already seen, both domestic and international political developments gave rise to a great deal of concern, and not just on the part of France's rulers. The attractively mendacious myth of *égalité* – the idea that all men (if not women) were equal as citizens and that the mere existence of the Republic was a guarantee of progress and prosperity – fooled only its perpetrators. The so-called *belle époque* was a society deeply divided by inequalities of class and gender and characterized by social conflict as much as by social harmony.

Enonomic Growth

Perhaps the best evidence for the period's claim to be a *belle époque* comes from the performance of the French economy. No longer do economic historians talk in terms of its 'backwardness' and seek explanations for French economic retardation, though none would deny the lack of a real industrial revolution in the nineteenth century, the continuing importance of the agricultural sector (in 1891 17.5 million people, some 46 per cent of the population, still depended on agriculture for their livelihood), and the reality of stagnant population growth. Despite the sluggishness of certain sectors, dynamism was apparent in others and, overall, the performance of the economy was complex and somewhat ambiguous.

The demographic slump was certainly a source of anxiety for nationalist-minded politicians, fearful of its military implications, especially when set beside the rapid expansion of the German population. In 1871 France had a population of 36.1 million people; by 1911 it had reached 39.6 million, an increase of only 9.7 per cent. (In the same period the German Empire developed from 41.1 million to 64.9 million, an increase of 57.8 per cent.) By 1911 France had the smallest population of young people (under 21) in Europe (34.9 per cent, as against 43.7 per cent in Germany). France also had the most old people (over 59): 12.6 per cent, by comparison with 7.9 per cent in Germany. The slow increase in population was the direct result of marital infertility, caused by the deliberate limitation of families through birth control (the most common method being *coitus interruptus*). Between 1898 and 1913 France had a birth rate of 19.5 per 1,000, compared to Germany's 29.1. From 1901 to 1911 the annual rate of population increase was 0.2 per cent. That the population grew at all was a consequence of a drop in the death rate, which between 1911 and 1913 averaged 18.2 per 1,000, whereas it had been 21.5 per 1,000 between 1891 and 1900. On several occasions between 1890 and 1914 the number of deaths exceeded that of live births.

Agriculture, too, was stagnant, and had been since the 1880s, despite a slight recovery in the years before 1914 (when growth took place at a rate of 0.5 per cent per annum). Given the tremendous diversity of the French countryside, however, any generalization about the state of French agriculture is hazardous. The wealthiest farms were those of the large tenant farmers of the Paris basin, who increased their productivity by recourse to fertilizers and new machinery. In 1906 there were about 250 large-scale farms which each employed more than 50 labourers, though in all there were some 1.3 million capitalist farmers, mainly in the north of France, who had the help of at least some waged labour and oriented their produce towards an urban market. Much more typical, especially in the south, were the numerous family farms given over to polyculture and subsistence farming (perhaps as many as 2½ million in 1900, concentrated in Provence, Brittany and Champagne). In other regions, like the centre and south-west, farming was carried on essentially by sharecroppers *(métayers)*, who did not own the land they worked but supplied labour for the owner and, more rarely, some of the equipment and working capital. The wine-growing areas of the Midi, devastated by the phylloxera epidemic in the 1870s, staged a recovery in the early twentieth century, only to suffer a crisis of over-production, which underlay the 'revolt of the Midi' in 1907. Prices of agricultural produce in general rose slightly before 1914, but an atmosphere of crisis clung to French agriculture in these years. In the 1890s tariff legislation was introduced to protect farmers from foreign competition – a political necessity, no doubt, given the politicians' need to woo the support of the massive rural electorate, but one whose consequences were to bolster uneconomic units and to reduce further the competitiveness of French agriculture.

Industrial growth on the other hand, which had made impressive progress under the Second Empire only to slacken off in the 1870s and 1880s, began to rise rapidly from about 1896, and even more so after 1905, inaugurating a period of expansion that lasted until 1929. Industrial production grew at a rate of 2.6 per cent per annum between 1896 and 1906, and at a rate of 5 per cent between 1906 and 1913. Considerable gains were made in productivity and in capital investment, with the fastest growth taking place in technologically advanced industries such as chemicals, electricity and car manufacture. Electrical production, for instance, expanded from 340 million kilowatt hours in 1900 to 1,800 million in 1913, while the power generated by steam multiplied by 1,360 per cent. In the motor industry, France became Europe's leading producer, thanks to the dynamism of such pioneers as Louis Renault and André Citroën. There, too, some manufacturers began to show an interest in introducing American methods of 'scientific management' (or the

'Taylor system' as the French called it after its chief American exponent).
These were the years of France's 'second industrialization'.

Nevertheless, progress was by no means uniform. Industrial growth varied
a great deal from sector to sector. The most striking achievements were
precisely in the new fields – electricity, cars, aeronautics – or in the older
industries, like iron and steel, which they helped to revitalize. The basic
structure of French industry remained largely unchanged, with the bulk of
the workforce (42.4 per cent) still concentrated in the traditional sectors of
textiles, clothing and leather, and engaged in producing high-quality, frequently handmade, goods. Even motor cars remained a luxury product, aimed
at a wealthy bourgeois clientele. In effect, France had a dualistic industrial
structure, which, side by side, ranged industries with many features derived
from pre-capitalist modes of production and others remarkable for their modernity and receptivity to technological change.

In many respects the most striking evidence of economic dynamism was in
the tertiary (service) sector, which grew in terms of its proportion of the
active working population from 21.4 per cent in 1856 to 28.1 per cent in 1906.
Perhaps the most obvious sign of this expansion was the emergence of the
large department store, which came into existence under the Second Empire,
but it was in fact the growth of the small shop or the small business which
was the more typical development. The ideal of working for oneself, making
one's fortune and then retiring to live off investments was at once an incentive
to economic expansion and a powerful force for social conservatism. Here,
again, one can see the ambiguities inherent in discussing French economic
growth.

The Inequalities of Class

France of the *belle époque* was still predominantly a peasant society. In 1911
some 56 per cent of the population still lived in the countryside. The drift
away from the land took place relatively slowly, and, since most of those who
left were rural labourers, in either industrial or agricultural trades, rather
than peasant farmers, the depopulated areas of Brittany, the Massif Central
and the departments of the centre became, even more than in the past,
regions of small cultivators.

Yet the 'peasants' were far from forming a solid, homogeneous class, conscious of their common interests. The rural world was characterized primarily
by its diversity, and reflected wide varieties of wealth and status as between
prosperous tenant farmers, sharecroppers, small peasant proprietors and village labourers. 'Peasantism' – the idea that France was, in a special way, a
peasants' republic – was a myth, put about by the politicians who were obliged
to woo the rural voters at election times. They liked to represent France by
the symbolic figure of the peasant girl Marianne, and they also made real
concessions to the countryside in the form of tariff legislation introduced in
the 1890s to prevent French agriculture from suffering excessively from
foreign competition. In the long run, arguably, these measures did more
harm than good, by postponing rather than solving the problems of French
agriculture and by forcing the urban population to accept artificially high food
prices. Perhaps even more damaging was the way in which peasants learned
to look to politicians to resolve their difficulties, rather than tackling them

themselves. Yet, in the short term, protection did help to preserve the balance between town and country and may, therefore, have contributed something to the maintenance of a certain social stability in France.

Not that the countryside was a contented, depoliticized, arcadian world, insulated from the turbulence of national political life. Even before 1870 rural France had a long history of involvement in national politics, stretching back at least to the French Revolution and evident also in rural responses to the establishment and defeat of Republicanism between 1848 and 1852. Politicization intensified after 1870, as peasants acquired a deeper sense of their stake in the national community through better schooling, the development of roads and railways and military service, though even in 1914 there were communities where rural people were peasants first and French second. In any case the countryside was torn by its own special conflicts and tensions, as peasants grappled with the perennial problems of debt, land hunger and rural depopulation. On occasion, impelled by desperation, peasants might resort to violence, as in the case of the winegrowers of the Midi in 1907. Following a catastrophic fall in prices, itself brought on by over-production, the producers of cheap wine in four of the southern departments (Aude, Gard, Hérault and Pyrénées-Orientales) staged a series of riots under the demogogic leadership of an ex-actor named Marcellin Albert. The Clemenceau government was as ready to use force against peasants as against workers. Troops were sent in and five lives lost before order was restored.

The Third Republic, then, was no peasants' paradise. Peasants suffered from their own anxieties, discontents and hates. Many also seem to have had an increasing sense of their inferiority *vis-à-vis* town dwellers. For many of the younger generation, education offered a passport out of the countryside to what they hoped would be a less rude and more civilized life in the towns.

Urban France embraced only 44 per cent of the total population in 1911 – and, it is worth remembering, for French census-taking purposes a town was a centre of habitation with more than 2,000 inhabitants. In 1900 only 15.4 per cent of the population lived in towns with more than 100,000 inhabitants (in England and Wales the comparable figure was 39 per cent, in Scotland 30.8 per cent). Paris with its three million inhabitants (most of them not native Parisians) easily dwarfed all other centres of population, of which only Lyon and Marseille numbered more than 500,000. Yet urbanization was changing the face of France. Limoges, a town of 25,000 inhabitants in 1821, had grown to 85,000 in 1911. At the same time, urbanization also changed the consciousess of the people who experienced it. Inequalities in the material conditions of life led to serious conflicts and struggles for power and access to resources between workers and bourgeois, both imbued with a highly developed sense of class consciousness.

Much has been written on the subject of *la France bourgeoise*. The phrase's implication that, over the course of the nineteenth century, the bourgeoisie established itself as the dominant political class is broadly accurate. Some historians, however, prefer to dwell on the divisions within the ranks of the bourgeoisie rather than on its sense of class cohesion. They question whether its heterogeneous groups of people – industrialists, businessmen, bankers, members of the professions, bureaucrats – constituted a coherent, self-conscious class, let alone one which also included a *petite bourgeoisie* made up of small *rentiers*, small businessmen, self-employed artisans and white-collar employees. To suggest the endless diversity of the bourgeois class, however, is not to refine it out of existence. What matters for understanding the dynamics of social relations is how different groups of people define themselves in relation to other groups. By this criterion, one can indeed recognize a bourgeois mentality and an extremely powerful sense of bourgeois class solidarity, whether manifested as a code of social behaviour or through the implacable defence of private property and political hegemony.

The older ruling élite, the aristocracy, had long relinquished the direct exercise of political power, except in a few remote areas mainly in the west of France. The prefects of the Third Republic no longer feared any noble-inspired attempts at restoration of the monarchy and Republicans could congratulate themselves on the highly successful propaganda campaign conducted against the aristocracy in the 1870s, by which they had persuaded the peasantry that 'feudal' landlords were their enemies, whereas bourgeois landlords were the best guarantee of order and stability. Though no longer a ruling class, however, nobles retained a great deal of wealth. Over the century 1815–1914, in the department of Loir-et-Cher, total landed property receded by 15 per cent, but noble property by only 10 per cent. The heirs of the Count of Chambord (the Princess of Parma and her children) were still the biggest landowners in the area, with 5,000 hectares. It was the wealthiest landlords, many of whom were noble, who best survived the general reduction in the value of land in the nineteenth century, though it is true that smaller noble families fared less well, some even dying out altogether and others forsaking the land to lead an urban existence.

Nobles, of course, like other social classes, were made up of different elements. Apart from those who could trace their descent back to the *Ancien Régime*, there were many bourgeois who appropriated the aristocratic *particule* 'de' and others who had acquired papal or imperial titles. In consequence there were roughly 20,000 families who claimed to be of noble stock in the mid twentieth century. Distinctions must be drawn, too, between rural *hoberaux* and the wealthy aristocrats who inhabited the noble faubourg Saint-Germain in Paris. Even before the French Revolution, some nobles had already assimilated themselves to the world of the *grande bourgeoisie* – the élites of finance, commerce and industry. The trend continued in the nineteenth century. One finds examples of great noble capitalist entrepreneurs, especially in mining and the manufacture of iron, while by the end of the nineteenth century nobles sat on the boards of directors of insurance companies and, like the playboy Boni de Castellane, were ready to marry an American heiress to repair or extend a fortune. Yet the fusion of aristocrats and *grands bourgeois* into an élite of notables was not total. Nobility retained much of its sense of separateness and exclusiveness. Nobles enjoyed status if not power. Their existence confirmed the reality of a social hierarchy, of which they were the apex. They conferred prestige, and received deference. Their dedication to a life of leisure and idleness gave them an aura of distinction, at least among social snobs. The latter cannot be ignored, since they included Marcel Proust.

For the vast majority of Frenchmen, however, the aristocracy was an exotic and marginal survival from another age. It was bourgeois Frenchmen who most evidently enjoyed wealth, status and political power in the early years of the twentieth century. Most fundamental was the factor of wealth. Certainly, money alone did not make a bourgeois, but without it there was no possibility of maintaining a bourgeois way of life. By 1900 most Frenchmen were better off than they had been in the middle of the nineteenth century, but some were much better off than others. In 1900 2 per cent of the people who left legacies on their deaths bequeathed more than half of the total value of all bequests made in that year, a figure which indicates the existence of a small number of immense fortunes. In the same year, however, 13 per cent of the people who made bequests left sums in the order of 10,000–100,000 francs – amounting to 30 per cent of the total – which points to the existence of a reasonably widespread and comfortable bourgeoisie. Patterns of income tell the same story. One tenth of Frenchmen took 40 per cent of total income in 1900. As many as half a million people lived off investments as *rentiers*, increasingly drawing their income from shares rather than land. For these, the idle rich, especially given the stability of the franc, the period has some claims to be truly a *belle époque*.

Industrialists, bankers and big businessmen formed the top stratum of the bourgeois class. The big capitalists, whether textile manufacturers in the north or ironmasters in the east, exhibited considerable traits of individuality and diversity as to business strategy and political outlook, but in common they wielded enormous economic power. The family firm remained overwhelmingly the dominant form of enterprise, but by the beginning of the twentieth century a shift towards concentration and monopoly was evident in certain sectors: metallurgy, chemicals and banking, for instance. Thus, in the iron industry 12 firms produced 80 per cent of the output, while in the *Comité des Forges*, founded back in 1864, the ironmasters had the most famous and powerful of employers' pressure groups. In an era of economic expansion, the profits realized by the big capitalists were huge. In iron and steel, they rose in some cases by as much as 100 per cent between 1896 and 1914.

France, however, was not overtly a plutocracy. The correlation between the economic and the political power of the notables was much less direct than in, say, the days of the July Monarchy. Some did go into politics – industrialists like Méline, Motte, Jules Siegfried, Schneider and Wendel; financiers like Henri Germain, the founder of the Crédit Lyonnais – but they rarely emerged as politicians of the front rank. Nevertheless, business was able to influence State policy through pressures from chambers of commerce and the like. The protective tariffs of the 1890s were enacted to placate not only the peasants but also textile manufacturers. Some of the biggest businessmen in France – Prince d'Arenberg, of the Suez Canal Company, Florent Guillain, president of the *Comité des Forges* – were among the most active directors of the groups which made up the extremely influential colonial lobby. The Union of Economic Interests, founded in 1910 by Baron Guillaume Cérise, devoted much time and money to lobbying MPs to oppose the extension of State 'monopolies'. It took Joseph Caillaux seven years to pass legislation introducing a graduated income tax. Press barons also wielded real, if indeterminate, power through their newspapers; Jean Amaury's *La Pétite République*, Jean Dupuy's *Petit Parisien* and the other two big Parisian dailies, *Le Matin* and *Le Journal*, had a combined circulation of 4.5 million, and accounted for 75 per cent of the Parisian market. Some of the press magnates went into politics themselves. Dupuy was closely linked with the Republican moderates of the *Alliance démocratique*, becoming a senator and a minister. Humbert, director of *Le Matin*, was in turn deputy and senator. During the First World War, while *rapporteur* of the war budget, he was paid a handsome fee by an armaments factory and used his newspaper to whip up patriotic fervour that, from his point of view, could be translated into lucrative military contracts.

If, then, the *grande bourgeoisie* had no monopoly of power under the Third Republic, it is clear that its interests were well represented by the regime. The politicians tacitly accepted that there could be no serious tampering with the social order. Some key figures, indeed, such as Poincaré or Maurice Rouvier, Finance Minister 1902–5 and premier 1905–6, made themselves the spokesmen for the property interests of the French upper classes. As a body, the ministers of the Third Republic were mostly men of considerable wealth. Their bequests at death show them to have been among the richest 2 per cent of the French population. One third of them were franc millionaires, while the median fortune was half a million francs. About 30 per cent of the deputies came from a *grand bourgeois* background. It was the upper middle class, too, that staffed the top posts of the state bureaucracy, since they alone could afford to give their sons the long, expensive and élitist education required to pass the entrance exams. The advent of democracy may have mitigated, but it did not end, the decisive sway of privilege.

Closely linked to the *grande bourgeoisie* and even more prominent among the political élite of the Third Republic was the professional middle class. There were 72 doctors in the Chamber of 1898 and lawyers (Waldeck-Rousseau, Millerand, Poincaré) were always well represented. After the First World War, Albert Thibaudet was to draw attention to the number of *universitaires* and graduates of the École Normale Supérieure (Jaurès, Herriot, Daladier) by dubbing the regime the *République des Professeurs*. Within the professions themselves, there was great variation as to rewards and status. Engineering was regarded as risky; medicine, despite its associations with science and progress, suffered from the presence of quacks and incompetents; civil servants had prestige but not necessarily high financial remuneration. But, in general, professional people were among the most comfortable and characteristic of the bourgeoisie. The liberal professions were quintessential bourgeois preserves, in that they not only conferred financial independence, but also required the exercise of qualities such as initiative, intelligence and authority. Formed by a long education, usually of a literary kind, with Latin still playing an important role, the bourgeois erected cultural barriers between himself and his social inferiors which confirmed his sense of superiority.

The lower middle classes were a crucial sector of the population by dint of their numbers. In 1900 it was estimated that there were about 4 million small businessmen in France. Of these, only a quarter employed one or more salaried workers. The majority were 'independents' working alone or with their wives or other members of the family. Frequently small shopkeepers, they bitterly resented the advent of large department stores like the *Bon Marché* and successfully demanded of parliament that such stores should pay stiff taxes from which small shopkeepers would be exempt. High profit margins ensured that many small *commerçants* achieved their ambitions of early retirement and, perhaps, of social promotion for themselves or at least for their children. In addition to these, the petty bourgeoisie included State officials: some 130,000 primary schoolteachers, for instance, as well as an army of 500,000 minor civil servants. The village schoolmaster or schoolmistress was not well paid, but enjoyed a certain prestige in most rural communities (clerical areas were an exception). Petty bureaucrats, too, were badly paid and clashed with governments over their right to belong to unions, but they were consoled by the thought that they occupied a station in life above that of the proletariat and enjoyed a certain security and independence. For all their grievances these lower-middle-class elements were not unsusceptible to the appeals of Republican – especially Radical Republican – politicians, who knew how to suggest that the regime was, in a special way, that of the 'small man' in French society. The *nouvelles couches sociales* ('new social strata') did not take over power, as Gambetta had predicted, but at least men from modest backgrounds (like Combes or Delcassé) could now make it to the top of national politics. In the Chamber of Deputies, the proportion of MPs from a lower-middle-class background advanced from 10 per cent in 1893 to 15 per cent in 1919.

Industrial workers were the least favoured section of the French community. Commensurate with the rapid progress of industry in the mid 1890s, significant expansion and change took place within the composition of the French working population. The older, artisanal, forms of production declined, while factory production increased. By 1914 there were around 4.5 million industrial workers. Textiles was still the main industry, but its relative importance had diminished steadily since the mid nineteenth century. In the *belle époque* it accounted for roughly two-fifths rather than half of the total industrial workforce. By contrast, numbers in metallurgy had doubled to about 600,000, while those in the chemical industry, though numerically fewer, were rising even more rapidly (to 130,000 in 1913 from 30,000 in 1870). Female labour constituted an important element in the industrial workforce: in 1906 there were 1,097,000 women workers classified as *ouvrières*. Foreigners, too, played an increasingly vital role in the French economy. Overall, they constituted only 3.2 per cent of the economically active population of France but in certain departments, such as the Alpes-Maritimes, they amounted to as much as 30 per cent. Italians predominated in the east and south-east, Belgians in the north, working in key industries such as metallurgy, chemicals and construction. Their presence was strongly resented by native workers: at least 30 cases of industrial conflict in the Lyon area between 1890 and 1913 arose over the use of non-French labour.

As within every class, there was a wide diversity of material conditions and political outlook. The wool workers of Mazamet in the Tarn, while ready to engage in militant action, as in the great strike movement of 1909 led by the CGT, still voted for parties of the Right in national and local elections, mainly because, as Catholics, they were opposed to the Protestant *patronat*. Even miners, arguably one of the most homogeneous groups of workers, did not all evince a high degree of class consciousness, as expressed through political action. At Carmaux, the other main industrial town of the Tarn, a majority eventually supported Jaurès by 1914, but others voted for the Marquis de Solages. Potentially, miners were among the most powerful sections of the working-class community, and they certainly had a highly developed sense of solidarity forged both by their conditions of work and by their frequently violent confrontations with ruthless coal-owners. The fundamental issue of mine safety alone helped to sharpen class antagonisms. Yet, on the whole, the miners' trade-union movement was led by moderates like Basly, secretary of the Northern Federation. Believing not in revolutionary syndicalism but in reform by social legislation, he himself became deputy of Lens.

The declining fortunes of the artisan class were evident in such industries as clothing, luxury goods, printing, bronze-working and jewellery. In the clothing and footwear industries, tailors and cobblers suffered from the introduction of readymade clothes and shoes by the large department stores (and also from the competition of Jewish immigrants from eastern Europe who were prepared to work for derisory wages). What disappeared in this process was not simply a highly skilled job but a whole way of life. Artisans prided themselves on a certain level of education and had a healthy sense of their own worth. They had long thought of themselves as distinct from, and superior to, the rest of the working class. Faced with proletarianization, they were capable of mounting strenuous resistance, as in the strikes of glass-workers at Carmaux in 1895 and file-workers and glass-workers in the Loire at the turn of the century.

Factory workers were an altogether different breed. The development of mechanization created a new sector – that of the semi-skilled machine operator who worked at a fairly simple, tedious and repetitive job. Known (misleadingly) as *ouvriers spécialisés* (OS), these workers comprised perhaps as much as a third of the industrial labour force in the early twentieth century and were subject to ferocious discipline imposed by supervisors and foremen, especially in the larger factories. Fines were exacted for lateness, absence or insufficient production. Habitual offenders were dismissed. Factory discipline was what the older, artisanal, workers most bitterly resented, and they despised their new OS or unskilled colleagues for their submissiveness and deference. They tried, nevertheless, to mobilize them in their struggle against the devaluation of skill. But, even without artisanal leadership and exhortation, the new workforce was not insensible to the indignities of its condition. In the Lyon area, there were serious confrontations in the mining and metallurgical industries at the turn of the century at Monceau-les-Mines and Le Creusot, where workers demanded the right to organization and representation. Nor were protests confined to strikes. Resistance was also expressed in absenteeism and high turnover rates. At the Decazeville iron works five workers left for one who stayed. In the mines of Carmaux 30 workers left for one who remained. The emotive image of the factory as prison was also common in working-class propaganda, and eloquent testimony to the alienation of factory workers.

Industrial workers worked long hours – at least 10, sometimes as many as 14, more usually 11. By 1914 one of the most important trade-union demands was for the eight-hour day and a shorter working week. Factory workers were also preoccupied with improving conditions at their places of work. The introduction of machinery on a larger scale increased the risks of industrial injuries. Wages, as always, were a sensitive issue. It is true that they increased steadily after 1890, perhaps by as much as 30–60 per cent. Adjusted for rises in the cost of living, 'real' wages were still rising, at least until about 1909. Diet improved, as workers both spent a lower percentage of their earnings on food and at the same time ate a little more meat, vegetables and fruit. But the economic conditions of working-class life remained precarious. Wages were still too low to allow for any saving, or planning for the future, on the bourgeois model. Poverty receded, but anxiety and insecurity were endemic.

Workers inhabited a different physical world from that of the bourgeoisie. They even looked different, being on average much shorter in height. In terms of housing, there was virtual segregation. In Paris workers lived either in poor districts such as Vaugirard or Gobelins or, increasingly, in the working-class suburbs which since the Second Empire had begun to sprout around the periphery – places like Ivry, Pantin, St Denis. It is true that, in Paris, housing was a general, not just a working-class, problem. A survey of 1912 revealed that only 50 per cent of Parisians were comfortably housed (that is, with one room for each person in the household). Some 300,000 people lived in overcrowded accommodation, sometimes with whole families crushed into one room. In the suburbs 45 per cent were deemed to be badly housed. Death came more quickly to the inhabitants of these areas where mortality rates were inevitably higher than in the more salubrious quarters.

The working class also manifested a strong class homogeneity. One was born into it, married in it, died in it. Workers were a class apart, undifferentiated, unknown and even feared by members of the bourgeoisie. Crowd psychologists, masquerading as objective social scientists, well articulated bourgeois terror of the masses. Following on from Taine, who had depicted the popular classes of the Revolutionary period as barbaric, bloodthirsty hordes, Gustave Le Bon in his phenomenally successful *The Psychology of Crowds* (1895) identified workers with vice, alcoholism, disease, insanity and decadence, a prey to subversive ideologies such as anarchism, socialism, and feminism. Haunted by memories of the Commune and traumatized by the more recent murder of Watrin, a hated company official, during a strike at Decazeville in 1886 (hence the verb *watriniser*, to kill an employer), such writers spoke for those who refused to address themselves to the legitimate claims of trade unionists, preferring rather to dismiss them as the ravings of madmen. The Watrin case was the only murder to issue from some 2,700 strikes between 1870 and 1890, yet it was precisely the one upon which the 'crowd psychologists' seized. Fewer than 4 per cent of the strikes in this period gave rise to any violence at all, the great majority being defensive in character.

The reality was that workers set a high store by the value of respectability. They detested idleness and lack of cleanliness – hence their prejudice against such as gypsies and vagrants, and, increasingly, their demands for better, especially cleaner, working conditions. Work was an affirmation of dignity, not a stigma of degeneracy or inferiority. It is not true that they were generally out of sympathy with the more militant, revolutionary syndicalist leaders of the CGT. Certainly, when they went on strike, it was usually for some tangible objective – better pay, job security, a fairer share of the nation's wealth – rather than to start a revolution. But the fact that they consistently elected outspoken militants to be their leaders indicates that they approved of those who most vigorously articulated the sense of grievance experienced by class conscious proletarians. For their part, the leaders did not regard their task as being to stir up industrial strife. Rather, they were there to lend their organizational talents to workers engaged in a conflict and to educate them into seeing the wider implications of industrial disputes. The fact that workers struck ostensibly over pay, conditions of service and the desirability of social legislation is not necessarily an argument for their basic acceptance of the existing social order. What workers demanded in the course of a strike was not necessarily what a strike was really all about, particularly at a time when procedures for arbitration and conciliation were virtually non-existent. Strikes had a symbolic value, allowing workers to demonstrate their strength and solidarity. In this sense, they were either implicitly or overtly political, testifying to the workers' commitment and challenging not just employers but also governments to take cognisance of their demands. It is no accident that some of the greatest strike waves occurred at times of political crisis, for instance in 1899 (in the midst of the Dreyfus/Millerand affairs) and in 1906, when a record number of Socialist deputies were returned to parliament.

In the event, the French State did little to alleviate, let alone eliminate, the inequalities of material existence. Inspired by the doctrine of solidarism, some social legislation did find its way onto the statute books. By a law of 1893 the State committed itself to providing *assistance* for the indigent requiring medical care, though not for incurables until after another law of 1905. A series of laws was passed between 1898 and 1902 to provide workers with some compensation for industrial accidents. A law of 1900 stipulated that in factories where women and children were employed, no worker should work more than a 10-hour day: it was frequently ignored by employers. Miners secured the eight-hour day in 1905. Old-age pensions for those over 65 were introduced in 1910. Most workers, with a life expectancy of below 50, would not live to collect them. The legislators of the Third Republic certainly did not ignore the 'social question' – how could they? – but their attempts to grapple with it were neither bold nor impressive.

One area where the Republicans liked to think that they had achieved a considerable degree of success was education. It was the belief of the founders of the Republic that universal education was the great social reform to be accomplished in order to establish a viable democracy. It was also seen as the key to social harmony and social progress, paving the way to a meritocracy in which careers were open to talent. In practice, the 'school laws' of 1879–84, even if they introduced free, secular and compulsory elementary education for boys and girls and also established State secondary schools for girls, preserved a two-stream system of education which rigidly segregated primary and secondary schooling. There was no automatic progression from the primary to the secondary sector: even for those children (usually the sons and daughters of peasants rather than of workers) who required post-elementary school education, there existed a 'higher primary' sector. Behind a democratic façade (made somewhat more credible in the 1880s by the anti-clerical thrust of the school laws and consequent 'clerical' and 'reactionary' opposition to them) a highly élitist, class-biased educational system was maintained. Less than 3 per cent of boys aged between 11 and 17 were able to attend a State *lycée* – a not altogether surprising figure when fees amounted to roughly 1,000 francs a year. In the State's – or the Church's – secondary schools, bourgeois children acquired the culture, based on study of the classics, French literature and philosophy, that distinguished them from the herd. The children of workers learned to read, write and count. But they did not always learn to defer to their social superiors, even if they entertained few illlusions about breaking out of their cultural ghetto.

The Inequalities of Sex

Class alone did not determine social conditions. For the women of France, who constituted more than 50 per cent of the population, gender was another decisive influence. All women were denied the rights of citizenship. They could neither vote nor stand as candidates in parliamentary or local elections. As far as French law was concerned, women – in particular married women – were inferior beings. The Civil Code required wives to obey their husbands, and assigned to the latter responsibility for the administration of the couple's property. A number of legal reforms were enacted in the years before 1914, such as the law of 1907 which gave wives the right to dispose freely of their own earnings (a purely theoretical advance, in that most husbands appear to have been unaware of their formal entitlement to appropriate their wives' pay). But, in the eyes of the law, women continued to be viewed as minors. The Penal Code likewise discriminated blatantly against women, regarding female adultery as a much more serious offence than that of men and generally sanctioning a double standard of morality, epitomized by the official regulation of prostitution. On the assumption that male extra-marital sexual activity was inevitable and acceptable, the State elaborated a system of controls over prostitution with a view to minimizing the spread of disease and infection. In the era of the *belle époque*, at the behest of a powerful lobby of doctors and parliamentarians who were alarmed by the extent of clandestine, 'unofficial' prostitution and the consequent dangers to the future of the 'race' posed by the venereal peril, the regulatory system was refined and reinforced through the development of *maisons de rendezvous*, in place of the older *maisons closes*.

Moralists constantly preached that women's place was in the home. Yet in 1906 women constituted 36.6 per cent of the total active population, not counting agriculture. Women's participation in the world of work, however, was on terms of massive inferiority. Their representation in top managerial or professional posts was infinitesimal. The legal profession, for instance, opened its doors to women in 1900 but only 0.29 per cent of the profession was female in 1910. Women doctors formed less than 3 per cent of the medical profession. A fundamental obstacle confronting aspiring professional women (quite apart from the weight of cultural prejudice) was unequal educational opportunities. Though the Sée law of 1880 introduced State secondary schools for girls, the curricula of the female *lycées* and colleges prepared their pupils not for the *baccalauréat*, the passport to higher education and the professions, but for a largely honorific diploma. After 1905, following the example of private schools such as the Collège Sévigné and a number of Catholic establishments, some State schools did begin to subvert the aims of the legislator by teaching Latin and entering their pupils for the '*bac*', but equality with boys' schools still lay far ahead. The number of native French female students who entered higher education also remained small, though it increased from 624 in 1900 to 2,547 in 1914. Typically, bourgeois parents showed little interest in the academic achievements of their daughters. As for the women teachers in State secondary schools, the *femmes professeurs*, they had to accept conditions inferior to those offered to male teachers: they were widely regarded as oddities and an affront to the natural order of male supremacy.

As we have already seen, women constituted an important element in the industrial workforce. Their presence, however, was more apparent in some sectors than in others. Only in textiles did they make up a sizeable factory proletariat, forming 55.2 per cent of the total labour force in 1906. In metallurgy by contrast, they accounted for only 5.8 per cent of the workforce. Domestic servants were more numerous than textile workers in the non-agricultural labour force (19 per cent as against 14 per cent of the total in 1896), while women workers in the clothing industry outnumbered both (26 per cent in 1896). Many of these were employed in sweat shops, where they were obliged to put in inordinately long shifts in the busy season, only to be thrown out of work in the 'dead' season. Wages were pitifully low – usually less than subsistence level. Domestic workers were usually the poorest paid of all. In general, even the best-paid female industrial workers could hope to earn only about 50 per cent of the pay of a skilled male worker.

Arguably, it was only in the countryside that women approximated to a relative equality with men. Despite the all-pervasive ideology of male supremacy in peasant society, women were far from being domestic drudges or mere ancillary workers on the farm. Rather, they were partners in the running of the enterprise, with well-defined responsibilities, and essential to its economic viability. *De facto*, they enjoyed both power and prestige, whatever misogynist proverbs or folklore might say. The image of the dominant woman inspired awe and fear among countrymen, and loomed large in peasant customs and rituals: there is every reason to believe that, often enough, it coincided with social reality.

The more blatant forms of gender discrimination did not go unchallenged in the period before the First World War. France had its own feminist movement which, to be sure, never attained the degree of militancy or notoriety of the English suffragettes but, rather, resembled the moderate British suffragists of Mrs Fawcett's National Union of Women's Suffrage Societies. In the early years of the twentieth century mainstream feminism in France was represented by the National Council of French Women, the CNFF, founded in 1900, and the French Union for Women's Suffrage, the UFSF, founded in 1909. By 1914 the National Council boasted roughly 100,000 members, the French Union 12,000. There was also a Catholic feminist movement directed by Marie Maugeret, who gradually converted her members to the campaign for the suffrage and built up a substantial following in the provinces. Radical feminists were few in number, the most outstanding being Madeleine Pelletier, who called for sexual liberation as well as political emancipation. Socialist women, like Louise Saumoneau, regarded the agitation of 'bourgeois' feminists as a diversion from the essential business of the class struggle.

The leadership of the mainstream feminist movement did indeed consist of wealthy, upper-class women, not infrequently from a Protestant background and often having close links with the male Republican élite. Many of these women came to feminism as an extension of their philanthropic activities. Given their character, it is hardly surprising that they developed a moderate, legalistic, gradualist movement which feared male ridicule and shunned suffragette-type tactics. Nevertheless, they had a certain impact on public opinion, not only through their own newspapers, such as Marguerite Durand's *La Fronde* and Jane Misme's *La Française*, but through the big Parisian dailies, such as *Le Journal*, which by 1914 had begun to devote more space to feminist issues. The suffrage issue was raised in parliament. But, most important of all, the feminists squarely posed the question of the continuing validity of assumptions about gender-based roles; and in so doing they added a 'feminine' dimension to all the great national issues of the day: depopulation and the 'future of the race', which obsessed nationalists and imperialists, the various sides of the 'social question' – poverty, sweated labour, bad housing – which preoccupied social reformers of all shades of opinion. The fact that the feminists did not score striking successes does not show their irrelevance, or testify solely to their ineffectiveness as a political lobby. Rather, it points to the degree to which the forces of anti-feminism were deeply embedded in French society.

Male support for the ideal of 'woman by the hearth' came from all points of the political spectrum, from clerical reactionary, through establishment republican, to revolutionary socialist. 'Nature', they all claimed, predestined women for a domestic role. Church leaders looked to women to preserve the Catholic faith in an increasingly secular world. Conservatives worried about the undermining of masculine authority in the family, should women be given the vote. Moderate Republicans expressed fears that women's suffrage would reinforce 'clericalism' and therefore the very safety of the regime. Socialists and syndicalists denounced the exploitation of women workers and demanded the right to domestic bliss for the working-class family. Novelists such as Marcel Prévost depicted, with revulsion, the emergence of a new, sexually-emancipated woman. Doctors countered the feminist demand for the abolition of state-controlled prostitution with calls for even tighter regulation. Most men were reluctant to contemplate an order of gender relations different from that which they took to be natural, traditional and immutable.

Likewise most women. As the feminists themselves were only too well aware, feminism raised at least the possibility of a clash between women's needs and interests as individuals and their responsibilities as wives, mothers and organizers of households. Extremely sensitive to the charge that they were attacking marriage and the family, mainstream feminists insisted rather that it was precisely because women were primarily destined to be wives and mothers that they should have a bigger say in the running of society. Thus, for instance, the vote was sought not as an end in itself but to allow women to make their own special, feminine, contribution to politics. But however much the feminists tried to proclaim the perfect compatibility of motherhood and feminism, most French women seem to have been unresponsive to their arguments. For bourgeois women, marriage represented an important economic arrangement (hence the importance of marriage contracts) but also an institution from which they might derive emotional fulfilment and status. Foreign observers were often impressed by the influence and power exercised by bourgeois women, through their domestic role, whatever the Napoleonic Code might have intended. Their cult of domesticity was not imposed upon them by men but developed out of their own culture and experience.

Working-class women, confronted with the intensification of the sexual division of labour in an increasingly industrialized society, preferred, when they could afford it, to accord priority to family life rather than to seeking work in the form of paid employment outside the home. The vast majority of the female labour force was made up of young, single women: and if France had proportionately twice as many married women in the labour force as, say, Britain (20 per cent as against 10 per cent) an important reason for this was the much more widespread practice of domestic work. The ideal of man as the breadwinner, woman as the homemaker, was deeply implanted in working-class culture. Working-class women were by no means insensitive to political issues, but their political participation was most likely to assume the form of defending the collective interests of the working class as a whole rather than making any specifically feminist demands. Peasant women shared the general political apathy of the countryside and were in any case probably too engaged in their economic role as partners in a commercial venture to be able to respond to the individualistic appeals of feminism. The great mass of French women seem thus to have remained unpersuaded that the pursuit of feminist goals was worth the risk of jeopardizing the material and moral advantages offered to them within the context of the family. But whether they would have regarded the period before the First World War as a *belle époque* seems at least open to question.

II

1914–1940 The Stalemate Society

7
A Nation at War

It is often suggested that the peoples of Europe went to war in 1914 with a light heart. Whatever the truth of this claim for other countries, it certainly does not hold good for France. Most Frenchmen were genuinely surprised when the assassination of an Austrian archduke set in motion a series of events which culminated in the outbreak of a European war. The order to mobilize was received calmly, but it created no small degree of consternation. If the troops went off willingly, it was not because they were thrilled at the prospect of *revanche* but rather because the overwhelming majority of French men and women were convinced that the war had been needlessly provoked by the aggression of the Kaiser's Germany and that the inviolability of French soil had to be defended. A sense of French national consciousness was sufficiently widespread and deep-rooted to be activated by the demands of the *patrie en danger* and, fired by the traditions of 1792 and 1793, had little difficulty in equating the cause of freedom and justice with the independence and greatness of France.

In the sense that there existed a universal commitment to the defeat of the enemy, President Poincaré rightly spoke of 'a sacred union' (*union sacrée*) which bound the whole nation together. Frenchmen of all persuasions had a good idea what they were fighting against. What they were fighting for, in terms of concrete war aims, was by no means as clear. Governments, only too conscious of the fragile nature of national unity, deliberately refrained from any explicit articulation of war aims throughout the duration of hostilities and maintained a flexible, ambiguous position. It is clear, though, that both inside and outside government circles some thought was given to the shape of the post-war world. Thus the French accepted Italian expansion in the eastern Adriatic as the price of Italy's entry into the war on the Allied side in 1915. The French Right made no secret of its desire to see Germany dismembered and reduced to its pre-1870 status. The colonial lobby hoped for new gains in German-controlled parts of Africa and in the Middle East. Delcassé acquiesced in Russian aspirations to acquire Constantinople. When Russia collapsed in 1917, the French military wanted to intervene in the Russian civil war to rebuild the Eastern Front, while French diplomats were more worried about saving the huge French investments in Russia by defeating revolution and re-establishing normal diplomatic and economic links.

That economic considerations might enter into French calculations was most clearly revealed by the blockade of Germany. Though not envisaged to begin with, on the assumption that the war would be short, the blockade was eventually erected into a complete doctrine of economic warfare with the objective of destroying the enemy economy. The Allies tried to deprive Germany of access to markets and raw materials: Germany replied with the U-boat campaign in 1915. Britain and France brought immense pressure to bear on neutral countries such as Holland, Switzerland and Sweden to comply with their attempts to restrict the shipping movements of the Central Powers. The blockade was not the weapon that won the war, but the French developed an enthusiasm for it and mobilized considerable diplomatic efforts in favour of it.

The long-term aims of French policy, however, remained a matter of academic interest while the war had still to be won. The immediate preoccupation was with victory in battle, which, at the outset, was expected to be rapidly forthcoming. Instead, France almost succumbed to an early defeat. As the Germans swept through Belgium and northern France in the first weeks of the war, the military authorities suppressed all information about the reversals sustained by the French army. The gravity of the situation, however, could not long be concealed. On 1 September the government itself was forced to flee to Bordeaux and large numbers of Parisians followed suit, joining citizens from northern towns such as Abbéville and Beauvais who had already preceded them in flight before the invading German army. In the provinces, the arrival of the dead and wounded back in their native towns and villages profoundly shook the inhabitants, especially the older ones, who remembered 1870. Only Joffre's 'miracle of the Marne' – by which the French commander-in-chief exploited tactical errors on the part of the invading German armies to halt their advance on 9–12 September – succeeded in restoring morale and in reviving hopes of victory. Increasingly, however, it was apparent that, far from being over by Christmas, the war was likely to drag on into an indefinite future, though few people realized the magnitude of the horror which lay ahead.

The Soldiers' War

After the battle of Marne and the subsequent failure of either side to obtain open space in the 'race to the sea', France found herself engaged in a war that bore no resemblance to any for which pre-war military strategists had planned. The French High Command, intoxicated with their belief in the superiority of the offensive, had prepared for a war of movement. Instead, they had to confront a situation of deadlock, a war of attrition in which the Germans held the hilly territory of northern France while the Allied armies tried to dislodge them. Yet, in the face of all the evidence, Commander-in-Chief Joffre's faith in the offensive remained undiminished. All through 1915 he attempted in vain to wear down the enemy by means of repeated attacks. The result was that, pounded by the superior German artillery, not infrequently the victims of their own defective shells, and further hampered by atrocious weather, the French infantry sustained casualties in the order of two million, including 600,000 dead, before the end of the year.

The slaughter continued throughout 1916, the year of Verdun. From the strategic point of view, the loss of the great fortress would not have been disastrous. Not only would the Germans still have been unable to force a decisive breakthrough, but also, unbeknown to the French people, who still imagined the fortress to be a key element in the country's defence, it no longer even contained any guns. Thus when the bombardment began in February, Joffre saw no good reason why he should divert resources from the massive Anglo-French offensive which he was planning on the Somme. Prime Minister Briand thought otherwise. In his view, the loss of Verdun would be a crushing blow to French morale and would also jeopardize the survival of his own ministry. Joffre was over-ruled and as the Germans had hoped, the French committed themselves to the all-out defence of an empty fortress which was made to stand as the symbol of their resolve to see the fight through to the finish. General Pétain, reckoned to be the outstanding exponent of the defensive, promised that 'they shall not pass'. The heroic resistance of his men enabled him to keep his promise, but when the fighting finally ended in June 1916, France had lost another 300,000 men, the Germans 280,000.

The pyrrhic victory of Verdun all but broke the spirit of the *poilu*, the ordinary French soldier. While it was poorly trained and untried British troops who sustained the heaviest casualties in the other great battle of 1916, on the Somme, the French still managed to lose another 200,000 men. As Joffre had nothing to propose apart from a continuation of the war of attrition (though he took comfort in the thought that more British than French troops might now be sacrificed in the interests of France) Briand skilfully manipulated him out of the supreme command. Unfortunately, General Robert Nivelle, Joffre's successor, was a man with even more faith in the mystique of the offensive and in his own ability. Having persuaded not only Briand but also Lloyd George that he had a formula which would force a decisive break-through, in the spring of 1917 he launched what he guaranteed would be the vital attack. By this time, however, the Germans had discovered full details of his plans and had prepared accordingly. At Chemin des Dames the French infantry were ordered to advance to certain death, Nivelle having reneged on his promise to break off the attack in the eventuality of anything other than immediate success. At last the *poilus* had been driven past breaking point. From the end of April to mid May 1917 mutiny was rife in the French army. Some 40,000 men in 68 divisions behind the line simply refused to go to the front. Some of the leaders sang the *Internationale* and called for an immediate end to the war, which allowed the generals to blame the troubles on pacifist agitation in the rear rather than on their own incompetence. Most mutineers, however, were neither traitors nor defeatists but brave soldiers who were not prepared to be massacred for no purpose other than to gratify the criminally insane delusions of callous and ambitious generals. Excessively harsh military discipline, quite inappropriate to the realities of life in the trenches, was another major complaint. Pétain, who replaced Nivelle, understood these grievances. He committed the French army to the defensive, preferring, as he put it, to wait for the Americans and the tanks. He saw to it, too, that material conditions were improved. Better food was provided and more leave granted. Repression was also used to restore discipline but on a much smaller scale than used to be thought. Twenty-seven men were eventually shot after court-martial for acts of *indiscipline collective*. Another 2,873 were given prison sentences. Slowly, Pétain nursed the French army back to being an effective fighting force.

French tribulations, however, were far from over. Following the decimation of the British army at Passchendaele, the routing of the Italians at Caporetto and the complete collapse of the Eastern Front, General Ludendorff, the principal architect of German military strategy, was confident that he could deliver a final blow against France. In an attack launched on the Somme on 21 March 1918, the Germans threatened to take Amiens and to split the French and British forces apart. A second main thrust carried the Germans to the Marne and to within 40 miles of Paris, again causing panic-stricken Parisians to take flight. General Foch was given control of the Allied armies in order to halt the advance. His own role in the successful containment of the offensive is a matter which continues to divide military historians, but at the time it earned him a Marshal's baton. Having held back his reserves while the German attack over-reached itself, he was able eventually to launch a counter-offensive which began on 24 July and continued through August and September. The initiative had now definitely passed to the Allies. By the end of September, Ludendorff was ready for an armistice, although the German defensive line remained intact. The Kaiser wanted to fight on, but his fate was sealed by the German Revolution which began at the end of October. On 11 November Foch was in a position to dictate the terms of an armistice to the Germans in his railway carriage at Rethondes in the forest of Compiègne.

The Civilians' War

How did the civilian population react to all the suffering and slaughter in the trenches? As already related, public opinion in France was not prepared for a period of protracted warfare and yet throughout the four long years of the conflict the people of France showed themselves to be solidly behind the war effort. The intensity of their commitment to the *patrie* is not something the historian should take for granted. Rather, it is a matter which calls for some explanation.

In part, the answer lies in the fact that the French State was itself acutely conscious of potential difficulties and took prompt remedial action. To forestall the discontent which might arise among families deprived of their principal breadwinner, a law was passed on 8 August 1914 to provide them with an allowance of 1.25 francs a day, with a supplementary payment of 50 centimes for each child under the age of 16. As a result, a large number of families in the countryside were probably better off than they had been before the mobilization. In the towns, it is true, the allowance would not usually have been enough to compensate for the loss of earnings of a skilled male worker, but urban working-class families did benefit from the government's decision to freeze rents. As well as seeing to the population's material needs, the State also sought to create the right climate of opinion to make people support the war. Rigid censorship of the press was imposed, while a barrage of patriotic propaganda sought to convince French civilians of the valour and heroism of their own troops in contrast to the cowardice and brutality of the 'Boche'. In the long run, however, it may well be that the campaign of *bourrage de crâne* ('eyewash') was counter-productive, for there is some evidence that in time people came to have little confidence in the official version of how the war was going. Certainly soldiers themselves when home on leave were never deceived by patriotic propaganda. On the contrary, they bitterly resented the illusions fostered in the rear about the war, which could only serve to deepen the alienation of the *poilu* from civilian life.

The prolongation of the war posed problems for the State which had never

been envisaged previously. Industrial resources had to be mobilized on a
hitherto unprecedented scale. Improvisation was at first the order of the day,
as ways were devised to meet the demands for munitions, skilled workers,
raw materials, finance and food. Wherever possible, the politicians avoided
creating new bureaucratic structures, preferring to rely on the market and the
co-operation of business. Boards and committees were set up, some simply to
gather information, others to take decisions. By 1916 a system of consortia
(groups of employers attached to executive committees) facilitated collaboration between State and industry. In 1917, with considerable reluctance,
initiatives were taken to control prices and capital movements as well as to
manage production. Rationing of bread and sugar was introduced in 1918.

Direction of the war economy was concentrated in the hands of a small
number of ministers and their teams. The most imaginative was at the Ministry of Commerce, held by Etienne Clémentel between 1915 and 1919. Son of
an Auvergnat miller and hitherto more drawn to painting and writing than to
business, he revealed himself to be a formidable administrator and headed a
remarkable team which included the former businessman Jean Monnet, about
whom a great deal more would be heard in the context of reconstructing
Europe after the Second World War. It was Clémentel who was largely
responsible for the development of the consortia system, in order to control
raw materials and imports, much to the displeasure of most businessmen,
who resented any tampering with prices and profits.

The other key ministry was that of Munitions (until December 1916 a
subdepartment of the War Office). Its first head was the unlikely figure of
Albert Thomas, a socialist and *normalien* who nevertheless threw himself
with relish into the task of producing armaments. His enthusiasm, however,
was not always matched by his achievements. The army complained frequently about the quantity and quality of French shells, while damaging
stories got around about the vast profits made by arms manufacturers. It is
certainly true that, given the State's reliance upon the co-operation of industry, the situation conferred enormous power on the employers, notably on
Robert Pinot, general secretary of the *Comité des Forges*, who was spoken
of as a kind of unofficial minister of munitions. Thomas was also responsible
for the disastrous decision to build a model state arsenal at Roanne, which
cost 203 million francs yet produced only 17 million francs' worth of arms.
Thomas's successor at the ministry in 1917 was a very different individual.
Louis Loucheur was a graduate of the École Polytechnique and had already
made a fortune out of construction in the pre-war period. During the war, he
turned himself into a highly successful arms manufacturer and was Thomas's
assistant on technical matters before taking over the ministry himself. Essentially a technocrat, he was a firm opponent of nationalization and believed
only in selective State intervention. Nevertheless, the achievements of French
industrial mobilization were impressive. At the armistice, the armaments
industry employed some 1.7 million workers, comprising 497,000 men subject
to military discipline; 430,000 women; 425,000 civilian male workers; 133,000
children under 18; 108,000 foreign workers; 60,000 colonials; 40,000 prisoners
of war; and 13,000 *mutilés*. Productivity had also been increased, perhaps by
as much as 50 per cent, as a result of the adoption of Taylorist methods of
scientific management.

State action, whether on the material or moral plane, cannot alone explain why French men and women managed to stay loyal to the choice made in August 1914. Too many people suffered too much for their patriotism to be attributed merely to manipulation. In particular, for the people of the invaded regions of northern and eastern France, the war represented an unmitigated calamity. Families were broken up, property destroyed, goods of every description requisitioned. Thus when Lille was finally liberated it was found that very few homes still possessed a mattress. By order of the Germans, the flour content of the bread was reduced to one third from the end of 1914: the threat of starvation seemed very real. The German authorities also used every means at their disposal to try to break the morale of the indigenous population, not excluding terror. Death was the penalty for those who dared to harbour Allied soldiers on the run. During Easter week of 1916 thousands of men and women from Lille, Roubaix and Tourcoing were deported to the countryside of the Ardennes and forced to do heavy manual labour in the fields. All this is not to say that the average German soldier conformed to the brutal stereotype of the Hun developed in French propaganda. As is clear from the vivid novel *Invasion '14*, by Maxence van der Meersch, German troops often suffered the same material privations as the French civil population and even formed liaisons with French girls. The fact remains, however, that in the invaded regions the war brought little except suffering and ruin.

Parisians had a less harsh experience of the war. But they too could hardly erase it from their consciousness, when troops were constantly to be seen passing through the railway stations. There, too, the wounded were returned in their thousands, while the rapid growth in the number of hospitals in all the major cities widely publicized the fate of many who went off to the combat. Women lived in permanent dread of hearing ill tidings about a husband, a son, a brother, a lover. The comfort brought by a soldier's return on leave was invariably short-lived and could make the pain of separation all the harder to bear. Nor were the sufferings of the civilian population purely moral. In March 1915 Parisians had their first experience of a Zeppelin raid. In 1918 they were shelled by 'Big Bertha', a railway-mounted gun of huge calibre. In addition, the war created economic difficulties for many people. Middle-class families on fixed incomes grew alarmed at the effects of inflation and deplored what they (mistakenly) believed to be the exhorbitantly high wages paid to workers (especially women workers) in the war factories. A number of products became increasingly hard to obtain, notably petrol and sugar. Other items, such as coal and meat, remained relatively plentiful, but as they began to spiral upwards in price they moved beyond the purchasing power of poorer families. In December 1915 the Prefect of Police in Paris noted that without question the greatest preoccupation of the housewife was the high cost of living.

On the other hand, it must be admitted that at least for the first two years of the war life on the home front continued much as in the days before 1914. Few places were quite so indifferent to the war as the proprietors of the Royal Hotel at Evian spa, who, when issuing their prospectus for the summer season of 1915, regretted that wounded soldiers could not be catered for, but guaranteed that service would be maintained with 'all its usual charm'. Nevertheless, to the disgust of army officer and diarist Michel Corday, the good life was still to be had in the bars, restaurants and nightclubs of Paris. Corday also commented bitterly on the number of women who seemed to be profiting from the absence of their husbands to form adulterous liaisons. Even the economic hardships which affected many citizens have to be seen in perspective, for France, cushioned by Allied control of the seas, never experienced the same privations as Germany where already from the beginning of 1915 the government had been obliged to introduce food rationing. Indeed, some sections of French society suffered precious few hardships at all. In the countryside, peasant families prospered as never before, while in Paris the wealthy jewellers of the Rue de la Paix had no lack of custom from the new rich who were doing well out of the war.

In the end, however, neither indifference nor war profiteering can explain why the nation as a whole committed itself to a war which it had not wanted. Ultimately, it was patriotism and a highly developed sense of nationhood which sustained French men and women in the last two terrible years of the conflict. But before an armistice was signed, civilian morale was to be tested to the utmost.

Gradually, sections of the French Left had begun to build up what became a serious challenge to the war aims of the *union sacrée*. One of the first and most indefatigable opponents of the war was the militant socialist Louise Saumoneau, who attended an international conference of women socialists held at Berne in March 1915. Revolutionary syndicalists associated with the newspaper *La Vie Ouvrière* also opposed the war from the outset. In September 1915 two of their number, Merrheim and Bourderon, attended the anti-war conference organized at Zimmerwald in Switzerland by dissident socialists among the belligerent nations. The French delegates were not prepared to back Lenin's strategy of 'revolutionary defeatism' (by which the war was to be turned into revolution), but they backed the common declaration against the war and on their return established a Committee for the Resumption of International Relations which attracted strong support from certain sectors of the labour movement, notably the metalworkers and the primary schoolteachers. Within the SFIO Zimmerwaldiens were few, but a minority tendency in favour of a negotiated peace was orchestrated by the deputy Jean Longuet and the new SFIO newspaper *Le Populaire*, with considerable backing from a number of the provincial federations (Haute-Vienne, Isère, Rhône). Three Socialist deputies attended the Kienthal conference of April 1916 called by the Zimmerwaldien movement (Merrheim and other syndicalist delegates were refused passports by the government) and on their return refused to vote for war credits.

By the spring of 1917 signs of war weariness in the country at large were unmistakeable. Agitation was general throughout the clothing industry in May and June, following a successful strike by Parisian dress-makers for higher pay and the 'English week'. At the same time, there was a wave of strikes in the war factories, with women again well to the fore. Although the basic cause of these strikes was the soaring cost of living, anti-war slogans were also chanted sporadically. The right-wing press spoke of sabotage and treason, while the government was greatly alarmed. In June 1917 only three prefects could report that morale in their departments was 'good'. Seventeen, on the contrary, judged it to be positively 'bad', the larger towns being the most disaffected. Had the military authorities been unable to restore discipline and confidence in the army after the mutinies, it is possible that the French State might have fallen apart. As it was, the high morale of soldiers home on leave seems to have comforted and reassured the civilian population, so that the situation eased considerably by the end of 1917.

Pacifist agitation, however, was yet to reach its peak. After months of unrest, particularly among the metal-workers of the Loire, a massive strike wave ran through the metal industry in the spring of 1918. Unlike the strikes of the previous year, these were overwhelmingly strikes of male rather than female workers, with political rather than economic goals. Orchestrated by a committee of revolutionary syndicalists, they were inspired by the example of the Bolshevik Revolution and aimed both to end the war and to start a revolution. But France under the Clemenceau regime was a far cry from Russia, and the movement was ruthlessly suppressed. Even so, it would not be true to say that the strikers had failed only because they were confronted by the superior forces of the French State. At bottom, the rank and file workers shared neither the pacifist nor the revolutionary aspirations of their leaders. Though heartily sick of the war, they had no wish to see France lose the fight, and therefore refused to jeopardize the chances of victory by industrial sabotage. Thus in the Isère both individual workers and peasants were prepared to contemplate a continuation of the war into 1919 or even 1920. The reservoir of patriotism among the least privileged citizens of the Republic is perhaps the key to understanding why the French nation was able to go *jusqu'au bout*.

Politicians at War

In the face of what was universally deemed to be naked German aggression, French politicians of all persuasions agreed to suspend their own internal quarrels and to rally to the 'sacred union' proclaimed by President Poincaré in his address to the Chamber of Deputies of 4 August 1914. The only political issue became how best to crush the common enemy. All the major political figures wanted to serve the *patrie* in its hour of need and at the end of 1914 Prime Minister Viviani put together a 'sacred union' cabinet, which included such diverse politicians as Delcassé (recalled to the Foreign Office), Millerand (Minister of War), Briand (Keeper of the Seals) and Ribot, a conservative Republican who had been unable to form a ministry in June 1914 because he was considered too moderate. Perhaps even more indicative of the new spirit of reconciliation was the entry into the cabinet of the doctrinaire Marxist Jules Guesde, as Minister of State, while the appointment of Marcel Sembat to the Ministry of Public Works confirmed socialist commitment to the common cause. Poincaré himself was all for including a prominent member of the Catholic Right (such as Albert de Mun or Denys Cochin) in the cabinet, but Viviani and Malvy, the anti-clerical Radical–Socialist Minister of the Interior, convinced him that the Chamber was not yet ready to go to quite that length in pursuit of sacred union. Even so, it was certainly encouraging that Edouard Vaillant and Albert de Mun, two parliamentary colleagues who had never greeted each other, having been on opposite sides of the barricades during the Paris Commune of 1871, now agreed to shake hands. The prudence shown by Minister of the Interior Malvy in not arresting the left-wing figures on the file known as *Carnet B* was amply vindicated.

It should not, however, be imagined that the formation of the *union sacrée* obliterated all the great issues, religious, political and social, which had divided Frenchmen before 1914. The sacred union was really a political truce, an agreement to postpone domestic conflicts for the duration of what everyone anticipated would be a short war. Once it became clear that the war was going to be a much more protracted affair, the politicians were able to return to their trade, and notably to the question of the loss of parliamentary control over government, only too evident in Joffre's assumption of virtually dictatorial powers for the conduct of the war. Millerand, at the War Office, was content to act as the spokesman for the Commander-in-Chief. Although Joffre's prestige as the victor of the Marne was such that he could not be attacked overtly, in the course of 1915 the mismanagement of the war was turned into a political issue. A storm of protest followed the Generalissimo's dismissal of General Sarrail from the command of the Third Army. Joffre claimed that Sarrail had failed in the field, but it was known to a number of Socialist deputies that officers in the Third Army had been highly critical of Joffre's handling of the war. Worse still, Sarrail was the epitome of the political general, a militant anti-clerical with many friends in the higher reaches of the Radical party, and they were not slow to allege that Sarrail had been victimized for his political opinions by the reactionary Commander-in-Chief. If Joffre himself was still beyond attack, the same was not true of his protector, Millerand, who came under increasing fire, as did the virtually senile Delcassé at the Quai d'Orsay. These pressures forced the resignation of the Viviani government in October 1915.

Viviani's successor was Briand, who sought to strengthen the *union sacrée* by the inclusion of Denys Cochin in his cabinet alongside the man who personified anti-clericalism, Émile Combes. His other preoccupation was to restore civilian control of the conduct of the war, ultimately by the removal of Joffre. The consternation provoked by the slaughter of Verdun gave him his opportunity. Aware of the government's increasing unpopularity from the voting returns in the secret sessions of parliament, Briand made Joffre a Marshal of France and effectively kicked him upstairs at the end of 1916. At the same time he carried out a cabinet reshuffle, bringing in the imperious Military Governor of Morocco, General Lyautey, as Minister of War. Lyautey proved to be a singularly unfortunate choice since, unaccustomed to parliamentary ways, he soon managed to infuriate the Chamber by questioning the right of deputies to discuss the conduct of the war even in secret session, thus precipitating the fall of Briand in March 1917.

The new Prime Minister was the octogenarian moderate Ribot. Formally, he kept the *union sacrée* in existence, retaining Denys Cochin and also the right wing Socialist Albert Thomas as Minister of Munitions. Confronted with the most critical phase of the war, however, the Ribot cabinet proved short-lived. The failure of the Nivelle offensive at Chemin des Dames, followed by the mutinies in the army, the massive industrial unrest in the spring of 1917 and the disintegration of Russia all led to renewed secret sessions of parliament in which the government was subjected to severe criticism. On the one hand, many Socialists now wanted to try to end the war by a negotiated peace and demanded that the government allow them to send a delegation to hold talks with fellow socialists at an international congress to be held at Stockholm. On the other hand, the extreme Right bayed for the blood of Interior Minister Malvy, whom they denounced as a German agent responsible for the spread of defeatist sentiments among mutineers at the front and strikers at the rear. Georges Clemenceau, without subscribing to the hysterical charges brought against Malvy by the zealots of the *Action Française*, had also blamed the minister for his indulgence towards the Left ever since his refusal to round up the trade-union suspects on the notorious *Carnet B*. Now he was able to allege that Malvy was guilty of criminal negligence in failing to pursue the pacifists associated with the newspaper *Le Bonnet Rouge*, which, since the arrest of a shady journalist named Duval in May 1917, was known to be subsidized by the Germans. In a public session of the Senate on 22 July 1917 Clemenceau indicted Malvy of having betrayed the interests of France.

The atmosphere of crisis was intensified when the editor of the *Bonnet Rouge*, an anarchist known variously as Vigo and Almeyreda, was found dead in his cell two weeks after his arrest in August 1917. The official explanation was suicide, but the *Action Française* was not slow to allege that he had been murdered before he could reveal ugly truths about prominent politicians. In these circumstances, the Ribot government was forced to resign at the end of August, to be followed not by Clemenceau, who according to the Socialists was likely to provoke the working class, but by the mathematician and Republican–Socialist Painlevé. The formation of the Painlevé cabinet formally marked the end of the sacred union at ministerial level, for the Socialists, indignant both at not being allowed to send representatives to Stockholm and at the treatment of their protector Malvy, refused to participate.

Painlevé lasted only two months. Formed on 13 September 1917, his ministry coincided with the routing of the Italians at Caporetto and with the victory of the Bolsheviks in Russia. At home, more scandals came to light, one involving a deputy named Turmel, another the senator and newspaper magnate Humbert, a third the shady but well-connected Bolo Pasha. The demand for a negotiated peace was by this time no longer confined to socialist circles, but was being advocated by ex-premier and Finance Minister Joseph Caillaux. Even Briand had begun to explore ways of bringing the war to an end. Outraged by these tendencies, Clemenceau forced Ribot, Painlevé's Minister of Foreign Affairs, to tell parliament in secret session that no terms acceptable to France had been offered and that in any case France considered herself bound by treaty obligations not to conclude a separate peace. Manifestly lacking in both authority and determination, the Painlevé government was overthrown on a vote of confidence in the Chamber in November 1917. Poincaré now felt that he had no option but to call upon a man whom he cordially loathed but who, more than any other French politician, embodied the national resolve to see the fight to a finish: 'the Tiger', Georges Clemenceau.

Clemenceau was 76 when he came to power. Throughout the war, he had in his newspaper *L'Homme Enchâiné* been an unremitting though not always realistic critic of the French failure to win a decisive victory. As his political adversaries pointed out, many of his articles reappeared as propaganda in the *Gazette des Ardennes*, the paper inflicted upon the inhabitants of the northern territories under German occupation. For a scourge of defeatists, Clemenceau, on occasion, though doubtless unwittingly, came close to purveying defeatism himself, as when he made the sensational claim that Verdun had fallen on 3 March 1916. Of his patriotic ardour and iron determination there could, however, be no question. In the course of a heated debate in the

Chamber in March 1918, he summed up his policy: 'Internal policy, I wage war; foreign policy, I still wage war'. Such was the outlook of a man who came to be known as *Père-la-Victoire*.

The Clemenceau ministry has passed into socialist mythology as a repressive, even dictatorial, regime. Yet Clemenceau's biographer relates that, to Poincaré's great chagrin, he was in reality much less tough than he had promised to be in opposition. Duval, Bolo and others, including the celebrated female spy Mata Hari, were tried and executed, but as most of the main treason cases were already *sub judice* when Clemenceau took office his advent to power had little influence on their outcome. Clemenceau also proved much more conciliatory towards organized labour than Poincaré had expected. Talks were arranged with syndicalist leaders such as Jouhaux and Merrheim, while employers were encouraged to make concessions to the unions' demands for higher wages.

There is, nevertheless, plenty of evidence of a new and harder line towards political opponents. A considerable number of people, guilty only of wishing to see an end to the senseless slaughter, found themselves clapped in jail. The feminist Hélène Brion was only one of many militant schoolteachers who were sacked and tried for their pacifist sentiments. Parliamentary life was effectively stifled, since Clemenceau, who had been foremost in the demand for secret sessions of parliament while he himself chafed under the wartime censorship, saw to their abolition once in office. Caillaux, whom Clemenceau regarded as a dangerous political opponent, had his parliamentary immunity removed and was then arrested in January 1918. (Brought to trial only in 1920, he was convicted of the bizarre crime of treason with extenuating circumstances.) As for Malvy, whose negligence had opened the way for Clemenceau's assumption of power, when tried (at his own request) before the Senate sitting as a High Court, he was found not guilty of treason, but was convicted of a dubious crime called 'improper conduct' with which he had not been charged. Clemenceau also made no pretence of maintaining the sacred union. The Socialists were now treated openly as the opposition, and however much Clemenceau might like to think of himself as an apolitical figure, towering above party, his was in essence, if not in composition, a government of the Right. It was certainly a government dominated by a single man. Pichon, the Foreign Minister, for instance, was a mere cypher. Clemenceau alone decided policy and relied upon his faithful henchmen Mandel and General Mordacq to see to the execution of his orders.

It would, however, be wrong to suggest that Clemenceau was a dictator who compelled a reluctant people to fight on against their will at a time when the war could have been ended by a negotiated peace. For one thing, no terms which would satisfy French honour and justify the sacrifice already made were on offer. Exploratory talks carried on with emissaries of the Austrian government had already come to nothing when Clemenceau indignantly repudiated the suggestion of Count Czernin, the Austrian Foreign Minister, that France had made approaches for a separate peace. As for being a dictator, Clemenceau was able to govern as he did only because he enjoyed the support of the great majority of the French people, who shared his commitment to outright victory. Far from being the enemy of parliamentary institutions, he ensured that power remained in civilian, rather than in military, hands. Here he was helped by the fact that neither Pétain nor Foch aspired to the supremacy exercised by Joffre in the first two years of the war and that differences between them allowed Clemenceau to play one off against the other. Nevertheless, however much certain elements on the far Left may have dreamt of emulating the Bolsheviks, it seems far more likely that a French collapse in the war would have been followed not by the establishment of French soviets but by a takeover by the generals, backed by the extreme Right. It was not the least of Clemenceau's achievements to further consolidate the legitimacy of the Republican form of government, even if in doing so he contributed heavily to the swing to the Right which was to be the dominant factor in French politics in the immediate post-war years.

8
The Aftermath of War

The Harvest of Victory

Having won the war, France faced the no less daunting task of winning the peace. Clemenceau, who maintained decisive control over French policy in peacetime as in wartime (to the distress and frustration of President Poincaré and of military leaders, among them Foch), had one overriding objective at the peace conference which opened at Versailles in January 1919: to guarantee French security against any future threat from Germany. This not to say that he wished to impose draconian terms on the defeated Germans: the legend of the 'Carthaginian' peace (whose fabrication owed much to the British economist J. M. Keynes) has been exploded by recent research on the Versailles settlement, especially in its financial and economic provisions. Nevertheless, Clemenceau and other French statesmen were only too well aware that, in order to ensure the continuing independence and great-power status of France, serious limitations had to be set upon Germany's sovereignty. Such had been France's objective in fighting the war and, given the price of victory in terms of lives and material damage, it was not unnaturally what she expected of the peace, even if French claims manifestly clashed with the ideals of national self-determination championed so ardently and with such disastrous consequences by President Woodrow Wilson of the United States.

In the first instance, France demanded the destruction of German militarism: the German army was reduced to a token force of 100,000 men and Germany deprived of her navy. France also insisted upon a reduction of German territory: ideally, for sections of the Right and the military, headed by Marshal Foch, German unification would be undone. Neither Wilson nor Lloyd George would contemplate the dismemberment of the German State but they did agree to strip Germany of her colonial possessions. In Europe, Germany lost comparatively little territory, most of it in the east to the resurrected state of Poland and the new state of Czechoslovakia. France recovered Alsace and the lost parts of Lorraine, and was also ceded the Saar coalfields for 15 years. The Saarland itself went not to France but to the newly created League of Nations for the same period, after which time a plebiscite was to be held to settle its fate definitively. With regard to the Rhineland, Clemenceau pursued a hardline but flexible diplomacy which envisaged its detachment from Germany in some form, most probably as a separate Rhenish Republic. In the end, he had to settle for a demilitarized, temporarily occupied, but still German Rhineland, though as the price of conceding on this issue, he was delighted to extract from America and Britain a guarantee of French security in the event of a German attack.

While Clemenceau conceived of 'security' primarily in strategic terms, it was also the intention of French policy-makers to curb the economic power of Germany. Clémentel in particular argued that without a real and permanent redistribution of economic resources France could well be threatened once again by Germany's sheer industrial might. His idea was not to saddle Germany with crippling reparations but rather to effect a bold reorganization of the whole world economic order by the continuation of the inter-Allied cooperation of the war years and the integration of Germany into the new system. German industrial strength would thus be made to work for the general good of the world economy.

Clémentel's vision became the basis of French government policy. Only when these schemes were rejected by the Americans did the French begin to talk seriously about large reparations payments, in the first instance as a ploy in negotiations to win over the Americans, and then, when that failed, as a realistic and fairly modest demand to which even Wilson could adhere (the sum in question was about 120 milliard gold marks). It was not the French but the British who insisted in raising the cost of reparations by calling for the inclusion of pensions and separation allowances, as well as compensation for material damage. The huge amounts now bandied around, not surprisingly, produced outrage among the Germans, who had agreed in principle to contributing something to the cost of rebuilding Belgium and northern France. In the end, the Treaty did not stipulate a fixed sum but set up a Commission of Reparations to determine the appropriate figure by May 1921. The historical record, therefore, does not show a victorious and vindictive France determined from the outset to ruin the German economy and to restore French finances on the principle of *le Boche paiera*. Rather, more than most, it was the French who showed some understanding of the fact that a successful return to peace would involve reorganization of the whole world economy.

In addition to the military, political and economic provisions of the Versailles Treaty which aimed at constraining Germany, France acquired the former German colonies of Togo and the Cameroons in Africa along with Syria and Lebanon in the Middle East, and thus reached the zenith of her overseas expansion. Clemenceau could contemplate with some satisfaction that, in the event of a future war, he had provided for another contingent of black colonial troops to fight on France's behalf. In Morocco, Marshal Lyautey consolidated French authority by a combination of diplomacy and force, though in 1925 Marshal Pétain had to be sent to put down a serious revolt in the Rif led by Abd el Krim. In 1921 the Minister for the Colonies, Albert Sarraut, drew up a grandiose plan for the economic development and exploitation of France's overseas possessions, which in the event was never implemented. Nevertheless, French investors began to show much more interest in the colonies as an investment proposition than they had done before 1914. By 1939 the empire accounted for 45 per cent of all French overseas investment, compared with 9 per cent in 1914. Thirty per cent of all French foreign trade was also with the colonies by the mid 30s. The existence of a huge overseas empire contributed not a little to French delusions of grandeur.

The Price of Glory

France had won a great victory. But, on the morrow of her triumph, France had to count the cost at which victory had been purchased. It was frighteningly high. Frenchmen, parsimonious with their seed, had been prodigal with their blood. One million three hundred and twenty-two thousand soldiers perished, 16.6 per cent of all those mobilized – the highest proportion of all the major belligerent countries. Forty-two per cent came from a rural background: the countryside was bled white. In terms of age, the worst affected were young men aged 20 in 1914: more than 25 per cent of this cohort was killed. The sorrow and suffering engendered by such slaughter cannot be measured, but it can be imagined. An indication of the scale of the tragedy is that it left 600,000 widows eligible for State pensions and more than 750,000 orphans who required to be officially 'adopted' by the State.

As well as the dead, France had to reckon the cost of the three million wounded. Of these, at least a third suffered from a permanent disability which qualified them automatically for a pension. More than 125,000 had lost at least one limb. Another 42,000 had been blinded. Countless others would suffer recurrent nervous disorders induced by the abiding effects of shell-shock. Once again, it is beyond the powers of the historian to recapture the physical and moral suffering experienced by *mutilés* and their families: but one does not doubt that it was immense.

A more precise appraisal can be made of the demographic and economic impact of the human catastrophe. In a country where the birth-rate was already alarmingly low, as the death toll rose, the number of births plunged to a record low in 1916 (in keeping with the inevitable decline in the marriage rate). That year there were only 313,000 live births in the non-invaded regions, giving a birth-rate of 9.5 per 1,000 as against 18.2 (for the whole of France) in 1912. In 1919 the corresponding figures were still only 403,500 and 12.6. Between 1909 and 1913 just over four million births were registered for the 87 departments. Between 1915 and 1919, in the same departments, the total dropped to just under 2.25 million. That is, some 1.75 million babies were 'lost'. The full effects of these losses were to be felt only later, when these unborn children would have been young adults. As it was, in 1938, there was only roughly half the normal number of 19- to 21-year-olds. The shortage of manpower reached its peak when France faced a new, and even more dangerous, threat to its existence.

The demographic damage inflicted by the war had immediate consequences for the structure of the French labour force. In 1919 it was estimated that France was short of three million workers. To make good the deficiency, it was necessary to have massive recourse to the recruitment of immigrant labour. In contrast with the pre-war situation, where immigrant labour was largely unregulated, the State itself took charge of organizing the supply of foreign workers, just as it had done during the war. Between 1919 and 1924 the State helped to settle more than a million foreign workers in France (mainly Italians, Spaniards and Belgians) who played a crucial role in the post-war reconstruction of the devastated areas. In addition, a commercial immigration company, the *Société générale d'immigration* (SGI), specialized in the recruitment of Polish workers to work in mining and agriculture. In the 1920s it supplied more than 500,000 workers, or 28 per cent of the total foreign labour force in France. Just under two million foreign workers came to work in France between 1920 and 1930. Non-communist labour leaders such as Léon Jouhaux accepted that the foreigners were a necessary addition to the labour force in France but only on condition that they were strictly regulated. Native workers, however much they may have benefited from being released from the dirtiest and most menial jobs, strongly resented the presence of foreigners in their midst and rarely extended a hand of welcome or friendship.

The material damage sustained during the war was staggering. Ten departments of the north and east had been invaded and finally laid waste by the Germans when they retreated. Mines, blast furnaces, roads, railways, agriculture – all were ravaged. Seven and a half per cent of existing buildings were destroyed. Sometimes whole towns lay in ruins. Reims was left with 17,000 inhabitants out of 117,000, Soissons with 500 out of 18,000. Close to three million hectares of fertile farm land were devasted. Much of the livestock had been slaughtered.

The war also wreaked havoc with French public finances. The French State had paid for the war by quitting the gold standard, borrowing massively and printing money, which had produced an enormous debt and soaring inflation. The debt now stood at 175 billion francs, a figure more than five times greater than in 1913, while prices had risen by more than 400 per cent since 1914. France was no longer in a position to be one of the world's major creditor nations. During the war it had proved necessary to liquidate foreign investments in the order of some 700 million US dollars. Private investors in government securities in central and eastern Europe sustained losses of a staggering four billion dollars. In all, France lost about 50 per cent of her pre-war overseas investments – one reason for the high figure being that the new Soviet regime in Russia refused to honour the debts incurred by the Tsars. Reconstruction (reckoned to cost about 100 million francs) and paying compensation to the victims of the war would inevitably add to the financial burdens of the State. In the circumstances, it is not difficult to see how the cost of reconstruction and reparations emerged as the burning political questions of the immediate post-war period.

The war effectively dealt a body blow to the liberal economic order which had prevailed in France before 1914. By the end of the war, most aspects of economic life had become subject to controls and intervention on the part of the State. Even before hostilities were over, ministers like Albert Thomas and Clémentel had begun to think ahead to the problems of demobilization and reconstruction. Thomas chaired a committee whose membership included labour leaders such as Jouhaux, Merrheim and Keufer, as well as industrialists like Renault, and whose brief was to devise ways to streamline, rationalize and modernize the French economy in a spirit of class collaboration. Clémentel's department prepared various schemes for post-war economic reorganization, aimed at equipping French industry for success in the struggle for world markets and at preventing the resurgence of Germany as an economic power capable of dominating France. In Clémentel's view, the victory in the field had to be consolidated by the perpetuation of the wartime pooling of resources and raw materials practised by the Allies. He also invisaged a new, corporatist, partnership between State, industry and labour, along with the extension of Taylorist 'scientific management'. For Clémentel and his team, the old economic liberalism was incompatible with the ambition of France to remain a power of the first rank.

Most French businessmen, on the other hand, viewed the economic dirigisme of Thomas and Clémentel with intense suspicion. The wartime consortia came under fire from chambers of commerce and employers' associations. Clémentel failed to become Clemenceau's Minister of Industrial Reconstruction. The post was awarded to Loucheur, who did everything possible to thwart Clémentel's grand designs. The rebuilding of France was to be accomplished by private initiative, not State direction. Wartime restrictions on trade were speedily abandoned. The consortia were formally abolished in 1919. Britain and America showed no interest in continuing with co-operation in sharing raw materials. Business returned to 'normal' – which included the imposition of high protective tariffs, since apologists for the 'liberal' economy were highly selective about the freedoms they wished to defend.

Yet a full return to pre-1914 ways was not possible. The enlargement of the role of the State could be seen, for instance, in its direction of the new immigrant workforce. Its increased involvement with industry was also evident in a number of mixed companies formed in certain key sectors such as mining and hydro-electricity. The railways were placed under a *Conseil supérieur des chemins de fer* in 1921. The *Compagnie française des pétroles* (CFP) was established to exploit former German shares in the Turkish Petroleum Company, which gave France its own petroleum industry, though it is true that at this stage the State was a reluctant partner in the enterprise.

In a number of sectors the demands of total war acted as a powerful economic stimulus: in metal-processing and chemicals, for instance. France was obliged to compensate for an iron and steel industry which produced only about a third of Germany's output and for the lack of ammonia and nitric acid essential for the fabrication of explosives. The French also began to produce their own electric dynamos, tubes and carbon steel wire. Output of hydro-electric power doubled. Pioneers of the car industry transformed their factories to the needs of war production. The Citroën factory in the fifteenth *arrondissement* of Paris, which did not exist in 1914, employed nearly 10,000 workers in 1918. Renault, which employed 6,300 workers in 1914, had 22,500 in 1918, engaged in producing tanks, lorries and aircraft, as well as cars. Daily production of 75mm shells increased from 10,000 in 1914 to 300,000 by May 1917.

Yet it would be a mistake to view the war as a vital stage in the industrialization of France. Sectors of secondary importance to the war effort were allowed to languish. The labour force in the building industry was halved between 1914 and 1917. Textiles and food also underwent decline. The war thus checked as well as stimulated economic growth and shifted production towards activities which were not always readily reconvertible to the requirements of peacetime. It revealed the underlying dynamism of the French economy, which boded well for recovery, but the war was not responsible for an industrial revolution.

Just as there was no economic revolution, so there was no social revolution – though, as we shall see, in 1919 and 1920 the French bourgeoisie was frightened by the prospect of a Bolshevik-style seizure of power by the Left. The social structure of France remained substantially unchanged. The bourgeoisie suffered its share of the war dead: 19 per cent of the officer class, as opposed to 16 per cent of the troops, perished. Two hundred and twenty-seven pupils or ex-pupils of the École Normale Supérieure from the promotions 1894–1918 were killed (20 per cent of the total). The École Polytechnique lost 661 (14 per cent). But inheritance patterns reveal very little modification to the concentration of wealth observed for the *belle époque*. One per cent of those who left legacies accounted for 50 per cent of the total value of bequests. France, like Britain, had its class of 'new rich' – hard-faced men who had done well out of the war – but their numbers were insufficient to transform the basic character of French society. The introduction of income tax was not entirely without some effect here. Renault, who made profits of 31 per cent in 1915, saw this figure diminish to 7 per cent by 1918. The *rentier* class was badly hit by the loss of overseas investments (especially of Russian bonds) and by inflation, but, having wisely diversified their portfolios, few people were completely ruined, however loudly they complained about the cost of living and the impossibility of affording servants. Members of the liberal professions, too, found that their incomes had failed to keep pace with inflation: between 1911 and 1930 the purchasing power of top civil servants declined by 26 per cent. More than anything else, it was the loss of financial stability which made the pre-war era seem, in retrospect, a *belle époque*.

Bourgeois class consciousness seems to have been intensified by the sense of privation among the middle classes, many of whom believed that, while they suffered, the working classes – and most gallingly working women – had made fabulous gains. Consequently, bourgeois French men and women showed considerable determination to hold on to such advantages as they possessed, notably in the sphere of education. Against the (mainly Radical and Socialist) proponents of the *école unique* (who wished to end the segregation between the primary and secondary sectors of the educational system) middle-class parents, along with most of the teaching profession and education officials, argued successfully for the retention of the two-tier system. It is true that they favoured an expansion in the number of secondary schools. Between 1913 and 1939 the number of boys in State secondary schools doubled, from 69,000 to 140,000. The number of girls likewise increased from 30,000 to 64,000. It is precisely this female increase, however, that points to the real motives underlying the expansion. The Bérard Law of 1924, which granted the formal equality between boys' and girls' schools long sought by feminists, instituting the right to take the *baccalauréat*, was championed by the author of the law not on the groups of promoting sex equality (Bérard was a notorious anti-feminist and opponent of women's suffrage) but because of his commitment to the study of the humanities and the formation of an educated élite, now broadened to include bourgeois girls as well as boys. The fact that a few bursaries allowed some children from underprivileged backgrounds to obtain secondary schooling did not alter the general effect of the secondary-school system. The French bourgeoisie after the First World War did everything in its power to maintain class barriers, all the more so in that it feared for its own impoverishment and the gradual erosion of social distinctions.

No class was more affected by the war than the peasantry. Almost 700,000 peasants were killed, another 500,000 wounded. For the French countryside the war was a human disaster of truly staggering proportions. Nevertheless, alongside the tragedy, the war also brought about a number of beneficial changes in rural economic and social structures. Although there was only limited progress in the mechanization of agriculture, inflation generated a new peasant prosperity, wiping out much peasant indebtedness and enabling peasants to purchase land and property. In 1919 farmers could sell their produce at four times the prices charged in 1913: even allowing for inflation, they were markedly better off. In the years after the war, as prices continued to rise, the fortunes of the peasantry continued to improve.

The conditions of working-class life were also modified by the war. The extension of mass production was one notable development which affected industrial workers in huge factories such as those of Citroën and Renault. In certain establishments, such as Peugeot, Renault and the repair workshops of the Paris–Orleans Railway, elements of the Taylor system were applied, leading to greater mechanization and rationalization of production, with consequent intensification of the division of labour and the creation of more semi-skilled workers paid at piece-rates. In the war factories, workers developed a powerful sense of being exploited. Constantly exhorted to produce ever more for the war effort, they contrasted their harsh conditions with the huge fortunes being made by industrialists and war profiteers. They too emerged from the war with a heightened sense of class consciousness. Male workers complained bitterly that the introduction of female and foreign workers freed men to be sent to the slaughter. The lack of enthusiasm for the war among workers in the war factories was at odds with the image manufactured by the press and by government propaganda of a patriotic labour force cheerfully turning out cannons and munitions. As we have already seen, the great strikes of 1917 and more especially 1918 gave vent to their pent-up frustrations and grievances.

Yet at the same time many labour leaders believed that the war presented new possibilities for advancing the interests of the working classes within the context of a new, corporatist relationship with the State and the employers. And, indeed, the new reformist line, espoused notably by Jouhaux, brought some rewards. Although real wages did not attain their level of 1914 until 1921 or 1922, from 1916 workers at least had the sense of catching up on the pay front, as ministers like Albert Thomas showed a new sensitivity to workers' demands. In some war factories shop stewards (délégués d'atelier) were permitted to facilitate contact with representatives of the State and to help resolve industrial disputes. The crowning triumph for reformism was the enactment of the law of 23 April 1919, which instituted the eight-hour day and the 48-hour week.

On the negative side, however, workers still had to contend with truculent bosses who brooked no interference with their right to be masters in their own factories and imposed an iron work discipline. The labour inspectorate was not always able to make them comply with the law, notably in the matter of the eight-hour day, whose implementation was left to individual industries. Recalcitrant employers also benefited from the complicity of ministers like Loucheur who had grave reservations about the law in any case, because of its allegedly damaging impact on national production. Workers were still the outsiders of French society and the corporatist aspirations of Jouhaux and other reformist leaders of the CGT met with precious little support from the State before 1936.

One of the most commented upon social developments of the war was the massive participation of women in war work. Almost 25 per cent of the 1.5 million munitions workers were female. The example of the Renault works at Billancourt illustrates the transformations which took place. In January 1914 the factory employed only 190 women who formed less than 4 per cent of the total labour force. By December 1916 there were 3,654 (18.12 per cent) and by the spring of 1918 6,770 (31.63 per cent). The generalization of female labour led many contemporaries to suppose that a social revolution in the status of women was well under way by the end of the war. But such claims exaggerated a great deal.

For one thing, women's experience of war work was frequently anything but emancipatory. They were employed usually at menial, routine and at best semi-skilled jobs, sometimes in dirty and indeed dangerous circumstances. Nearly 70,000 industrial accidents involving women were reported in 1917, of which 59 proved fatal and 756 resulted in permanent incapacitation. Legislation on the 10-hour day and the ban on night work for women were frequently ignored. Male colleagues, especially skilled workers, resented the 'dilution' of skill and the freeing of more men for combat in the trenches. Sexual harassment was common. Thousands of women found war work intolerable and left the munitions factories after only a very short period of employment.

A further consideration is that women's entry into the war factories did not bring about any permanent change in the sexual division of labour. Whereas women came to constitute over 40 per cent of the industrial workforce during the war, by 1921, after demobilization, fewer women were found to work in industry than had been the case in 1906. For example, the numbers in textiles were down by 270,000 (a drop of 18 per cent). Likewise, numbers in the clothing industry declined by 55,000 (with a further fall of 162,000 between 1921 and 1926), while domestic service, which employed 17.7 per cent of all working women in 1906, accounted for only 14.8 per cent in 1921. In metallurgy, by contrast, numbers tripled. Equally, the number of women employed in the tertiary sector increased from 344,000 in 1906 to 855,000 in 1921. Thus, what happened during the war and its immediate aftermath was an acceleration of trends visible before the war, namely a decline in participation in older industries, such as textiles, and an increasing involvement in new ones, such as light engineering, electricity and chemicals, along with a rapid expansion in female white-collar jobs. Women were redistributed within the labour force, but without any serious alteration of the sexual division of labour. The 'feminine' sector was merely reclassified.

Nor was there any notable shift at the level of attitudes. Indeed, if anything, the ideology of separate spheres was reinforced by the wartime experience. Male workers clung as tenaciously as ever to their belief in a natural sexual division of labour, partly out of an atavistic attachment to patriarchy and the cult of masculinity but also out of a concern for the preservation of a distinctive proletarian family unit in which working-class consciousness could be passed on from generation to generation. The bourgeois ethic, we have seen, was all the more strenuously championed by middle-class people who considered their way of life threatened. They too continued to be votaries of the cult of 'women by the hearth' and of family life. From the point of view of the French State, the loss of manpower in the war was not only tragic but, coupled with the decline in the birth rate, potentially disastrous for the continuing great-power status of France. Hence its renewed support for the pro-natalist campaign and the introduction of punitive legislation against the neo-malthusian lobby. A law of 31 July 1920 stipulated both imprisonment of up to six months and a fine for anyone convicted of distributing birth-control propaganda or making contraceptives available. Another law of 27 March 1923 tried (unsuccessfully) to curb abortions by making both the woman involved and any other party to the operation liable to imprisonment. In the eyes of the legislators, women existed to be wives and mothers: maternity was their mission. In such an intellectual climate it is hardly surprising that a parliamentary bill to give women the vote, carried by the Chamber of Deputies in 1919, was thrown out by the Senate in 1922, ostensibly on the grounds that to enfranchise women would be to add significantly to the clerical enemies of the Republic, more fundamentally to perpetuate gender-based roles in a deeply conservative society.

In the end, it seems most likely that the greatest impact of the First World War was made not at the level of social and economic structures but of individual and collective psychology, among those who took part in the fighting and managed to survive. What the experience of trench warfare was really like for the ordinary soldier cannot be fully comprehended by the historian, any more than it was appreciated by the civilians at the time. For four long years men knew the hell of living in the constant shadow of death. Caught up in an event outside of the control or understanding of any individual, all they could do was try to accustom themselves to the squalor and routine of the trenches, in the hope that, somehow, they would be spared. Many of those who survived were never to recover from 'shell neurosis', the nightmare of being buried alive by a heavy shell. Sometimes combatants seem to have recognized that they had more in common with the enemy than with the officers who ordered them to suicidal attacks or with the civilians who could never begin to imagine the horrific sights and sounds of industrialized war. For some there was at least the consolation of comradeship and a sense of achievement and purpose. The French *poilu* had the additional satisfaction of having been on the winning side, which may have been a not inconsiderable factor in the preservation of political stability in the post-war world.

On the other hand, there can be no mistaking the widespread bitterness and disillusionment among ordinary soldiers like Louis Barthas, a barrel-maker from a small village in the Aude, who recorded in notebooks his horror and outrage at the slaughter of so many innocent men, along with his resolution to do everything in his power to prevent any repetition of the catastrophe in the future. A profound pacifism animated many French war veterans who, while remaining patriotic and loyal to the Republic, were transformed into ferocious partisans of peace at virtually any price. Almost 3.5 million of them, mainly from rural and small-town France, joined ex-servicemen's leagues, through which they preserved the spirit of the trenches, the memory of the dead and hatred of war. Their size and influence meant that makers of French foreign policy had to be sensitive to their outlook: their mentality helped to shape the destiny of inter-war France.

The Menace of Bolshevism

War, according to Lenin, was the mother of revolution, and events in Russia in 1917 seemed to have proved him right. He anticipated that other countries of Europe would soon follow the Russian example: and France, with its long revolutionary tradition, was to have been no exception. From a different perspective, the French Right agreed with him. In the election campaign of 1919, to alert the voters to the red menace in France, the Union of Economic Interests covered the country with its notorious poster depicting the Bolshevik as the man with a knife between his teeth. Fear of revolution was intensified by the new mood of militancy evident in sections of the labour movement. CGT membership had grown throughout the war until it reached 1.6 million, three times as many members as in 1911. The wartime strikes of 1917 and 1918 were followed by a massive strike wave in 1919 and by further action in 1920. In 1919 the ferment began with a strike of miners in Lorraine against savage wage-cuts and continued throughout the spring with demonstrations against the acquittal of Villain, the assassin of Jaurès, and a huge show of strength on May Day, involving some 500,000 workers, many of whom carried red flags and chanted revolutionary slogans. One worker was killed in the course of clashes with the police. A strike of bank employees and shop workers from the large department stores followed, before the movement reached its crescendo with the great strike of the Parisian metal-workers. In 1920 the initiative was taken by the railwaymen, led by Monmousseau. As discontent swelled, the CGT, admittedly with some reluctance, called for a general strike on 1 May 1920.

That the temper of the workers was in some sense revolutionary was apparent in a number of ways: in their disenchantment with the moderate leaders of the CGT, their frustrations at the dislocations caused by the return to peacetime conditions (unemployment, price rises, shortages of raw materials) and, above all, in their aspiration to see a better world replace the old, if need be by resorting to revolutionary action, as in Russia and in central Europe. The most active and militant syndicalists were the *minoritaires*, those who were disgusted with the CGT's official policy of class collaboration during the war: it should be emphasized that the great post-war strike movements were all 'unofficial', and to a considerable degree, spontaneous. The reappearance of Monatte's *La Vie Ouvrière* in April 1919 and the creation of *Clarté* in May by Raymond Lefebvre and other radical intellectuals keen to publicize the Russian Revolution added to the atmosphere of the crisis.

Revolutionary aspirations alone, however, could not create a revolutionary situation. Clemenceau's France was not Kerensky's Russia. The authority of the French State never looked like disintegrating. On the contrary, to meet the challenge of the metal workers, in June 1919 the government put together a force of 17,000 men, 4,000 of them on horseback, some armed with sub-machine guns and others assigned to tanks. Merrheim, secretary of the Metalworkers Federation and a Zimmerwaldien, was bitterly reviled by other *minoritaires* for seeming to have passed into the reformist camp because he drew the obvious and realistic conclusion that a successful revolution was simply not possible in 1919. In 1920 the State again demonstrated its strength in the ruthless way it suppressed the railwaymen's strike. The ringleaders were arrested and when the workers capitulated at the end of May some

18,000 railwaymen were sacked, the State setting the example on its own network. A court declared the CGT to be an illegal organization on 11 May 1920, though the judgement was later quashed.

It was not only the State that was well equipped to deal with potential revolutionaries. Employers, too, emerged from the war better organized, having established the CGPF (General Confederation of French Production) in July 1919, to add to older pressure groups like the *Comité des Forges*. But the basic problem was that the workers themselves were divided, and not simply as between reformists and revolutionaries: the railwaymen refused to support the metalworkers in 1919, and in turn were not joined by the latter in 1920. But reformism was a significant current among the CGT leadership, as we have seen. Jouhaux was desperately keen to continue the wartime policy of collaboration with the State in a postwar *politique de présence*. In his view, if the State could not be overthrown, it could be penetrated, and the working class should be prepared to assume a directing role in the economy through the realization of a programme of nationalizations and the establishment of a National Economic Council, on which labour would be represented alongside civil servants and employers and thus have a say in developing the planned economy. Or so at least it was hoped.

The defeat of the great strike movements had a disastrous effect on union numbers. Almost a million members left within a few months, leaving in the region of 600,000–700,000 in 1921. By this time the Left generally was in disarray. Like the syndicalists, the Socialists were badly divided by the war. Every year of carnage added to the ranks of those disaffected with the policy of supporting the *union sacrée* and increased support for the minority tendency of Longuet, Faure and Frossard, which favoured a negotiated peace (though there were few Zimmerwaldiens in the SFIO). Again, the bitterness and rancour occasioned by the war were far from dissipated by the return to peace. Discontent among the Socialist rank and file with the bourgeois character of the leadership also became more open (a maximum of 17 per cent of the party's deputies could be classified as coming from a working-class background), while the electoral defeat of 1919 (the Socialists lost 30 seats) compounded the sense of disillusionment and frustration, particularly among the 34,000 younger and more impatient recruits who joined the party between 1918 and 1920. In the circumstances, it was not surprising that many Socialists began to look eastwards for inspiration, seeing in the Russian Revolution the realization of their own aspirations.

Few people in France had any real idea of what was going on in Russia. Anarchists, like Péricat, believed that the Bolshevik revolution was a triumph for their brand of spontaneous revolution and direct democracy. Revolutionary syndicalists, such as Rosmer, equated the soviets with French *syndicats* and were excited by what they took to be a genuine proletarian revolution. SFIO leaders inclined to a 'Jacobin' interpretation, believing that in certain respects the Russian Revolution was a development and refinement of the French Revolution: 'Blanquism with tartar sauce', Charles Rappoport called it. However much all these elements disagreed as to the nature of the new regime in Russia, they were completely at one in defending it. Clemenceau's decision to send 40,000 French troops to support the White Russian forces in Odessa and the Crimea in December 1918 gave rise to a storm of protest, which culminated in the mutiny, animated by André Marty, of the Black Sea fleet in April 1919. As ever, when the revolt spread to the military ports of Toulon and Brest in June, government repression was savage, but the French 'hands off Russia' campaign could claim a victory.

Given the French Left's general discontent and its widespread infatuation with Soviet Russia, it is hardly surprising that, once the Bolsheviks decided to replace the Socialist Second International with a third, Communist, International, French Socialists were tempted to join. The pacifists of the former Committee for the Resumption of International Relations (Loriot, Louise Saumoneau, Péricat, Monmousseau, Monatte) took the initiative in forming a Committee of the Third International. In February 1920 the national congress of the SFIO at Strasbourg supported a resolution proposed by the former *minoritaires* to separate from the Second International and to reconstruct a new revolutionary International. Two delegates, Cachin and Frossard, were dispatched to Russia to report on the desirability of adhering to the Third International: and, suitably impressed by the Bolshevik leaders, they duly recommended adherence. Moscow, however, laid down such stringent conditions for membership that a section of the SFIO headed by Renaudel and the newly elected deputy Léon Blum refused to submit. (Among other stipulations, the Bolsheviks wanted the French Socialists to subscribe to the doctrine of revolutionary defeatism, to acknowledge the complete supremacy of the International, and to accept the total subordination of trade unions to the Communist party.) At the Congress of Tours in December 1920, despite desperate attempts by Longuet and the centrists to avoid a schism, the issue of whether or not to adhere to the Third International on Moscow's terms split the old SFIO, a majority of the delegates voting in favour (3,427) and a minority against (1,398). Blum led the rump of those who believed in reconstructing the 'old house' of Jaurès and Guesde: the majority formed the PCF, the French Communist Party. Less than a year later (in September 1921) the split in the Socialist ranks was followed by a schism within the CGT. Disillusioned with the failures of syndicalism both during and immediately after the war and turning now to Moscow as the mecca of revolution a number of militants broke away from the CGT to form their own Communist CGTU (*Confédération Générale du Travail Unitaire*). In the end the menace of Bolshevism produced not a revolution but deep and damaging divisions on the French Left which were to last for the next 15 years.

9

The Game of Politics in Post-War France

After the upheavals of the war and its immediate aftermath, the French people, in their great majority, longed for a return to what, in retrospect, appeared to be a lost, golden age; a time of stability at home and confidence in France's status as a great power. The social conflicts of 1917–20 and the difficulties of first devising and then implementing a satisfactory peace treaty demonstrated that such a return to what the pre-war élite, especially, liked to think of as normality was not to be taken for granted. The world had changed in 1914, even if for more than a decade the French lived under the illusion that tranquillity had been restored to domestic life and peace to the international arena. The 1930s would soon reveal that their quest for stability and security had proved something less than a complete success.

The Context of Politics

During the 1920s, however, Frenchmen were not wrong in thinking that politics had a very familiar look. Continuity was all too apparent in personnel: Poincaré, Millerand, Briand and Painlevé had all been prominent before 1914. It became a standing joke that France had 80-year-old leaders because all the 75-year-olds were dead. The political system itself remained the same (apart from a temporary alteration of the electoral law in 1919, to bring in a bastardized form of proportional representation using a departmental list system). Ministerial instability was still endemic. Clemenceau's two leading disciples, Mandel and Tardieu, believed that the time had come to overhaul an out-moded political system to make it conform more to the Anglo-Saxon model based on two parties and stronger executive power, but the vast majority of the nation's politicians disagreed. Their most telling argument was that the existing system had been resoundingly vindicated by France's victory in the war.

The rules of the game in parliamentary politics in France had not changed. It was tacitly accepted that governments would not attempt to challenge the interests of the industrial and financial bourgeoisie, who were the country's true ruling élite, controlling the economy, the civil service and the press. Parliamentarians confined themselves to oratorical battles over ideology and the pursuit of office. These, of course, could be heated. It was not unknown for blows to be exchanged in the Chamber, as in 1930, when the venerable Hellenist and Socialist deputy Bracke fought with a Radical over the question of whether a government headed by Tardieu was morally entitled to organize the centenary celebrations of Jules Ferry's birth. Certain politicians, indeed, seemed to excite personal, as well as ideological, animus. Tardieu was punched by his opponent during the election campaign of 1928. Mandel was another who came in for constant vilification, especially in the right-wing press.

The press played a large part in amplifying for a wider public the ideological clashes in parliament. The laxity of the 1881 law permitted vile and vicious remarks to be printed about political opponents. Maurras could write of Blum that he was a man to be shot – but in the back. Roger Salengro, Minister of the Interior in the Popular Front government, was to be hounded to suicide by the false accusations of desertion during the First World War. One would not wish, therefore, to dismiss too readily the importance of the ideological divisions in France. They mattered above all where material interests were at stake, as over questions of taxation. *Le Temps* spoke for the *rentier* class as a whole when it denounced 'confiscatory' socialism. *L'Humanité*, taken over by the new PCF, and *Le Populaire*, the organ of the Socialist party, used the language of class warfare as a matter of course.

At the same time, however, one should be wary of accepting the intensity of ideological battles at face value. France was not divided into two blocs, of Left and Right, Red and White, 'Resistance' and 'Movement'. A fair degree of consensus existed at the Centre, which parliament faithfully reflected. Even the more conservative parties, like Louis Marin's Republican Federation or the *Alliance démocratique*, felt obliged to include words such as 'republican' or 'democratic' in their titles. For historical reasons, because of the power of republican myth, government by the Right alone was impossible: that way lay 'reaction' and 'clericalism'. On the Left, Communists and even Socialists did not accept the rules of 'bourgeois' politics, which meant that the Radicals were the chief representatives of the Left in government. The Radicals, however, were no longer a force for change, but champions of the *status quo*, with which they had good reason to be satisfied. Governments tended therefore to be either of the Centre–Left or Centre–Right. Ideological clashes generated much rhetoric but little social or political change. Robert de Jouvenel was not wrong to label the Third Republic a *république des camarades*, 'a republic of pals'.

The constraints within which parliamentary politics operated did not place deputies in the pockets of the financial obligarchy: but the power of money was always a factor to be reckoned with. Parliament had to contend with pressure from the likes of the *Comité des Forges*, the CFPF and the Union of Economic Interests, the last of which contributed heavily to the electoral coffers of the Right. Big industrialists, like the steelmaker and deputy François de Wendel, aspired to influence governments, even if they did not always succeed. On certain occasions, they were only too successful, as in 1926, when Wendel himself was largely instrumental in bringing down the *Cartel des gauches* government of Herriot.

The press was another means by which big capitalists chose to exercise influence. The press was not free. Its proprietors had definite ideas about what was news and what should and should not be discussed in their papers. They were therefore in a position to influence how issues were presented and debated. The financial press in particular was notoriously corrupt. Bankers and financiers paid journalists handsomely both for flattering articles and, equally important, for their silence. The small investor had no means of distinguishing between genuinely independent comment and concealed publicity. Governments made no attempt to legislate against such corruption but rather engaged in similar practices, subsidizing newspapers from secret funds in return for favourable reports. Journalists shamelessly presented themselves at the end of the month at the Ministry of the Interior for their 'envelopes'. Even an upright statesman like Poincaré made liberal use of this system, especially for bribing foreign pressmen, in the interests of French foreign policy. A certain amount of graft was thus inevitably built into the fabric of French politics.

Nevertheless, the relationship between money and politics was by no means straightforward. Money could be a handicap to politicians, as well as an asset, as Joseph Caillaux had discovered on account of his contacts with shady financiers. Few of the very wealthy entered the parliamentary arena, and fewer still obtained cabinet posts (Louis Loucheur was a notable exception). It is probable that the French Left exaggerated the power of the *mur d'argent*, the 'wall of money', which they always claimed was erected against governments of the Left, most notoriously in 1924 and 1936. Internal divisions and distrust of the State vitiated the capacity of French businessmen to act in concert and made organized business a less effective pressure group than in, say, Weimar Germany. Even the regents of the Bank of France were divided among themselves and open to government manipulation and pressure. Some financiers, like Horace Finaly of Paribas, were known to be well disposed towards the moderate Left. Power may not have been completely in the hands of the representatives of the people, but neither was parliament the poodle of big capital.

Democracy in France, then, was not a mere sham, nor was it in a state of 'decadence', reflecting a chronic incapacity for government on the part of the French. As acute a political observer as André Siegfried even argued that the fragmentation of political opinion in France was not a malaise but a sign of vigour and diversity in French public life, which contrasted favourably with the 'ponderous discipline' of British party politics. The French political system seemed to provide the type of government which most French people wanted. It had its critics and its faults; but, then, what regime has not? It did not produce strong, positive and dynamic leaders committed to action. But at a time when the principal advocates of 'action' were Mussolini and Hitler, perhaps this was not altogether a bad thing.

From Clemenceau to Poincaré

After the war, Clemenceau postponed parliamentary elections until November 1919 so as to be able to negotiate the peace treaty without having to concern himself unduly with public opinion. His Minister of the Interior and ruthless henchman, Georges Mandel, took charge of 'making' the elections through the application of pressure on the prefects. A variant of the proportional system was introduced by which voting was by departmental list and a single ballot in order to favour the parties best able to organize electoral alliances rather than the independent local candidate favoured by the previous system. The parties of the Centre and Right accordingly formed themselves into an electoral coalition presided by Clemenceau and led by Millerand with a programme that included 'religious peace'. With the Left in disarray, fear of Bolshevism rampant and chauvinistic confidence in *père-la-victoire* high, the *Bloc National* swept to a resounding triumph, winning 400 out of 616 seats in the Chamber of Deputies. The largest parliamentary group was found to be the *Entente Républicaine Démocratique*, many of whose members were Catholics. The new 'horizon blue' Chamber, as it was called, was the most right-wing since 1876.

It was the hope of Mandel and of Tardieu, Clemenceau's two leading disciples, that the overwhelming victory at the polls would provide the occasion for a transformation of the political system, to shift the balance of power more towards the executive and to create an Anglo-Saxon type two-party model. The first step to be taken was to elect Clemenceau to the Presidency of the Republic, so that he could appoint a Prime Minister capable of turning the *Bloc National* into a truly united and disciplined political grouping. The plan miscarried, however, in January 1920, when the National Assembly elected Deschanel rather than Clemenceau to the Presidency. Probably 'the Tiger' could have obtained the post had he campaigned openly for it. Instead, he was the victim of a whispering campaign orchestrated by his old adversary Briand, who reminded Catholics of Clemenceau's vitriolic anti-clericalism and stirred up concern for the preservation of parliamentary sovereignty. Clemenceau withdrew into bitter retirement. Mandel and Tardieu were left isolated and the moment for reform passed. It was small consolation that Deschanel soon went mad and had to be replaced by Millerand.

The general swing to the Right produced no profound change in the political situation in the country. The new conservative deputies were mostly inexperienced (more than half of those elected in 1919 entered parliament for the first time) so that the old hands retained ministerial power. Millerand, the first premier of the *Bloc National*, was succeeded by the insignificant moderate Leygues, who lasted only four months before being replaced by Briand in January 1921, who in turn gave way to Poincaré in January 1922. The recall of Briand in particular clearly illustrated that not a great deal had changed, since he owed his pre-eminence entirely to his skill as a parliamentary operator.

The key to the political situation, in fact, lay not with the Right but with the Centre, crucially with the moderate Republicans of the *Alliance démocratique* who had organized the *Bloc National* coalition in the first place. They were ready to throw sops to the Right in the form of a policy of 'religious appeasement'. They cheerfully joined in the celebrations which accompanied the canonization of Joan of Arc in 1920 and, more concretely, re-established diplomatic links with the Vatican in 1921. They also exempted Alsace from the Separation Law of 1905 and chose not to enforce the legislation against the 'unauthorized' congregations. The Church was further enabled to devise 'diocesan associations' which were deemed to comply with the stipulations of 1905. Yet the Right received only minimal and nominal representation in government, while the moderates of the Centre refused to break completely with the Radicals to their Left. The 'politics of principle' had little appeal for the moderates: after all, in a genuine two-party system, the Left might win. Knowing that Radicals were at bottom conservatives, they preferred to resort to combinations that would isolate extremists of both Left and Right. Gamesmanship and the blurring of ideological divisions suited them much better, not least from the point of view of obtaining jobs in the *République des camarades*.

The principal concern of the *Bloc National* was with the implementation of the Treaty of Versailles and the collection of reparations from Germany. Foreign affairs, however, could not be divorced from domestic politics, above all not from the financial problems bequeathed by the Great War. These were by no means insoluble, provided that the French people were prepared to shoulder a greater burden of taxation. But there, precisely, was the rub, for opposition to higher taxes was voiced not only by the spokesmen of the Right but by Radicals and Socialists. Politically, it was so much easier – or so it seemed – to make Germany pay. Moreover, Finance Ministers and the Bank of France still adhered to pre-war notions of financial orthodoxy and cherished the illusion that somehow the franc could be restored to its former parity. They refused, therefore, to make any concessions to inflation by accepting the stabilization of the franc at a level reflecting the productivity of the French economy. In consequence, government revenue was low and the Treasury was obliged to meet its needs through the issue of short-term bonds, which placed governments at the mercy of their creditors, both at home and abroad, should bond-holders fail to renew the issues. Lack of liquidity and general financial vulnerability were crucial elements in determining the fate of domestic reform and French diplomacy.

Until 1923 the precarious state of French public finances was masked from view by the business depression which began in the autumn of 1920, leaving idle capital free to take up the Treasury's bonds. But once the economy took an up-turn investors began to look for more attractive propositions. On 11 January 1923 Finance Minister Lasteyrie felt that he had no alternative but to ask for a temporary tax increase. Parliamentary opposition to his proposals was furious: and, at this junction, Poincaré was not prepared to risk the survival of his government on the issue. A year later, however, when the franc was considerably weaker in the wake of the Ruhr occupation, Poincaré himself saw no alternative to a package of tax increases and special powers. The Chamber gave its consent in February 1924 but the refusal of the Senate to ratify the deal brought the franc under still greater pressure. But for a loan from the American banker J.P. Morgan, the currency might have collapsed: and the price of the loan was ratification of the fiscal package in the Senate.

The financial crisis of 1923–4 along with the problems associated with the Ruhr occupation helped to bring about the disintegration of the *Bloc National* coalition. Already its 'clericalism' had offended some moderate as well as Radical Republicans, while the latter also took strong exception to a speech by President Millerand at Evreux in October 1923 in which he made no secret of his ambition to strengthen the powers of the Presidency. Poincaré's strategy of uniting the centres became impossible. As the elections of 1924 approached the Radicals and Socialists began to draw together again in an electoral coalition of the Left, which also had a certain appeal for the Centre–Left. In May 1924 the *Cartel des Gauches* scored a famous victory at the polls, winning 328 seats to 226 for the Right and Centre. The door seemed open for a return to the palmy pre-war days of the *Bloc des gauches*.

The Radicals formed the new government, with 13 out of the ministerial posts in a cabinet led by Edouard Herriot. But they were no longer a genuine party of the Left. For them, politics consisted largely in the preservation of historical memories and the re-enactment of historical rituals. Their philosopher, Alain, expressed their deep-seated distrust of power and bigness in his *summa*, *Elements of a Radical Doctrine*, published in 1925. Radicals liked to present themselves as champions of the 'small man' in French society, ever viligant against the depredations of big business and the State (which did not prevent some of their number entertaining relations with dubious financiers and certain press barons).

Their partners in the Cartel coalition, the Socialists of the SFIO, had made a remarkable recovery since their defeat in the elections of 1919 and the split at Tours in 1920. It was above all the rural sections which had seceded from the party to join the PCF, which meant that it retained its bases in the industrial Nord and Pas-de-Calais regions, lending some credibility to its claims to be the party of the French proletariat. The Socialists, however, had little following in Paris, while in the provinces they recruited much of their support among schoolteachers and petty government officials, along with a good number of small peasants and share-croppers in certain Republican areas. These tended to be interested mainly in local issues and to dislike the parliamentary group. It was fortunate for the Socialists nationally that they returned most of the ablest and best-known figures from the old SFIO. No one could take the place of Jaurès, but in Léon Blum they had a new leader who was distinguished, upright and intelligent. In 1924 they had 110,000 party members and won 104 seats, twice as many as in 1919. But they had joined the Cartel coalition only with extreme reluctance, having had unfortunate experiences of electoral pacts with Radicals in the past, and fearing to lay themselves open to Communist accusations of being dupes of the bourgeoisie. In consequence, against the wishes of a minority headed by Joseph Paul-Boncour, they refused to participate in the Cartel government, a decision which boded ill for the survival of the Left in power.

The Herriot cabinet had little to offer other than symbolic gestures. Millerand was removed from the Presidency for allegedly overstepping his constitutional powers, his successor being Gaston Doumergue rather than Paul Painlevé, whom the Radicals would have preferred. Amnesties were voted for Caillaux and Malvy. The ashes of Jaurès were transferred to the Panthéon in an impressive procession which terrified the more jumpy elements of the Parisian bourgeoisie. Once again, clericalism was identified as the enemy *par excellence*. True enough, reactionary militant Catholicism manifested itself anew in the National Catholic Federation founded by General de Castelnau in 1924. But that a more conciliatory spirit was abroad in the Vatican, if not among some of the diehard, integrist, French bishops appointed by Pius X, could hardly be denied, especially when the successor of Benedict XV, Pius XI, condemned the *Action Française* in 1926 and forced the resignation of the Jesuit Cardinal Billot for resisting papal policy.

In addition, Catholics could and did point out that, if the religious orders had come back in 1914, it was to serve with the armed forces. A break with the political Right was also evident on the part of at least some Catholics, in groups such as *La Jeune République*, founded by Marc Sangnier and animated by some of his former collaborators in the Sillon, and the Christian Democrats of the Popular Democratic Party (PDP), founded in 1924 and from 1932 associated with the newspaper *L'Aube*. In the 1930s two publications of the Dominican Order, *La Vie Intellectuelle* and *Sept*, also spelled out new directions for Catholic participation in politics, though Emmanuel Mounier's *Esprit*, founded in 1932, showed a marked hostility to parliamentarism as practised by the Third Republic. It was in the inter-war period, too, that Catholic trade unionism began to emerge as a significant force in the political and social life of the nation. The CFTC, founded in 1919, had around 300,000 members in 1936. There was even a small group of anarcho-Christians who aired their views in the newspaper *La Terre Nouvelle*. But perhaps the most striking witness to a renewed and reinvigorated Catholicism, more open to the world and ardently seeking a new alliance of Church and people, was the growth of Catholic Action. The dynamic *Jeunesse Ouvrière Chrétienne* (JOC), created in 1927, led the way, soon to be followed by other groups which concentrated upon a particular milieu (the JAC in the countryside, the JEC among students). Not the least of the contributors to these burgeoning movements were the separate feminine sections. Thus, when Herriot attempted to resurrect the clerical bogey, threatening to close the embassy at the Vatican and to introduce the Separation Law in Alsace, his manoeuvre badly miscarried. The real problems facing the country could no longer be swept away by anti-clerical rhetoric.

The ineluctable financial problem did not take long to surface. Herriot, Mayor of Lyon for as long as anyone could remember and the very type of the amiable, back-slapping Radical politician, was a man of wide culture as well as wide girth, but he had little interest in, or understanding of, economics. He had a shrewd political brain, and knew all the rules of the game of politics as played under the Third Republic: but he lacked the energy and expertise to master complicated financial and diplomatic questions. Ignoring the advice of Pierre de Moüy, director of the Treasury, to terminate the policy of deflation and to abandon the chimera of trying to restore the franc to its pre-war parity, he and the Finance Minister Clémentel resorted to further borrowing and to doctoring the reports of the Bank of France. For eight months the government led a hand-to-mouth existence, hoping somehow to stave off the day of reckoning. In vain. The debt got larger, the franc fell and the confidence of French investors, large and small, was undermined. Capital went on strike and sought more profitable outlets abroad, as right-wing newspapers like *Le Temps* counselled. (A number of Catholic newspapers such as *L 'Ouest-Eclair* and *La Nouvelliste d'Alsace* also paid the government back for its anti-clericalism by advising readers not to subscribe any new loan.) The government also came under strong pressure from the regents of the Bank of France, headed by François de Wendel, who threatened to reveal the government's false declarations about the money supply. In desperation Herriot was forced to advocate measures pressed upon him by Blum and the Socialists, which included a 10 per cent tax on capital. These were unacceptable to the Senate, which overthrew him on 10 April 1925.

A new government was formed by Painlevé, who appointed Caillaux to the Ministry of Finance. But not even the legendary financial wizardry of that celebrated conjurer could restore confidence among the financial community. His attempt to raise a new loan failed and the government fell. In dizzying succession France went through another five short-lived cabinets, none of which could stop the franc from falling – in July 1926 there were 243 francs to the pound sterling, as opposed to 76 in May 1924 – or prices from rising. In desperation, in July 1926, the Cartel-dominated Chamber had to turn to

Raymond Poincaré, so recently repudiated at the polls, as its saviour.

Poincaré headed a government of 'national union' in which he included Radicals (notably Herriot), a few right-wingers and Briand as Foreign Minister, which helped to ensure some left-wing support on account of his allegedly conciliatory foreign policy. Poincaré himself took charge at the Finance Ministry and implemented measures from which Herriot had shrunk in 1924. He increased taxation across the board, with the exception of 'supertax' on the rich, which he reduced to reassure them. He raised foreign loans and succeeded in balancing the budget. Benefiting from a combination of a general economic upswing, which affected Germany as well as France and enabled her to pay some reparations, Poincaré, by his very presence at the helm, persuaded businessmen, financiers and investors that the ship of state was in safe hands. The franc was stabilized at one-fifth of its former value, though not formally until after the elections of 1928. Held once again under the old system of *scrutin d'arrondissement*, these amounted to a solid vote of confidence in Poincaré's government. The parties of the Centre and Right won 330 seats, against a bitterly divided Left. Poincaré, with Radical votes, could muster support from over two-thirds of the Chamber. He remained in power until 1929, when ill-health forced him to retire. Under him, the French began to believe that they had rediscovered the elusive tranquillity, stability and prosperity for which they had been searching since 1918. They were soon to be cruelly disappointed.

The Quest for Security

In the international arena, the French quickly discovered that the Versailles Treaty was, in itself, no guarantee of security. Having abandoned territorial safeguards in return for the Anglo-American Treaty of Guarantee, they were understandably shattered by its repudiation, first by the US Senate, then by 'perfidious Albion'. At a stroke, the French seemed to have won the war only to lose the peace. Disillusionment with the British was aggravated by the Chanak incident in 1922, when Lloyd George backed the Greeks against the dynamic new Turkish leader Kemal Pasha, with whom the French were keen to remain on good terms. It may, perhaps, seem strange that the French were neurotic about Germany, given that France retained a massive military superiority over a German army reduced to a token force of 100,000 by the Treaty. But French policy-makers lived in dread of resuscitated Germany: not surprisingly, they adopted an increasingly hard-line stance on reparations.

They also cast around somewhat desperately for suitable alliances. The Bolshevik Revolution had ended confidence in any revival of the old Franco-Russian alliance, but it was hoped that some of the new states of eastern Europe might provide an alternative. After concluding a military agreement with Belgium in 1920, France signed another military pact with Poland in 1921. An alliance with Czechoslovakia followed in 1924, which associated France with the 'Little Entente' powers of Czechoslovakia, Yugoslavia and Rumania, which had banded together to protect the new order in south-eastern Europe against any attempts to revive the Habsburg Empire.

None of the arrangements gave France the real sense of security she craved. Serious rivalries between France's eastern allies reduced their usefulness as a counter-weight to Germany. They in turn rightly suspected the genuineness of the French commitment to eastern Europe. The fact was that France was not ready to sever all links with Britain, which had no liking for the new states in the east, nor had France ruled out forever a reconciliation with the Soviet Union, regarded by the Poles as at least as great an enemy as Germany. France's eastern diplomacy was deeply resented in Germany, possibly increasing her determination to obtain revision of the Versailles settlement, widely regarded by German public opinion as a harsh *diktat* imposed on Germany by an intransigent and belligerent France.

French fears of Germany were hardly allayed by the survival of the old imperial bureaucracy, the domination of the German economy by great industrial magnates and the rapid revival of the German steel industry. In the absence of any satisfactory alliance system, the French fell back upon the strict implementation of the Versailles Treaty and the payment of reparations – all the more so since the Americans and the British insisted on the full repayment of wartime loans. By the Spa Conference of 1920, the French share of German reparations payments was fixed at 52 per cent of the total, itself finally set at 13,200 million gold marks in April 1921. Strict application of the Treaty, it should be noted, was agreed by French politicians of all political persuasions. The contrast often drawn between, say, an intransigent Poincaré and a more conciliatory Briand is essentially false. When Germany defaulted on an interim cash payment in 1921, it was Briand who, as premier for the seventh time, was ready to send French troops into the Ruhr, though he settled instead for Franco-British occupation of the ports of Dusseldorf, Duisburg and Ruhrort.

On replacing Briand at the beginning of 1922, Poincaré maintained, rather than inaugurated, the tough stance on reparations. He would have preferred not to invade the Ruhr in 1923. Nevertheless, he was alarmed by the Treaty of Rapallo, concluded between Germany and the Soviet Union in 1922, and exasperated by Germany's claim that she was unable to meet her repayment schedules, all the more so when Britain appeared ready to grant her a four-year moratorium. Accordingly, he did not flinch from sending a force of French and Belgian troops to seize Ruhr coal. At the same time he gave French backing to the separatist movement in the Rhineland, in the hope of detaching the region from Germany. The Rhenish separatists, however, lacked any real popular support, while the occupying forces were met with passive resistance on the part of the German population, strongly encouraged by their government. A grim, protracted, struggle ensued which brought about the collapse of the mark and placed the franc under severe pressure.

In the end, given French unwillingness to reform the nation's fiscal system, France had to bow to the conditions set by American bankers for both the loan she needed and for the resumption of reparations payments by Germany. The plan drawn up under the aegis of Charles G. Dawes was in one sense a victory for France, in that it did provide for the continuation of German reparations, though on a reduced scale. Essentially, however, the outcome was a serious defeat for France. The adoption of the Dawes Plan, agreed to at the London Conference of 1924 by Poincaré's successor, Herriot (who went into the conference chamber extremely ill-prepared), signalled the failure of the Treaty of Versailles to contain Germany and prevent her eventual recovery of economic and financial hegemony in Europe. France, clearly, was in no position to compel adherence to the treaties by force. Her only hope lay in diplomacy.

From 1925 to 1932 French diplomacy was essentially in the hands of Aristide Briand, the most flexible and subtle of French policymakers. Briand was only too well aware of the constraints within which he had to operate: in the absence of an Anglo-American guarantee, heavily dependent on international finance and confronted with an economically resurgent Germany bent on the destruction of Versailles, France seemed to have no option but to seek some kind of accommodation with Germany. The reactionary Right protested that Briand was consistently out-manoeuvred by Stresemann, the formidably skilful German Foreign Minister. The Left praised him as a genuine internationalist, faithful to the spirit of Geneva and the League of Nations. More accurately, he remained what he had long been, a realist and the servant of the interests of France as a great power, but now pursuing nationalist goals by international means. His hope was that by integrating Germany fully into the economic and political life of the European community she would become so wedded to the existing structures that she could not possibly contemplate another conflict with France.

It was fortunate for Briand that, between 1924 and 1929, most unusually, Britain had a francophile Foreign Secretary in the person of Austen Chamberlain. Without wishing to go all the way towards the military alliance which the French wanted so badly, Chamberlain had some understanding of French fears of Germany and wanted to do something to allay them. Through him, in October 1925, Briand and Stresemann were brought together at Locarno in Switzerland. In what, ostensibly, appeared to be a relaxed, friendly atmosphere, epitomized by a communal boating trip on Lake Maggiore, the representatives of France, Germany and Belgium pledged their solemn commitment to the frontiers established by the Treaty of Versailles. Germany also accepted the permanent demilitarization of the Rhineland and was invited to join the League of Nations. The provisions were guaranteed by Britain and Italy, with all future disputes to be resolved though the League.

Back in Paris, Briand received a hero's welcome. In both France and Britain, Locarno was hailed as the dawn of a new era of peace. Briand knew otherwise. Behind the façade of conviviality at Locarno, hard bargaining had taken place in which the real winner was Stresemann. While prepared to guarantee Germany's frontiers in the west, he would give no undertaking with regard to the east. Poland and Czechoslovakia, France's eastern allies, were threatened, exacerbating the French dilemma as to whether they were an asset or a liability. Stresemann also secured a further reduction in the occupying forces in the Rhineland. Briand had conceded a great deal in order to obtain a diluted British guarantee, which in 1936 was to prove worthless.

But for the time being the illusion of peace was nourished by the outward maintenance of the 'Locarno spirit' in international relations. Briand formally welcomed Germany into the League of Nations at Geneva in September 1926. More informally, he and Stresemann met for a *tête-à-tête* at an inn in the village of Thoiry, near Geneva, where they held wide-ranging talks on the obstacles in the way of Franco-German reconciliation. Accounts of what they said to each other vary, but it seems likely that Stresemann offered to step up reparations payments in return for French evacuation of the Rhineland and the return of the Saar to Germany. Nothing came of the talks, but once again the image of cordiality exuded was encouraging for those who believed in peace. Growing economic co-operation between France and Germany, especially coming at a time of general prosperity, inspired similar hopes. In 1926 France and Germany joined an international steel cartel and shortly afterwards a Franco-German commercial treaty was signed.

Perhaps the most characteristic accomplishment of the Locarno era was the signing of the Kellogg–Briand Pact. Ever anxious to entangle other powers in guaranteeing French security, however obliquely, Briand proposed to the US Secretary of State Kellogg that France and America make a declaration renouncing war against each other in perpetuity. An unenthusiastic Kellogg pressed by pacifists at home, suggested instead a multilateral international Treaty for the Renunciation of War as an Instrument of National Policy, which he and Briand, followed by Stresemann and a host of other countries, signed in 1928. The pact was little more than a declaration against sin, since it made no practical provisions to achieve its purpose, but once again it raised people's hopes for peace in their time.

But mere rhetoric could not make the real problems go away. French security, reparations, disarmament and German revisionism continued to plague good relations between France and Germany. By 1928 Briand and Stresemann were increasingly at odds. The efforts of the idealists at Geneva to prepare a conference on disarmament were constantly undermined by French intransigence on the issue of security, Germany's insistence on equality and British concern for her interests as a naval power. The issues remained unresolved when the Disarmament Conference finally met in 1932. Reparations aggravated the bitterness and mistrust. Germany would agree to the amounts stipulated under the Dawes Plan only in return for the evacuation of the Rhineland, which Briand, under strong pressure from the military in France, would not concede. Yet another committee of experts was set up, this time under the American banker Owen D. Young, to try to find a way out of the impasse. At the Hague Conference of 1930 German repayments were further reduced to roughly a third of the 1921 figure. To the detriment of Anglo-French relations, pressure from the new Labour government in Britain forced Briand to give way on the Rhineland and to accept a financial modification of the Young Plan which benefited Britain rather than France.

To the end, Briand went on scheming of ways to contain Germany. In 1930 his ever fertile brain devised a plan first for Franco-German economic cooperation as a prelude to European integration, then for a federal European Union. Even less than in 1919, Europe was not ready for the establishment of a French-dominated Common Market. The Wall Street crash of 1929 had already begun to make its impact felt in Germany, while the force of unregenerate nationalism revealed its strength in the elections of 1930, in which the National Socialist party of Adolf Hitler won 107 seats to become the second largest party in the Reichstag. Joint Anglo-French pressure frustrated a German – Austrian plan for a customs union, portending *Anschluss*. But by the time Briand died in January 1932, in a rapidly deteriorating economic and political climate, Germany was pleading her inability to pay reparations and France her inability to repay war debts to the United States. President Hoover granted both a moratorium of one year in 1931, but in

July 1932 the Lausanne Conference finally cancelled German reparations, motivating France to welsh on her payments to the US in December. Even before Adolf Hitler became the German Chancellor on 30 January 1933, French illusions of peace and prosperity had been shattered.

10
The Depression and its Consequences

In 1929 France was still enjoying the benefits of the economic boom which had begun in the late 1890s and had continued, more or less without interruption, right through the 1920s. Between 1913 and 1929 rapid expansion took place in industries such as electricity, metal processing, chemicals and paper. Real, but more modest growth, took place in textiles, leather, food, iron and steel, building and some other sectors. Investment in new plant and machinery rose by 84 per cent between 1913 and 1929, while between 1924 and 1929 the average growth rate was 5 per cent a year.

In the 1920s too, there was a certain vogue for 'rationalization' or 'taylorization', that is for mass production of standardized goods and an intensification of the division of labour. Before the war the Taylor system had been applied in fewer than 10 establishments in France and was usually – wrongly – understood and as *chronométrage*, or timing the work rate of the labour force in efforts to increase their productivity – something that was bitterly resented by the unions and gave rise to a serious strike at the Renault factory in 1913. In the 1920s, however, enthusiasts for 'scientific management' included not just conservative businessmen and politicians, such as Ernest Mercier and André Tardieu (both of whom were prominent figures in the *Redressement français*, a movement that wanted to promote the modernization of the whole French economy), but also a number of trade-union leaders, such as Hyacinthe Dubreuil, whose personal experience of working in the United States made him a strong advocate of American methods. Raoul Dautry, the engineer mainly responsible for the reconstruction of the Nord after the devastation of the First World War and appointed by Tardieu in 1928 to carry out modernization of the State's railway network, was another firm believer in scientific management and of fruitful collaboration between capital and labour.

The Wall Street Crash of 1929 unleashed the greatest economic crisis that the world had yet witnessed, but at first its impact on France was minimal, failing to destroy the predominant mood of optimism. For one thing, the very archaism of some sectors of the French economy meant that France was to some extent insulated from the world recession. Thus the policy of self-financing practised by many firms left them less vulnerable to the collapse of banks than their counterparts in America and other European countries. Another factor was that, especially after the stabilization of the franc by Poincaré, France was considered a haven for capital, which boosted the reserves of the Bank of France to some 80 milliard gold francs in 1930. But the arrival of the Depression in France was only delayed: and then, when it came in 1931, its effect persisted through to 1938, even after the upswing inthe world economy from 1935. Nineteen twenty-nine long stood as the peak year for French economic activity and France entered a period of crisis marked by a sense of political, social and moral, as well as economic, malaise.

The Depression

The crisis manifested itself in two principal ways: the decline of French over-seas trade and the development of a huge balance of payments deficit. Especi-ally after the devaluation of sterling in 1931, French goods – especially luxury items – were overpriced in the world market. Consequently exports fell (by 50 per cent between 1929 and 1938). Whereas between 1927 and 1931 the French balance of payments was in surplus by 3 milliard francs, thereafter it sustained a deficit of the same order.

Production dropped dramatically, bringing about a sharp fall in profits and prices. By 1935 output was down by one fifth compared with the figure for 1929. The price of ordinary shares fell by more than a third between 1929 and 1934, while dividends were down by 52 per cent between 1930 and 1935. Investments fell by 37 per cent in the same period. Agricultural incomes declined by 16 per cent between 1930 and 1932, and by a further 17 per cent between 1932 and 1934. Self-employed businessmen in industry and commerce saw their incomes dwindle by 23 per cent between 1930 and 1932. Bankruptcies rose from 6,500 in 1929 to 13,370 in 1935.

Governments had few ideas as to how to manage the crisis. Before 1932, with elections pending, the tendency was to avoid unpopular measures. Thereafter, both left- and right-wing governments resorted to the traditional remedy of deflation, cutting public expenditure, and notably the wages of state employees and the pensions of ex-servicemen. In 1935 the Laval govern-ment carried this policy to its extreme point when it slashed the wages of civil servants by 10 per cent. Devaluation of the franc, championed by the lonely voice of Paul Reynaud, was ruled out on the grounds that it was politically unacceptable after the devaluations of the 1920s which had so traumatized the French bourgeoisie. The State also resorted to protection and subsidies, both with regard to agriculture and certain manufactured goods, in order to try to sustain price levels. One consequence of this policy was the acceleration of progress towards greater State intervention and a 'mixed economy', as, inadvertently and reluctantly, in order to rescue certain companies in deep financial difficulties, the State expanded its own holdings in them. In 1933 the Treasury acquired 25 per cent of the shares of the newly founded Air France company. The same year, it provided 83 per cent of the capital to refloat the failing *Compagnie Générale Transatlantique*. In 1937 it similarly assumed responsibility for the whole of the railway network, creating the SNCF (*Société Nationale des Chemins de Fer*).

The impact of the Depression varied considerably in the different sections of French society. In many ways the countryside was most affected. Peasants were dismayed at the steep drop in prices, brought about partly by over-production and partly by the general fall in demand and the diminution of purchasing power. Wheat, quoted at 152 francs a quintal in 1930, fetched only 74 francs in 1935. Wine, quoted at 183 francs a hectolitre in 1930, was down to 64 francs in 1935. Many peasants-found themselves driven back on a more or less subsistence economy. Discontent and agitation were rife throughout rural France. All sections of political opinion were obliged to take heed of peasant protest, whether to propose 'corporatist' solutions to their problems (like Jacques Leroy-Ladurie) or to woo them for fascism (like Henri Dorgères) or the Left (like the Socialists and Communists). Undoubtedly, peasant grievances contributed very substantially to the generalized sense of crisis.

By contrast with the peasants, the urban working classes gained from the fall in prices, which raised their standard of living. Unemployment, too, though severe by French standards, never became a problem on the scale experienced by Germany, the United States or even Britain. From zero unemployment in 1929 the official numbers out of work rose to 260,000 by 1932 and then to 426,000 in 1935, the first victims being immigrant and female workers. Many more workers, however, though not fully out of work, were put on 'short time' as employers reduced the number of working hours. Wages may have fallen by an average of 15 per cent between 1930 and 1935. So workers also experienced anxiety about the future and had every reason to be concerned about defending their rights against an embattled and often frightened *patronat*.

Fear was the main product of the Depression among the possessing classes. Materially, the crisis touched all elements of the bourgeoisie, including great industrial magnates like François de Wendel, who found that he had less cash available to subsidize right-wing political activity. Small shopkeepers and the like may have been, relatively speaking, hit less hard, since the State, sensible to their interests, acted to protect them against the worst effects of the fall in prices. Equally, the professional classes and minor civil servants (despite the wage cuts sustained by the latter) probably maintained or increased their purchasing power. But what was common throughout the ranks of the middle classes was a collapse of confidence and a growing sense of insecurity, perhaps best represented statistically by the declining birth rate, which fell from 18.2 per 1,000 in the period 1926–30, to 16.5 in 1931–5 and 14.8 in 1936–8. From 1935 the number of deaths exceeded the number of live births. Pessimism, rancour and fear were rife throughout bourgeois France by the mid 1930s, producing a notable deterioration in the psychological and social climate which manifested itself strongly in the bitter political confrontations of the Popular Front era.

Crisis Politics

The onset of the Depression did not have an immediate impact on French political life. When Poincaré left the stage in 1929 his successor, after another brief Briand interlude, was André Tardieu. As a former civil servant and brilliant and influential journalist on *Le Temps*, he had long been a forceful figure in French politics. Before the First World War, Bülow, the German Chancellor, called him the seventh great power in Europe. During the peace negotiations at Versailles, he was Clemenceau's closest collaborator, and thereafter the Treaty's most implacable defender. Like Mandel, 'the Tiger's' other leading disciple, he had spent the first half of the 1920s in the political wilderness, but returned to office in Poincaré's 'national union' cabinet, where in 1928 he eventually moved to the Ministry of the Interior and adopted a notably hard line towards the Communists. A man of superb intellect and surpassing arrogance, a Parisian in the midst of provincials, he sat ill in the 'Republic of Pals', loathed by the Left and by no means completely trusted by the Centre and Right, who grudgingly supported him. It was his ambition to transform the political system into a more effective means of government and to make the French economy dynamic and modern. Neither of these aims recommended him to the Radicals, who refused to participate in his government, obliging him to seek his majority on the Right.

Unlike the barons of Radicalism, Tardieu believed not only in taking power but in using it. To their further indignation, he gave every sign of intending to put through the Radical programme, if not with them, then against them. He announced an ambitious Five Year Plan for 'national retooling', which envisaged the modernization of French agriculture and industrial plant, a vast programme of public works to build houses, schools and hospitals, and the equipment of the countryside with electricity, telephones and better communications. Social reform, in the shape of a social insurance scheme, was also proposed. The Left was incensed, but Tardieu blithely asked them whether they were going to shoot him 'at the very moment when I come before you bearing your children in my arms'. To reassure the Right, he continued to crack down on Communism. With a slight interlude in February 1930, he continued as premier until February 1932, and again prime minister from February to May 1932, was the central figure in French politics in the early years of the Depression.

Little came of his great projects, however. Virtually no one in the French parliament could be found to support his proposals for national retooling. The PCF wished the Soviet Union to retain a monopoly on Five Year Plans; Radicals and Socialists were indignant at the mere idea that reform could be carried through without them, the 'progressives'; the Right balked at the concept of deficit finance and at the spending of money on public works rather than on reducing the national debt; the Centre feared the polarization of politics into a clash between Left and Right, which Tardieu threatened to accomplish as much by his personality as by his policies. Politicians, in short, wanted no truck with someone who threatened to change the rules of the game. Seizing on government collusion with the failed Oustric Bank, the Senate overthrew him. The Left branded him as an authoritarian tyrant bent on the destruction of French democracy. That was not true in 1930, though failure of the 'Tardieu experiment' left him embittered and increasingly contemptuous of parliamentary rule.

Disappointment also lay in store for another leading statesman of the era. Aristide Briand, so often the kingmaker in the past, failed to crown his own career by becoming President of the Republic in 1931, when, partly thanks to the machinations of Tardieu, he was passed over in favour of the dull Paul Doumer. Doumer was to last only until May 1932 before being assassinated by a fanatical White Russian – the right-wing press tried to make out that he was a Red – and being replaced by the even more insipid Albert Lebrun.

In the meantime, a new left-wing Cartel emerged victorious at the polls in 1932, winning 344 seats to the Centre and Right's 259. But the Left had failed to learn any lessons from its experiences of 1924–6. Herriot became Prime Minister and once again demonstrated his incapacity in the face of financial problems – now much more serious than in the earlier period, in that the

economy itself was no longer buoyant but had begun to take a steep down-
ward turn. As in the past, the SFIO refused to participate in government and
broke with the Radicals over their dismal, if predictable, policy of deflation.

Herriot escaped from his thankless task by contriving to fall on the issue
of paying war debts to the United States, irrespective of Germany's refusal
to pay reparations. Herriot maintained France had an obligation to pay but
even the internationally minded Socialists voted against him. Daladier, the
rising star of the Radical party, once a pupil of Herriot's and like him a
normalien, took over, but fared no better in coping with the crisis. His pro-
posal to cut the salaries of government officials only antagonized many of the
very people who had voted for the Cartel and made Socialist support even
less forthcoming. Ludicrously short-lived governments under the archetypal
Radicals Sarraut and Chautemps followed, prescribing the same medicine,
which the Socialists were forced to swallow. But in December 1933 the Chautemps cabinet was confronted with a new charge to add to that of incompetence: namely, corruption. The Stavisky scandal was about to break.

The name of the crooked financier Serge Stavisky, or Monsieur Alexandre,
as he liked to call himself, became known throughout France when, on
8 January 1934, news of his suicide was blazed across the headlines of the
national press. Wanted for questioning in the 'Bayonne Affair' involving the
arrest for fraud of a local bank manager and the town's deputy mayor, he
was reported to have taken his own life as the police closed in on him at a
villa near Chamonix. What fascinated the newspapers, and their public, was
that, for a crook, Stavisky appeared to have many friends in high places,
including Albert Dalimier, Minister of the Colonies in the Chautemps cabinet, not to mention various other Radical deputies and senators. Thanks to
his powerful friends, and not least to the fact that the public prosecutor was
the brother-in-law of the Prime Minister, Stavisky had already succeeded nine
times in avoiding trial since the police first began to investigate him back in
1927. The Right was enraptured at these revelations of Republican graft:
Action Française lost no time in alleging that Chautemps had had Stavisky
murdered to keep his mouth shut, and the *camelots du roi* took to rioting in
the streets. Throwing dirt at the Republic was of course nothing new for the
right-wing press, but what gave added force to their accusations in 1934 was
the by now generalized sense of crisis and the menace of ruin posed to the
middle classes by the Depression and the incompetence of the politicians.
Someone or something had to be blamed and *Action Française* had no doubt
that it was the feeble, corrupt parliamentary regime itself. Yet in parliament
Chautemps resisted all attempts to institute an enquiry, before being forced
to resign, leaving Daladier to try to clear the air of scandal.

Daladier, doubtless thinking to win over the Socialists, decided to act
against Chiappe, the Prefect of Police, who not only had associations with
Stavisky but had shown an indulgence to right-wing demonstrators which
contrasted sharply with his heavy-handed treatment of the Left. But the
dismissal of one of their favourite officials, allied to a sense that Daladier
intended to sweep the Stavisky Affair under the carpet, brought the extra-
parliamentary Right onto the streets in an unprecedented show of force. On
6 February 1934 right-wing demonstrators congregated outside the Chamber
of Deputies, chanting anti-republican slogans and apparently bent on invading
the House. The demonstrations soon became a full-scale riot which the police

were forced to quell by firing into the crowd, killing 14 people and wounding another 236. Deputies were manhandled as they left the Chamber and the rioting continued spasmodically into the night. Next day, Daladier, belying his reputation for being a 'strong man', resigned, and Gaston Doumergue emerged from retirement to head a new cabinet of national union.

It would be difficult to exaggerate the sense of shock felt by the Republican politicians on the morrow of the 6 February riots. Then, and for long afterwards, they believed that the rioters were part of a co-ordinated conspiracy on the part of the Right to bring down the regime and to replace it with a French version of Mussolini's or Hitler's dictatorship. The notion of a fascist plot became, if anything, even more credible in the light of events after 1940, when a good number of the activists of the 6 February proclaimed themselves Vichyites or collaborators with the Nazis. And, in truth, France was not without its share of fascists in the 1930s, even if they were not concentrated in a single movement as in Italy or Germany.

Action Française was not fascist, but it had recognizably fascist traits. In its anti-parliamentarism, anti-communism, integral nationalism, xenophobia, anti-Semitism and cult of violence it belonged to the same family as Italian fascism or German nazism. In 1934 it had about 60,000 members, of whom about 7,000 were based in Paris. Its newspaper had a circulation of about 100,000. Its leader, Charles Maurras, was no Mussolini or Hitler: he was an intellectual, not a man of action. Many of the more genuinely Catholic readers of the newspaper ceased to take it after the papal condemnation of 1926, while a younger generation of right-wing militants complained of the movement's lack of dynamism. One of them, George Valois, as early as 1925 founded a new movement, the *Faisceau*, which looked to Mussolini rather than Maurras for inspiration. Not that fascism, for Valois, was un-French: on the contrary, if Mussolini had invented the word, the thing itself was French, rooted in a fusion of nationalism and socialism, of Barrès and Georges Sorel. For a brief period Valois's movement appealed to a number of war veterans and anxious bourgeois – though few workers – but the advent to power of Poincaré and then Tardieu rendered its services redundant. Much the same thing happened to the *Jeunesses patriotes*, a neo-bonapartist league founded by the champagne magnate Pierre Taittinger in 1924, though by 1934 it had rallied again to number 90,000 members.

Maurras, too, was the original mentor of a new school of right-wing intellectuals who, if few in number, had considerable influence in the literary world and helped to shape the intellectual climate of the 1930s. Men like Robert Brasillach, Maurice Bardèche and Lucien Rebatet and their confrères on the newspaper *Je suis partout* (founded in 1930), novelists like Drieu la Rochelle and Céline, journalists on the weeklies *Gringoire* and *Candide* combined a maurrasien loathing of degenerate democracy with a new, romantic faith in 'fascist man' and fascism's cult of youth and virility. Other signs of the spread of the 'fascist spirit' were the secession of Marcel Déat and the 'neo-socialists' from the SFIO in 1933 and the evolution of the prominent Radical Gaston Bergery (who invented the term Popular Front) from staunch anti-fascist to eventual Vichyite.

The crisis bred more than a 'fascist spirit' among intellectuals. There were also the leagues. In 1933 the perfume manufacturer François Coty, ever prodigal with his fortune in subsidizing right-wing movements and newspapers, founded the *Solidarité Française*, whose blue-shirted militants, commanded by Jean Renaud, were the leading rioters of 6 February. Likewise in 1933 the war veteran Marcel Bucard, a former associate of Valois, created his *Francisme*, a straight replica of Mussolini's fascist model, though his collaborator Paul Guiraud gave the organization certain religious overtones. But by far the most important of the fascist groups was Jacques Doriot's *Parti populaire français*, founded in 1936 by the ex-communist mayor of Saint-Denis who carried large numbers of his working-class supporters with him when he effected his political transition and thus revealed the capacity of fascism to recruit on the Left as well as the Right. In 1937 he had perhaps 100,000 members. Intellectuals such as Drieu, Bertrand de Jouvenel, Paul Marion and Alfred Fabre-Luce were impressed by Doriot and joined the PPF. Pierre Pucheu, steel executive and future Minister of the Interior at Vichy, raised finance from industrialists and businessmen, while Mussolini himself contributed to the party's coffers. A smaller but more sinister organization than the PPF was the *Cagoule*, or 'Hooded Men', a secret society founded by Eugène Deloncle and ready to further its aims by murder. It had some links with army officers and staged an abortive *coup d'état* on the night of 15 November 1937. Finally, there was the 'peasant fascism' of Henry Dorgères's Green Shirts, who demanded a return to a more virtuous, agrarian way of life. It had at least 10,000 active militants and thousands more (many of them rural labourers) who sympathized with its aims, particularly in the north and west of France, along with Nice, Algeria and the Paris basin.

Back in 1934, however, the group deemed by the French Left to be the most dangerous incarnation of the fascist threat was the veterans' association the *Croix-de-Feu*, founded in 1927, and after 1931 transformed by its president Colonel de la Rocque into a mass movement with around 450,000 members by 1936. In reality, though it did have its para-military side, the *Croix-de-Feu* was much less active than *Action Française* and *Solidarité Française* in both the riots that preceded 6 February and on the day itself. During the rioting De la Rocque gave orders not to attack police barricades. Although there was something fascist about his style of leadership, especially its authoritarian personality cult, he always denied the charge of fascism and in 1936 accepted the dissolution of his movement and its transmutation into a political party, the *Parti Social Français* (PSF). Nevertheless, the size of his organization and the ambiguity surrounding its ultimate aims made it the most obvious target for left-wing denunciations.

In retrospect, it is clear that the French Left greatly exaggerated the possibility of a fascist takeover in France. Fascism, though certainly not 'unFrench', was fragmented, incoherent and badly co-ordinated. Even on 6 February there was no concerted action, certainly no plan to seize the key instruments of power. Most of the demonstrators went off to catch the last metro home. Yet it would be a mistake to underestimate the extent of the economic, social and political malaise experienced by the French at this time. Discontent with the politicians and the parliamentary system ran deep. A street demonstration did remove a Prime Minister, if not the regime. French democracy was shown to be vulnerable and by no means predestined to escape the fate of Italy, Germany or Spain. More effective leadership of the fascist organizations would have tested its limitations even more severely. But at least the French Left did not make the fatal error of their German counterparts in underestimating the danger from fascism. Ultimately, the survival of the regime depended on a readiness to break with the politics of the 'stalemate society': to countenance change and to embrace reform. This is what the Left did in forming the Popular Front alliance.

The Rise of the Popular Front

Before the 6 February riots a coalition of the three major parties of the Left seemed far removed from the realm of practical politics. The ambiguity and shortcomings of the Radicals have already been outlined. Their credentials as a part of the Left were much in question, despite the best efforts of the 'Young Turks' – Daladier, Pierre Mendès-France, Jean Zay, Pierre Cot and others – in the late twenties and early thirties. The Socialists, under the leadership of Léon Blum and Paul Faure, continued their recovery since the dark days of 1920, winning back many of the schismatics of Tours who had been tempted and then disappointed by communism. They had also begun to make inroads on Radical support south of the Loire, especially among peasants and minor civil servants. Party membership remained small, but was increasing (60,000 in 1924, 137,000 in 1932). By the elections of 1932 the SFIO could poll nearly two million votes and returned 131 deputies. A number of the party's leading lights – Renaudel, Ramadier, Marquet and Léon Blum's great hope for the future, the *normalien* Marcel Déat – were in favour of participating in government, but Blum repudiated any such resuscitation of *millerandisme*. Instead, while the 'ministerialists' quit the SFIO to form the 'neo-Socialist' party in 1933, Blum developed his famous distinction between the 'conquest of power' – the ultimate goal for which Socialists were striving – and the 'exercise of power' by which Socialists might assume office, either alone or as the senior partner in a coalition, in order to defend and promote the interests of the working class.

Even more isolated and much more intransigent were the Communists. From the start, it was intended that the PCF should be an entirely new type of political party, not just another addition to the ample selection already on view. Its aim was to emulate the Bolshevik, democratic – centralist model, and it looked to Moscow for both inspiration and direction. The Communist International was not reticent with its advice. In 1921 it prescribed a 'single proletarian front', by which communists were exhorted to capture the mass support of democratic movements while waging war against their treacherous leaders. In 1922 Trotsky vetoed communist participation in such 'petty bourgeois' organizations as Freemasonry and the League of the Rights of Man. Moscow also kept a watchful eye on the French party through the Comintern's representative in Paris, J. Humbert-Droz. Before long, disillusioned socialists and revolutionary syndicalists were making their way back to whence they came. Others were summarily expelled, especially once the party began its 'bolshevization' drive in 1924. The party attached small priority to electoral successes. Instead of building up territorial bases, it concentrated on forming cells within factories and other places of work, making most headway among metalworkers and railwaymen. The party was strongest in the Paris area, above all in the working-class, 'red' suburbs – places such as Ivry and Saint-Denis – which elected Communists to control of municipal government and returned the vast majority of Communist deputies (19 out of 26 in 1924). The industrial Moselle (rather than the industrial Nord, which remained loyal to socialism) was another area of Communist strength, though the PCF also implanted itself in certain rural departments – Allier, Gard, Vaucluse, Var and others – with a tradition for voting for the extreme Left. The success of Renaud Jean in the Lot-et-Garonne was a striking illustration of this tendency and of the potential impact of a charismatic individual.

'Bolshevization' did not proceed smoothly. The power struggles in Moscow which followed the death of Lenin in 1924 had repercussions for the French party. 'Leftist' elements in France, such as Boris Souvarine and two of Trotsky's leading French admirers, Monatte and Rosmer, were purged. So too were Treint and Suzanne Girault, who earlier had conducted a witch-hunt against the 'Right' deviationists. Already noted for its uncompromising opposition to the occupation of the Ruhr in 1923, its refusal to join the Left Cartel in 1924 and its denunciation of the Rif war in 1925, the PCF attained new heights of notoriety when, for the election campaign of 1928, it adopted the International's 'class against class' tactic, predicated on the belief that the final crisis of capitalism was at hand and that the proletariat must be given a clear lead, to prevent it from being duped by fascists, Radicals and, above all, Socialists, who were increasingly condemned as 'social fascists' and 'social-democratic vomit'.

Abandoned to an intransigent sectarianism, the PCF won only 12 seats in the 1928 elections (having refused the traditional practice of 'republican discipline' at the second ballot) and saw its membership figures dwindle steadily, from 52,000 in 1928 to 28,000 in 1933. These were also years of bitter internal conflict, but in the end Maurice Thorez emerged as the party's dominant figure. Born the illegitimate son of a grocer in a mining village of the Pas-de-Calais, Thorez proved to be a bright pupil at school, which saved him from the usual fate of having to go down the pits when he left. Attracted to the new PCF, he became a full-time party official and began to climb steadily up the hierarchy, developing close links with Moscow, which he visited several times, on the way. Like Stalin himself, Thorez achieved pre-eminence more on account of his bureaucratic talents than on account of any personal charisma. Always a Stalinist, he maintained extremely close links with the Comintern representative, Fried. Together, they kept the party to its 'class against class' line into 1934. Alongside the right-wing demonstrators of 6 February was a contingent of Communists who likewise hurled their abuse at the corrupt and decadent Republic.

Against this distinctly unpromising background, it was remarkable that it was the PCF which should take the lead in putting together an anti-fascist coalition of the Left. On 9 February the Communists defied a ban on a demonstration which they had called and clashed violently with the police. Eight people died and several hundred were injured. Significantly, on this occasion, PCF militants were joined by other left-wing elements and then when the CGT called a general strike for 12 February, not only the Socialists but also the Communists decided to participate. Once again there were brutal, and fatal, confrontations with the police. The protests clearly revealed concern among the rank and file of the French Left about the spread of fascism, but party chiefs hesitated to engage in talks about unity or any further concerted action. One exception was Jacques Doriot, the Communist mayor of Saint-Denis, who called for the Left to stand together against fascism, but was in consequence disowned and expelled from his party. Earlier attempts at unifying the Left had also come to nothing. The pacifist and communist intellectuals Romain Rolland and Henri Barbusse, alarmed by the rise of Nazism, organized two congresses, one in Amsterdam in 1932, the other in Paris at the salle Pleyel in 1933, to try to bind together the struggle against fascism and the crusade for peace in a common movement. They obtained the support of a number of politicians, trade unionists and intellectuals, but neither the CGT nor any political party would give its backing. Similarly, the left-wing Radical deputy Gaston Bergery obtained a poor response to his appeal for a 'Common Front against Fascism'. The only sequel to the protests of 12 February was the formation of a committee of anti-fascist intellectuals, which represented all three Radical, Socialist and Communist tendencies.

What altered the situation dramatically was Hitler's smashing of the German Communist party and Stalin's growing fears of Nazism. Thorez, who had been privately sympathetic to breaking out of the 'class against class' ghetto but had hesitated to identify openly with a policy espoused by the heretic Doriot, obtained a signal from the International to proceed with an attempt to construct a common front. The new line became official party policy at the party conference held at Ivry in June 1934. Socialist leaders were inclined to treat the Communist conversion with extreme suspicion, but left-wing Socialists, such as Marceau Pivert and Jean Zyromski, were much more enthusiastic, and forced the pace. A joint Communist–Socialist pact of unity of action was negotiated in June 1934 which agreed on the need for concerted action against fascism. By the autumn Thorez had begun to employ the term *'Front populaire'* and also sought to extend the alliance to the progressive elements of the bourgeoisie (meaning the Radicals). As he told the Chamber of Deputies in a speech of 13 November 1934, the Popular Front was 'for bread, for liberty, for peace'.

In May 1935 Socialists and Communists made important gains in the municipal elections, which demonstrated plainly that, in the countryside, distressed peasants blamed the Radicals for the ills that beset them. Daladier and Left Radicals such as Jean Zay and Pierre Cot were more than ever convinced that their party could not remain outside the coalition of the Left, whose star was plainly in the ascendant. In July 1934 Radicals joined the committee of the *Rassamblement Populaire* set up under the presidency of Victor Basch of the League of the Rights of Man and, amidst great euphoria at the recovery of long-lost unity on the Left, Radicals, Socialists and Communists participated in the huge demonstrations of 14 July called for by the Amsterdam–Pleyel committee. In October 1935 the Radical congress endorsed the party's adhesion to the programme of the Popular Front. Earlier, in July, Communist commitment to the idea of a united front had been endorsed by the official strategy of the Comintern at its Seventh Congress. The way was clear for the Left to fight the forthcoming parliamentary elections of 1936 in unison.

It should, however, be emphasized that the Left's common programme contained little in the way of concrete proposals for structural reforms, which the Socialists wanted and the Radicals opposed. Anxious above all not to alienate Radical support, deemed essential both for the defence of democracy at home, and even more so, for the creation of an effective anti-fascist alliance at the level of international relations, the Communists agreed to confine the programme to the dissolution of the leagues, nationalization of the armaments industry, some moves to curb the excesses of the press and reorganization of the Bank of France, to strike at the '200 families' and the 'wall of money'. With regard to the economic crisis, an end would be put to the ruinous policy of deflation pursued since 1934 by the governments of Doumergue, Flandin and, especially, Laval, but there was to be no devaluation of the currency, which, alone among politicians of any standing, Paul Reynaud prescribed as the only remedy capable of stimulating demand and raising prices.

The Left entered the election campaign in a spirit of euphoria, heightened by the fact that at the end of 1935 the syndicalist movement had agreed in principle to reunification, which was formally agreed at the Congress of Toulouse in March 1936. Like the Socialists, the leaders of the CGT had initially been hesitant, but had bowed to pressure from militants at the grass roots. As with the PCF, the CGTU was ready to make plenty of concessions for the sake of unity. The Communists went to enormous lengths to project a favourable image of themselves as a truly French and patriotic party, incarnating the French revolutionary tradition and, as Thorez put it, reconciling the tricolour of their fathers with the red flag of their hopes. Much to the indignation of anti-clerical Radicals, in a speech of 17 April 1936 broadcast on the radio (the radio was extensively used in the campaign and Thorez emerged as a particularly skilful exponent of the medium) the Communist leader even proferred a hand to French Catholics, which was not, in the event, clasped. In marked contrast to the new mood of optimism and fraternity on the Left, the Right contemplated a victory of the Left with mingled hatred and fear. The bitterness of the times was embodied not just in the poisonous filth pumped out by the right-wing press but by a brutal physical assault on Léon Blum on 13 February by an *Action Française* mob.

The intense interest in the outcome of the elections was reflected in the extremely high turn-out at the polls (over 84 per cent) in the first ballot in April 1936. The Left polled 5.5 million votes to the Right's 4.5 million, but what was most striking about this result was where the left-wing votes came from. Whereas, by comparison with elections of 1932, the Radicals lost 400,000 votes and the Socialist 30,000 (while still topping the poll with almost 2 million votes) the Communists secured almost 1.5 million votes – an increase of 800,000. The Left experienced considerable anxiety as to whether or not the Radicals would defect at the second ballot, but in the end Republican discipline held up. At the final count, the Radicals had 106 seats (a loss of 50), the Socialists had 147 (a gain of 15) and the PCF 72 (a gain of 61). The Left had won its most famous victory and, as the leader of the largest party from the winning coalition, it fell to Léon Blum to form the government of the Popular Front.

11
The Popular Front Era

The Blum Experiment

Léon Blum was nothing if not legalistic. He therefore did not begin to form his government until after the formal expiry of the life of the former Chamber on 2 June. But before then the caretaker Sarraut cabinet was confronted by the biggest demonstration of working-class protest France had ever seen. Beginning in mid May in the aviation factories of Le Havre, Toulouse and Courbevoie, a gigantic strike wave spread through the whole of French industry, bringing production to a halt and leaving factories in the hands of some two million sit-in strikers. This 'social explosion' was the workers' response to the victory of the Left in the elections. At last it seemed that a new day had dawned for the urban masses, so long the outcasts of the regime and now filled with immense hopes for the future, expressed as much in song and carnival as in the strikes themselves. The strikes were essentially spontaneous and unorganized. Indeed, they had not been envisaged even by trade-union leaders, though revolutionary elements on the Left – Trotskyites, *pivertistes*, and anarcho-syndicalists, but not the PCF – sought to develop the movement. On 27 April Marceau Pivert wrote in *Le Populaire* that a genuinely revolutionary situation had been created: all was possible, he claimed. The propertied classes were aghast. Employers fumed at the occupation of the factories and demanded government intervention to put an end to the strikes.

It was amid these extraordinary circumstances that the Blum government took office on 5 June. Born in 1872 into a well-off Jewish family, Blum had abandoned his studies at the École Normale to move in *avant-garde* literary and anarchist circles before establishing himself as a legal expert at the Council of State. Having entered parliament in 1919, he rapidly emerged as the outstanding figure in the reconstructed Socialist party: upright, highly intelligent, a brilliant journalist and formidable debater, but aloof and lacking the warmth and popular touch of Jaurès. When the Communists announced that they would not participate in his government, but only support it from the backbenches (much as the Socialists themselves had been wont to do with the Radicals), Blum put together a Socialist–Radical cabinet in which Socialists assumed responsibility for the ministries of the Interior (Salengro) and Finance (Auriol), while Foreign Affairs (Delbos) and Education (Zay) went to the Radicals. He also caused a certain stir by including three women as undersecretaries of state, despite the general exclusion of women from the suffrage, and by the creation of a new department of Sports and Leisure, headed by the Socialist Léo Lagrange.

His first priority was to deal with the occupation of the factories. Bringing together representatives of the CGT and the employers' CGPF at the Hôtel Matignon, the prime minister's residence, Blum secured the signing of the Matignon Agreements on 7 June 1936 by which the workers obtained pay rises of up to 15 per cent, acceptance of the principle of compulsory collective bargaining and recognition of trade-union rights. These were followed on 11–12 June by social legislation instituting the 40-hour week and paid holidays for workers. When some workers still showed a reluctance to return to work, Blum was able to obtain Communist support for his call to end the strikes. The PCF, in truth, had been much embarrassed by the sit-ins, and on 11 June Thorez came out strongly against their continuation, declaring that 'one has to know when to end a strike once satisfaction has been obtained'.

Having got the country back to work, the Blum government set to implementing its programme. On 18 June it dissolved the leagues though the *Croix-de-Feu* reformed as a legitimate political party, the *Parti Social Français* (PSF), whose membership soon far outstripped that of either the Socialists or the Communists (at its peak it numbered about 800,000). On 2 July Zay raised the school leaving age to 14. On 24 July the Bank of France was 'democratized'. An assembly of 40,000 shareholders replaced the '200 families', while a council of experts, some of whom represented the State, took over the Regency Council. This reform fell far short of the full nationalization which ideally the Socialists and Communists would have preferred, but it was as much as they could persuade the Radicals to wear. The one case of nationalization was in the war industries, brought under State control by a law of 11 August. For the Left, this represented a vital blow struck against the 'merchants of death' and a veto on their capacity to dictate to the State in the matter of arms supply: it also served notice of the Popular Front's intention to resist further aggression on the part of Germany, and the military supported it. With regard to the problems of the countryside, a law of 15 August set up a Wheat Office to fix the annual price of wheat.

While carrying out its domestic reforms, the Popular Front had also to grapple with the problems of the international situation. These will be considered at greater length later, but for the moment it is necessary to appreciate how the conflict in Spain opened up a serious breach between the Blum government and the mass of its working-class supporters, and also created bitter divisions within the coalition itself. When civil war broke out in Spain in July 1936, the desire to show solidarity with the Spanish Republic against the Nationalist rebels was strongly felt throughout the ranks of the Left in France. For reasons that will be elaborated in the final section of this chapter, Blum, though strongly sympathetic to the government of the *Frente Popular*, declared in favour of non-intervention on 1 August 1936, with the result that the Spanish government was refused the right to purchase arms from France. Indignation among Socialists and trade unionists ran high at what was seen as a betrayal of the French government's commitment to fight fascism. Jean Zyromski, the left-wing Socialist leader closest to the rank-and-file, articulated the general dismay in *La Bataille Socialiste*, though there were those like the more revolutionary Marceau Pivert and the more moderate but ultra-pacifist Paul Faure who congratulated Blum in keeping France out of an imperialist war. The Communists, for reasons of their own (including genuine anti-fascism), were also highly critical of the government's position. Solicitous above all to promote an effective anti-Nazi alliance between France and the Soviet Union and concerned to demonstrate the bona fides of their 'united front' strategy to defend democracy, they directed much of their propaganda effort at the Radical party in the hope of resurrecting a new *union sacrée*. At the same time, the Spanish issue provided Communists with a weapon to attack the Socialist government and possibly to win over disillusioned Socialist militants for Communism: never did the PCF lose sight of its long-term ambition to be the dominant, even the sole, party of the proletariat. In December 1936 the Communists refused to support Blum in the Chamber on the question of non-intervention.

Though resolved to keep France out of the Spanish Civil War, the Blum government was far from insensitive to the problem of French security. Rearmament was high on the Popular Front's agenda. At the Ministry of Defence Daladier initiated a vast programme of modernization of the country's land forces, raising military spending to 14 milliard francs. By 1938 national defence claimed a third of the whole French budget and absorbed 50 per cent of French tax returns. But, however salutary from the point of view of national security, these measures could not but exacerbate the financial and economic crisis which had not ceased to deepen since Blum's assumption of power. Speculation against the franc had been going on since May 1935, when rumours began to circulate in financial circles that France might, after all, be obliged to go off gold and to devalue. In 10 days 6.3 milliard francs were exported abroad. The trend accelerated in the winter of 1935, mainly because speculators, believing a devaluation to be inevitable, hoped to make a killing: but certainly the prospect of a left-wing victory in the elections did not help matters. Perhaps as much as 13 milliard francs were placed abroad between May 1935 and June 1936. On taking power, Blum was confronted with a strike not only of labour but of capital. At the same time, the budget deficit continued to grow and inflation mounted sharply. Against all his promises, in the hope of encouraging capital to return, Blum, after consultation with the Americans and the British, devalued the franc in September 1936 by an 'elastic' amount of between 25 and 35 per cent.

But French investors were in no hurry to repatriate their funds: the very existence of the Popular Front government put them off. The franc remained under pressure, increasing Blum's dependence on financial assistance from the Anglo-Saxon powers. At their insistence, France had to refrain from introducing exchange controls and other measures that might have curbed speculation against the franc, such as the Governor of the Bank of France, Labeyrie, was urging Blum to adopt. By February 1937 the Socialist leader saw no alternative to a 'pause' in the reform programme of the Popular Front. Plans to introduce old-age pensions for workers and a National Unemployment Fund were shelved as the government sought to restore the 'confidence' of French capital holders.

Left-wing reactions to the retreat from the social and economic goals of the Popular Front were predictable. The Communists and the far Left of the Socialist party denounced the government's craven capitulation to the power of money. Workers, initially so ecstatic at the triumph of the Left, shed their enthusiasm when the government not only refused to help its sister republic in Spain but appeared impotent before the class enemy. The rapid rise of the cost of living, along with the workers' determination to resist widespread attempts on the part of employers to renege on the Matignon Agreements, produced another crop of strikes in the autumn of 1936. A civil servants' strike in August was followed in quick succession by strikes of textile workers in the Nord and then of miners, metalworkers and dockers. In the last third of 1936 France recorded its highest ever level of strikes (2,428), involving some 295,000 workers. The only comfort Blum could offer the strikers, in the face of intransigence among employers and their spokesmen in the Senate, was a law on compulsory arbitration, passed on the last day of 1936. It was not enough to reassure an increasingly disenchanted workforce, all the more so in that under the Arbitration Act workers never received full compensation for the steep rise in the cost of living. The 'pause' completed the breach between labour and the Popular Front.

On 16 March 1937 the breach became a chasm. When the government refused to ban a rally of De la Rocque's PSF held at a cinema in Clichy, left-wing protesters staged a counter-demonstration which ended in a violent clash with the police. Seven people were killed and several hundred injured. Even a People's Front government had spilled the blood of workers in the defence of order. A fresh wave of strikes broke out in Paris and the CGT called a general strike for 18 March. Blum considered resigning, but eventually lingered in office for another three months. Refused full powers to deal with the continuing financial crisis, he finally went on 22 June. The 'Blum experiment' was over.

The reasons for his failure continue to provoke controversy among historians. Some blame Blum himself and his timid, hesitant policies, which allegedly destroyed the revolutionary *élan* of the workers. In this view, the Popular Front was yet another *révolution manguée,* a failure to exploit the possibilities opened up by the mass sit-in strikes of June 1936. Such a verdict seems hard to justify in the light of the attitude of the Communists, who refused to attempt to turn the strikes into a revolution. It is hard to see how a successful revolution in France could have been carried through without them, let alone against them; that of course may be seen as a betrayal of the Communists' own revolutionary ideals. Historians sympathetic to Blum and the Socialists also criticize the Communists' ambivalent attitude to the government. Their non-participation and 'ministry of the masses' could be interpreted as an attempt to create a 'dual power' situation, as in the Russia of Kerensky in 1917. Certainly, the Communist stance did not make life easier for the Socialists. Nor were the Radicals any more reliable as allies, since many of their number had joined the Popular Front only with extreme reluctance and with the aim of checking, rather than promoting, the structural reforms sought by the Socialists.

For economic experts such as Alfred Sauvy, the crucial failure of the Popular Front was its allegedly disastrous financial and economic policies. Devaluation was too long delayed, its extent was insufficient, and, worst of all, its benefits were wiped out by a doctrinaire insistence upon the rigid application of the 40-hour week, which stifled the short-lived economic revival, limiting production, increasing wages and boosting inflation. An extension of this argument is to say that, in any case, the country could not afford the social programme of the Popular Front, given the precariousness of the economic situation and the overriding requirements of foreign policy. Such purely economic arguments do not do justice to the political realities of the position of the Popular Front government. It was committed to doing something for the workers: they expected it, and it was no more than their due after years of governmental indifference, if not hostility. Moreover, in conformity with its fundamental pledge to fight fascism, the Blum administration spent much more on rearmament than on social reform. The cost of national defence, rather than the cost of social legislation, was what strained the resources of the State.

At bottom, the financial community's lack of confidence in the government stemmed less from what it did, but from what it was: the reactions of the extreme Right and of investors leave no doubt on that score. The constant vilification of Blum and his ministers in the right-wing press exemplified French gutter journalism at its worst. Its saddest outcome was the suicide of Roger Salengro, falsely accused of desertion during the Great War. As for investors, their confidence was only restored when Paul Reynaud took over the Ministry of Finance in the Daladier government in 1938 and set about undoing the Popular Front's legislation. The 'wall of money' was a reality which Blum could not overcome. Perhaps his greatest failure was to duck a showdown with the monied power and to believe, naïvely, that it could be reconciled to his premiership by gestures of moderation and conciliation. In consequence, he forfeited the support of his most genuine and ardent supporters among the working classes. Honest, reasonable and tolerant, but over-sensitive to the social and ideological divisions which beset France, Blum lacked the inner conviction that he was the man to resolve the country's problems by bold and imaginative leadership.

The spirit of the Popular Front died with the fall of the first Blum government, even though its successors were still supported by the Popular Front Chamber. Blum was replaced by the Radical Chautemps, who put together a predominantly Radical cabinet, with Socialist participation (including that of Blum). The leading figure in the government was not the prime minister but the new Finance Minister, the increasingly right-wing Radical Georges Bonnet, known at home and abroad (he was recalled from the embassy in Washington) for the 'orthodoxy' of his financial views. Not even Bonnet, however, could prevent a further devaluation of the franc at the end of June 1937. The Socialists, uncomfortable in the new government, quit in January 1938, opening up another ministerial crisis. Bonnet was unacceptable to the Socialists, while Léon Blum's suggestion of a government 'from Thorez to Paul Reynaud' was too much for the Radicals.

The only solution was a second Chautemps cabinet, this time without the participation of the Socialists (a decision which threw the SFIO into even further disarray). Brought down by the Socialists on his handling of the endemic financial crisis in March 1938 (which saved him from having to respond to the *Anschluss*) Chautemps left Blum to form his second cabinet. Ideally, Blum wanted to put together a government of national unity which would have stretched all the way from Thorez to Louis Marin of the Republican Federation, but the Right would have nothing to do with an administration that included Communists. After only a month in office, Blum resigned, bowing once again to the Senate's opposition to his financial policies. The time had come for a new man and new measures, and the most appropriate figure appeared to be the 'bull of the Vancluse', Edouard Daladier.

The Daladier Regime

Already a veteran of 15 cabinets and three times Prime Minister, Edouard Daladier was no stranger to government. Yet another product of the *République des professeurs*, he liked to present himself as a Republican in the Jacobin mould, democratic, patriotic and authoritarian. By contrast with Léon Blum, whose very name was synonymous with the ideological and social divisions afflicting France, Daladier enjoyed an exceptionally widespread popularity. On 12 April 1938 his government was endorsed by all but a handful of deputies in the Chamber. Like Clemenceau and Poincaré before him, he possessed a personal authority, which, if anything, increased during his tenure of office, commensurate with the impression he gave of steering France safely through a succession of grave international and domestic crises.

Unquestionably, it was the exigencies of the international situation that commanded most of his attention. As we shall see in the next section, Hitler and Nazi Germany resurrected the dreaded spectre of war and plunged the country into even deeper depths of ideological and political conflict. Paradoxically, however, the divisions engendered by the Nazi menace tended to enhance Daladier's standing as the nation's leader in a time of crisis. Hence, on the domestic front, when he turned to the problems of the economy and demanded the full financial powers the Senate had refused to grant to Léon Blum, he had no difficulty in obtaining them for a period of three and a half months. Inheriting a situation in which production was stagnant and prices rising, he devalued the franc by 10 per cent in May 1938 and started a public works programme, with special emphasis on housing.

For Daladier, the critical obstacle to increased production was the rigid implementation of the 40-hour week, and in August 1938 he began an assault upon it, authorizing derogations in the armaments industry and thereby provoking the resignation of the Socialist ministers Ramadier and Frossard. The appointment of Paul Reynaud to the Ministry of Finance confirmed the new direction in economic policy. At a personal level, there was no love lost between the premier and his Finance Minister, but in the assault on the 40-hour week, which Reynaud had always opposed, they were as one. In mid November Reynaud promulgated a series of decree laws, with the objective of stimulating the economy by unblocking controls on both prices and the length of the working day and by cutting public spending. Derogations from the 40-hour week became ever more frequent. For their part, the unions strenuously opposed this tampering with the precious gains they had made in 1936 (though they were prepared to treat the armaments industry as a special case). Conflict was inevitable, despite the desire of CGT leaders to avoid a showdown. In the face of Reynaud's implacable refusal to negotiate, they had no choice but to strike, particularly since the Reynaud decrees were viewed as the culmination of a concerted attack on the legislation of 1936 by intransigent employers. For two years many had been reneging on collective bargaining agreements, firing shop stewards and union officials and refusing to increase wages in line with prices. Some firms chose to implement the Reynaud decrees in a deliberately provocative manner. Hutchinson's at Puteaux, for instance, introduced a 44-hour week, with a seven-hour day Monday to Friday and nine hours on a Saturday. Renault imposed the 40-hour week over six days rather than five and further aroused the ire of their workers by lockouts and dismissals. Egged on by right-wing newspapers like the *Echo de Paris*, the government, too, prepared itself for a fight with the unions. Troops and police were mobilized and the radio waves commandeered to broadcast its resolution. The CGT, by contrast, prepared badly for the conflict. Its call for a 24-hour general strike on 30 November was ill-timed and ill-conceived. In any case too short and symbolic to achieve any real impact, the strike gave the government and the bosses plenty of time to plan their strategy. On the day, it failed to bring out the whole workforce, notably in the public sector, where the State had not scrupled to threaten and intimidate its own employees, though the strike was supported by miners, seamen, dockers, printers, metal-workers and workers in textiles and the building industry. The outcome was a serious defeat for the CGT, whose numbers plummeted yet again, as workers were dismissed, disciplined and even prosecuted in the aftermath of the strike. By 1939 the CGT was on the point of a second schism, divided among those, like George Dumoulin, René Belin and the group associated with the anti-communist newspaper *Syndicats*, who openly favoured class collaboration with the *patronat* and defended the Munich agreements, centrists like Jouhaux, and the Communists. Yet another nail had been hammered into the coffin of the Popular front.

The Daladier regime marked an important turning point in the political history of France. The centre of gravity of the Third Republic shifted decisively to the Right. Nowhere was this more apparent than in the evolution of the Radical party itself, which broke decisively with the Popular Front and began to attract support from the provincial bourgeois circles which had hitherto inclined more towards the conservative opponents of Radicalism. De la Rocque, who would have liked his *Parti Social Français* to usurp the place of the Radicals as the champions of the peasantry and small and middling bourgeoisie, was unable to match Daladier in popularity and, to his dismay, saw many of his supporters come to accept the authority of their former opponent of 6 February 1934. George Bonnet, the Radical Foreign Minister, became the chief hope of pacifists and out-and-out appeasers of Hitler. The new tendency was expressed in the newspaper *L'Ère Nouvelle*, which increasingly vented chauvinistic and anti-Semitic sentiments. Significantly, Jewish ministers were excluded from the reception for German Foreign Minister Ribbentrop in December 1938. Laws were passed subjecting foreigners to more stringent security controls. *L'Ère Nouvelle* also called for a new spirit of co-operation between Radicals and the Catholic Church, on the grounds that they shared a mutual, abiding, anti-communism. The era of the historic, nineteenth-century, Radical party was over.

All this is not to say that the Third Republic was already dead, reduced to a dictatorship under Daladier, and ripe for replacement by an even more overtly dictatorial regime like that of Pétain's. Rather, what was happening was that the Third Republic was moving into a new phase, both in terms of its style of government and in its bases of support. If the Left was more alienated than ever, the regime enjoyed a new degree of confidence on the Right. On Daladier personally were focussed the aspirations of many people who believed in political and social renewal. One indication of the government's apparent readiness to try to find new solutions to old problems was its introduction of the Family Code on 28 July 1939, by which, in the hope of arresting France's demographic decline, the State undertook to pay family allowances. Daladier himself seems to have been conscious of incarnating a strongly felt desire for positive leadership at a time of exceptional international tensions. Whether he was capable of supplying it is another matter.

The Shadow of War

With the benefit of hindsight, we can see plainly enough that Hitler's advent to power was a decisive turning point in the history of Europe. This was less obvious at the time. For France, already obsessed with the threat to her security posed by Germany, Hitler was only the latest incarnation of the German menace. Few Frenchmen had read *Mein Kampf* (it was not translated into French until 1934), otherwise more might have been alarmed by the visceral hatred Hitler openly entertained for France. One of the few to have read *Mein Kampf* was ambassador François-Poncet in Berlin, but he refused to take it seriously. He and others were encouraged by the assurances Hitler gave over the next three years about the maintenance of peace. Hardly anyone in France – including at first the PCF and Socialist leader Léon Blum – had any idea of the real expansionist and aggressive drives of Nazism.

Naturally there was concern and consternation when, in October 1933, Germany quit the Disarmament Conference in Geneva and at the same time left the League of Nations. Paul-Boncour, Foreign Minister between December 1932 and January 1934, realizing that Mussolini, too, was alarmed by the rise of Hitler and the prospect of *Anschluss* with Austria, entered into negotiations aimed at reconstructing the old pre-1914 'concert of Europe' in a Four Power Pact of Italy, France, Britain and Germany to guarantee the peace. But Mussolini's revisionist attitude to Versailles was deeply suspect in the eyes of France's eastern European allies. To reassure them, the French diluted the Four Power Pact to the point of meaninglessness. Franco-Russian talks, initiated by the Soviet Union, also went ahead, but the French, unlike the Soviets, were not ready to commit themselves to a full-scale military alliance.

In France the most resolute partisan of a Franco-Soviet alliance was Louis Barthou, who assumed responsibility for French foreign policy in 1934. Something of a mystery man, with many enemies, Barthou was immensely able, cultured and dynamic, and an old-fashioned Germanophobe. A supreme realist, he had no faith in Briandism or the League of Nations and believed that only an effective alliance system could guarantee French security. For the sake of that paramount aim he was ready to jettison the Anglo-French entente, as he saw clearly that Locarno was as far as Britain would go with any guarantee to France. While keeping open channels to Italy, he saw the Soviet Union as an altogether more attractive proposition. The Poles, of course, objected, but Barthou was able to point out to them that they had themselves compromised their alliance with France by signing a non-aggression pact with Germany in January 1934. Nevertheless, to allay the fears of France's eastern neighbours somewhat, he suggested that they try for an 'Eastern Locarno'. Realistically, he knew well enough that such negotiations were likely to founder on the rock of Polish–German differences, but he hoped that they might prove a useful ploy for winning over those who required a Franco-Soviet alliance to be wrapped up in a larger and more acceptable package.

Whether or not Barthou could have brought his 'Grand Design' of encircling Germany to a successful conclusion remains a matter for conjecture. It collapsed when he himself fell the accidental victim of an assassin's bullet – intended for King Alexander of Yugoslavia – on 9 October 1934. His successor, Pierre Laval, had little liking for the Soviet Union. In May 1935 he did sign the long-gestating treaty with the Russians, but refused to follow it up with staff talks and a military convention. His strong personal preference was for reaching an understanding with Mussolini. At the beginning of 1935 he went to Rome and on 7 January signed the Rome Agreements which proclaimed an end to the differences separating the two countries. It was Mussolini's understanding (if not Laval's real intention) that France thereby agreed not to oppose Italian designs on Abyssinia. In April 1935 Britain, France and Italy met at Stresa to reaffirm their commitment to Locarno and to the maintenance of an independent Austria. When Italy eventually did attack Abyssinia in October 1935, Laval and the British Foreign Secretary, Sir Samuel Hoare, meeting for talks in Paris in December 1935, decided that Abyssinia should be ceded to Italy. But when news of their pact was leaked to the press, the furore aroused in Britain obliged Hoare to resign while the Left in France indignantly repudiated Mussolini as a potential ally.

As well as wooing Mussolini, Laval also hoped to achieve Franco-German reconciliation. In January 1935 arrangements were made to hold a plebiscite to decide the fate of the Saarland. By an overwhelming majority the voters opted for Germany. Hitler now began to show his true colours, announcing his rearmament programme, with the introduction of conscription, the creation of the *Luftwaffe* and the establishment of a navy fixed, by a bi-lateral agreement of June 1935 with Britain which greatly infuriated the French, at 35 per cent of British tonnage. The rift between France and Britain had the further effect of emboldening Hitler to proceed earlier than planned with the remilitarization of the Rhineland. While France was in the hands of a caretaker government under Sarraut in the run-up to the elections of 1936 Hitler, in defiance of the advice of the German High Command, ordered troops into the Rhineland on 7 March. His gamble that, despite this flagrant violation of the Treaty of Locarno, France and Britain would take no retaliatory action proved amply justified. British policy-makers in particular did all in their power to restrain France, though in any case the weight of French public opinion, at least as expressed in the newspapers, was also against unilateral French retaliation. Furthermore, the military chiefs, headed by General Gamelin, advised the cabinet that the French army lacked a suitable strike force to carry out reprisals and, worse, was inferior in strength to the military might of Germany (which was not in fact true). French policy-makers, as much as their British counterparts, had come to the view that there was no real alternative to appeasing Hitler.

It was also their belief that, however much they might complain about it and resent it, there was no better bet for French security than the British entente. For one thing, given her financial and economic weakness, the French needed material help from Britain if they were to rearm on the scale deemed necessary to meet the renewed German menace. For another, French strategists, contemplating only a defensive war against Germany, counted on the British navy and the resources of the British Empire to enforce the blockade that would, in the long term, bring the enemy to its knees. The task of the French army was to prevent any invasion of French soil, holding back the enemy at the Maginot Line – the continuous front of massive fortifications constructed, in accordance with military, parliamentary and public opinion, from the late 1920s – and then to advance and finish off the debilitated and demoralized aggressor. On ideological grounds, too, Britain appeared as the least controversial ally for France, since the Soviet Union was suspect in the eyes of the Right while Mussolini's Italy was unacceptable to the Left.

Thus, while Mussolini drew closer to Hitler, announcing the Rome–Berlin Axis in 1936, the Popular Front government in France worked, with some success, to improve Anglo-French relations. Blum's decision not to intervene in the Spanish Civil War undoubtedly helped, even though it cost him much personal anguish, since he was genuinely concerned with the fate of the Spanish Republic and also understood the conflict symbolically in terms of the struggle between democracy and totalitarianism. French non-intervention, however, should not be seen as yet another instance in which a reluctant France gave way, against her better judgement, to the imperious wishes of the 'English governess'. For Blum, the essential consideration, alongside how best to prepare against the Nazi threat, was the domestic situation in France. where, as we have seen, existing ideological and social divisions had been intensified by the victory of his own Popular Front coalition in the elections of 1936. Haunted by the nightmare of civil war in France and perhaps unsure how the army would react to intervention in Spain, Blum resisted the pressure from the Communists and from some sections of his own party to give assistance to the Spanish Republic, though individual Frenchmen – almost all of them Communists – did enlist in the International Brigade.

Equally, Blum and his Foreign Minister Delbos remained deaf to the overtures of the Soviet Union. Stalin understood Hitler's real intentions better than any western stateman and very much hoped that the main outcome of the Popular Front electoral victory in France would be a military alliance between France and the Soviet Union. Blum, however, had an innate antipathy to Communists, which the ambiguous attitude of the PCF towards his government served only to reinforce. He also knew that the French General Staff, like their British counterparts, entertained serious doubts about the Red Army's strength and capacity for offensive action – doubts which Stalin's purges did nothing to allay. Again, to ally with the Soviet Union posed problems for France's relations with her eastern allies. Lacking a common border with Germany, Russia could only come to French assistance if she moved her troops through Poland – a situation the Poles were resolutely determined to avoid. In the end, it was the Franco-British entente that made the most sense. Or so it seemed.

In fact, the entente was a huge mistake, guaranteeing France against a war which Hitler had no desire to wage. Never was it his intention to re-open the war of attrition fought in the trenches between 1914 and 1918. Rather, he planned for *Blitzkrieg* – short, lightning war. In the long term his aim was to create a vast new German Reich greater and more powerful than ever before. In the short term he proceeded piecemeal and in the manner of a born opportunist. After achieving *Anschluss* with Austria in March 1938, without any effective protest from France and Britain, he then turned his sights on Czechoslovakia, on the pretext of resolving the question of 'Germans abroad'. His target here was the 3.5 million Germans in the Sudetenland. The new

French premier, Daladier, well appreciated that French obligations to her Czech ally were clear. His Foreign Minister, Georges Bonnet, however, had a regard for international treaties that was of the same order as Hitler's. An out-and-out appeaser, Bonnet's view was that if the price of avoiding war was the abandonment of Czechoslovakia and the acceptance of German domination in eastern Europe, he was prepared to pay it. While protesting that French policy was hamstrung by Britain, he effectively used the entente as a pretext for seeking to renege on French commitments in central and eastern Europe.

Thus, in September 1938, on behalf of France, Daladier signed the Munich agreements, which forced the Czechs to make concessions to Hitler so as to avoid the possibility of a general European war. The Sudetenland was to revert to Germany, while Polish and Hungarian claims on Czech territory were also to be met. Daladier had few illusions about the shamefulness of the deed to which France had been party at Munich, but at this juncture the French policy of appeasement was supported by majority opinion in the country. On his return from Munich, Daladier was fêted as a hero, the man who, with Chamberlain, had stemmed the tide that threatened to engulf France in another war. The only political party firmly opposed to appeasing Hitler was the PCF. The Socialists were divided, with one group supporting the secretary-general Paul Faure in his belief that war must be avoided at any price, while even on the far Left of the party the *pivertistes*, too, were pacifists. On the extreme Right, hitherto noted for its bellicosity and ultranationalism, *Action Française* led the swing towards a new commitment to pacifism based on a belief that the principal beneficiaries of a war might be the Soviet Union and the cause of Communism generally. In the aftermath of the Popular Front experience, for considerable sections of the French bourgeoisie, Hitler began to appear less as a threat to France and more as a barrier to Bolshevism – an outlook encapsulated in the chilling slogan 'better Hitler than Blum'. Nevertheless, it is true that within a relatively short space of time many Frenchmen came to sense the extent to which Munich was a disaster. Whereas one opinion poll taken immediately after the resolution of the Czech crisis showed 57 per cent in favour of the agreements, with 37 per cent against, another, conducted a few weeks later, revealed 70 per cent in favour of resistance by France and Britain to any further German exactions, with only 17 per cent opposed. Munich left a lingering stench, which few could ignore. It was the smell of decadence, of the long disintegration of France as a great power.

In the short term, Munich marked the end of France's eastern European strategy. Having abandoned Czechoslovakia, Bonnet's next objective was to try to pull out of the Franco-Polish alliance of 1921. It was something of a paradox, therefore, that when Hitler showed his real plans for Czechoslovakia with the occupation of Prague on 15 March 1939, France and Britain together should give a formal guarantee to Poland (as well as Greece and Rumania). Before then, the French persisted with their policy of appeasement, searching in vain for accommodation with Italy and an understanding with Germany. A Franco-German Declaration of 6 December 1938, without giving Hitler an entirely free hand in the east, recognized that Germany should have room for expansion. But the British were now resolved to stand up to Hitler – even if Hitler, understandably, believed that the new hard line was mere bluff.

French policy-makers were unenthusiastic, but, wedded to Britain, felt that they had little choice but to go along with the new commitment. On the far Right, Marcel Déat launched the cry that it would be folly to die for Danzig – the next object of Hitler's aggression.

Danzig itself, however, was hardly the real issue. The point of the Polish guarantee was rather to try to put a halt to limitless German aggression and expansionism. When, therefore, in the face of Polish defiance, Hitler prepared to take by force what he could not obtain by negotiation, even Chamberlain recognized that appeasement had had its day. Not so Bonnet, who, to the end, hoped for a second Munich, to be arranged through the good offices of Mussolini. But war was not to be avoided. On 23 August Hitler and Stalin stunned the world by concluding their Nazi–Soviet Pact. At a stroke, Stalin thus rebuffed the overtures France and Britain had been making to him (this time seriously on the part of the French, but still with no great conviction on the part of the British) and left Hitler free from the worry of having to fight on two fronts, should the western powers persist in regarding Poland as a *casus belli*. On 1 September Germany invaded Poland. Only two days later did Britain and France declare war on Germany, on 3 September. The delay was caused by French reluctance to meet their commitments. Conditioned by years of slippery '*pactomanie*', they hoped somehow to avoid the inevitable. The British, however, took their treaty obligations seriously and France had no choice but, with the greatest reluctance, to follow the British lead. Ironically, the long-sought British alliance dragged the French into a war they had dreaded since 1918.

12
The Strange Defeat

In 1939 France found herself involved in a war that she had neither wanted nor sought. British statesmen had reached the conclusion that something had to be done to stop Hitler, though they had no idea what. The French, to their surprise and dismay, discovered that they had to fight because of the Franco-British guarantee to Poland, which they had hoped would prevent the outbreak of war and which, in the event, proved worthless to the Poles in the face of the Nazi *Blitzkrieg*. The French army, geared for defence, could be mobilized only slowly: its role was to contain the German attack until the British were also able to mobilize massively and more modern weaponry – especially aeroplanes – could be produced. Poland was thus abandoned to her fate, to be repartitioned between Germany and the Soviet Union. The French fulfilled their pledge to take action within 15 days of mobilization by launching a token offensive in the Saar on 9 September. Both civilian and military leaders were determined that there would be no repeat of the First World War, with its slaughter and material destruction on French soil. A blockade, enforced by British maritime supremacy, would eventually bring Germany to her knees. In the meantime, France settled into a 'phoney war' in which it was hoped that victory could be obtained without fighting.

The 'Phoney War'

In retrospect, it can be seen that the period of the 'phoney war' (from September 1939 to May 1940) was disastrous for France, in that the illusion of normality prevented the development of any real sense of national unity or resurrection of the 'sacred union' of 1914. As a result, the country was rendered all the more vulnerable to the shattering experience of *blitzkrieg* in the summer of 1940. In the autumn of 1939, however, there were few Frenchmen who believed that France would soon lie prostrate before the might of Nazi Germany. French inertia in the 'phoney war' did not mean that France was paralysed by fear or engulfed by a wave of defeatism. Rather, to some extent at least, inactivity sprang more from a false sense of security, based on confidence in the impenetrability of the Maginot Line, the massive defence network constructed along the Franco-German border since the late 1920s. Had not General Weygand, in a widely publicized speech at Lille in July 1939, proclaimed that the French army was stronger than at any previous point in its glorious history? That he may well have thought exactly the opposite hardly mattered, since his aim was to reassure the general public.

The French people badly needed some reassurance. They could surely be forgiven if they evinced little enthusiasm for the war or if they appeared somewhat perplexed as to what it was supposed to be about. The choice of the diplomat and writer Jean Giraudoux to be head of the French propaganda effort was unfortunate. Instead of full-blooded denunciations of Hitler and Nazism, the public heard academic and literary disquisitions on the true Germany of musicians, thinkers and poets. Many Frenchmen, especially peasants, filled with an understandable horror of war, remained to be persuaded that France was engaged in a vital, necessary and just struggle and not a conflict brought about by bungling politicians. Visiting upper-class French friends in April 1939 General Sir Louis Spears noted their bitter opposition to war over Poland and their deep resentment of the new-found British resolution to stand up to Hitler, who, however repugnant, could still be considered as a barrier to Bolshevism. Spears was probably not exaggerating when he wrote that, as a class, the French bourgeoisie seemed to be 'gibbering with fright'. The working classes, at least as represented by the CGT, were still smarting from the defeat of the general strike of November 1938 and preoccupied with trying to rehabilitate militants who had been victimized in its aftermath. It was a deeply divided, weary and dispirited French nation that faced Hitler in the autumn of 1939.

Yet public opinion seemed to be waiting for some kind of initiative from the nation's leaders, which is what makes their shortcomings all the more serious. Despondency may have been widespread, but defeatism was confined to the relatively ineffectual circles of the extreme Right, the *munichois* section of the SFIO and certain pro-German organizations such as the *Comité France –Allemagne* (founded in 1935 by Fernand de Brinon and other future collaborators). Studies of French public opinion in the period between Munich and the fall of France are as yet few and their conclusions necessarily tentative, but some evidence has been adduced to suggest that, even more than in Britain, and at an earlier date – after Munich, rather than Prague – a significant psychological shift took place in the outlook of large numbers of the French population. A sense of shame and anger at Munich, combined with a belief that the time had come to stand up to Hitler, could be discerned among such disparate shades of opinion as Socialists of the Blum tendency, some of the hitherto pacifist *instituteurs*, among groups of war veterans and even among sections of the *patronat*, including the *Comité des Forges*. One indication of the new tendency was the difficulty that Déat had in being elected in Angoulême in April 1939, where his notorious pacifism lost him half of the votes of his predecessor. The order to mobilize met with no serious opposition, even if it aroused no enthusiasm: after all, the outbreak of war in 1914 had not been greeted with wild enthusiasm.

Pacifism, it is true, persisted even after war had been declared. Even within the Chamber of Deputies and the Senate there was a network of parliamentarians – most notably Bonnet, de Monzie, Flandin, Laval and Caillaux – who intrigued against first Daladier and then Reynaud. Some pre-war pacifists of the far Left tried to campaign against the war, but their efforts were feeble and posed very little threat to the security of the State. Likewise, the pro-Nazi sympathizers of the *Comité France–Allemagne* were powerless to prevent the prosecution of the war, though subsequently they furnished Republicans with the scapegoat of a 'fifth column' responsible for plotting the defeat of France and engineering the collapse of the Third Republic. It would be wrong to underestimate the extent of pacifism during the *drôle de guerre*, but it hardly added up to a more serious challenge than the French State had coped with in 1917. In 1939–40, however, there was no Foch and no Clemenceau. And there was the PCF.

Until the eve of the war no other party in France had been more consistent in its denunciation of Hitler. Resistance to Nazi aggression lay at the very heart of the Popular Front strategy and, even after the overthrow of Blum and the defeat of the general strike of November 1938, the PCF refused to accept that its strategy had been wrong. On the contrary, given the growing reaction against Munich and above all, the rape of Czechoslovakia in March 1939, Communists could argue plausibly that they had been right all along and that an increasing number of people were coming round to their point of view. News of the Ribbentrop–Molotov Pact of August 1939, therefore, came as a thunderbolt, throwing the party into utter disarray and bringing about the deepest schism in its history. Twenty-one out of 72 deputies quit the party, along with one of their two senators, and the trend was followed by a sizeable number of their local government officials. Leading communist intellectuals, like Paul Nizan, voiced their disapproval, while party militants also expressed their disgust at what they regarded as the treason of the Soviet Union.

Amidst the confusion, the party's chiefs attempted to put a brave face on things. In the columns of *Humanité*, while maintaining their unswerving devotion to Moscow and attempting to justify the Pact, they also reiterated their hostility to Nazism and their loyalty to the *patrie*. On 2 September the Communist deputies voted for war credits and on 6 September they passed a resolution congratulating the 22 PCF deputies (including Maurice Thorez) who had gone off to join their combat units. On 20 September, however, Raymond Guyot came back from Moscow with the latest directives from the Comintern. The war was now to be denounced as an 'imperialist' war, fought on behalf of the financial interests of the City of London. On 4 October Thorez deserted from the army, and with the assistance of the Comintern, eventually reached Moscow, where he added his voice to the Communist clamour against the war.

Even before the party began to adopt its new pacifist line, the Daladier government had decided to act against it. Profiting from the wave of revulsion which swept the country in the wake of the Nazi–Soviet Pact, Daladier embarked on a policy of draconian repression, starting with the seizure of the party's newspapers and culminating in the dissolution of the party itself on 26 September and the arrest of 40 Communist deputies on 8 October. The latter were accused of 'intelligence with the enemy', on the grounds that, after the Soviet Union's invasion of Poland, Russia was at war with France's ally. Effectively, the Communist party was driven underground. As always, persecution served to foster solidarity among party members, who observed bitterly and correctly that the Daladier government showed a great deal more energy and enthusiasm for persecuting Communists than for waging war on the Nazi enemy.

Meanwhile, the 'phoney war' dragged on. After subjugating Poland and repartitioning her with Stalin, Hitler launched a 'peace offensive' on 28 September 1939, arguing that the right conditions for peace now existed in eastern Europe. The insidious offer was more attractive to Daladier than to Chamberlain, and its impact on French public opinion may have been unsettling. In any event, it was rejected by both France and Britain, though nothing was done to step up the prosecution of the war. Only at the end of November, when the Soviet Union invaded Finland, did the government show an interest in assisting the Finns, whose stout resistance captured the imagination of the French people. Daladier and Gamelin saw not only an opportunity to engage in military action far away from France, but also to stop German supplies of Swedish iron ore, which might bring Hitler to the negotiating table. But it was still all of a piece with winning the war against Germany without a real fight. Finland received inadequate help from France and Britain, and, after heroic resistance throughout the winter of 1939–40, capitulated to the Russians in March 1940 – a disaster that finally precipitated the fall of the Daladier government on 21 March 1940.

The new Prime Minister was Paul Reynaud. A wealthy, well-connected lawyer, with a considerable reputation for financial expertise, Reynaud was able, energetic and confident, but he lacked the popular appeal of his predecessor. Nor, as an *anti-munichois*, was he an entirely reassuring figure for the French upper classes. The weakness of his politicial position was evident from the size of his cabinet (21 ministers and 14 secretaries of state), and by his need to keep Daladier (whom he loathed) at the Ministry of Defence as the price of Radical support. The well-informed also had good reason to be suspicious of his entourage, above all of his redoubtable mistress, Hélène de Portes, who moved in defeatist circles and may well have been responsible for bringing one of their number, Paul Baudouin, an intimate of Bonnet, into the government. Reynaud was to prove no man of destiny. He did, however, inspire a greater degree of confidence among the British, especially when France and Britain signed a pledge that neither country would conclude a separate peace with Hitler.

On the other hand, the British were distinctly cool towards his grandiose plan for a great pincer movement, from Scandinavia in the north to the Caucasus in the south, with the objective of cutting off Swedish iron ore and Russian oil from Germany, which at the very least, it was hoped, would divert the Germans northwards rather than westwards, To forestall any such move, the Germans occupied Denmark and attacked Norway in April 1940. Anglo-French efforts to support the Norwegians were badly bungled, and testified eloquently to the ineffectiveness of the Supreme Inter-allied Council as a co-ordinating agency for the joint conduct of the war. (In contrast to the First World War, it was the British who wanted a real war to be waged against Germany – needless to say by France in the first instance – while the French preferred a waiting, peripheral war.) While the Allies dithered, Hitler at last launched his long-awaited offensive in the west on 10 May. The 'phoney war' was over and *Blitzkrieg* had begun.

The Débâcle

On paper, the French army looked at least a match for the Germans. In the matter of tanks, if the French had no Panzers, they nevertheless had numerical superiority, thanks to increased production since 1936, and, in the famous *Char Bs*, qualitative superiority. The airforce, it is true, gave more cause for concern, since the French had only really begun to produce modern planes in

1938 (as compared to 1935 in Britain and 1934 in Germany). French aviation amounted to only about one fifth of the strength of the *Luftwaffe*. On the other hand, Commander-in-Chief Gamelin did not envisage that planes would have to play a crucial role in battle. The British Expeditionary Force (BEF) under Lord Gort added another nine divisions and some aircraft, but not Spitfire fighters. The British turned a deaf ear to French pleas for more air support, since Chamberlain wanted to keep British planes for the defence of London and British industry. Ominously, it was the British view that the collapse of France, like the collapse of Poland, would not spell the end of the war.

Nevertheless, the French problem was not essentially *matériel* but strategy. Had the Germans stuck to their original 'Plan Yellow' by attacking via northern Belgium in a re-run of 1914, the French High Command would perhaps have been better able to cope. What they did not bargain on was *Blitzkrieg* waged in accordance with the brilliant plan of General von Manstein to annihilate France after an attack through the hilly, wooded Ardennes, deemed inpenetrable by Pétain and other French military planners. For Manstein (and Hitler) the key to victory lay in mobility, through the use of tanks to smash the enemy lines and of planes to drop paratroops who could prepare the ground ahead. The French High Command, wedded to the tactics, time-scales and technology of operations in the First World War (they still relied on telephones rather than radio for communications) had no effective reply and were simply outclassed. Unlike the Germans, they had not absorbed the writings of the Englishman Captain Liddell Hart on modern war (he had, after all, had the temerity to attack the reputations of Joffre and Foch) nor had they heeded the criticisms of the purely defensive mentality voiced by such as their own General Estienne and a certain Colonel Charles de Gaulle, whose book *Vers l'armée de métier* was published in 1934, ironically with a dedication to Pétain.

Not that the outcome of the battle of France was a foregone conclusion. The French collapse in the fight was, as Marc Bloch wrote, a 'strange' defeat: unexpected, swift, shattering. It was all the more strange because, contrary to what was later alleged, the French fought bravely and well. If some generals were excessively pessimistic and others simply incompetent, there were those like Prioux and Giraud whose valour and leadership were exemplary. If the morale of certain troops – especially the reservists – left much to be desired, it is a myth that the mass of the French soldiers were spineless, unworthy successors of the *poilu* of 1914–18. The Germans knew otherwise. Defeatism and subversion had less to do with the result of the battle than, on the one hand, the technical brilliance both in conception and in execution of the Manstein Plan, and, on the other, errors committed and opportunities squandered by the French High Command.

Gamelin's first and fatal error was to fail to perceive that the main thrust of the German offensive would be through the Ardennes. When they attacked the Low Countries simultaneously with France, he was deceived into sending the crack troops of the French army along with the whole of the BEF into Belgium, while Giraud took the most valuable reserves up to Holland. Hitler is reported to have 'wept for joy' when he heard of Gamelin's decision. Its consequence was that the decisive German thrust, aimed at crossing the river Meuse at Sedan, was countered only by inexperienced reservists under

Huntzinger, who were no match for Guderian's Panzer divisions and Richthofen's divebombers. The decisive breakthrough came on 14 May, leaving Guderian free (if exposed) to make for the Channel coast. That same evening, north of Dinant, Rommel succeeded in crossing the Belgian Meuse. On 15 May Gamelin informed Daladier, his Minister of War, that the French army was broken and that he had no reserves to throw in. On 20 May the Panzers reached the sea.

Prime Minister Reynaud's response to these disasters was to remove Daladier and take over the Defence Ministry himself. He also appointed the aged Marshal Pétain, the victor of Verdun, to be his personal military adviser and Deputy Prime Minister, and replaced Commander-in-Chief Gamelin with another ancient, the 73-year-old Weygand, recalled from Syria. Neither of these old warriors knew how to halt the German advance. Weygand's counter-offensive at Arras, on 21–3 May, failed, partly because of appallingly bad co-ordination between the British and French commands. The Belgians surrendered on 28 May; Allied forces were trapped at Dunkirk, and but for the German Command's decision to halt the advance of the Panzers, would have met with total, rather than partial, disaster. As it was, the delay allowed the evacuation of 338,000 troops in a motley armada of boats which plied their way between France and the southern English coast. The fact that 139,000 of the evacuees were French did not prevent a further deterioration of Anglo-French relations and the resuscitation of the old accusation that the English would always fight to the last Frenchman. (It was indeed 40,000 French troops who surrendered when Dunkirk at last fell.)

The end came swiftly. To compound French misery, Mussolini treacherously declared war on 10 June, hoping for a share of the spoils. The government fled from Paris, first to Tours, then on 11 June to Bordeaux. On 12 June Weygand ordered a general retreat. Between 10 and 14 June some 2 million Parisians abandoned their homes and fled, in cars, on bikes, on foot, joining the other 6 million men, women and children from the north of France and Belgium who were already clogging the French roads in a general exodus southwards. All too often abandoned by the political and administrative authorities in their regions, millions of the French were panic-stricken and gripped by a *grande peur*, a prey to the wildest rumours including the story that the Communists had seized power. On 14 June the Germans entered Paris. On 16 June Reynaud resigned, after a stormy encounter with Weygand, in which the latter demanded an immediate armistice and threatened to disobey any governmental order to fight on. Reynaud's successor, Pétain, a defeatist from the beginning, sued for peace and obtained an armistice on 22 June, effective from 25 June. The mighty French army had capitulated in just six weeks.

The End of the Third Republic

Few regimes can sustain a disaster of the order of the French collapse and survive. So it proved with the Third Republic. The generals blamed everything and everyone but themselves for what was first and foremost a military defeat. The more credulous saw it as an act of divine retribution, visited upon a sensual and materialistic people. Some singled out the primary-school teachers as the corrupters of French youth, instilling pacifism rather than patriotism in the classrooms. All agreed that the politicians and their 'decadent' political system had left France ill-prepared for her ordeal.

Much of the mud slung at the Third Republic in 1940 has stuck. Most histories of the period incline to the view that the defeat was a verdict not simply on the army but on the regime itself. From the grandeur of 1914, the Republic is reputed to have declined to the depths of 1940, already moribund before it fell apart. Evidence for such a view is hard to find. It would be difficult, for example, to prove that the Republic was more rotten or corrupt in 1939 than it was in 1914. At the beginning of 1940 the Third Republic no more appeared to be in its death throes than the Second Empire at the beginning of 1870. The shortcomings of the regime were plentiful, and have already been listed. But the idea that the Republic had effectively ceased to exist under Daladier's rule by decree law is untenable, not least because of the authority and popularity of the Prime Minister (outside of labour circles) and because of the widespread aspirations for reform and renewal which he seems to have stimulated. Nor, before the defeat, were the enemies of the Republic in any position to mount a serious challenge to its continued existence. The extreme Right, if anything, was in decline. Without the *débacle*, they would never have come to power.

The crucial factor leading to the demise of the regime was Weygand's insistence upon an armistice, in defiance of the civil authority of Reynaud. Invoking the honour of the army, he maintained that the government that had started the war should also sue for peace. For the first, but not the last, time in the twentieth century France was threatened with a military takeover and possible civil war. Reynaud's resignation averted these eventualities, but opened the door to Pétain and the partisans of capitulation. The armistice terms were humiliating. The French held out for only two conditions: that a sovereign French State should continue to exist and that the French fleet should not be handed over. Otherwise, they were subjected to a *diktat* which disarmed the French army, reducing it to a minimal force necessary for the maintenance of order, and which obliged the French to pay the vast costs of a German occupation. The country was divided into two by a 'demarcation line' into an 'occupied' and a 'free' zone: the north and the eastern seaboards being taken over by the Germans to facilitate the pursuit of operations against Britain, the southern zone being the seat of the French government. Since Bordeaux was in the occupied zone, on 29 June the Pétain regime installed itself in the spa town of Vichy, hitherto famous only for the restorative effects of its waters on the livers of the French bourgeoisie.

Some of the nation's leaders, it is true, wanted to continue the fight after the loss of the battle of France. They argued that France could continue the struggle alongside Britain by mobilizing the resources of the French empire and the French fleet, and by transferring the government to North Africa. Some 27 parliamentarians – among them Daladier, Delbos, Zay, Mandel and Mendès-France – set sail for Casablanca aboard the *Massilia* on 21 June, only to discover that they had been outmanoeuvred by the pro-armistice lobby, which had wanted to get them out of the way. The British attack on the French Fleet at Mers-el-Kebir on 3 July, which cost 1,200 French sailors their lives, was another blow to the hopes of those who wanted to carry on the war in partnership with the British, even though the attack was prompted by fear that the Germans might seize control of the French navy.

The enemies of the Republic could now move in for the kill. No one was more determined to be rid of the regime than Pierre Laval, who stalked the corridors of power in Bordeaux and then Vichy cajoling and threatening any parliamentarians opposed to constitutional revision. Some resisted: even defeatists like Baudouin and Flandin saw no reason to dispense with the constitution of 1875, quite apart from convinced Republicans such as Jeanneney, the president of the Senate. But once Laval persuaded Pétain to declare in favour of revision, the Republic was doomed. Amidst the chaos and the bewilderment of the French people in the summer of 1940, the aged war hero seemed the only credible source of leadership and stability. On 10 July 1940 the National Assembly voted by 468 votes to 80, with 20 abstentions, to give Pétain full powers to revise the constitution. The Third Republic gave way to the *Etat Français*.

III

1940–1991 The New France

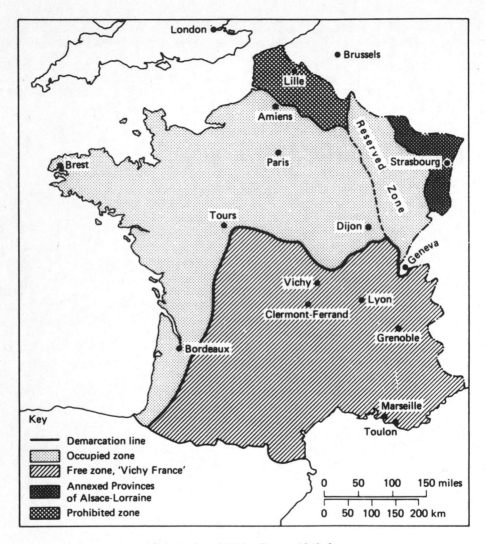

Key

— Demarcation line

Occupied zone

Free zone, 'Vichy France'

Annexed Provinces
of Alsace-Lorraine

Prohibited zone

Occupied and Vichy France 1940–2

13
The Vichy Regime 1940–1944

In the summer of 1940, for most French men and women, Philippe Pétain appeared as the country's saviour in its darkest hour, a supreme patriot summoned to assume the burdens of high office at the age of 84. After the nightmare of defeat and the chaos and panic of the *exode*, Pétain seemed to be a benignly reassuring father-figure who could restore confidence and stability to a shattered nation. The collapse of Republican administration, especially at the local level, had left people bitter as well as bewildered, and there is no mistaking the genuine and widespread goodwill which was extended to the Marshal and his new regime in its early days. For his part, Pétain was not in the least embarrassed by all the adulation he received. An immensely vain man, he spoke in all seriousness of making a gift of his person to the French nation and readily adopted a monarchical style, heading official documents with the words, '*Nous, Philippe Pétain, chef de l'État*'.

Yet, with remarkable speed, Vichy forfeited the initial goodwill. Instead of uniting the country under the banner of patriotism, as it claimed to do, the regime opened up deep divisions among Frenchmen which long outlasted its own duration. For the French, its history is still a sensitive and controversial subject: it is no accident that the best work on it has been done by foreigners.

Pétain, the *État Français* and the National Revolution

The *État Français* was consciously authoritarian and virulently antiparliamentary, since Pétain entertained no doubts that the military defeat was a verdict on the bankruptcy and corruption of the Republican regime rather than on the shortcomings of the army. Though not himself a Maurrasian, Pétain shared many of the prejudices and preconceptions of the *Action Française*. To maintain some contact with public opinion, he replaced parliament with a Veterans League, on the reckoning that ex-soldiers were better guides than deputies to what ordinary people were thinking. To provide a forum for the élites, a National Council was established in January 1941, which grouped various representatives of the aristocracy, the French Academy, the bench of bishops and even several ex-ministers of the Third Republic. Officially, Vichy affected to be above politics, preoccupied solely with what it took to be the national interest. In practice, it was a hotbed of political intrigue, providing ample scope for old Third Republic hands such as Pierre Laval and Flandin to exercise their talents for backstairs manipulation. Despite its lofty pretensions, the Vichy regime came nowhere near eliminating the 'politicking' with which it reproached its predecessor.

Pétain was no figurehead. The American ambassador wrongly represented him as 'a feeble, frightened old man, surrounded by self-seeking conspirators'. Pétain was far from being a gaga octogenarian, a mere puppet manipulated by his entourage. Retaining a certain earthy sensuality, he insisted on being kept fully briefed by his ministers and saw to it that overall control of policy rested with himself. Pétain was by no means a disinterested, apolitical patriot, reluctantly forced to assume power in order to rescue France from disaster. He had long been a political general, hungry for office and prepared to seek it in cabals and intrigues with right-wing opponents of the Third Republic. The point about his ultimate responsibility for policy is important. Older histories sometimes speak of a 'Vichy of Pétain' and a 'Vichy of Laval', contrasting the 'real', neutralist, Vichy of the Marshal with the collaborationist designs of Pierre Laval, bent on integrating France into the new Hitlerian order in Europe. Put on trial at the Liberation, Pétain would plead that, having failed to be the sword of the French people, he had at least tried to be their shield. In reality, Pétain was the ultimate arbiter of policy at Vichy and therefore the principal architect of its ever-increasing compromises and collaboration with the Nazis.

But there was much more to Vichy than a personalist authoritarian state. Essentially, it served as a rallying point for all those who reviled and feared the Popular Front and everything it stood for. Thus, certainly, Vichy was welcomed by all sections of the extreme Right, delighted at last to be rid of the Republic which they had been impotent to overthrow and impatient to wreak vengeance on their old enemies. But, more generally, Vichy represented security for a bourgeoisie still resentful of the concessions made to workers in 1936 and relieved by the ending of a war whose eventual outcome might have been the triumph of Bolshevism. The *État Français* spoke the language of national unity, but it pursued policies geared to defending the propertied classes. It sponsored a 'National Revolution' which, in the name of moral and political renewal, paid off old scores and promoted sectional interests. It replaced the Republican watchwords of 'liberty, equality and fraternity' with the motto 'family, country and work'. In practice, it declared war on those elements – anti-clericals, Freemasons, Protestants, Jews, foreigners – that it conveniently deemed responsible for the decadence of the 1930s and the capitulation of 1940.

The first institution to which Pétain turned in the endeavour to create a new moral order was the Catholic Church. The Marshal himself, it should be said, was not particularly religious. Though educated by the Dominicans, he was not a practising Catholic. His civil marriage to a divorcee in 1920 (when he was 64) had put him outside the communion of the faithful: the irregular situation was rectified with a religious ceremony only in 1943, after his wife had finally obtained an annulment. Nevertheless, Pétain believed that religion was good for the people. The Church had centuries of experience of trying to instil moral precepts into recalcitrant populations – and Church leaders, for their part, were only too willing to take on the role assigned to them by Vichy. Grateful clerics were foremost in manufacturing a veritable cult of the Marshal as the saviour of France – 'the Frenchman without reproach', Cardinal Suhard, the archbishop of Paris, called him, the instrument of Providence, according to Mgr Piguet, bishop of Clermont-Ferrand, the leader who would bring the nation back to its Christian roots, in the view of Cardinal Gerlier of Lyon.

The regime's clericalism was most apparent in its education policies. Education was taken out of the hands of the allegedly left-wing and pacifist schoolteachers, whom Vichy accused of corrupting French youth: the war, it was assumed, had been lost on the benches of the primary schools rather than on those of the École de Guerre. Thus, at first, even the 'godless' State schools themselves were required to provide religious instruction, while Church schools received State aid and the religious orders, banished from the classrooms by Combes, were summoned back. A witch hunt was conducted against politically active *instituteurs* and, as a mark of official reprobation, primary teachers received no salary increase for two years, despite the soaring cost of living.

Vichy's preoccupation with the moral regeneration of French youth also led to the creation of a number of organizations designed to mobilize young people to the cause of the National Revolution. Jean Ybarnégaray, a well-known Basque sportsman and right-wing deputy, was appointed Minister of Youth, the Family and Sport. Subsequently, General Georges Lamirand, a devoted Pétainist and Catholic, became Secretary-General for Youth, with a wide brief to oversee the moral, social, civic and vocational training of young people over school-leaving age. It was never his intention, however, to build up a single youth movement on the totalitarian model, as fascists such as Déat advocated. Instead, a number of Vichyite youth organizations came into being alongside existing Catholic movements such as the ACJF and the scouts. The *compagnons de France*, established in 1940, was a voluntary organization recruiting among the uprooted and the unemployed and setting them to work in the general field of reconstruction. The *chantiers de la jeunesse*, on the other hand, was an obvious attempt to replace military conscription with compulsory civilian service. Young men of military age were set to work on hard, physical tasks, not simply to experience the benefits of manual labour but also to be exposed to the right sorts of moral influence. A number of leadership training schools, the most famous of which was at Uriage, were established to train an élite of young intellectuals and civil servants.

It cannot be said that the moral dimensions of the National Revolution made much headway. An overtly clerical policy in education was pursued for only a year. Jean Carcopino abandoned it on becoming Minister of Education in 1941, while his successor, from April 1942, the agnostic and collaborationist homosexual Abel Bonnard, was an altogether unlikely figure to spearhead a moral revolution. His attempts to convert schoolteachers to his vision of a German-dominated 'new order' in Europe met with a notable lack of success. As for raising the moral standards of the nation's youth, Vichy failed to make young people conform to its dubious values. Promiscuity was rife, while official figures for juvenile delinquency doubled between 1940 and 1942. Such an outcome was hardly surprising, given that a regime which extolled honour and duty made a virtue of spying and informing. A quite staggering 3 million to 5 million letters, signed and unsigned, were sent to the Vichy bureaucracy to denounce fellow Frenchmen – not just strangers but sometimes other members of the same family.

Vichy's own promotion of the family amounted to little more than an obsession, inherited from the Third Republic, with the need to boost the birth rate. Building on the anti-malthusian legislation of the previous regime and in particular on Daladier's Family Code, Vichy introduced measures to favour large families (something of a paradox in that Pétain himself was childless). Women were represented primarily as baby machines and attempts were made to drive them from the labour force. Divorce, though not outlawed completely, was made more difficult to obtain. The fact that the birth rate did begin to rise before the Liberation should not, however, necessarily be attributed to the success of Vichy's family policy but to the change in the collective psychology of the French which was to produce the post-war 'baby boom'.

Undoubtedly, the ugliest side of Vichy's abortive moral revolution was its vicious racism, and in particular its own special brand of anti-Semitism. Recent research has established beyond question that, far from being a Nazi imposition, Vichy's anti-Semitism was entirely home-grown and in certain respects even exceeded German requirements. Hatred of the Jews, as we have seen, was deeply implanted in the French right-wing mentality at least from the time of the Dreyfus Affair. The influx of refugees into France in the 1930s, many of them fleeing from persecution, contributed to an upsurge of xenophobia, already apparent in the measures enacted against foreigners by the Third Republic, notably by Daladier's decrees of May 1938. Even before 1940, French cabinet ministers were discussing what to do about the 'Jewish problem' – Bonnet for one favoured shipping them to Madagascar. In a sense, therefore, Vichy's policy towards the Jews represented an intensification of an existing, indigenous anti-Semitism. Vichy differed, however, in showing a willingness to go much further than the previous regime, partly in order to curry favour with the Germans but more to try to lend substance to its claims to be an autonomous state, aspiring to exercise influence even in the occupied zone.

Vichy's racial laws were essentially a reaction to the catastrophic defeat of 1940. A scapegoat had to be found, and more than the venal politicians, more even than the morally bankrupt schoolmasters, the Jews were singled out as the agents of France's downfall. From the autumn of 1940 a series of laws was passed attacking the civil rights of Jews. French Jews were excluded from a number of professions: foreign Jews were interned in special camps or exiled. The Commissariat-General for Jewish Affairs, established under the fanatically anti-Semitic Xavier Vallat, prepared a new *statut des juifs* in June 1941 which applied to the whole of France and ordered a census to be taken of all Jews resident in unoccupied France along with the 'aryanization' of their property, an application of the German model already in force in the Occupied Zone. The summer of 1942 brought a further turning-point. As the Nazis moved towards their 'final solution' of exterminating Jews in death camps in eastern Europe, the Vichyite authorities collaborated in supplying victims from France. French policemen gave invaluable assistance to the Germans in rounding up Jews for deportation. In the summer and autumn of 1942, more than 42,500 Jews – among them 6,000 children – were sent to Auschwitz. Only a handful survived. In all, some 76,000 Jews – a quarter of the country's Jewish population – perished in the Holocaust. If the percentage was lower in France than in other Nazi-occupied countries like Belgium and Holland, what remains particularly shameful was the extent to which the

French authorities colluded with the Occupier in rounding up victims among the foreign Jews who had fled to France as refugees. For Pierre Laval, Pétain's Prime Minister from April 1942, these unfortunates were expendable pawns in his power game of trying to negotiate the best possible deal for France with the Third Reich. That they were not being sacrificed on the altar of racist ideology was, however, no comfort to those at the receiving end. In any case, Laval's strategy wrung few concessions from the Nazis. Once again, Vichy's sordid methods were drastically at odds with its professed goal of a national moral revival.

The National Revolution also had an economic dimension, and it is here that the regime's class bias becomes most obvious. The official ideology was corporatism, by which it was intended that all economic activity should be divided up into natural, self-governing groups, or corporations. In this way, a community of interest would replace artificial divisions between, say, labour and capital, created by apologists of the class struggle. The State would interfere as necessary to promote economic harmony. Thus, in conformity also with its professed peasantism, Vichy sought to provide a corporatist solution to the problems of French agriculture. Vichyite traditionalists, starting with Pétain himself, were content to encourage a 'back to the land' movement, but corporatists such as Jacques Leroy-Ladurie won government backing for the Peasant Charter of December 1940, which gave producers the right to regulate production. Under the impetus of food shortages and rationing, however, the State effectively took control of the corporations and used them to run French agriculture more efficiently. In the end, Vichy came to show a distinct bias in favour of large-scale producers ready to adopt modern techniques and equipment rather than the small peasant farmer.

In theory, at least, the workers might have benefited under the reorganization of labour relations within a genuinely corporatist system. Such, indeed, was the hope of Vichy's first Minister of Industrial Production, the ex-deputy-secretary of the CGT, René Belin. In practice, Vichy systematically favoured business, especially once Belin was succeeded by economic magnates such as Pierre Pucheu and François Lehideux. Vichy's Labour Charter, promulgated on 4 October 1941, was principally a device to smash the unions by banning strikes and trade-union activities. The bosses, on the other hand, were invited to staff the organization committees intended to supervise and co-ordinate economic activity in their respective sectors. At least some of the *patronat*, supported by powerful civil servants, welcomed the defeat as the opportunity not so much for moral regeneration as for transforming France into a dynamic, modern, highly technological economy. These technocrats came into their own when Admiral Darlan became Pétain's chief minister in February 1941. Men such as Jean Bichelonne, who headed the Ministry of Industrial Production, acquired vast power and influence over the whole of French economic life. Civil servants and employers were brought together in a new partnership, under the overall supervision of the ministry, in a new experiment in economic planning. So great did the influence of the technocrats appear that their enemies spread fantastic rumours about the existence of a 'synarchy' – a conspiracy of economic magnates reputed to have seized control of the French economy after first arranging the defeat of France. Pétain himself resented their power and prestige but could do little to resist the drive for economic efficiency, especially when it was so much appreciated by German economic overlord Albert Speer.

Vichy France and Hitler's Europe

It was Pétain himself who decided that France had to seek active collaboration with the Third Reich. Certainly, Pierre Laval, Pétain's first 'dauphin', had been a long-standing advocate of Franco-German *rapprochement* and was the Frenchman with the best access to the Nazi authorities, notably to Otto Abetz, the German ambassador in Paris. But the Marshal, convinced that Britain, too, would soon be prostrate before the rampant German army, required no persuasion that France had to reach an agreement with Hitler. He therefore arranged to meet the Führer at Montoire in October 1940, following which he publicly broadcast that 'I enter into the way of collaboration'. Pétain's hope was that, in consequence, he would be able to soften the terms of the Armistice, especially with regard to the release of prisoners, the return of the seat of government to Paris, the costs of the occupation and the problem of movement between the two zones. Hitler, in fact, had no intention of making any such concessions to the French, and deliberately concealed from Pétain that he planned to maintain France in a state of impotence, powerless ever to launch a war of *revanche* against Germany.

The removal of Laval from office in December 1940 did not represent any real turning-point in Vichy's foreign policy, however much it aroused the suspicions and resentment of the Germans. Pétain's objections to Laval were largely personal, though he also blamed him for the failure to achieve any breakthrough consequent on the Montoire talks. Laval's replacement as Foreign Minister, Flandin, tried even harder to reach accommodation with Hitler, but he soon had to be sacrificed (in February 1941) to appease German wrath. His successor, Admiral Darlan, was an all-out collaborationist, who tried in vain to interest the Nazis in according France a naval and imperial role within the context of the German Reich, to be achieved primarily at the expense of the British Empire. In May 1941 he went to see Hitler at Berchtesgaden and, in return for making military concessions to Germany in the Middle East, he obtained a slight reduction in the occupation costs, easier movement between the two zones and the release of First World War veterans held by the Germans as prisoners of war. Opposition from Hitler and Ribbentrop again frustrated the fulfilment of Darlan's 'grand design' and his failure precipitated the return of Pierre Laval to office in April 1942, this time as Prime Minister.

To the end, Laval pursued his dream of carving out a special place for vanquished France in the new order established by the Nazi conquerors. France, he hoped, would become 'the favourite province of Germany'. Though he became the living embodiment of *collaboration d'état* – especially after his speech of 22 June 1942 in which he affirmed his desire for a German victory in the war – he received the constant and public backing of Pétain, who entirely shared his view that the only alternative to collaboration was 'polonization', subjugation to the horrors of direct Nazi rule. Priding himself on his realism and deluded as to his influence with Hitler, who in reality despised him, Laval was ready to make whatever sacrifices the Germans might demand. To supply the Germans with skilled labour, he devised a '*relève*' system whereby one prisoner of war was released for every three workers dispatched to Germany. After the entry of the Soviet Union into the war (22 June 1941) and the consequent upsurge in PCF resistance activity, Laval resorted to arresting and shooting Communists in an effort to forestall German reprisals. As we have already seen, French police co-operation in the rounding up of Jews for deportation was also readily forthcoming.

Appeasement brought little or no return, all the more so when the fortunes of war began to veer against Gemrany. In 1941 the entry of first the Soviet Union and then the United States into the war on the side of Britain were crucial turning points. In October 1942 Montgomery halted Rommel's penetration of North Africa at El Alamein. In November the Allies landed in Morocco and Algeria. On the Eastern Front the German Sixth Army was cornered at Stalingrad. In response to these reverses, especially the threat of an invasion of southern France from the springboard of North Africa, the Nazis extended their occupation of France to the whole of the national territory. Overnight, Vichy effectively ceased to exist. The German presence in the northern zone had always been a considerable limitation on its freedom of action but now it became virtually a Nazi puppet state. Its ability to bargain and manoeuvre with the Germans was all the more diminished by the decision to scuttle the French fleet before it fell into German hands and by the extent to which the Allies succeeded in gaining control of much of the empire.

At least some Vichyites read the signs of the times and began to desert the sinking ship. There had always been a certain *attentiste* – or 'wait and see' – mentality at Vichy, which had accepted the Armistice and collaboration with Germany as necessary but short-term expedients. Into this category came army officers such as Generals Weygand, Georges and de Lattre de Tassigny, as well as high-ranking civil servants like Maurice Couve de Murville. But few of Vichy's leading lights went over to the Allied cause. Darlan, accidentally caught in North Africa at the time of the Allied landing, was reluctantly prevailed upon to head a Pétainiste but anti-Nazi administration along with General Henri Giraud, but he fell to an assassin's bullet in Algiers on Christmas Eve 1942. Flandin too changed sides, but Pucheu, Vichy's Minister of the Interior, notorious for his readiness to hand over Communist hostages to the Germans, was not welcomed when he reached North Africa via Spain in February 1943. Rather, he was arrested, tried and eventually executed in March 1944. His fate may well have deterred others from seeking any alternative to collaboration with Germany. In any case, neither Pétain nor Laval were *attentistes*. It was never their aspiration to take France back into the war on the Allied side. Instead, they hoped that France might be instrumental in bringing about a compromise peace and that she would re-emerge as a major power within a new European order.

Collaboration d'état thus continued to the end. To feed the insatiable demands of the German war economy, French workers were conscripted to work in Germany from February 1943. France became the principal source of skilled labour for the Germans in the whole of occupied Europe, much to the satisfaction of German economic supremo Albert Speer, who valued French men and Russian women as the two most productive elements in his slave labour force. The entire French economy was made subservient to Germany's military needs. As well as cash payments which amounted to some 42 per cent of Germany's 'special income from abroad', the French furnished agricultural products and foodstuffs, raw materials and the use of French communications – by January 1944 the Germans controlled 85 per cent of French train movements. By 1944 'Vichy' existed only in name. Only when the Allied armies closed in on Paris and Pétain and Laval were forcibly removed by their German masters, Pétain to the castle of Sigmaringen, Laval to Belfort, did they finally refuse to exercise any office. By this time, Vichy's initial popularity had long evaporated.

The French Nazis

Vichy was not overtly fascist and was at first the only state to retain some semblance of autonomy in Hitler's Europe. This was merely because it suited Nazi policy, not because there were no French fascists ready and willing to assume power. Quite the contrary. As we have seen, France had spawned an impressive number of fascist organizations in the inter-war years and the defeat presented them with the opportunity to demonstrate their commitment to building a new Europe along Nazi lines.

The ideological collaborators were a heterogeneous lot. Tending to congregate in Paris rather than at Vichy, they included fascist intellectuals like Brasillach and the editorial team of *Je Suis Partout*, mingling their romantic notions of the new heroic fascist man with vicious anti-Semitism and gutter journalism. Others, such as the journalists Fernand de Brinon and Jean Luchaire, both of whom had close pre-war links with Abetz from the days of the *Comité France–Allemagne*, welcomed the Occupation for the prospects it opened up for careers and personal advancement. De Brinon became the official representative of Vichy in Paris, while Luchaire edited the *Nouveaux Temps* and headed the Paris press association. Both prospered through the liberal slush funds with which Abetz sought to turn the French press into organs of Nazi propaganda.

The ideological collaborators also included fugitives from the French Left. Apart from the prominent figures like Déat and Doriot, there were anti-Communist trade unionists who rallied to the idea of a new, corporatist era in labour relations: Belin, Rey, of the Metalworkers, and Dumoulin, of the Miners' Federation, the two last contributors to the pro-Nazi labour newspaper *L'Atelier*, founded in December 1940. Ex-Socialists as well as ex-revolutionary syndicalists accommodated themselves to the new order. Charles Spinasse, a minister in the Popular Front cabinet, edited the weekly *Le Rouge et le Bleu*, 'a review of French socialist thought', which preached class reconciliation. René Château, editor of *La France Socialiste*, exemplified the extreme pacifism which led many pre-war intellectuals to accept the consequences of the defeat, deluding themselves that Hitler would inaugurate the peaceful and united Europe of their dreams.

It was, however, the pre-war fascist activists who pressed for the closest collaboration with Nazi Germany. Déat was the most persistent advocate of a single party on the fascist model – a proposition consistently vetoed by Pétain. Instead, he had to settle for the *Rassemblement National Populaire* (RNP), the first major political organization to be created after the defeat, in January 1941. In 1942 Déat expanded the movement into the southern zone and entertained great hopes of being summoned to power by Laval. Overtly critical of Vichy, Déat hailed Hitler as a man of genius and constantly called on France to take her place in the new Europe. Doriot, on the other hand, at first declared himself to be '*un homme du Maréchal*', though he did not conceal his aspirations for a totalitarian state. When the invasion of Russia presented the opportunity for a great anti-communist crusade, he broke with Vichy and founded the Legion of French Volunteers against Bolshevism (LVF). Doriot himself set off for the Russian front in September 1941, but fewer than 3,000 others – all recruited from fascist groups in the occupied zone – followed his example. Nevertheless, the threat of imposing a Doriot regime was always a useful card in the Germans' hand to keep Vichy in line, though in practice Abetz preferred Laval to the excessively 'active' and 'nationalist' Doriot.

The gap between Paris collaborators and Vichyites, never as great as apologists for the latter like to make out, narrowed considerably over the years between 1940 and 1944, as Vichy developed into a repressive police state, at one with the Nazis in persecuting Jews, Communists and all who refused to accommodate themselves to the new order. Epitomizing the evolution of the regime was the career of Joseph Darnand, who, despite a slavish devotion to Pétain, by whom he had been personally decorated for extraordinary bravery in the First World War, ended up as the head of the hated *Milice*, the French police force which, alongside the Germans, waged implacable war against the French Resistance. An ultra-nationalist and ex-cagoulard, Darnand had fought with distinction during the battle of France, but thereafter he was recruited into Xavier Vallat's *Légion de Combattants*, within which, with Pétain's encouragement, he established his own *Service d'Ordre Légionnaire* with a special mission to pursue jews, Communists and Freemasons. This was the organization that in January 1943 was transformed into the *Milice Française*. By 1944 it operated also in the northern zone and numbered some 30,000 members, mainly youths aged 16–25, often from fairly humble social backgrounds. Its services were appreciated by the Germans, who made Darnand an SS *Sturmbahnführer*. At the end of 1943 he entered the government of Vichy as Secretary of State for the Maintenance of Order. Perhaps more than any other organization, Darnand's *Milice* symbolized the horror of French ideological collaboration. The presence of Frenchmen in the Gestapo (many of them former criminals recruited by Henry Lafont, himself in the pay of the Abwehr) and in the Waffen SS (the Charlemagne division) form part of the same story of perverted idealism.

On the other hand it should be stressed that the out-and-out collaborators were a rarity in the French population as a whole. A film such as *The Sorrow and the Pity*, which implies that France was close to being a nation of collaborators, is misleading. In terms of its numerical support, the extreme Right declined throughout the Occupation: even in Paris the French Nazis were pushed to find recruits. In Clermont-Ferrand (the focus of Ophuls's film) the PPF struggled to achieve a membership of around 50, while Déat's RNP was all but non-existent. The Milice numbered between 150 and 200. If these figures are representative, it seems unlikely that the French Nazis amounted to more than 15,000 in the country as a whole. Moreover, even the leadership (let alone the rank and file) of these groups were rarely motivated purely by admiration for Nazi ideology. In Marseille, Simon Sabiani, leader of the local PPF, had, like Doriot, begun as a communist and ended up as a collaborator, but his politics have been shown to be less those of ideology than of clientelism, intrigue, revenge and ambition in the context of a marginal and criminal milieu.

Founded on the fundamental error that the war was over, Vichy ended its life a discredited and divisive regime. In the end, few people could be found to fight for it. Yet it cannot be written off as a brief, alien, German-imposed break in France's Republican tradition. Its links with the French past were important. But so too were its links with the future. After the trauma of Vichy there could be no return to the 'stalemate society' of the inter-war years. In that sense, Vichy helped prepare the ground for the emergence of a new France.

14
The Resistance

The history of the Vichy regime is not the whole story of France in the years between 1940 and 1944. In shining contrast to the shame and moral compromise with which Vichy is forever tarnished, there was another France with which Frenchmen would later identify and in which they could take legitimate pride: the France of the Resistance, of those who refused to be crushed by the Nazi jackboot and who worked in a thousand different ways for the liberation of their territory. Surprisingly, however, in view of the popular literature and television serials it has inspired, few professional historians have attempted to grapple with the Resistance as an historical problem. Did resistance really matter? What did it achieve? What was its impact? This chapter will try to provide some answers to these questions.

Resistance, it must first be understood, took many forms. It might amount to no more than the cold-shouldering of German soldiers in bars; it might be a question of tuning in to the BBC; it could involve the extremely dangerous business of sheltering Allied airmen or British SOE (Special Operations Executive) agents; or it could mean engaging in industrial sabotage or acts of terrorism and ultimately full-scale armed struggle. In the first instance, however, the French will to resist was represented to the world at large less by internal resistance movements than by the defiance of General de Gaulle and the Free French.

De Gaulle and the Free French

In 1940 de Gaulle was one of the most junior generals in the French army, known within military circles mainly for his unorthodox views on the conduct of modern warfare. On 5 June 1940 Reynaud had brought him into his cabinet as under-secretary at the War Office, but by comparison with Pétain he was a nobody. Yet, even while Pétain, with the full support of other top-ranking army officers, sued for peace with Germany, de Gaulle escaped to London from where he made his subsequently celebrated, though at the time little noticed, broadcast of 18 June on the BBC, to the effect that France had lost only a battle, not the war itself, and must at all costs remain in the fight. All true, free Frenchmen were invited to join him and thus rally to the *patrie* in its hour of gravest need.

On learning of the broadcast, most senior army officers were incensed by the claim of the unknown de Gaulle to personify France more than Pétain, the legendary hero of Verdun. Only one high-ranking officer with experience of war on the Western Front – de Hautecloque – was prepared to fight on.

The others denounced de Gaulle for having committed the cardinal military sin of disobedience: a military court sentenced him to death for desertion. Nor did de Gaulle have much success in his efforts to win over the colonies. An attempt by the Free French and the British to take the port of Dakar in French West Africa was driven off by French forces loyal to Vichy in September 1940.

De Gaulle's biggest problem was how to make others take seriously his claims to be representative of French public opinion. Those who did rally to him consisted mainly of junior officers, colonial soldiers and administrators, and on the whole men of the French Right who were nationalists but not Vichyites. The presence in his entourage of at least a number of people known to be reactionaries and opponents of the Third Republic did not enhance his image as a spokesman for Republican France, and raised doubts about his professed political impartiality. Like Vichy, de Gaulle tended both to blame 'politics' for the defeat of France and to assert the possibilities it had revealed for some kind of renewal of the French spirit. Nevertheless, if an appeal to a mystical, undying patriotism, linked to a projection of himself as a man of destiny, in part explains the secret of his own ultimate success, his personal mastery of the art of politics was no less important.

De Gaulle justified his action on the grounds that there existed a political void in France. The Third Republic had not been abolished but it could no longer govern. Vichy on the other hand was not a real sovereign government, placed as it was in a client relationship with Nazi Germany and its legitimacy unconfirmed by consultation with the electorate. In collaborating with the enemy it betrayed rather than safeguarded vital French interests. It was to be some time before the Allies were won round to the Gaullist viewpoint. In some ways, Churchill could recognize in de Gaulle a kindred spirit yet he always found him personally difficult to deal with. For the Americans, de Gaulle was simply impossible. Roosevelt found his arrogance unbearable and harboured deep suspicions as to his ultimate ambitions, fearing that he would reveal himself to be a military dictator. The Americans accepted Vichy as the legitimate French government and, in so far as they came to envisage an alternative to Pétain as head of state, at first looked not to de Gaulle but to a much more senior army officer, Henri Giraud, a five-star general, brought out of France on board a British submarine on 6 November 1942.

Giraud represented that tendency in the French army which was not only *Pétainiste* but *attentiste* – that is, living in the hope that the Marshal was playing a double game and was waiting for a suitable moment to get back into the war. In Giraud the Americans saw the man they believed could lead *attentiste* officers in the French colonies, given his well-publicized loyalty to Pétain, reaffirmed on his return to Vichy after a spectacular escape from imprisonment in Germany. The idea was essentially to establish a 'neo-Vichyite' regime in North Africa sympathetic to the Allied cause.

De Gaulle, understandably, was outraged at the notion that Giraud, and still worse Darlan, briefly his associate, should head the French effort to defeat Hitler. Giraud made no secret of his Vichyite sympathies and maintained all of the regime's repressive legislation intact in North Africa, including its decrees against the Jews. Gaullists he treated as rebels and subversives. Fortunately for de Gaulle, as even the Americans came to appreciate, Giraud was a political innocent – 'perfectly incompetent', in his own candid words –

which made de Gaulle's task of ousting him as leader of the pro-Allied colonial movement easier than it might otherwise have been.

The Internal Resistance

While de Gaulle concentrated on establishing his legitimacy with the British and Americans, within France itself there had been stirrings of resistance almost from the outset of the Occupation. In the northern zone there were groups of people – intellectuals, university students, priests, – who refused to accept Nazi rule and who conceived of resistance as any form of action which might help to liberate French territory. Of necessity, resistance in the north was a dangerous activity: arrests, torture and executions were frequent. The group formed around Paul Rivet, Director of the Musée de l'Homme in Paris, was smashed by the Germans in the course of 1941, and other northern groups were condemned to an extremely precarious existence.

In the south, too, resistance followed no very clear pattern but was at first the result of isolated personal choices or, at best, of small and poorly organized groups. In the southern zone, however, resistance was invested with a political significance it did not necessarily carry in the north, for the decision to resist was not just a repudiation of Germany but also of the Vichy regime. People's responses may have varied enormously, but, almost inevitably, resistance in the south was tinged with a left-wing stance in politics. Some, reacting to the catastrophe of 1940, saw it as a witness for the need to break with the past and to construct a new and better world. Others, like the small group of Christian Democrats, regarded resistance as a natural consequence of their pre-war attitudes. Those who had opposed Munich were likely to oppose the Armistice. But, whether the spur was a sense of continuity with the past or a need to break with the past, Resisters in the south were as one in linking their anti-Nazi activity with a strong desire for political change within France once Hitler had been defeated.

Gradually, several distinct groups began to emerge in the southern zone. The group *Combat*, directed by Captain Pierre Frenay, was strong in the Lyon area and the south-east of France, recruiting essentially among professional people and intellectuals – army officers, engineers, industrialists, civil servants, university teachers. *Libération*, whose leading light was the radical ex-naval officer Emmanuel d'Astier de la Vigerie, was more overtly left-wing. Its aim was first of all to mobilize the mass of French workers through the institutions which had traditionally sought to represent their interests – the PCF, the Socialist party, the trade-union movement – and then to stage a general strike and a popular revolution. *Franc-Tireur*, though based in the south, was led largely by Parisian intellectuals (among them the historian Marc Bloch) and again grouped people of leftist views. Notable among the smaller groups were *Libérer et Fédérer*, a socialist group based at Toulouse, and *Témoignage Chrétien*, which brought together Christian Democrats and radical Catholics. Their leader, Fr. Chaillet, devoted much of his energy to trying to save Jewish children from deportation.

Equally, in the north, resistance activity also became co-ordinated in larger, better-organized groups. The Socialist Jean Texcier succeeded in building up *Libération-Nord*, a movement based on both Socialist and Catholic trade unions. *Organisation Civile et Militaire*, on the other hand, recruited mainly soldiers, civil servants and professional people. In time, however, the principal resistance movement in the north came to be *Front National*, which succeeded in developing its network into the southern zone and was organized with different sub-groups, including a women's section, a peasants' section and so on. *Front National* aspired to ressurrect a popular front against Nazism and therefore grouped representatives of all shades of resistance opinion. But, in the main, and especially after June 1941, the principal animators of FN were members of the French Communist party.

The entry of the PCF into full-scale resistance activity is still a subject that engenders bitter historical polemics. Non-communist historians and former party militants allege that before the Nazi invasion of the Soviet Union, Communist involvement in Resistance was either non-existent or negligible. Party historians and sympathizers tend either to gloss over the events of 1939–41 or to distort them by crediting the party with a coherent and consistent strategy which, in the circumstances following its dissolution, it seems unlikely to have possessed. A number of points are clear. Officially, the PCF reversed its anti-Nazi stance after the signing of the Nazi–Soviet pact. In 1940 it opposed the war as imperialist and adopted a position of neutrality towards Germany. The Communists also applied formally to the Nazi victors to be allowed to resume legal publication of *L'Humanité*, certainly with a view to rebuilding their organization, but much less obviously with the idea of preparing an eventual revolution. Still leading an underground existence, the party claimed that it alone embodied the true aspirations of the French people. It would have no truck with Vichy, nor did it want the triumph of Anglo-American imperialism or forced incorporation into the Nazi Reich. In their eagerness to emerge from the underground (and at the same time pay off old scores) some leading Communists even expressed their willingness to testify against Daladier, Blum and other Third Republican luminaries whom Vichy eventually put on trial in shameful court proceedings at Riom in February 1942 (where the accused effectively turned the tables on their accusers, causing the trials to be postponed indefinitely).

The official party line, however, was not always accepted at the base. Just as a sizeable number of militants refused to accept the Nazi–Soviet pact, so, too, at the local level, patriotic Communists rejected the neutralist position towards the Nazi occupation and began to engage in resistance activity. By June 1941 the party hierarchy (dominated by Jacques Duclos in the absence of Thorez) was under pressure from bold militants such as Charles Tillon and Auguste Lecoeur to renew its commitment to the struggle against fascism. The German invasion of the Soviet Union resolved the problem. Overnight, the PCF became the foremost element in the Resistance, specializing in acts of terrorism and guerrilla warfare, which in turn provoked merciless reprisals on the part of the Nazis. At the Liberation, the Communists would claim to be the party of the 75,000 shot: an exaggeration, but still an indication of the scale of Communist heroism and martyrdom after June 1941.

Perhaps the most remarkable achievement of the Resistance was that, out of so many diverse groups, it proved possible to forge a broad-based, united movement. If any single person can take the credit for this unification, it was one of de Gaulle's most heroic associates, Jean Moulin, the ex-prefect of Chartres. Exiled to Provence after clashing with the German authorities in 1940, he joined resistance groups which were eventually to link up with

Combat, and at the end of 1941 made his way to London to establish contact with de Gaulle. Parachuted back to France, he spent the next 18 months trying to bring the different elements of the Resistance together. The first step was to establish the MUR, the United Movements of the Resistance, to link up organizations in north and south. His greatest achievement, however, was to persuade the Communists to come into a united movement prepared to accept de Gaulle as the replacement for Pétain at the Liberation. In May 1943 he organized the first meeting of the CNR, the National Resistance Council, which represented all the major shades of Resistance opinion. Six weeks later he was betrayed, captured and brutally tortured to death at the hands of the infamous 'butcher of Lyon', Klaus Barbie.

The success represented by the creation of the CNR did not mean that most Frenchmen were now on the side of the Resistance. Even in 1942 the number of those actively involved was extremely small. What turned Resistance into more of a mass movement was, above all, the introduction of STO, compulsory labour service, in February 1943, which drove all sections of French youth – workers, peasants, students – into hiding to avoid being drafted to work in Germany. Many sought refuge with the *Maquis*, the most dynamic element of the secret army, especially strong in isolated regions of mountains, hillside and forest, and increasingly engaged in guerrilla warfare. Even then, Resistance remained a minority activity, relative to the French population as a whole. Accurate figures for the number of activists are, in the nature of things, impossible to come by. After the war ended the State officially recognized some 300,000 people as Resistance veterans, along with another 100,000 who sacrificed their lives in the struggle. At best, however, this suggests that only a maximum of 2 per cent of the French adult population can be deemed to have been 'in the Resistance' – a figure strikingly at odds with the myth of *la France résistante* developed at the Liberation. On the other hand, it would be wrong to belittle the very real achievements of the Resistance. Even if numbers remained relatively small and the purely military or economic impact of acts of terrorism and sabotage was modest, the Resistance was important as an enormous boost to French morale. In refusing to bow to the verdict of 1940, the Resistance kept alive the flame of hope that Germany would ultimately be defeated. In permitting Frenchmen to have some share not only in their own liberation but in setting the whole of Europe free from the Nazi yoke, it gave back to a great nation its sense of dignity and pride.

Liberation and *Épuration*

By 1944 it was certain that the Reich would not last a thousand years. Following the smashing of the Axis in 1943 and the steady Soviet advance on eastern Germany after the battle of Stalingrad, the Allies were finally in a position to unleash their long-planned invasion of western Europe across the Channel. On 6 June 1944 they began their gigantic operation with a landing on the Normandy beaches, and within two months most of Normandy and Brittany was liberated. On 15 August, in conjunction with the First French Army, the Allies staged a supplementary landing in the south of France, from where they drove swiftly up the Rhone valley to Lyon. As the Germans retreated, France was delivered from four years of bondage.

In planning the liberation of Europe, the Allied strategists, in particular the Americans, had attached little importance to the contribution that internal resistance movements might make to freeing their own countries. Their role was to be confined to sabotaging German reinforcements and providing useful local intelligence. For leaders of the French Resistance such a role was deemed to be far from adequate to expunge the cruel memories of 1940. De Gaulle and the Free French abhorred the idea that not only might France be liberated solely by American and British troops but, even worse, the liberated *patrie* would be placed under an Allied Military Government of the Occupied Territories, as in the case of Sicily in 1943. Equally, within the internal Resistance, all shades of opinion had been won over to the PCF view that liberation required to be accomplished by a mass uprising both to free the country from the invader and to remove the taint of Vichyite collaboration. From early 1944 pressure was mounting on Resistance leaders to unleash a national insurrection. Acts of sabotage and terrorism increased, matched by ferocious reprisals. When the Allies landed in Normandy, resisters, from the end of 1943 grouped collectively in the *Forces Françaises de l'Intérieur* (FFI), were ready to embark on full-scale guerrilla warfare in addition to rendering all possible assistance to the invasion. In some regions Resistance committees took over as the Germans pulled out; in others, such as the Glières plateau and the Vercors, their risings were ruthlessly suppressed by the Germans. The butchery carried out by the 2nd SS Panzer division '*Das Reich*' (including the massacre of 642 men, women and children at the village of Oradour-sur-Glane) also served as a horrific reminder of the destruction that Nazism could wreak even in its death throes.

Among internal resisters, none was more committed to the idea of a national insurrection than the PCF. By August 1944 the PCF controlled the key posts within the 'secret army'. Two of the three delegates on COMAC, the military commission of the CNR, were Communists, while the other member was a fellow traveller. The overall head of the FFI was General Koenig in London, but, on the ground, the Communists furnished the bulk of the Partisan leadership. In the Paris region, the FFI were commanded by the Communist Colonel Rol-Tanguy, while the leader of the local liberation committee was another Communist, Tollet. At least a third of the local committees were made up of party members. As much as the imposition of an Allied military government, de Gaulle dreaded the prospect of a Communist takeover. His representative, Alexandre Parodi, was unable to prevent the Paris committee from launching an insurrection at Communist instance on 19 August 1944. Preceded by a police strike on 16 August, in the course of which striking policemen occupied the Prefecture of Police, the Paris insurgents of the FFI occupied the Hôtel de Ville. A short-lived truce was arranged between non-Communist Resistance leaders and the Military Governor of Paris, Dietrich von Choltitz, but on the 22 August barricades were erected and the fighting resumed.

News of the events in Paris did not please the Allied generalissimo Eisenhower: the liberation of Paris was not high up on the scale of Allied priorities, since the city was of little strategic importance beside the task of smashing the Siegfried Line. But persuaded that, after all, Paris must be liberated, Eisenhower dispatched American and French troops (the latter commanded by General Leclerc) to relieve the FFI. On 25 August von Choltitz surrendered to Leclerc, though Rol-Tanguy insisted that his name be added to the document on behalf of the FFI. On his arrival in Paris that afternoon de Gaulle was feted by the cheering crowds. But, in a significant gesture to show that he represented the continuity of the French State and was not the prisoner of the Resistance, he drove straight to his old office at the War Ministry, where, he said, he found everything just as he had left it in 1940. The next day he staged a triumphal procession from the Arc de Triomphe to Notre Dame which he regarded as his own 'apotheosis' and which confirmed him as the new master of France.

Subsequently, de Gaulle developed the myth that he had foiled a Communist plot to seize power at the Liberation. Certainly, among a good number of the armed Partisans, especially in the south-west, there existed the hope that the expulsion of the Nazis might be followed by a genuine revolution. André Marty, François Billoux and others articulated the aspirations of this tendency at Algiers. But the leaders of the party had other ideas. Thorez, who spent the war in Moscow, was in a good position to know that Stalin had no plans to foment communist coups in western Europe, and accepted the division of the world into two distinct power blocs, as agreed at the Tehran Conference of 1943. In any case, it was apparent to the party's chiefs that Communist strength was insufficient to permit a Bolshevik-type seizure of power. The party's numbers and prestige had both risen dramatically since 1941, clearly because they succeeded in representing themselves as the patriot party *par excellence*, not because they offered the prospect of revolution. Furthermore, the leaders rightly concluded that the circumstances of 1944 did not favour a coup, since it was scarcely credible that the Americans would have been prepared to stand idly by and allow the Communists to take over. For the Communists, it seemed, there was no real alternative to co-operation with de Gaulle: hence their agreement to the incorporation of the militia forces into the regular army and, later, their newfound willingness to participate in government. De Gaulle's main achievement at the Liberation was less to defeat the Communists in a race for power than to obtain American recognition of his ready-made government in exile.

Myth, too, surrounds the *épuration*, or purges, which followed the Liberation. The figure of 100,000 summary executions of former collaborators is still bandied about. True enough, in certain parts of France, notably in the south and in the Dordogne, there was a virtual reign of terror. Local Resistance leaders clearly took the law into their own hands, inevitably, in some cases, profiting from the opportunity to pay off old scores against personal enemies. Nevertheless, all Resistance leaders, de Gaulle as well as the chiefs of the PCF, agreed that some examples had to be made. Seven hundred and sixty-seven people were executed after trial. Summary executions were probably in the order of 9,000. No doubt the figures would have been considerably higher had not de Gaulle's Commissioners of the Republic made preventive arrests and internments of about 126,000 people.

In the eyes of the law, the worst collaborators were those who could be most easily identified: that is, those who had advertised their position through political or ideological commitments. Pétain, Laval, Darnand, de Brinon, Luchaire and others were tried and sentenced to death (in Pétain's case the sentence was commuted to life imprisonment). Some fortunate ideological collaborators escaped down various 'rat-lines' – to Spain, South America or, in the case of Déat, to a monastery in Italy. Another form of collaboration to be dealt with severely was 'horizontal collaboration'. Women who had formed liaisons with occupying German soldiers were publicly humiliated, often forced to parade naked through the streets with their heads shaved.

Yet, given the intention of the Resistance to sweep away all traces of Nazism and the Vichy regime, perhaps the most remarkable feature of the *épuration* was its relative moderation. Partly this was because de Gaulle was determined to prevent the outbreak of anarchy or civil war: violence had to be curtailed and minimized and the authority of the State upheld. Partly, too, it was a question of preserving the myth of *la France résistante* in the interests of national unity. Hence, collaborators could be presented as a handful of guilty men (or women) unrepresentative of the nation as a whole.

In consequence, there was no wholesale purge of the administration. The prefectoral corps (the most obviously politicized section of the bureaucracy) was hardest hit, with some 50 per cent dismissals; but of the *inspecteurs de finances*, 97 per cent of those in place in 1948 had been employed in 1942. Only about a fifth of the counsellors of state and a third of the diplomatic corps were purged, and almost no judges. Among the economic collaborators, Renault was the only large firm to be nationalized. Even political collaborators survived to make their mark subsequently in French public life. Pétain's lawyer and indefatigable apologist, Jacques Isorni, was elected to parliament in 1951, and, after a general amnesty proclaimed in 1953, some 14 ex-Vichyites sat in the Chamber of Deputies in 1958. The ex-director of Vichy radio, Tixier-Vignancour, became a deputy in 1956 and was a candidate for the Presidency of the Republic in 1965. Such survivals guaranteed that the 'new France' of the post-Liberation period would not mark the altogether clean break with Vichy that Resistance leaders had dreamed of.

15
The Fourth Republic

The First Phase 1944–1947

Paris was liberated on 25 August 1944. For the next 14 months de Gaulle ruled France as a virtual 'dictator by consent', paying little heed to the Consultative Assembly, made up of various shades of Resistance opinion, which was supposed to help him. Some critics of the General allege that his failure to embrace sweeping change in this period allowed the Resistance spirit to be dissipated and encouraged the return of party squabbles. But such cirticism, on balance, seems unfair. Quite apart from the fact that the Resistance itself was only nominally united and far from agreed on the shape that the new France should take, de Gaulle was confronted with enormous problems in trying to rebuild the authority of the State and to repair the shattered economy. Also, there was still a war to be won. Fighting, indeed, was still taking place on French soil. Paris may have been liberated but the war against Hitler was by no means over, and it was de Gaulle's intention that France should pay an honourable part in the final destruction of the Third Reich.

In the military sphere de Gaulle could claim a resounding success. In exile he had raised a colonial army of eight divisions numbering 300,000 men. By a decree of 23 September 1944, the combatants of the FFI were incorporated into the regular army. New troops were also mobilized under the general mobilization order of 1939. At the end of the war France had an army of 18 divisions which had acquitted itself well in the protracted closing stages of the fighting. No victory was more satisfying or symbolic than General Leclerc's retaking of Strasbourg on 23 November 1944. The first French army, with American support, recaptured Colmar at the beginning of February 1945. On 30 March General de Lattre crossed the Rhine and began a remorseless advance into Germany. Such triumphs tasted sweet and helped to wipe out the bitter memories of 1940. But, to de Gaulle's immense indignation, they were not sufficient to win France a place alongside the 'Big Three' at the peace talks at Yalta and Potsdam which decided the fate of the post-war world.

With regard to the internal reconstruction of the country, de Gaulle from the first successfully reaffirmed the authority of the State. In exile he had prepared the men – his *commissaires de la République* – and the administrative machinery for a takeover of power at the Liberation, while his own tours of the provinces contributed greatly to the establishment of his personal ascendancy. On 9 September 1944 he constituted a 'government of national unanimity' which reflected all shades of Resistance opinion and, through its inclusion of uncompromised figures from the Third Republic, such as Jules Jeanneney, the former president of the Senate, provided continuity with the Republican past.

Economically, the country lay in ruins. The damage to property was greater even than in 1914–18. Nearly half a million buildings were destroyed and almost another two million damaged. Communications – especially the railway network – had been devastated. Raw materials, notably coal, were in short supply. Inflation was rampant. Food was strictly rationed, though peasants still managed to eat well and made impressive profits on the black market. Hunger intensified traditional antagonisms between town and country and made the urban population highly critical of the new government. Given the circumstances, it was no mean achievement on the part of the authorities to return the country to some semblance of normal economic life within a comparatively short space of time.

The fundamental political problem was to equip France with a new constitution. The omens for change and renewal at first looked favourable. A referendum held in October 1945 established overwhelmingly (96 per cent) that there was no desire to resuscitate the Third Republic, while the elections to a Constituent Assembly (in which women voted for the first time) produced a Chamber whose composition differed very significantly from those of the previous Republican regime. The Radicals, for so long the dominant force in French parliamentary politics, were reduced to 10 per cent of the deputies, and the Right accounted for only another 16 per cent. Instead, the Assembly was dominated by three large, roughly equal, power blocs controlling between them almost three-quarters of the seats. Topping the list were the Communists, followed by the Socialists, and then came a completely new party, the MRP (*Mouvement Républicain Populaire*), a party of Christian Democrats under the leadership of Georges Bidault, the successor to Jean Moulin as the head of the National Resistance Council. Many commentators believed that a new era in French political life was opening up in which a more coherent party system would form the essential framework.

But to put together a constitution on which all parties could agree proved no easy matter. De Gaulle, refusing to associate himself with any one party, favoured a presidential-style system, that is, with a strong head of state and an executive power that would not be at the mercy of the legislature, as under the Third Republic. (De Gaulle of course assumed that he himself would become President.) The three main political parties were united in their opposition to any such Gaullist regime but could agree on little else. The PCF, posing as latter-day Jacobins, demanded a unicameral assembly, one sovereign chamber which would not be subject to checks from a 'reactionary' upper house. The Socialists agreed with unicameralism in principle, but in practice they remained intensely suspicious of the Communists, fearing to be absorbed by them. The MRP on the other hand, dreaded that in the 'direct democracy' envisaged by the PCF one single party might end up dominating the Assembly, and that the party in question might turn out to be the Communists. Disgusted by what he saw as the return of party squabbles, de Gaulle resigned in January 1946. No doubt he hoped that his absence would soon demonstrate his own indispensability and the incompetence of the professional politicians. In the event, he found himself in the political wilderness for the next 12 years.

In May 1946 a constitution proposing a one-chamber assembly was submitted to the electorate for approval. By a narrow majority (10½ million to 9½ million, with 6 million abstentions) it was rejected and the whole process of constitution-drafting had to be gone through again by a second Constituent Assembly, elected in June 1946. This time the MRP emerged as the party with the largest share of the vote (28 per cent) with the Communists also gaining slightly and the Socialists losing ground. The best that the Assembly could do was to devise a constitution remarkably similar to that of the despised Third Republic. Wooed by the MRP the Socialists agreed to the creation of a second chamber, to be called the 'Council of the Republic', a Senate in all but name. Certain cosmetic changes were introduced which prevented the Chamber of Deputies from being an exact replica of that of the Third Republic – for example, the system of interpellation was dropped and parliament itself was to be dissolved if a government lost a vote of confidence – but in its everyday operation the Fourth Republic looked very like the Third, notably in the matter of ministerial instability (between December 1946 and June 1951 eight ministries were formed, with the average government lasting seven months). Submitted to the electorate in October 1946, the proposals were endorsed by 9 million to 8 million, though significantly there were 8 million abstentions. Already the Fourth Republic aroused a good deal of apathy if not hostility: it cannot be said that the new regime got off to a good start.

The era of tripartism, maintained through the fresh elections of November 1946 (where the Communists topped the poll, though they did not get to form the government) proved short-lived. The experiment in coalition government made up of representatives drawn from the three main political parties ended abruptly in May 1947, when the Socialist Prime Minister Ramadier sacked the Communist members of the cabinet. The ministerial participation of the PCF had been one of the most striking political novelties of the post-war era, but there were many people, including their Socialist colleagues in government, who remained unconvinced of the sincerity of their commitment to parliamentary democracy. In 1947, whatever their intentions in 1944, it was widely feared that the Communists had used their years in power to infiltrate the State and to prepare the ground for the kind of political takeover practised so successfully by communists in eastern Europe.

Whether the French Communists were really planning to seize power or not is still a matter for lively historical debate. Doubtless, the party was frustrated at having failed to obtain outright control of any of the key ministries (Interior, Foreign Affairs, Defence) and at the National Assembly's preference of Léon Blum to Maurice Thorez for premier despite the PCF's success in the elections of November 1946. It is also true that relations between Communist and non-Communist ministers became increasingly fraught, as the party, after preaching austerity to the French workers, increasingly identified itself with their protests against economic hardship, food shortages and black marketeering. It was Communist support for striking workers at the Renault plant that prompted Ramadier to fire his Communist ministers. Nevertheless, it appears that the party was genuinely shocked by the expulsions. Thorez and his ministerial colleagues seem to have enjoyed the exercise of office and to have hoped that their exclusion would be only temporary. They were slow to realize that their fate was being determined in the larger world arena, with the onset of the Cold War. On 12 March 1947

US president Harry S. Truman enunciated to Congress his 'doctrine' that Communism had to be 'contained'. In June his new Secretary of State, Marshall, divulged details of a massive programme of aid to promote economic recovery in Europe. In agreeing to accept American assistance, France effectively committed herself to the Western bloc. At the same time, Moscow, too, was adopting a harder line. In September 1947 the newly established Cominform banned all participation in government on the part of communist parties. The French party was singled out for particularly stern criticism for its class collaboration since 1944 and responded with grovelling apologies. Perhaps with a view as much to propitiating Moscow as to seizing power in its own right, the PCF orchestrated a series of strikes in late 1947 and 1948 through the CGT: there was no mistaking their political, and possibly revolutionary, overtones. The point remains, however, that the Communists had not so much wrecked tripartism as become the principal victims of its demise. They were to wander in the political wilderness for the next 34 years, regaining office only under the Socialist government formed by François Mitterrand in 1981.

The real wrecker of tripartism was de Gaulle. Increasingly exasperated by the re-emergence of party politics, he welcomed the rejection of the first draft constitution, and in a speech of 16 June 1946 at Bayeux outlined his own proposals for a strong presidential system. He then campaigned vigorously against the second draft constitution, not in the end successfully, but effectively enough to make many voters abstain, notably previous supporters of the MRP, which prided itself on being the 'party of fidelity' to the General. Thoroughly disgusted by the establishment of a Fourth Republic which largely resembled the Third, de Gaulle made no secret of his antipathy to the new regime. Speaking at Strasbourg in April 1947, he founded the RPF, the 'Rally of the French People'. This, he insisted, was not yet another political party but a genuine popular movement united behind de Gaulle as Leader and Man of Destiny. The obvious parallels with fascist movements of the 1930s were not lost on parliamentarians, especially when de Gaulle took up an implacably anti-Communist stance and resorted to mass rallies on the Nuremberg model. Fears that a de Gaulle regime would end parliamentary democracy were intensified by the initial success of the RPF, which in October 1947 captured 40 per cent of the votes in the municipal elections.

Confronted with de Gaulle's assault on the new Republican edifice, both the MRP and the Socialist party were thrown into some disarray. The MRP was essentially a party of leaders, without a natural, well-organized base. Overnight, it lost its credibility as the 'party of fidelity' to de Gaulle, which had a disastrous effect on its ability to win support at the grass-roots. The Socialists, in many ways the key element in the working of tripartism, were genuinely alarmed by de Gaulle's recourse to demagogy. They had tried to steer a difficult course away from their pre-war alliances with the Radical party but without aligning themselves too openly with the Communists, of whose motives Socialists retained a deep-seated distrust. Hence their somewhat unlikely and uneasy alliance with the MRP, a party whose leaders, at least, were avowed Christian Democrats, whereas many Socialists remained hardened anti-clericals. In the circumstances of 1947, with both the PCF and the RPF mobilizing against the new Republic, it seemed appropriate for the Socialists to fall back on the classic device of organizing a 'Third Force', that is rallying the Centre against threats from the extreme Left and the extreme

Right. Radicals who had been frozen out of the political system under tripartism now had a chance to make a political comeback and a new day dawned for the politics of immobilism.

Immobilism, *Mendésisme, Poujadisme*

The emergence of the 'Third Force' combined Socialists, Radicals and MRP in governments which, in their instability and ineffectiveness, reminded people of the ministerial musical chairs and parliamentary intrigues of the Third Republic. The need to rally centrist and even moderate right-wing support increasingly shifted the political centre of gravity towards the Right. When the Ramadier government fell in November 1947, an attempt to replace him with Léon Blum failed and his successor was Robert Schuman of the MRP, who took the Radical René Mayer as his Minister of Finance. Schuman lasted only until July 1948, when he was replaced by the even shorter-lived administration of the Radical André Marie, whose Finance Minister was none other than Paul Reynaud. A second Schuman government survived only a farcical two days in September 1948, before giving way to a government formed by the Radical Henri Queuille, the very embodiment of the old-style machine politician, who before 1940 was a veteran of some 20 cabinets of the Third Republic. Before the elections of 1951 it proved necessary to re-shuffle the pack several times between Queuille, Bidault and Pleven.

Not surprisingly, some commentators viewed these developments as a return to the old 'gamesmanship' of the Third Republic, in which politics was largely a game played for personal advancement and the spoils of office. Decision-making and action were very much last resorts, since waiting and avoiding responsibility were far safer bets for retaining friends and jobs. Ideological divisions were minimal. The gamesmanship explanation for the immobilism of the French system, however, though not without its element of truth, understates the ideological cleavages in French political life and the consequent difficulties involved in putting together an effective coalition government. Even within the 'Third Force' itself there were tensions and antagonisms. The confessional aspect of the MRP, most clearly evident in its advocacy of State subsidies for Catholic schools, antagonized anti-clerical Socialists and Radicals. The Socialists, moreover, were unwilling to accept deflationary financial policies for dealing with the problem of inflation. Foreign and colonial policies also produced splits in the 'majority' parties, as the questions of German rearmament and Indo-China were to reveal.

Much more apparent, however, was the divide between those who favoured 'the system' and those who opposed it. In the French Communist party, the Fourth Republic had to contend with a party that rejected the dominant political culture and that presented itself as a class party, on the Bolshevik model, embodying the revolutionary aspirations of the French proletariat. To their enemies, especially in the Cold War era, they were less a genuinely French party than the agents of the Soviet Union: and certainly there can be no mistaking the slavish subservience of the leadership to Stalin and Stalinism. But the great majority of those who joined the party, and still greater majority of those who voted for it, were far from being Marxist ideologues. While it is true that the party could not claim to represent the majority of the French industrial workforce, it was easily the party which had the highest working-class membership and the most *ouvriériste* image. It had a strong appeal for many of the underprivileged in French society, who aspired to a better life for themselves and their children. In the party they could find comradeship, warmth and a helping hand as well as an outlet for idealism and political commitment. At the other end of the political spectrum, the Gaullist RPF also stood for a wholesale rejection of the new Republic: and, following its sweeping gains in the municipal elections of 1947, the 'Third Force' had every reason to fear that the forthcoming legislative elections of 1951 might turn into a plebiscite for de Gaulle.

In the face of the twin threats from Left and Right, the politicians were at least agreed on the need to defend the regime. They therefore tampered with the electoral system, shamelessly modifying the system of proportional representation settled on in 1946 so as to favour Centre parties at the expense of larger parties (Communists and Gaullists). The RPF still won the largest number of seats (107) with 21.7 per cent of the votes, and the Communists 97 seats with 25.9 per cent, but the Centre parties, including the conservatives, still mustered over 50 per cent of the votes and took 340 seats. The price of survival, however, was an accentuation of the swing to the Right. After two typically short-lived governments under Pleven and the Radical Edgar Faure, Antoine Pinay succeeded in forming a government of the Centre–Right in March 1952 by luring some 27 Gaullists from the RPF into his majority. To the General's disgust, his Rally ended up behaving much like other parties and he himself withdrew from active politics to write his memoirs. The challenge from the RPF collapsed, but the Republic was now in the hands of those, Radicals and conservatives, who were supposed to have been swept away by the new broom of 1944–6. The Pinay cabinet, indeed, marked an important stage in the rehabilitation of ex-Vichyites. Pinay himself had voted for Pétain in 1940 and included Flandin as one of his advisers. Another indication of the swing to the Right was the election of the obscure conservative René Coty to succeed the Socialist Vincent Auriol as President of the Republic in December 1953. He, too, had voted for Pétain and required 13 ballots to be elected. The Socialists were in opposition from January 1952 and the Centre–Right monopolized office until the advent to power of Pierre Mendès-France in June 1954.

Nothing highlighted the debility of the Fourth Republic more than the failure of the Mendès-France experiment of 1954. Mendès was a rare breed: a Radical politician of integrity, who stood for policies rather than the mere pursuit of office. Once the youngest deputy in the Chamber, he had been active in the Resistance and served in de Gaulle's post-war cabinet, resigning in 1945 when his advice on economic and financial reconstruction was rejected in favour of the more conservative measures advocated by Pleven. Out of office, he consistently expatiated on certain themes: the need for economic modernization; the priority to be attached to investment in industry over either consumer or military expenditure; the maintenance of full employment; and the disastrous impact of the war in Indo-China on both the prospects for economic recovery and on French foreign policy. To govern, said Mendès, was to choose. Problems had to be solved, not shelved. He was prepared to assume power only on his own terms, which cost him the premiership in 1953. But in 1954, following the military disaster at Dien Bien Phu in northern

Vietnam, he appeared to be the only politician capable of extricating France from the mess of the war in Indo-China.

In seven short but hectic months France was subjected to dynamic government such as it had rarely known. Mendès kept his promise to pull France out of Indo-China within 30 days, negotiating the Geneva agreements which divided the country into North and South Vietnam. Extending the new sense of realism in colonial policy to North Africa, he settled the conflict in Tunisia between the French and the Neo-Destour nationalist party by agreeing to self-government, and opened talks on the future of Morocco. True, he refused to concede independence to Algeria, where open revolt broke out in November 1954; but he appointed Jacques Soustelle as Governor-General charged with carrying out economic and social reforms.

Turning to foreign policy, Mendès applied the same decisive approach to the question of the European Defence Community (EDC), long allowed to hang fire by his predecessors. In the immediate aftermath of the war, Germany was still viewed as the principal threat to French security and de Gaulle at first believed that the Soviet Union would be the most useful ally for France to contain any future German aggression. With the onset of the Cold War, however, France was inexorably drawn into the 'Western' sphere of influence and forced to abandon the hard-line attitude towards Germany adopted by de Gaulle and Bidault. Faced with the unwelcome choice between America, the Soviet Union and isolation, France reluctantly opted for NATO in 1949. But, for the French, the German problem remained, the prospect of German rearmament being particularly objectionable. France was prepared to enter into economic agreements with the new West German state, but military co-operation was another matter. Thus the Schuman Plan of May 1950 to work out a common Western European policy on coal and steel was acceptable, whereas the Pleven Plan of October 1950 to devise a common European Army proved much more controversial. The EDC, mooted by the Bonn and Paris agreements of May 1952, had still not been ratified by the French parliament in 1954 when Mendès came to power. It was denounced not just by Communists, who opposed its manifest anti-Soviet orientation, but also by Gaullists, who regarded it as a threat to French national sovereignty. Their argument was strengthened by the attitude of the British, who made out that membership of the EDC was good for France but not for themselves. Public opinion was deeply divided. The influential newspaper *Le Monde* favoured a neutralist line. The trial in 1953 of former SS men from the '*Das Reich*' division reminded people of Nazi war atrocities. Many Radicals and Socialists who did not object to the EDC in principle disliked the fact that its main proponents were the leaders of the 'clerical' MRP and Christian Democrats in other European countries. The Americans, however, were determined that West Germany must contribute to the defence of Europe, and brought increasing pressure to bear on French governments. But these steadfastly refused to put the issue to the test in the French parliament until Mendès grasped the nettle. Despite his own untypical agnosticism on the question, he brought it before the Assembly in August 1954. By a majority of 319 to 264 it was resolved to postpone discussion indefinitely. In effect, EDC was dead, and to the right-wing enemies he had made over his colonial policies Mendès now had to add the outraged 'Europeans' of the MRP, furious at this refusal to engage the government's survival on the vote over their favourite project.

Within France, Mendès demanded special powers to tackle the problems of the French economy: he received them on 10 August 1954, and also began to initiate new policies in favour of French youth. Here, however, Mendès's dynamism began to appear somewhat misguided. Convinced that alcoholism was a serious threat to the economic as well as the moral life of the nation, he started a campaign to persuade the French to drink milk rather than wine, which not only made him an obvious target for satirists but won him the undying enmity of the *bouilleurs de cru*, the distillers of illegal alcohol, and the winegrowers' lobby. Moreover, the cult of Mendès's personality, promoted notably in the weekly magazine *L'Express*, intensely irritated all the machine politicians. In his short time in office he had managed to accumulate a remarkable number of enemies. By February 1955 enough of them were able to combine in the Assembly to bring down his government in the course of a debate on North Africa.

Besides, not all Frenchmen shared Mendès's passion for dynamic government and economic modernization. Many small businessmen, artisans and peasant farmers – in a word, the constituent elements of 'static' France – loathed and feared the shape he tried to impose on the country. Flourishing especially in parts of the south and south-west of France, the recalcitrants showed their capacity for resistance in the movement created by Pierre Poujade, a small shopkeeper from the Lot who first achieved prominence in 1953 when, drawing on long tradition of hostility to State 'interference', he mobilized opposition to governmental attempts to crack down on the tax evasion that was endemic among the *petits commerçants*. At first, the PCF itself backed the *poujadistes*, delighted with their denunciations of the 'system', technocracy and *les gros*; but very soon their true right-wing colours were revealed in virulent anti-communism and anti-Semitism (Poujade himself was the son of a member of the *Action Française* and was a former militant in the youth movements of both Doriot and Vichy. He was married to the daughter of a North African *colon*.) A natural demagogue, Poujade orchestrated a movement more than a little reminiscent of fascism, with its rallies and recourse to physical as well as verbal violence. In the elections of 1956 his party polled more than 2½ million votes and won 53 seats. Though powerless to force through their own legislation, the *poujadistes* were yet another negative element in French political life, aggravating the problem of operating a successful parliamentary democracy.

Colonial Problems and Collapse

The most serious consequence of immobilism was that it rendered the Fourth Republic impotent to deal with the problems of empire. In the end this is what destroyed the regime. The constitution had essentially fudged the issue of the colonies, referring not to the empire but to what it called the French Union. Nevertheless, it soon became evident that the regime intended to retain its overseas possessions and to resist the demands of indigenous nationalist movements. De Gaulle was far from alone in hating the British for having ended French rule in Syria and the Lebanon.

But, from the beginning, the French found themselves struggling to maintain their presence. In Indo-China, Vichy had managed to retain only nominal sovereignty in the face of Japanese aggression and the rise of a powerful nationalist movement, the Viet Minh. The leader of the Viet Minh, the communist Ho Chi Minh, was able to set up a provisional government at Hanoi in August 1945. It is a moot question whether the French and the nationalists could have negotiated a mutually satisfactory settlement which would have kept Vietnam within the French Union. Agreement was reached between Ho and de Gaulle's special emissary, Jean Sainteny, in 1946: but subsequent talks at the conference of Fontainebleau were sabotaged by the diehard colonial lobby – the so-called Saigon clique, headed by the High Commissioner, Thierry d'Argenlieu. The clique started a war against the nationalists that in the name first of nationalism and then of anti-communism received the backing of French policy-makers back in metropolitan France, and notably of the MRP chiefs who monopolized the Colonial Office.

It proved to be a war prodigiously wasteful of lives and money: ultimately, it disgraced and discredited the regime. While idealistic army officers died in defence of France and the 'Free World' the PCF was not slow to allege that the 'filthy' war was really being fought on behalf of the Saigon clique and the Bank of Indo-China. Some substance was lent to their allegations by revelations that among the troops of the Foreign Legion were former Nazi war criminals, and by the unseemly squabbling between the MRP and the Socialists over jobs and the control of policy. Public opinion long remained apathetic, largely because the war was being fought thousands of miles away from France and with a motley collection of foreign troops and legionaries rather than French conscripts. What transformed the situation dramatically, and raised the imminent and alarming prospect of the dispatch of native conscript troops, was the fall of the military fortress at Dien Bien Phu before the devasting attack of General Giap in 1954. As we have seen, the trauma was sufficiently great to permit Pierre Mendès-France to take power and to pull France out of the war.

In a sense, the Republic died at Dien Bien Phu, though its death certificate was not signed until four years later. Its graveyard in the end was Algeria. Mendès-France was able to make some headway in tackling the problems of French North Africa, granting autonomy to Tunisia and opening talks with Morocco, whose independence was recognized in 1956. Algeria, though, was another matter. There were over a million French settlers (in a population of 10½ million) who were determined to keep Algeria part of France to continue to enjoy the benefits of colonial rule. By 1954 the Muslim nationalist movement had come under the control of the faction favouring force as the only method of expelling the French. Encouraged by the success of Ho Chi Minh, the FLN opened a guerrilla war which was to be marked by appalling savagery on both sides and was to drag on until 1962. The insurgents resorted to terrorist bombs, both in Algeria and on mainland France. The French Army, especially General Massu's troops, did not scruple to use torture, notably in the pacification of Algiers in January 1957, and forcibly 'resettled' the Muslim population in what were, effectively, concentration camps. Altogether, it has been estimated that perhaps a million Algerians died in the struggle.

From the army's perspective, there could be no question of compromise or any 'sell-out' by cynical politicians, as in Indo-China. Badly in need of a boost to their morale and to their prestige, they convinced themselves that they were engaged above all in an ideological struggle, defending western civilization against the spread of communism: hence their immense efforts to win the minds of the Arab population through propaganda and genuine efforts to improve schooling, social services and the like. Intransigence on both sides barred the way to any peaceful settlement. Edgar Faure, who succeeded Mendès-France as premier in 1955, maintained Jacques Soustelle as Governor-General with a mandate to carry out reforms but these were insufficient to win over the Algerian nationalists. From 1955 the Socialists, now led by Guy Mollet, called for a negotiated peace, but when Mollet himself became Prime Minister following the elections of 1956 talks with the rebels broke down and the government reverted to a hard line, especially after settler demonstrations against Mollet in Algiers. A tough new Governor-General was appointed in the person of Robert Lacoste. On the pretext that Egypt was giving succour to the FLN, France joined with Britain in a punitive expedition against President Nasser occasioned by the latter's nationalization of the Suez Canal. Its abrupt termination, under international pressure, in November 1956 served only to fuel French determination to crush the Algerian rebels. Highly secret *pourparlers* with the insurgents still went on but Mollet and his two short-lived successors in office, Bourgès-Manoury and Gaillard, committed themselves fully to a military solution, sending a vast force of more than 350,000 men to Algeria.

By 1958, however, French public opinion had began to show signs of unease about both the cost and the conduct of the war. Despite the censorship, disturbing revelations about the use of torture leaked out in such disturbing publications as *La Question*, by Henry Alleg, an Algerian journalist who was himself a victim of army torture. The bombing of Sakhiet, a village in Tunisia, by French planes, in defiance of civilian orders, created a furore both at home and in the international arena, precipitating the downfall of the Gaillard government. At the end of yet another ministerial crisis Pierre Pflimlin formed a cabinet which was due to seek parliamentary approval on 13 May 1958. But on that very day rumours that the Prime Minister designate was ready to negotiate with the Algerian nationalists provoked a revolt among the 'Ultras' in Algeria. The *colons* and right-wing extremists seized control in Algiers and the army chiefs refused to act against them. On the contrary, General Salan called for the withdrawal of Pflimlin and on 24 May paratroopers invaded Corsica and looked poised to stage a coup on the mainland. The crisis of the regime, long predicted by de Gaulle, was at last on hand.

In the event only the General himself seemed capable of offering a way out. Whether or not he had secretly encouraged his supporters to plot against the regime remains a moot point, but what is not in doubt is that among the conspirators in Algiers were a number of Gaullist agents. With consummate political skill, de Gaulle proceeded to make himself the master of the situation. On the one hand, he refused to put himself at the head of a military coup, so as not to be the prisoner of the army; on the other hand, though invested legally by the National Assembly, de Gaulle demanded and obtained the right to draw up a new constitution. By voting for de Gaulle on 1 June 1958 the Fourth Republic effectively voted itself out of existence.

16
De Gaulle's Republic

De Gaulle, Gaullism and the New Regime

Throughout his years in the political wilderness de Gaulle retained his conviction that the Fourth Republic could not endure and that, in a time of crisis, the French nation would once again turn to him as its saviour. His faith in himself as a man of destiny had been confirmed above all by the war years, but in all probability it had been acquired at an earlier stage.

Born in Lille in 1890, de Gaulle grew up in a Catholic and royalist household with noble pretensions in which, most uncharacteristically, his father, a history master, was a supporter of Dreyfus. It was, in the first instance, to his family that he owed his sense of history and his strong individualism. After graduating from St Cyr, he served with distinction during the First World War, eventually ending up as a prisoner of war. In the inter-war years, as a lecturer at the École de Guerre, he made a name for himself in military circles as a somewhat unorthodox strategist and was appointed a junior minister at the War Office just before the fall of France in 1940. His years as leader of the Free French vindicated his belief in his destiny and brought him to the centre of French politics, where, guided by his own 'certain idea of France' he sought to make patriotism the basic and unifying force in French national life.

The certain idea of France had definite implications for the organization of the French State. If France were to assume her place as a great power and pursue the policy of *grandeur* which history demanded of her, the State had first to be placed under strong and resolute leadership. In de Gaulle's view the Fourth Republic had soon proved itself incapable of furnishing leaders equal to the task, since the parliamentary regime and the politicians worked only on behalf of sectional and selfish interests rather than for the common good. De Gaulle favoured a regime in which leader and people were in direct and dynamic contact, without the barriers interposed by parliament and political parties: hence his penchant for referenda and modern means of communication such as television, radio and press conferences. Critics were not slow to draw parallels between the gaullist style and that of bonapartism, if not fascism. Yet, in his defence, it must be said of de Gaulle that he never aspired to be a dictator. Not only did he ensure that, on assuming power in 1958, he did not become a prisoner of the military, but also, by his resignations in 1946 and 1969, he showed that he would not cling to power for its own sake when he sensed that he was no longer at one with the popular will.

If de Gaulle stood for certain principles and his gaullism aspired to represent a coherent world view, he also remained the master politician, supple, flexible and opportunistic, and gaullism itself underwent changes as it evolved from its wartime origins, through the episode of the RPF, towards institutionalization in the Fifth Republic. As far as de Gaulle's own gaullism is concerned, it is perhaps best understood as a style rather than as a doctrine. Stanley Hoffman has noted the 'ideological emptiness' of gaullism while stressing the talents of de Gaulle as a 'superb political artist'. His certain idea of France was both an ideal and a political device, designed to legitimate the authority of the French State and unify the French people.

Given his approach to politics, it is hardly surprising that on taking power de Gaulle accorded top priority to the elaboration of a new constitution, with the aim of strengthening the powers of the Presidency and of the executive at the expense of parliament. In the task of constitution-making, however, de Gaulle was not given an entirely free hand. He and his Minister of Justice Michel Debré had to draft a document acceptable to a Constitutional Consultative Committee, which included a number of prominent parliamentarians, who, not unnaturally, tenaciously defended the principle of parliamentary government against gaullist insistence on a presidential system. It was no easy task for the lawyers of the Council of State to reconcile the conflicting ideals, and in the end their text, adopted by the government on 3 September 1958 and approved by a large majority in a referendum of 28 September, retained a certain ambiguity both with regard to the relationship between President and Prime Minister, and more generally, between President and parliament.

Nevertheless, it was clear enough from the outset that the office of President had been uprated. At first the President was elected by a special electoral college, made up of some 80,000 political notables. After the referendum of October 1962, he was elected by universal suffrage, which immensely reinforced the idea that the head of state was specially entrusted by the people to exercise power on their behalf. As regards the executive branch of the constitution more generally, its increased strength was apparent in various new ways. Cabinet ministers no longer had to be MPs responsible to parliament. On the contrary, if appointed to the government, a deputy had to resign his seat, which would be taken by a substitute (*suppléant*) elected at the same time as himself. Parliament's power to unmake governments, such a noteworthy feature of the Third and Fourth Republics, was also radically curtailed. Instead of requiring governments constantly to seek parliamentary approval, the constitution of the Fifth Republic assumed that parliamentary approval was accorded failing evidence to the contrary in the form of a vote of censure carried by an absolute majority of the Assembly. Parliamentary sittings were themselves reduced in number while the right of parliament to initiate legislation was also curtailed. A variety of procedural controls gave the executive further powers at the expense of the legislature. In the end, however, government still had to seek parliamentary support, raising the possibility of a clash between President and parliament, and thus to an extent building the potential for a constitutional crisis into the system.

In practice, conflict was avoided because, to begin with at least, both Prime Minister and parliament accepted de Gaulle's pre-eminence. The fidelity of the Fifth Republic's first premier, Michel Debré, was legendary: the wits dubbed him Fidel Castrato. While the Algerian problem remained at the top of the political agenda, the Assembly, too, recognized the lack of any viable alternative. Algeria was in some respects an immense asset to de Gaulle in the consolidation of his rule in that it prevented the formation of any serious opposition to him in parliament: and de Gaulle was not slow to seize every opportunity to make presidential predominance the fundamental reality of French political life.

The Early Years 1958–1962

After the elaboration of a new constitution, de Gaulle's next priority was to try to end the Algerian war. '*L'Algérie bloque tout*', he would say: in other words, the war was an intolerable drain on French resources, human and material, which prevented France from embarking on the politics of grandeur he had taken office to pursue. The problem was to find a way of extricating France from the conflict without reproducing the kind of crisis that had led to the demise of the previous regime and thus undermining the authority of the French State. His hopes of an early peace settlement were soon dashed when the FLN rejected his secret overtures for a 'peace of the brave' on promises of massive economic aid to be pumped into Algeria. It was to take four long, difficult years before hostilities finally ceased.

It seems likely that de Gaulle had no precise solution to the Algerian question in mind when he came to power. Essentially, he adopted an evasive, wait-and-see, policy, visiting Algeria five times in the course of 1958 in order to make his own assessment of the situation. It was certainly not his intention to be beholden to either the Europeans or the army. On his first visit of 4 June he told the cheering Algiers *colons 'je vous ai compris'* – 'I have understood you' – a masterfully ambiguous statement which by no means necessarily implied sympathy for them or their cause. If the generals entertained the idea that de Gaulle might feel obligations towards them for putting him back in office, they were much mistaken. De Gaulle set about breaking up the whole 13 May movement. Salan was removed and replaced by General Challe and the Committees of Public Safety disbanded.

Though Challe was in some ways allowed to prosecute the war more vigorously than his predecessors, de Gaulle began to edge cautiously towards a political solution. On 16 September 1959 he announced that he wanted a ceasefire followed by a referendum in which Algerians would be free to opt for home rule, though not for complete independence. To concede even this much was going too far for the settlers and for army chiefs like Massu, who told a German newspaper that Algeria must remain part of France. Without hesitation, de Gaulle dismissed him, which in turn prompted the *colons* to try to organize a fresh revolt in January 1960. Crucially, however, this time they were not backed by the army and the rebellion collapsed after a week. Further secret but abortive talks were held with FLN leaders in June 1960, which helped to convince de Gaulle that the electorate had to be consulted as to the acceptability of self-determination for Algeria. In a referendum of January 1961 75 per cent endorsed de Gaulle's proposals but, once again, on 22 April 1961 the Algerian extremists, four generals at their head (Challe, Jouhaud, Salan and Zeller) replied by seizing power in Algiers. De Gaulle rose to the challenge by assuming emergency powers and making an impassioned, dramatic and highly successful appeal to the nation for its support. The isolation of the rebel officers soon became apparent: even in the army itself young conscript troops showed no stomach for a *coup*. A major crisis was surmounted, though de Gaulle still had to face desperate attempts on his life by dissident army officers, organized in the OAS (Secret Army Organization). Long and difficult negotiations were required with the rebel leaders before final agreement was reached, but eventually, on 18 March 1962, at the spa town of Evian, France recognized Algerian independence.

The Politics of Grandeur

Before 1962 de Gaulle was not free to devote himself fully to the question that most preoccupied him: the role of France in international politics. Nevertheless, from the outset he served notice of his intentions. His resentment of the 'Anglo-Saxon' powers was intensified when American and British troops were sent to Jordan and the Lebanon, where France still aspired to exercise the decisive influence, and by the unwillingness of the USA to accord France any share in the overall direction of NATO. Thus, in March 1959 he took French ships out of the NATO command structure, refused to give American bombers facilities in France and made plain his total rejection of military integration. More positively, he gave his full backing to the development of an independent nuclear deterrent: the explosion of the first French atomic bomb in the Sahara in February 1960 was a source of immense satisfaction to him. At the same time, he began to build up a new relationship with West Germany, exchanging visits with Chancellor Adenauer, and sought to spread French influence in the EEC.

From 1962 the main lines of his foreign policy emerged even more clearly. Starting from the existing division of the world into two blocs controlled by the super-powers, America and the USSR, he worked to make France the principal element in a third 'bloc', first by strengthening her ties with other European powers and, second, by trying to extend French influence in 'Third World' or non-aligned countries outside Europe. The *détente* between the super-powers in the wake of the near catastrophic Cuban missiles crisis seemed to facilitate his designs. Early in 1963 he gave a press conference at which he both spelled out his commitment to an independent French nuclear deterrent, rejecting an American invitation to purchase Polaris missiles, and turned down an application by Britain to join the EEC, on the grounds that British membership was likely to spread American influence in Europe by the back door. Ties with West Germany were strengthened by the signature of a treaty of co-operation on 22 January 1963. Most spectacularly, once confirmed in the Presidency of the Republic for another seven years after the presidential elections of December 1965, de Gaulle withdrew France from her military commitments to NATO and then visited Moscow in June 1966, to build bridges towards the Soviet Union and in pursuit of his ambition to construct a Europe from the Atlantic to the Urals.

De Gaulle also pursued his two-fold objective of challenging American hegemony and increasing French prestige in the world beyond Europe. In January 1964 he recognized communist China, to the embarrassment of the USA, the Soviet Union and the PCF. In September 1964 he toured Latin America with enormous *éclat*, fêted both on the spot and by the press at home. Other measures aimed at reducing American influence were his efforts to diminish the importance of the dollar as an international currency by converting French reserves into gold and his denunciations of the American role in Vietnam. In 1967, to the fury of the British, he seized the opportunity while visiting Canada to proclaim his support for the Quebec separatists in his cry of '*Vive le Québec libre!*' He also vetoed a second British application to join the EEC in May 1967.

Within Europe itself, de Gaulle had no time for supra-nationalism. His Europe was to be a Europe of nation states, in which France would play the decisive role. If necessary, he was prepared to bring the machinery of the EEC to a halt in order to block any progress towards European integration. In the second half of 1965 he boycotted its meetings for six months in order to maintain the right of individual states to a veto. In de Gaulle's view, France might speak for Europe, but the EEC commission must never presume to speak for France.

Whether de Gaulle had any real impact on international politics may be doubted. The super-powers remained pre-eminent, and the division of the world into their spheres of influence was brutally reinforced by the Soviet invasion of Czechoslovakia in 1968. France may have withdrawn from NATO, but she still remained part of the Western Alliance, since de Gaulle had no illusions about France's need for powerful friends in a dangerous world. French support for the USA was readily forthcoming in the Cuban missiles crisis of 1962. It is possible, therefore, to dismiss de Gaulle's foreign policy as mere posturing, striking attitudes at variance with the real capacity of France to influence events. Yet in his way de Gaulle did make France once again some kind of serious force in the world arena, a power not to be despised or ignored but recognized for the extra dimension she added to world diplomacy. In any event, the politics of grandeur were always designed more for domestic than for foreign ends. It was never de Gaulle's ambition to pursue power and glory in the manner of Louis XIV, but rather, by developing a renewed sense of national pride, to legitimize the Fifth Republic and to enhance the authority of the French State. In so far as his foreign policy – in particular his symbolic anti-Americanism – won overwhelming support among French public opinion, it well served his purpose in consolidating his regime.

17
New Social and Economic Structures

In 1945 the exultation produced by the Liberation and the final defeat of Nazism was necessarily tempered by a grim awareness of the devastation wreaked by war and military occupation. The economy lay in ruins. Industrial production was down to a third of its pre-war level. Agriculture was crippled by a lack of men and machinery. Food was strictly rationed, which encouraged the development of hoarding. There was in effect a dual economy, namely an 'official', controlled, price-fixed economy on the one hand and a flourishing black market on the other. Yet within a remarkably short period of time the French economy made a dramatic recovery. By 1947 industrial production had again attained its level of 1938. Between 1949 and 1963 growth took place at a rate of 4.6 per cent per annum. The problem for the historian is to explain how this transformation came about.

The French Economic Miracle

The answer, in part at least, must lie in the realm not of economics but of psychology and attitudes. The French, by way of reaction to the shattering blow of 1940 and the humiliating experience of the Occupation, finally began to face up to the problems of demographic decline and economic stagnation inherited from the 1930s. Perhaps the best indicator of the emergence of a new mentality was the striking increase in the birth rate. Between 1946 and 1955 some 8,352,700 babies were born in France. Whereas in 1935–9 the birth rate was down to 14.9 per 1,000, between 1946 and 1950 it rose to 20.9 per 1,000, and throughout the 1950s remained at over 18 per 1,000. The childless, or single-child, family of the inter-war years tended to disappear in favour of families with two or more children. The economic consequences of the abandonment of the old 'malthusian' mentality were not so much in the sphere of production as in the creation of demand.

Among industrialists and civil servants, evidence of a changed outlook was apparent in their desire to promote economic modernization. Shaking off the doubts and hesitations of the past, they launched a drive in favour of an expansionist capitalism in which the State itself would play an active role through economic management. The 'technocrats' of Vichy had already shown the way: in post-war France Jean Monnet and his team drew up a Five Year Plan, implemented between 1947 and 1953, designed to renew the infrastructure, or key industries, of the French economy, top priority being given to energy. The coal mines, gas, electricity, Air France, the Bank of France, some of the big clearing banks and several leading insurance companies were nationalized, as was the Renault car plant, for Louis Renault's alleged economic collaboration with the Germans. In general, however, the planners looked not so much to nationalization as to a close partnership between the State and industry in setting and implementing economic goals. The founding of the École Nationale d'Administration (ENA) in 1946 ensured that France would be well supplied with highly trained and dynamic administrators.

Financial assistance from America also helped to speed up the rate of French economic recovery. In 1947, as part of its general strategy to contain communism and to promote the expansion of American capitalism, the United States launched its European Recovery Programme, generally referred to as 'Marshall Aid'. But even before the French began to reap the benefits of Marshall Aid they had already received some $12,900 million in credits, grants and loans. The importance of Marshall Aid was that it permitted France to maintain the momentum of reconstruction at a juncture where, without it, funds would have been lacking to import raw materials and capital goods vital for full economic recovery. Between 1948 and 1952 France received another $2,500 million from the United States, a sum equal to one fifth of all the American credits made available to Europe. The planners and technocrats saw to it that American financial aid was put to the best possible use for the reconstruction of the French economy.

Throughout the 1950s and 1960s the French economy enjoyed unprecedented growth. The tenfold multiplication of the number of tractors in use between 1946 and 1958 was both cause and symbol of the modernization of the agricultural sector. French entry into the Common Market (the European Economic Community) in 1957 also contributed to agricultural progress. Industrial production increased by 85 per cent in the years 1950–8. A Second Plan, which embraced housing and regional development as well as the basic industries stimulated by the First Plan, was adopted and successfully implemented between 1954 and 1957. Certain industries – notably chemicals and engineering – were particularly dynamic. The Caravelle jet testified to the success of French aviation, while the expansion in the number of private cars from under three-quarters of a million in 1951 to four million in 1958, underlined the progress made in the car industry. By 1973 63 per cent of all French families owned a car.

As labour became concentrated in highly efficient and industrialized sectors of the economy and steady advances took place in economic rationalization and investment, productivity soared right through the 1960s, the peak year being 1967–8, when there was a 10.4 per cent increase. Again, for French industry as for French agriculture, entry into the EEC was a turning point, requiring businessmen to modernize in order to cope with foreign competition. Many had contemplated the idea of a Common Market with hostility and trepidation (just as some of the great steel magnates had opposed the creation of the Coal–Steel Pool in 1950) but the resultant benefits triumphantly vindicated the politicians of the Fourth Republic who negotiated the Treaty of Rome. Indeed, a great deal of the credit for the 'French economic miracle' must be attributed to the much maligned Fourth Republic, even though de Gaulle and the Fifth Republic reaped the political benefits that accrued from the generalization of prosperity.

Of course, the picture of tremendous economic progress overall has to be

nuanced. Not all of France participated equally in the drive towards modernization and efficiency. Certain regions, such as the south-west, continued to
belong to the old 'static' France and found in Pierre Poujade the spokesman
to articulate their hostility to the 'new' France. Older industries, such as
textiles, clothing and leather declined. Inflation consistently bedevilled the
financial policies of the governments of the Fourth Republic, some of which
(for instance those of Mayer in 1948 and Pinay in 1952) managed the problem
better than others without eliminating it. Inflation was again on the upsurge
at the end of the Fourth Republic's existence and among de Gaulle's first
measures on assuming power was a 20 per cent devaluation of the franc and
a deflationary package of tax increases and cuts in public spending prepared
by his veteran Finance Minister Antoine Pinay in collaboration with the
economics expert Jacques Rueff. These measures contributed significantly to
the creation of a climate of monetary stability, reflected in the confidence in
de Gaulle's new franc and the readiness of the business community to invest.
Nevertheless, the rate of inflation in France remained generally higher than
that of other industrialized countries and the franc was overvalued until after
the events of May 1968. A further worry, which greatly exercised de Gaulle,
was France's lack of oil and her need to import energy. But any general
survey of the performance of the French economy in the years after the
Second World War must conclude by emphasizing the transformation of
France into a major industrial power, manifesting the highest rate of eocnomic
growth among the countries of the EEC.

The Rewards of Prosperity

The new, mechanized, agriculture prospered as never before, but those who
continued to work the old inefficient peasant farms became increasingly conscious of the extent to which their standard of living fell short of that of the
urban population. The farmers suffered as agricultural prices lagged behind
those of industry. Throughout the 1950s, fomented by right-wing and Communist agitators, rural protest was rife at the price that the countryside was
forced to pay for the modernization of the French economy. The Fourth
Republic tried to fob off the farmers in time-honoured fashion, with subsidies
and price-supports. The powerful winegrowers' lobby prevailed on governments to buy up and destroy the surpluses produced in the Midi. But what
was really needed was a new, more radical approach to the problems of the
agricultural sector and in the late 1950s it came. JAC activists captured key
positions within the Farmers' Union, the FNSEA, and began to persuade
both peasants and governments of the need to promote modernization, but
also to ensure that it did not engender excessive human suffering.

Paradoxically, it was not the successful farmers of the north who became
the apostles of progress but dynamic younger men from the small farms of
the south, west and centre. Convinced that the small farm had to be kept
alive for the general health of society, they nevertheless saw the need for the
greater application of technology, for pooling the efforts of producers and
for more efficient structures of marketing. Between 1961 and 1966 they were
fortunate enough to have as Minister of Agriculture the dynamic ex-prefect
Edgar Pisani, who tried to implement much of the JACist programme. In
1961 he passed a law with the general aim of facilitating the purchase of land

by young, modern-minded farmers. Pensions were awarded to older farmers to encourage them to retire. The State set up an agency to buy and resell land to younger men, and it also introduced sanctions against absentee landlords as well as incentives for farmers to associate in producing and marketing. The Pisani Law undoubtedly contributed something to improving the lot of the small farmer. The high levels of prices fixed by the EEC's Common Agricultural Policy also helped the French countryside, though the bigger farmers tended to benefit more than the smaller ones from EEC policy.

If *la France paysanne* was dying, *la France bourgeoise* showed a strong capacity for survival and adaptation, and even expansion. Within the notoriously variegated ranks of the bourgeoisie, perhaps the most significant development was the new prominence attained by the *cadres*, the executive or middle-manager class, who were at the very centre of France's post-war economic boom, particularly in industries such as electricity, oil and car manufacture. In 1954 the *cadres moyens* accounted for just under 6 per cent of the work force; by 1975 they had more than doubled to 12.7 per cent. Much influenced by American methods of management (not infrequently as a result of direct experience) they could readily identify with the cult of efficiency promoted by the technocrats and experts in the service of the State. Their consciousness of their status and readiness to defend it were evident in the formation of their *Confédération générale des cadres* (CGC) in 1944 and their periodic recourse to strike action. Further up the social scale, the *cadres supérieurs* (top management) and the upper echelons of the liberal professions also enjoyed their full share of the new prosperity. The economic élites included fewer individual *patrons* and fewer *rentiers* than in the inter-war period, and more bureaucrats and managing directors (the latter not a class of new men but of *patrons* in a new guise). *Pantouflage* – moving between the State and the private sector – was increasingly common at this level.

In the lower reaches of the middle classes, however, many artisans and small employers in industry and commerce fared less well. In 1954 they were still an important element in the total labour force, numbering 1,300,000, and employing another 1,250,000 wage-earners. For the small independent craftsman, it is true, mechanization and the spread of technology sometimes opened up new opportunities – in maintenance work, repairing cars, television, radios and the like, and in the building industry. But the small shopkeeper felt increasingly ill at ease in the France of the technocrats, and was conscious, from about 1954, that the State was no longer ready to accord him a privileged status. As the supermarket and hyper-market chains spread in the 1960s, many *indépendants* were forced to shut up shop. (In 1960 France had a mere 40 supermarkets, by 1970 there were more than 1,000.) Some 108,000 *petits commerçants* and 18,000 artisans disappeared between 1962 and 1968. Small businessmen found themselves more and more on the defensive. As early as 1944 Léon Gingembre created the *Confédération genérale des petites et moyennes entreprises* (CGPME) and in the 1950s Pierre Poujade found a receptive clientele for his brand of demagogy. In 1969 Poujade's successor, Gérard Nicoud, a café-owner from Grenoble, was jailed for destroying documents in a tax office. Most of these 'independents' voted 'no' in the referendum of April 1969 and thus helped to bring to an end the political career of Charles de Gaulle.

The fortunes of the workers, the most numerous group (around six million) in the active population, were also mixed. Distinctions between the three million or so skilled workers and the rest were still important, both in terms of earning power and prestige. Increasingly, however, the typical worker was neither a skilled man nor a labourer, but a semi-skilled worker engaged in some routine, repetitive job on an assembly line. Many of these *ouvriers spécialisés* (OS) were immigrants and many more were women (by 1968 about 14 per cent and 25 per cent respectively). The development of automation in some industries (oil, electronics, car manufacture) led some sociologists to identify the emergence of a 'new working class', one in which individual skill had been devalued, but where the worker might be required to perform a highly technical and essential task in the plant. Despite their expertise (or rather because of it) such workers tended to be tied to a particular industry and chafed at their general lack of mobility. In a general way, most French workers suffered from a sense of their inferiority and a feeling of demoralization. Work, as for the old artisan class, could no longer confer dignity and pride but had become a burdensome daily grind. Many workers resented what they considered to be their subordinate place in the new technological society, all the more so as they could see no clear way towards ameliorating their situation.

One reason for the continuing marginalization and political impotence of the working class was the failure of the French trade-union movement to mobilize and articulate its grievances. As in the past, political and ideological divisions weakened the challenge of organized labour. In the immediate and euphoric aftermath of the Liberation, the CGT was able to swell its ranks to over five million members. The confessional CFTC, with 700,000 members, shared in the general aspirations for a new deal for labour, but kept its distance from the CGT, which, despite Léon Jouhaux's return to the post of general secretary in 1945, had effectively been captured by the Communists. Within the CGT itself, a faction hostile to the Communists soon developed: and after the expulsion of PCF members from the Ramadier government and the Communist organization of the great strikes of November–December 1947 the breach became an open schism. Those sympathetic to pure syndicalist or perhaps to Socialist (SFIO) positions set up a rival union CGT – *Force Ouvrière* (FO), with the aid of funds supplied by American unions and even by the CIA. The ideological isolation of the CGT, paralleling the political isolation of the Communist party, was reinforced by the government's brutal repression of the Communist-led miners' strike of 1948. Numbers plummeted drastically. By 1958 the CGT was down to a membership of 1.6 million. Unsure of their role in French society, the unions failed to provide leadership for the mass of French workers. In 1968 75 per cent of the workforce remained ununionized. The CGT still had most members, with 1½ million; FO had ½ million and another ½ million belonged to the CFDT (in 1964 the CFTC decided to drop its confessional ties by substituting the adjective 'democratic' for 'christian').

If class warfare was less naked and intense than in the past, class distinctions remained real and deep-seated. Workers were still marginalized, segregated from the bourgeois world not just by gaps in income and living standards but, more fundamentally, in mentalities and ways of life. As always, a strong element in maintaining both the class cohesion of the bourgeoisie and its social pre-eminence was the educational system. Despite the good intentions of Education Ministers under the Fourth and early Fifth Republics, the crucial barrier between primary and secondary education was not broken down. In 1963 a kind of comprehensive education was introduced in the form of the CES (*collèges d'enseignement secondaire*) and by 1968 there were some 1,500 of these schools. Even in these, however, streaming took place and it was bourgeois children who on the whole tended to obtain places in the academic sections while working-class children filled the technical sections. In the universities only 1 per cent of the students came from a working-class background. Bourgeois parents were not only more aware of the decisive stage that the secondary school represented for the future life chances of their children but in addition were able to initiate them into the social and cultural codes that teachers and employers recognized as skills. Earlier in the century, this 'cultural capital' was acquired by an education in the arts. In the 'new' France the bourgeoisie was quick to spot that the future lay with those competent in maths, either to obtain degrees in science and engineering or in economics.

Housing formed another barrier between the classes, segregating them physically. Under the First Plan housing received a low priority, with the result that the housing stock in 1954 remained at almost the same level as in 1914. Many working-class families were housed in ancient, overcrowded accommodation, including wretched furnished rooms with totally inadequate facilities. After 1954, it is true, a vast building programme was inititiated, so that in the 1960s some 400,000 dwellings a year were being created. Even so, the census of 1962 still classified one flat in four as 'overcrowded', while 60 per cent of all French housing still predated 1914, much of it in very bad repair. Another problem was that the number of low-rent flats (HLMs, *habitations à loyer modéré*) did not increase at the same rate as the luxury flats, affordable only by the well-off, and out of which property speculators made immense fortunes. Also, the standard of the new dwellings often left a great deal to be desired. The *grands ensembles*, suburban, commuter new towns, were criticized as dreary and soulless places, where families were housed in rows of box-like high flats and social amenities and community spirit were negligible. Young wives complained of isolation, while workers resented the extra travelling which added to the length of their working day. By far the largest and most notorious of the HLM suburbs was Sarcelles, established near Le Bourget airport, which despite housing a population of 40,000 had no secondary school or cultural centre, and which gave rise to a new form of depressive illness known as 'Sarcellitis' (well described in Christiane Rochefort's novel *Les petits enfants du siècle*).

Thus, while workers' wages rose steadily over the period, one should hesitate before talking of an 'affluent worker' embarked on a process of *embourgeoisement*. Certainly, by the 1960s, with the help of credit, workers could purchase the kinds of consumer goods – cars, televisions, refrigerators – once available primarily to the wealthier middle classes. To compensate for the long working week, French workers enjoyed an annual holiday (three weeks in 1956, raised to four in 1969) and some would make their way to the same resorts as middle-class holiday-makers. Such resemblances in living patterns, however, were for the most part superficial. In 1969 still only 49 per cent of the population took a holiday away from home. If 43 per cent of manual workers went on vacation, twice as many (88 per cent) professional people and *cadres supérieurs* did so. The working class largely inhabited a different universe and continued to reproduce itself: those born in the working class were likely to die in it. Social mobility (excluding rural depopulation) has not been a notable feature of French social life in the post-war years. In the consumer society, the universality of consumption and the availability of happiness reckoned in goods theoretically within the purchasing power of everyone are the main tenets of a seductive but lying ideology. Some remain more equal than others.

The Changing Face of France

In the period after the Second World War France became overwhelmingly an urban society. The population of town dwellers rose from 21.5 million in 1946 to 33.6 million in 1968, whereas the proportion of country dwellers fell from 46 per cent to 34 per cent in the same period. The French countryside was depleted by some 12 million people, leading to much discussion of the 'vanishing peasant'. The Paris conurbation swelled to eight million inhabitants, roughly a sixth of the whole French population. Other towns also grew rapidly. Grenoble, for instance, had a population of 80,000 in 1945, 360,000 in 1969.

Demographic expansion has also been a significant feature of the new society. France, a country of 40.5 million people in 1946, numbered 46.5 million in 1962 and 49.7 million in 1968. As in the past, immigration contributed significantly to the increase. By 1975 there were four million foreigners and their families residing in France, including 560,000 North Africans (mainly Algerians); 360,000 Portuguese; and 205,000 Spaniards. Constituting 8 per cent of the total labour force and 17 per cent of industrial workers, these immigrants for the most part worked in the dirtiest and most menial jobs and lived in the most squalid housing, sometimes in insalubrious shanty towns or *bidonvilles*. A decline in the death rate (itself partly a product of medical advances in such fields as antibiotics along with greater social security) also helped to boost the French population. But the most novel aspect of the French population explosion was the dramatic increase in the birth rate, already alluded to. The 'baby boom' of the post-war years was hailed, at least in official quarters, as an affirmation of national vitality.

Yet French attitudes to their enhanced numbers appear to have been ambiguous. Over the two decades from 1945 opinion polls discovered that many Frenchmen – and more especially many French women – had reservations about the 'baby boom'. While politicians, manufacturers of baby products and toys, and employers in general, remained enthusiastic, it emerged from a series of surveys carried out in the late 1950s and early 1960s that women and the majority of working-class people were opposed to any further population increase. Perhaps as many as one third of the children born to mothers between 1959 and 1962 were not wanted and were a consequence of unintentional pregnancies. Despite their illegality and attendant dangers, abortions remained shockingly high – perhaps as many as a million a year. The polls also revealed that the generous family allowances paid by the State provided a strong financial incentive to have children, without which many would not have been born. By the 1960s, despite an increase in the number of marriages the birth rate again began to fall.

At least as much as in the past, France's female population (51.3 per cent of the total in 1968) was subjected to strong ideological pressure to make women believe that happiness was to be found essentially through fecundity, that is by marrying and raising a family. And, by and large, French women did not contest the conventional wisdom. Despite the prevalent myth that women were going out to work on an unprecedented scale, by comparison with the early twentieth century there was in reality a slight decline in the proportion of women in the (official) labour force (38 per cent of the total in 1906, 35 per cent in 1968). In 1906 43 per cent of the female population was reckoned to be economically active; this figure had fallen to 28 per cent in 1972. The percentage of married women in the female labour force, however, did increase significantly, reaching 52 per cent by 1966. Yet, on the birth of a child, it was still common for a woman to give up work, and devote herself to the care of child and home.

The kind of work done by women did change significantly over time. In ever-increasing numbers women entered the tertiary sector of the economy, as office workers, shop employees and the like. The tertiary sector accounted for 42.3 per cent of all working women in 1946, but 59.6 per cent by 1968 and 63.5 per cent in 1972. Some entered the liberal professions, others became executives, usually at the junior rather than the senior level, but the vast majority occupied the lower reaches of the tertiary sector in terms of financial reward and status. Thus, in the *cadres supérieurs*, there were nine men for every one woman in 1974 and even these women still earned about a third less than their male counterparts. In general, married women with children earned 39 per cent less on average than men in the same 'socio-professional category' in 1974; the comparable figure for a single woman was 16 per cent.

On certain fronts it could be argued that women had made some progress. The legal disabilities of married women were finally removed by legislation in 1965. The older, arranged, marriage virtually disappeared. A woman doctor, Mme Weill-Hallé, led a successful campaign to change the law on the sale of contraceptives: by 1967 they could be purchased by those aged over 18. But it would be wrong to magnify these changes into a social or sexual revolution. For one thing, the pill was available only on medical prescription and young women under the age of 21 required parental consent. For another, doctors, at least the older generation, were reluctant to give contraceptive advice to patients. More importantly, French women were slow to avail themselves of the new facilities available at family-planning clinics. The old practice of *coitus interruptus* died hard. Within marriage itself, the 'modern' husband was chiefly one who agreed to help with the washing-up. Working wives still did the traditional household chores in addition to their waged labour. In the world of politics, women participated minimally. There were only 30 female deputies in 1945 and a mere 11 in 1967. Feminism attracted only an insignificant handful of intellectuals, their consciousness raised by Simone de Beauvoir's *The Second Sex* published in 1949.

The role of women in the new French society needs to be set in the context of the continuing prevalence of the family as a social norm. Families remain the key agents of socialization, and therefore of the transmission of ideological and cultural values. The basic family unit of mother, father, children, all with their disinctive roles, provided the model of a 'natural' and immutable order. Within the family, the individual was supposed to find warmth and support, no matter how hostile the outside world. The very idea of *the* family, rather than the very different family patterns distinguishable over time and place, reinforced the normative nature of the family, and by extension, legitimized the whole social order of which it was part. True, the divorce rate rose until, by the 1960s, one in ten marriages ended in divorce: families were apparently not always the havens of security and happiness that apologists made them out to be. In the 1970s marriage and family life were to lose some of their popularity, especially in the bourgeois class, but in the 1960s they still exercised enormous sway.

The strength of the family as both ideology and social reality was confirmed by the attitudes and behaviour of French youth. The rejuvenation of the population focused much media attention on *les jeunes* and the attitudes of French youth to all facets of life. An autonomous youth culture developed its own slang, popular music and forms of sociability. Groups of *copains* (pals) enjoyed going around together or staging *surprise-parties*. Yet the youth cult never made quite the same impact as in Britain or the United States. France produced no Beatles, and, even more assuredly, no Rolling Stones. French teenagers listened to the softer sounds of Richard Anthony, Françoise Hardy or Johnny Hallyday. Young people, in the main, continued to live at home, partly because of the powerful claims of the family and partly because of the housing shortage. In consequence, they showed fewer signs of open revolt against the existing social order – at least until May 1968.

18
May 1968

The liquidation of the Algerian War, the reaffirmation of France on the world scene, continuing economic expansion and the personal authority of de Gaulle seemed to indicate the advent of a new era of strong government and political stability in France. Unquestionably, the old Fourth or Third Republic style of politics had disappeared. Indeed, it became a charge against the Fifth Republic in the 1960s that political life had been effectively stifled. Yet, in May 1968, France was to experience a political and social upheaval that shook the regime to its foundations. A crisis which began as a wave of student protest escalated to the point where it was by no means inconceivable that the Fifth Republic would follow its predecessors into the void. How this came about is still not easy to explain.

The Political Background

After the elections to the Assembly in 1962, the Gaullist party (UNR) had 230 of the 482 seats. Alliance with the 35 Independent Republicans of Valéry Giscard d'Estaing clinched their majority. Giscard was rewarded with the Ministry of Finance and two other cabinet posts for his party. Georges Pompidou, a merchant banker from the Auvergne, was confirmed as premier and also looked after the running of the party machine, since de Gaulle continued to project himself as a national figure who towered above mere party politics.

The main focus of politics soon became the forthcoming Presidential elections of 1965, where for the first time the voting was to take place on the basis of universal suffrage. Anti-Gaullists were hopelessly divided as to who should be fielded against the General. The extreme Right, its ranks swollen by the arrival in France of former settlers from Algeria (the *pieds noirs*), favoured the ex-Vichyite lawyer Tixier-Vignancour. The Socialist mayor of Marseille, Gaston Defferre, was promoted by the weekly magazine *L'Express* as a candidate of the 'Third Force'. An implacable anti-Communist, Defferre was unpalatable not only to the PCF but also to many other Socialists, and notably the party leader Guy Mollet. He also failed to obtain the endorsement of MRP chiefs, and had to withdraw his candidacy when talks between the MRP and the Socialists broke down in June 1965. The Centre therefore turned to the MRP leader Jean Lecanuet, while the Socialists made common cause with the Communists behind the candidacy of François Mitterrand.

In the event, de Gaulle won only 43.7 per cent of the votes cast in the first ballot and was obliged to face Mitterrand in a run-off, which he duly won by securing 54.5 per cent of the votes cast (though only 44.7 per cent of eligible voters supported him). In the eyes of the electorate, charismatic leadership obviously had its limitations: routine issues could affect the General's standing and there could be no denying a certain amount of dissatisfaction with his policies. Further evidence of discontent emerged in the course of the campaign for the legislative elections of 1967. Mitterrand's FGDS (Federation of the Democratic and Socialist Left) attacked the government's record on social and economic policies, and in December 1966 reached agreement with the PCF for their respective candidates to stand down in favour of the best-placed left-wing candidate after the first ballot. In January 1967 the small but intellectually distinguished PSU (United Socialist Party) joined the coalition of the Left. Much of the pre-electoral debate focused on the constitutional question of whether de Gaulle would appoint a non-Gaullist to the premiership should the Gaullists be defeated. A good deal of indignation was aroused by the General's reluctance to signal clearly that he would in fact abide by the verdict of the electorate. The Ben Barka Affair (in which a prominent Moroccan opposition leader was kidnapped in Paris in October 1965 at the behest of the Moroccan Minister of the Interior with the collaboration of the French intelligence service) had already served notice of the regime's contempt for legality, though to be fair, de Gaulle personally was outraged by the incident and broke off diplomatic relations with Rabat in consequence.

In the March 1967 elections the Gaullists did reasonably well on the first ballot, winning almost 38 per cent of the vote. Their nearest rivals were the Communists with 22 per cent, followed by Mitterrand's Federation with around 19 per cent. The Centre polled only 13 per cent. In the second ballot, however, the Gaullists received a nasty shock when not only did the left-wing pact hold up, but in addition it benefited from votes transferred from the Centre which the Gaullists had reckoned would revert almost automatically to them. The Gaullists lost 35 seats, which reduced their numbers in the Assembly to 200. Several cabinet ministers (Couve de Murville, Messmer, Sanguinetti) were among the victims. The Left made impressive gains (the PCF 32 seats, the Federation and PSU 31). At the end of the day the government could muster a majority of only two in the Assembly and was now even more beholden to the Independent Republicans of Giscard d'Estaing, who had won an extra nine seats, giving them 44 in all. Giscard, who resented having been replaced by Debré at the Ministry of Finance in 1965, gave his support only grudgingly. During the election campaign he had already indicated that he meant to take a critical stance towards de Gaulle and the Gaullists in his well-publicized phrase 'Yes, but . . .' – that is, only qualified and conditional support for the majority in order to serve notice that in the far from distant future he saw himself as a successor to de Gaulle.

The government's response to the near electoral defeat was to resort to decree rule in economic and financial matters from April to October 1967, which helped to create a sense of unease, if not crisis. It also had to cope with three votes of censure, which it narrowly survived. Within the ranks of the majority Giscard went out of his way to dissociate himself from the more unpopular aspects of the regime, while even the Gaullists themselves were divided internally. Prime Minister Pompidou was increasingly out of favour with de Gaulle, who blamed him for the setbacks, and was resented also by the old 'Free French' Gaullists (Debré, Couve de Murville), loyal only to the General, as well as the more 'left-wing' Gaullists (Capitant, Hamon, Vallon), who considered him excessively conservative and too much of a machine politician. Pompidou it was, however, who set about reorganizing the party in 1967. A political realist, he knew that he had to plan for a day when the General would be no more and Gaullism would have to survive without de Gaulle. In Pompidou's view, the best way to ensure this was to develop a modern conservative party, with mass appeal, identified not with grandeur but with economic prosperity and political stability. Time was very soon to vindicate his political astuteness.

Not that the political difficulties experienced by the Fifth Republic in the years before 1968 gave any hint of the convulsions that lay in store. Communist intransigence made co-operation among the opposition parties difficult, while the Gaullists made full use of all the apparatus of a powerful modern state – including control of broadcasting and interference with the liberty of the press, quite apart from the illegalities revealed by the Ben Barka affair – to consolidate their hold on power. The situation was that, by 1968, there appeared to be no real alternative to the continuation of Gaullist rule. Politics were stagnant. The explosion of May 1968 took place against a background of political frustration.

The May Events

The sense of frustration in France was not confined to opposition politicians. It was shared by the young, and above all by the student population.

In part, student unrest in the late 1960s was a world-wide phenomenon, fuelled by American protests against US involvement in Vietnam and by a fashionable sympathy for Latin American revolutionaries such as Fidel Castro and Che Guevarra. In France itself, the 'baby boom' of the post-war era resulted in a student population in the 1960s 10 times larger than that on the eve of the Second World War. In the academic year 1938–9 there were some 60,000 students in higher education, in 1967–8 605,000. Unfortunately, the University had not evolved new structures to cope with the increased demand but was still that of Ferry and Lavisse, aiming to impart a general culture to the sons and daughters of the comfortably off bourgeoisie. But for the children of the middle and petty bourgeoisie who had secured university places, the old ideal was no longer good enough. They wanted an education that would guarantee them employment at the end of their studies in an increasingly competitive job market – without, however, reducing them to being mere lackeys of the capitalist system. French students also had legitimate grounds for complaint in the overcrowded classes in which they were taught, the lack of access to teachers, and the inflexible, centralized, bureaucratic university administration which treated them like a kind of academic proletariat. Failure rates were high, with only 30 out of 100 students succeeding in graduating in the Arts and Law faculties.

It was no accident that the student troubles of May 1968 began at Nanterre, a new campus in the Paris suburbs designed to cope with the overspill from the old Sorbonne. The site itself was hideous, its buildings the epitome of soulless modern architecture. Overcrowding was a particular problem, since numbers had grown from 2,000 in 1964 to 11,000 in 1968, without a corresponding increase in facilities: for instance, building work on the library was begun only in 1968. In consequence, students spent much of their time commuting between Nanterre and the Latin Quarter, all the more so because of ludicrous bureaucratic rules which, for example, obliged them to purchase tickets for the use of the Nanterre swimming pool in the centre of Paris. Though the regulations at Nanterre were more liberal than at some other faculties, students were irked by all kinds of petty restrictions, especially by attempts to segregate the sexes. Another feature of Nanterre was that it had a large sociology department (with about 700 students) who evinced a higher than average level of social awareness and politicization. Daniel Cohn-Bendit, a German national, soon to be known as 'Danny the Red', was only one of many student activists disillusioned with the orthodox Left, above all with the PCF, and attracted to more extreme leftist *groupuscules* of Trotskyites, Maoists and other dissident sects. There was also a certain amount of student support for left-wing Catholicism and *mendésisme*.

Protest against the Vietnam war was the issue that served to bring all of these disaffected elements together. In March 1968 bomb attacks were carried out on American targets in France, notably on the offices of the American Express Company. When one of the terrorists was discovered to be a Nanterre student, the militants orchestrated a campaign to protest at his arrest and 'victimization', which gave birth to the 22 March movement and led to clashes with the university authorities over proposed teach-ins on 'imperialism'. The administration closed the campus between 28 March and 1 April, which in turn produced further incidents for which leaders of the 22 March movement were disciplined, followed again by more protests. On 3 May all teaching at Nanterre was suspended.

The centre of student agitation then switched to the old Sorbonne in the centre of Paris, where attempts were made to mobilize support for Nanterre. The Rector, fearing violent confrontations between left-wing and right-wing students, suspended classes at the Sorbonne too, and called in the police to prevent disorder. That proved to be a fatal decision. When the police arrested a number of student demonstrators they were attacked by other students and responded with characteristic brutality, lashing out with their batons and making liberal use of tear gas. In the course of the fighting, numerous people were injured, including 80 policemen, and 590 people were arrested. Over the next 10 days similar scenes were to be re-enacted on an ever-increasing scale, to the concern and astonishment of television viewers not only in France but all over the world. The students erected barricades and demanded the release of arrested fellow-students, along with a ban on police on university premises and the reopening of classes. Protracted battles were fought on 6 May, when over 400 students were arrested, and again on 10–11 May, following the government's announcement that the university would remain closed indefinitely, and an order to the police to clear the barricades. The students hurled stones and Molotov cocktails at the police: the police battered students and even innocent bystanders, including Red Cross volunteers, indiscriminately. At the end of the long night of violence 460 arrests had been made, 367 people were wounded and 200 cars had been burned.

The sight of sadistic riot policemen (CRS) setting about their work with relish caused attention to be focused away from the student revolt and onto the issue of police brutality. The trade unions called a one-day general strike for 13 May, in which more than 750,000 workers and students marched together through Paris to register concern at the latest and most disturbing examples of the abuse of power in the Gaullist State. The entry of the workers onto the scene was ultimately what distinguished the French May events from other manifestations of student protest throughout the world. From small and spontaneous beginnings, some 10 million workers were eventually to come out on strike, inevitably posing the question of whether or not a revolutionary situation had thereby been created.

The workers' movement began not in Paris but in the provinces, first at the aircraft factory at Nantes, then at the Renault plant near Rouen. The spontaneous nature of the protests was seen in the lack of any mobilizing order from the principal trade unions. On the contrary, leaders of the Communist-dominated CGT were alarmed by workers' involvement in the affairs of 'adventurist' students, though CFDT militants were more sympathetic. No doubt the students' protest set an example for workers to follow, notably in the matter of sit-ins and occupations, and perhaps, too, student recourse to a rhetoric of struggle helped to rekindle some enthusiasm for the old *ouvriériste* revolutionary tradition. Essentially, however, the workers' action should be set against grievances of their own which they had long been harbouring. Low wages were one source of discontent: workers' pay had not kept pace with the great economic boom and the gap in income between workers and management had widened. Unemployment was another grievance, especially among the young and the unskilled. By May 1968 more than 500,000 workers were registered as unemployed. Young workers, too, were disaffected with the unions, particularly with the CGT, which, since the great strikes of 1947 and 1948, had given the impression of impotence, compensating for its inability to extract concessions from employers with the rhetoric of revolution and with ritualistic commemorations of previous struggles. Employers were every bit as obdurate as in the past. Like Peugeot in 1967, they were prepared, if necessary, to resort to the riot police; in the Peugeot incident the police cleared the factory and killed two workers in the process. Factory discipline was still exceptionally tough, and management, especially in car plants and in the engineering trades, consciously relied upon immigrant labour to keep the workforce divided and/or docile. But it was above all the sense of having no say in the running of the factories that alienated workers, none more so than the 'new working class' of the automated plants. Hence the constantly reiterated demand for 'participation' in May 1968, which the CGT rejected as class collaboration but which the CFDT, at least, recognized as an authentic *cri de coeur* on the part of workers who wanted to be treated with dignity and humanity. At Nantes, this demand was translated into reality by a Central Strike Committee, which, like a virtual soviet, was the real source of authority in the city for a week.

The Nantes example was not followed elsewhere, but never the less the aspiration for change was general. The theme of 'participation' was taken up by the professions. Doctors denounced their antiquated professional structures and the rigid, bureaucratic hierarchy which obtained in French hospitals. In the world of the arts, painters, critics, directors of art galleries, musicians, film-makers, actors and writers all protested at the State's organization of the arts in France. One of the most serious revolts was at the ORTF, whose employees demanded an end to political interference in broadcasting.

With protest evident on such a massive scale, the fate of the regime itself seemed to hang in the balance. Two related questions pose themselves. One:

was May 1968 a revolutionary situation? Two: was de Gaulle in real danger of being overthrown? The answers to these questions inevitably depend on how one interprets *les événements*: just what did they all add up to?

The Significance of May 1968

For some, May 1968 was not a revolutionary situation but a psychodrama. Thus, in *La révolution introuvable*, Raymond Aron contemptuously dismissed the student revolt as a vast, ego-boosting, adventure for young people who were merely acting, playing out roles, with no real desire to start a genuine revolution. Coming from the most privileged strata in French society, they had little enough to protest about and their recourse to anti-intellectual sloganizing – 'Rape your *alma mater*'; 'Be realistic, demand the impossible'; and so on – was an outrage to civilized values and reasoned discourse. Likewise Richard Cobb, Professor of Modern History at Oxford University and a long-standing and sympathetic student of France and the French, condemned the whole episode as a disgrace inspired by the 'prophets of the anti-culture', sub-marxist philosophers and dehumanizing, quantifying sociologists.

At the time, this point of view was put most forcefully by the PCF, which denounced the 'adventurism' of the would-be student revolutionaries. Georges Marchais, the party's secretary-general, dismissed Cohn-Bendit as a 'German anarchist' and generally branded the students as fascist *provocateurs* who basically despised the working class. Only the PCF stood for the real interests of the workers, recognizing the need to negotiate with the bourgeois State on their behalf and prudently avoiding giving the army an excuse to step in to smash the institutions of organized labour. Whether or not the Communist analysis was correct, it is fairly certain that the PCF, by adopting such a stance, made revolution extremely unlikely, if not impossible. The party consciously checked the development of the May movement, rather than leading it to revolution: hence Cohn-Bendit's accusations of 'betrayal' and far-Left condemnations of 'Stalinist filth'.

Those who persist in seeing May '68 as a case of *révolution manquée* point to the sheer scale of the revolt, indicating the massive dissaffection among the French people. Ultimately, they argue, the May movement amounted to a rejection of modern capitalist society, dominated by huge corporations and faceless, soulless, technocrats, slaves to the ideology of economic moderniz-ation and economic growth. Demands for 'participation' and *autogestion* were new and authentic articulations of the class struggle. Furthermore, the strikes and sit-ins placed power in the workers' hands: all they had to do was use it. The vacillation of the government in the crisis created the opportunity for a seizure of power, above all when de Gaulle 'disappeared' on 29 May. And indeed it seems to have been the case – though this was not known at the time – that de Gaulle's nerve had cracked and that he went off intending to seek refuge in Germany.

The crisis, undeniably, was a real one, but it was neither as great as the student revolutionaries made out nor yet as slight as the Communists claimed. De Gaulle's nerve may have failed momentarily, but in Baden-Baden his old adversary General Massu seems to have convinced him that he should return to France and resume command of the situation, which he did most effectively on 30 May, broadcasting to the nation that he himself would not resign and that he had no intention of changing his Prime Minister, as the leaders of the parliamentary opposition had been demanding. At the same time, he declared the National Assembly dissolved and ordered fresh elections. So began a Gaullist backlash. More than 500,000 supporters (mainly solid bourgeois citizens) marched down the Champs-Eylsées to express their solidarity with the General. The party changed its name to the Union pour la Defénse de la République (UDR) and, profiting form the disarray in the ranks of the Left as well as from widespread anxieties about public order, won a crushing electoral victory at the polls on 23 and 30 June 1968, with 358 seats out of 485. The fact was that there was no acceptable alternative to de Gaulle, with whom the most prominent of the opposition leaders, Mitterrand and Mendès-France, could not compete. It should be added that the strategy of calling fresh elections was that of Prime Minister Pompidou, and, even had de Gaulle remained in Germany, there is no evidence that the French State itself was on the point of collapse or that Pompidou could not have assumed responsibility for the maintenance of law and order.

Meanwhile, workers had begun to end their stoppages and to drift back to work. Student militants found themselves marginalized and harrassed as much by the CGT as by the CRS. The 'events' had failed to produce a revolution but they did produce some material gains for workers in the shape of the wage deals for which the PCF had been pressing. By the agreements signed at the Ministry of Social Security, situated in the rue de Grenelle (27 May), workers were offered an immediate pay rise of about 7 per cent, to be followed by another 3 per cent in October. The SMIC was to be increased by 30 per cent. More ambitious demands for 'participation' and the introduction of new practices in the field of relations between workers and management had to be dropped, to the dismay of the CFDT and many other non-CGT militants. May '68 left the trade-union movement in some disorder. As for the students, they had to be content with the law on educational reform of 12 November 1968, piloted through parliament by the veteran politician Edgar Faure in his new capacity as Minister of Education. The aim was to expand the higher-education system to create 67 universities nationally by 1972 (with 13 of them located in the Paris area). Elected student representatives were assigned places on the governing councils. A certain degree of decentralization was introduced into the administration of the higher-education sector.

In the short-term, the May events appeared to have generated a great deal of excitement, but little in the way of radical change. After the June elections, the Fifth Republic seemed more deeply entrenched than ever. The one surprise was that de Gaulle decided to remove the architect of the electoral victory, Georges Pompidou, and replace him with the technician Couve de Murville, formerly foreign minister. But the new order was not to last long. In April 1969 de Gaulle effectively committed political suicide when, in attempting to curb the powers of the Senate (an institution which reminded him of everything he disliked about the Fourth and the Third Republics), he unwisely called a referendum which conflated two distinct political issues – the Senate question and that of regional reform. Having put his prestige on the line, he felt obliged to resign when the electorate voted 'no' by 53.2 to 46.7 per cent on 27 April 1969. In a communiqué issued from Colombey, he announced.

Je cesse d'exercer mes fonctions de Président de la République. Cette décision prend effet aujourd'hui à midi.

The impact was profound. Many wondered if there could be life for the Fifth Republic after de Gaulle.

19
After de Gaulle: The Presidencies of Pompidou and Giscard 1969–1981

General de Gaulle did not long outlive his departure from office. After a trip to the west of Ireland, he had retreated to the seclusion of Colombey-les-Deux Eglises to continue writing his memoirs, but death overtook him on 9 November 1970. His passing marked the end of an era. It did not, however, contrary to what many feared and others hoped, spell the end of the regime.

The Pompidou Years 1969–1974

That there would be life for the Fifth Republic after de Gaulle had already been signalled by the arrangements made for an interregnum following the General's resignation. Pending fresh elections, the presidency was exercised by the President of the Senate, as provided by the Constitution, though it was ironic that the man in question had to be Alain Poher, a champion of parliamentary rights against presidential power and the leading orchestrator of the '*non*' vote in the referendum. Having discovered a taste for the presidential office after all, Poher decided to run in the elections of June 1969, but he was denied a seven-year term by de Gaulle's former premier, Georges Pompidou. Indeed, in the first ballot, Poher was lucky to finish second behind Pompidou, only marginally ahead of the strong Communist candidate, Jacques Duclos (Pompidou obtained 44.5 per cent of the vote, Poher 23 per cent and Duclos 21 per cent). The biggest losers, however, were the *gauchistes*, who were routed: Michel Rocard of the PSU won only 3.6 per cent of the vote, and the Trotskyite Alain Krivine 1 per cent. Evidently, the spirit of May '68 could not be translated into anything as substantial as votes. The other significant losers in the presidential elections were the socialists. Wracked by internal divisions, the SFIO could muster only 5 per cent of the vote behind its compromise candidate Gaston Defferre. After the second ballot, in which Pompidou won 57.6 per cent of the vote against Poher's 42.4 per cent, a Gaullist president succeeded de Gaulle. The institutions of the Fifth Republic were in safe hands.

Pompidou was well aware that de Gaulle would be a hard act to follow: as he told his prospective electors, France would have to settle for someone a little 'less great' than the General. Consolidation rather than grandeur was his main theme. The new president was no mere cypher, however, but a real political heavyweight. Born the son of an *instituteur* in the backward Cantal, Pompidou was a classic case of the scholarship boy of the Third Republic made good via the *lycée* and the École Normale Supérieure, and had finished up as a member of the Conseil d'Etat and a banker with Rothschilds. Brought to the notice of the General as a man of considerable administrative ability, from 1945 he served as a key policy advisor. Unknown to the general public when he was appointed prime minister in 1962, he used his six years in office to build up a strong power base, to the point where, by 1968, he seemed the obvious heir apparent to de Gaulle. Indeed, it may well have been the very strength of his position which prompted the General to dump him so unceremoniously in the aftermath of the May events in favour of the much less threatening Couve de Murville, a career diplomat. For a brief period, Pompidou found himself out in the cold, abandoned by the General and the object of rumours that he had connexions with the criminal underworld. When de Gaulle suddenly quit the political scene in 1969, however, Pompidou was still able to impose himself as the obvious Gaullist candidate for the succession.

For his premier, Pompidou chose Jacques Chaban-Delmas, a Resistance hero and a popular Gaullist parliamentarian with a youthful, *sportif*, image. The MRP veteran Maurice Schumann was appointed Foreign Minister, René Pleven went to the Ministry of Justice and the Independent Republican Valéry Giscard d'Estaing returned to the Ministry of Finance. The Chaban government was therefore by no means a strictly orthodox Gaullist team and it got off to a dramatic start when the prime minister announced his programme to the Assembly. Promising a 'new society' in place of the 'blocked society' deemed (at least by the sociologists) to be at the core of the malaise which had produced the events of May '68, Chaban announced that the state needed to open a 'dialogue' with its citizens, who had the right to be more fully consulted in the decision-making process. A far-reaching package of reforms was promised which, *inter alia*, envisaged a further reduction of government interference in the running of the state broadcasting service, the ORTF, and a series of initiatives in the social field designed to promote a more 'contractual' relationship between government and people. In consequence, several million workers were put on monthly rather than weekly wages: the minimum wage was to be modified in line with the cost of living: nationalized industries such as the railways, electricity and the Paris transport system were given greater autonomy: and by a law of 16 July 1971 workers were promised greater opportunities for training and development. In keeping with Chaban's commitment to decentralization and a reduction in the powers of what he called 'the octopus state', he also made gestures towards regional autonomy in a law of 1972 which prescribed the setting up of 22 regional assemblies to be elected by indirect suffrage and the introduction of advisory councils in each region.

Yet, for all the rhetoric, Chaban's 'new society' remained more of a publicity slogan than a social reality. The underlying sense of social crisis had not vanished. In 1969 some 2.25 million days of work were lost because of strikes. The figures doubled in 1971, a year of incessant industrial conflict, fuelled partly by rising expectations among workers. Moreover, in tandem with reform, the government pursued more traditional strong-arm methods to quell dissent. In 1970 the leftist group *Gauche prolétarienne* was suppressed and the journalists of the newspaper *La Cause du Peuple* brought to trial. Regional reform was pure window-dressing: none of the measures introduced removed overall state control in the regions. Above all, Chaban's vision of the 'new society' was not shared by his master at the Elysée. Pompidou never forgave his prime minister for having embarked on a reform programme without prior consultation with the President. Though Chaban received a vote of confidence in the National Assembly in May 1972, by July Pompidou was ready to replace him with a premier more in tune with his own thinking.

Pompidou, like his predecessor, had no intention of permitting a premier to build up support in the National Assembly or in the country in such a way as to allow a challenge to the supreme authority of the president. If anything, Pompidou increased presidential authority, intervening over the head of the prime minister to impose his own policies (especially in the area of finance and economic affairs). Thus it was Pompidou personally who sabotaged Chaban's regional projects. Parliament, too, was treated with some disdain – too much for even some Gaullist deputies. On the other hand, Pompidou remained faithful to the idea of 'non-party' government and sought to build up a majority that included non-Gaullists (despite the fact that after the 1968 elections the UDR had an absolute majority). Like de Gaulle, Pompidou wanted to be able to claim that he was the spokesman for 'the nation' rather than for any single party or interest group. He also maintained the General's practice of addressing the public directly through television and press conferences, though only once did he have recourse to another of de Gaulle's favourite devices: the referendum.

The conduct of foreign policy also gave Pompidou the opportunity to enhance both his personal authority and that of his office. The broad lines of Gaullist policy were maintained, but there were significant changes of style and detail. Pompidou, less confident, perhaps, about his ability to bestride the world stage, settled for a more 'European' approach to foreign policy. Thus, just as de Gaulle had twice personally vetoed British entry into the Common Market, Pompidou personally agreed to enlargement of the Community, though he subsequently went through the motions of testing public reactions in the referendum of 23 April 1972. Pompidou's enthusiasm for the EEC stopped well short of support for political integration, however, as was demonstrated in October 1972 at a meeting of the Nine in Paris, which broke up without reaching agreement on the issue of political union. As for de Gaulle, so too for Pompidou the concept of French national soverignty was sacrosanct.

French 'independence' in foreign policy was manifested also in Pompidou's opposition to a bi-polar world of two power 'blocs' under the domination of the United States and the Soviet Union, and in his attachment to a French nuclear deterrent. As de Gaulle had insisted, France alone should decide how best to respond to threats to its interests and the option of recourse to nuclear weapons continued to be viewed as essential to the maintenance of an independent policy. Pompidou therefore continued to carry out nuclear testing and sought to improve the capacity of French nuclear weapons. To underline the 'independent' profile of France, he travelled extensively to meet face to face with other world leaders, visiting the United States, the Soviet Union and China (twice) as well as other European countries. By way of resisting US leadership in the West, he refused to countenance a disarmament conference and rejected proposals that would have permitted a negotiated reduction of American and Soviet forces in Europe. Similarly, he stayed away from the Strategic Arms Limitation Talks (SALT) and, on the grounds that France had not been consulted, protested at the agreement reached by the US and the USSR in the summer of 1973 for preventing the outbreak of nuclear war. American proposals in the same year for a new Atlantic Charter also antagonized Paris and provoked a call for a 'European' policy that would frustrate American designs to exercise hegemony over the states of Europe. Anti-Americanism was possibly more rampant under Pompidou and his Foreign Minister Michel Jobert than it had been under de Gaulle.

Similarly, Pompidou followed the example of de Gaulle in cultivating better relations with Moscow, notably through economic ties. In the aftermath of the brutal Soviet invasion of Czechoslovakia in 1968, it was, however, difficult to see what France stood to gain by proffering friendship to the Soviets. In so far as the latter were interested in *détente*, they were much more tempted by the possibilities opened up through the *Ostpolitik* of West German Chancellor Willy Brandt than by Gallic goodwill. France was in no position to bargain with the Soviet Union on an equal footing and Pompidou's pro-Soviet gestures could only exacerbate Franco-American relations without winning new influence in the Kremlin. The result of Pompidou's posturing on the world scene was the increasing diplomatic isolation of his country.

Of course, as for de Gaulle, so also for Pompidou foreign policy was viewed primarily from the angle of its likely repercussions on French domestic affairs. His decision to hold a referendum on the enlargement of the European Community, for example, was inspired less by any genuine conviction that the public had a right to be involved in the making of foreign policy than by a crafty calculation that here was an opportunity both to demonstrate the popularity of his policies, and to boost his personal standing as president, while at the same time exposing the divisions in the ranks of the Left on the issue of Europe. In the event, the manoeuvre backfired, since only the Communists campaigned strongly for a 'no' vote and a Socialist call for abstention was heeded by 40 per cent of the electorate. Pompidou comfortably won 68 per cent of the votes actually cast, but the poor turn-out was widely interpreted as a rebuff. The president's prestige was dented rather than reinforced.

The setback in the referendum of April 1972 doubtless strengthened Pompidou's belief that it was time for a change of government. In July 1972 Chaban was replaced by Pierre Messmer, a premier more congenial both to himself and to 'orthodox' Gaullists. A Free French hero with a background in colonial administration, Messmer had served for 10 years as de Gaulle's Minister of Defence, and his cabinet included other hard-line Gaullists, one of whom took the sinister-sounding title of Secretary of State for Information. The appointment of another intransigent Gaullist deputy to head the ORTF was a further sign that Chaban's liberal experiment was over. As legislative elections loomed up on the horizon for March 1973, the government abandoned the language of *rassemblement* and, adopting a more openly right-wing stance, went on the offensive against the Left which, after its tribulations of 1968 and 1969, seemed once again to pose a serious threat to the Gaullist majority.

The transformation of the French Left was little short of remarkable. Its confidence boosted by the strong showing of Jacques Duclos in the presidential elections of 1969, the PCF under its new secretary-general, George Marchais, affirmed its commitment to a new policy of *ouverture* designed to establish its leadership over a united Left. Calling for the creation of an 'advanced democracy', the party also tried to loosen its ties with Moscow and proclaimed itself in favour of the 'Eurocommunism' already espoused by the Italians. The revival in the fortunes of the socialists was still more impressive. After the humiliation of Gaston Defferre in 1969, a number of militants, headed by Alain Savary, decided that the time had come for a clean break with the *molletiste* past and, abandoning even the name of the old SFIO, created a new Parti Socialiste (PS). Two years later, at the congress of Epinay, Savary's party was reinforced by the adhesion of the group known as the *Convention des Institutions Républicaines* headed by François Mitterrand, who in the process ousted Savary as leader of the party. Like the PCF, Mitterrand, too, was pledged to the unity of the Left, the elimination of the Centre and a return to bipolar politics in France. After protracted talks, agreement between socialists and communists was reached on a Common Programme for government, signed on 27 June 1972. Going well beyond the electoral pacts of 1924 and 1936, the *programme commun* contained specific proposals for legislation to be carried out by a government of the Left, notably the nationalization of some of France's leading industrial concerns. Revision of the constitution was also prescribed: the President would be elected for five rather than seven years, his right to resort to referenda would be circumscribed and his emergency powers eliminated. The Left also pledged its support for more liberal laws on divorce, contraception and abortion, and undertook to end private (meaning Catholic) education. Contentious issues, such as defence and foreign policy, where disagreements between the PCF and the PS remained, were left out of the programme. For the first time in 15 years, the parties of the Left began to sense that they were close to wielding power again. The belief that a new 'Popular Front' was in the making was further strengthened by the adhesion of some left-wing Radicals to the *programme commun*. One wing, the *Mouvement Réformateur*, led by the dynamic former editor of *L'Express*, Jean-Jacques Servan-Schreiber, believed that what the Radicals needed was a more modern and glamorous image, but despite the Kennedyesque rhetoric of Servan-Schreiber, the party maintained its conservatism and ties with the Centre. More left-wing Radicals, however, were ready to move closer to the socialists and the communists, and Robert Fabre's *Mouvement des Radicaux de Gauche* (MRG) signed the *programme commun* in July 1972.

In the run-up to the elections of March 1973, the Right tried to terrify the electorate with the twin evils of the expropriations and constitutional chaos that would inevitably result from a victory of the Left. Their propaganda was not in vain, since at the polls, despite gaining ground, the Left was unable to capture power. In a high turnout (81 per cent), the parties of the Left did well in the first ballot, the PCF polling 21.4 per cent of the vote and the PS 17.7, against 23.9 for the Gaullists, 12.5 for the *Mouvement Réformateur* and 10.3 for Giscard d'Estaing's Independent Republicans. In the second ballot, however, the fate of the Left was sealed when the Centre threw its votes behind the Gaullists, who topped the poll with 175 seats and 37 per cent of the vote. The socialists won 89 seats with 18.8 per cent of the vote: the communists 73 (15.4 per cent) and the Left Radicals 11 (2.3 per cent). The UDR no longer had an overall majority, but it could count on the support of the 54 Giscardian deputies and those of the 30 representatives of the *Mouvement Réformateur*. Pompidou had every reason to be satisfied with the outcome, and reappointed Messmer as prime minister. His one concession to the Left was to seek to implement their demand for a reduction in the presidential *septennat* to five years, but a bill laid before the two houses of parliament in October 1973 failed to mobilize the three-fifths majority required for constitutional change. Messmer shouldered most of the blame for the setback, but Pompidou also suffered a further loss in prestige.

What the French public did not know was that Pompidou was already a very sick man, stricken with a cancer that ultimately killed him on 2 April 1974. His presidency had successfully fulfilled the task he had set himself of preserving the institutions of the Fifth Republic and he also took pride in the economic progress which was such a marked feature of his years in power. Pompidou presided over the advent of a new and more dynamic France in the place of the old, static, rural order. But the transition was not effected without human and environmental losses to be set against the undoubted economic gains.

Expansion and Recession

From the mid 1940s France had enjoyed a period of spectacular economic growth, which continued, and indeed accelerated, during the period of the Pompidou presidency. French progress may have been matched, and sometimes bettered, by other countries in the EEC, but it was impressive nevertheless. Already by 1967 France had overtaken Britain in both industrial output and in the standard of living. The shock of 1968 brought only a temporary interruption to the expansionist trend. Expansion was not of course continuous, and checked by periodic, or cyclical, slumps. Inflation, too, had been a worry through the 60s, necessitating recourse to austerity packages such as that introduced by Finance Minister Valéry Giscard d'Estaing in 1963–4. The problem had been compounded by de Gaulle's stubborn refusal to devalue the franc, but Pompidou did not make the same mistake. On 8 August 1969 he allowed Giscard to carry out a swift and unexpected devaluation of 12.5 per cent, which gave a substantial boost to French exports and helped to cut the deficit on the balance of payments. Industrial growth continued at the high rate of 5.5 per cent a year. Giscard also made a point of balancing his budgets. True, inflation persisted at around 7 per cent a year until 1973, and rose above 14 per cent in 1973–4, but the *real* wages of workers rose even more dramatically (by at least 35 per cent between 1969 and 1973). Fewer than a million workers qualified for the minimum wage, the SMIC. Full employment was maintained, and a minority of workers even benefited from the extension of profit-sharing schemes in their industries. Under Pompidou, the French prospered as never before.

At the Elysée, the President did everything in his power to encourage economic development. Like a latter-day Napoleon III, he built on the well-established tradition of state intervention in the economy, investing massively in the infrastructure of the public sector – motorways, the Parisian transport system, the telephone service. In 1967 France had fewer than 500 miles of motorway – less even than Britain. Pompidou and his Minister of Equipment, Albin Chalandon, gave the go-ahead to private entrepreneurs to expand the network. In 1970 the *autoroute Sud* (Paris–Lyon–Marseille) was completed, along with the Boulevard Périphérique, the ring road around Paris. By the mid 1970s France was opening up new motorways at the rate of 350 miles a year, the highest in Europe. By 1981 six motorways stretched from the Boulevard Périphérique to other parts of France. Tolls were (and are) relatively high, but the gains for both trade and the well-being of the private motorist are difficult to deny.

Pompidou also helped to provide Paris with one of the best public transport systems in the world. In addition to the renovation of underground stations, the renewal of rolling stock and extension of the existing metro network, a new Regional Express Network (RER) was inaugurated with the objective of linking a number of suburban centres to Parisian metro stations. The first line, built at a cost of some 5,000 million francs, opened in 1977 and linked St Germain-en Laye in the west to central Paris and the suburb of Boissy-Saint Léger in the south-east. By 1982 there was a direct line to Roissy airport and to the suburbs of the south-west. The improvement in the telephone service was equally dramatic. In 1970 French telephones were still primitive. Local calls required the use of special tokens (*jetons*) and, given the lack of booths, often had to be made from crowded and noisy cafes. Long-distance dialling was a nightmare, involving long queues at the post-office. To have a line installed took, literally, years. Pompidou, along with his successor Giscard, appreciated that improved communications were a vital part of the drive for economic modernity. Thus, from 1970, vast sums were invested in the telecommunications industry. Between 1969 and 1979 the budget of the Ministry of Posts and Telecommunications (PTT) expanded ten fold and the number of lines more than quadrupled to some 17 million.

Another side of expansion was evident in what architects and town planners euphemistically term 'urban renewal'. Nowhere was this more apparent than in the capital. Pompidou believed that Paris required visible symbols of its status as the principal city of an advanced technological civilization and he was therefore an enthusiast for the erection of skyscrapers, or 'Manhattanization'. De Gaulle himself had already set precedents in this respect, having acquiesced in the tower-block schemes of his technocratic Prefect of the Seine, Paul Delouvrier, who had pronounced in 1963 that 'Paris must marry its century'. The most startling monument to this dictum was the Maine–Montparnasse tower, a huge glass and concrete edifice set between two other high-rise blocks, which went up between 1968 and 1970. Work had already begun on a new complex of shops and offices at the Porte Maillot, and also at La Défense, beyond the Champs Elysées, as envisaged by the planners of the Fourth Republic. Pompidou, however, authorized numerous other projects, with the result that in the early 70s the beautiful Parisian skyline was ruined. But for his untimely death, the damage to the Parisian environment might have been even greater. Fortunately, one person who became increasingly alarmed at Pompidou's depredations was Giscard d'Estaing, who from his window at the Finance Ministry in the rue de Rivoli was a daily witness to the horrors taking place at La Défense. Plans for a pair of gigantic towers to 'complement' the Arc de Triomphe were scrapped once he became President, though by 1981 La Défense had still grown into a high-rise city with 20,000 residents and 40,000 office workers. Giscard also vetoed the construction of an expressway on the Left bank of the Seine similar to that which had been built on the Right bank. Had it gone ahead, the foundations of Notre Dame cathedral could have been threatened. Under Pompidou, barbarity was the bedfellow of modernity.

It is perhaps fitting that Pompidou's own monument should be the Centre Georges Pompidou, or 'Beaubourg', a bizarre glass and tubular building which brazenly displays its innards as architectural features. Conceived by Pompidou in 1969 as a vast cultural space for a permanent collection of modern art and for staging multifarious artistic events, it cost 1,000 million francs to build before opening eventually in 1977. In addition to the modern art museum, it houses a substantial, open-access library, an avant-garde musical research centre, various auditoria and temporary exhibitions. As a crowd-puller, the building proved an instant success, immediately establishing itself as the single biggest tourist attraction in Paris. Likewise, its forecourt has become an animated stage for street spectacles performed by mimes, musicians, fireaters and the like. As a mixture of the extravagant, the brash and the new, it is a postmodernist memorial entirely appropriate to its begetter.

Not far from the Centre Pompidou an even more ambitious development got under way at Les Halles, the warren of wine and food markets that Zola described as 'the belly of Paris'. Because of the traffic snarl-ups it occasioned, de Gaulle himself had taken the initiative in closing down first the Halle aux Vins then, after a struggle, the meat market and the fruit and vegetables market, banished to La Villette and Rungis respectively. The question for Pompidou in 1969 was what to do with the old premises. True to form, he favoured business plans for a massive complex of shops and offices, the centrepiece of which would be a convention for world trade, though there was to be space also for a luxury hotel and a new metro station. The handsome wrought-iron pavillions of Victor Baltard were destroyed, but at Pompidou's death all that remained in their place was a huge hole in the ground, the *trou des Halles* – perhaps an even more appropriate monument to the deceased president than the Beaubourg. Once again it was Giscard who put a stop to Pompidou's vulgar schemes, though his own plans for a formal garden were blocked by the Paris Municipal Council headed by Jacques Chirac. In the end, the *trou* became the 'Forum', which opened in 1979 as an underground shopping and leisure complex built below a courtyard surrounded by structures of glass and aluminium.

As Richard Cobb has pointed out, however, the greatest damage inflicted on Paris has been human rather than architectural. The inexorable drift to the *banlieue* continued, emptying the city of its characteristic popular element and turning it into an ever more bourgeois (and aged) population. In 1970 Paris was a city of some 2.6 million people, while its suburbs numbered some 5.6 million. By the mid 1980s, the city's population had fallen to 2.1 million, losing 20,000 inhabitants a year. The popular classes who had inhabited areas like the Marais and enjoyed warm neighbourhood sociability found themselves exiled to the soulless *grandes ensembles* of the *banlieue*, their places taken in the renovated apartment blocks by the rich and upwardly mobile. Pompidou, impervious to the lessons of Sarcelles, authorized the construction of nine new towns, five of them in the greater Paris region. Even if there were a few improvements on the prototype, these dreary dormitory cities supply further evidence that the price of material prosperity was all too often paid in a diminution in the quality of life.

Prosperity, in any case, was itself under threat by the end of Pompidou's presidency. The long post-war boom, which French analysts refer to as *les trente glorieuses* (the thirty glorious years), was about to end. Changes in the world economic system were transforming the circumstances which had done so much to facilitate growth in the developed countries – cheap energy, raw materials and transport, along with a lack of competition from undeveloped countries. From 1974, the French economy, like that of all other advanced countries, entered a period of protracted difficulties, the principal symptoms of which were a sharp falling off in economic growth, rampant inflation and a steep rise in unemployment. The fourfold hike in the price of oil imposed by a cartel of oil-producing Arab states in 1973 was both a cause and a manifestation of the crisis. Its impact on France was immediate, since in 1973 France imported more than three-quarters of its energy needs (considerably more than competitors like Britain [47 per cent] and West Germany [50 per cent].

Furthermore, even without the advent of the world recession, there are grounds for thinking that the great era of expansion was over for France. During the Pompidou presidency, when growth was at its height, problems persisted in the midst of prosperity. Inflation mounted after 1969. By 1973 there were 300,000 unemployed. The performance of French exports of manufactured goods still lagged behind that of its major competitors. Foreign investment by French investors was much less than that of foreign (especially American) investment in France. To survive, let alone thrive, in an increasingly competitive world, further painful adjustments were necessary in sectors such as textiles and the steel industry. Had he survived, Pompidou rather than his successor would have been obliged to confront all of these problems. As it was, the task fell to Giscard d'Estaing.

At first, neither Giscard nor his prime minister, Jacques Chirac, seem to have been fully cognisant of the magnitude of either the French or the world crisis, regarding it as a particularly nasty cyclical upset (largely attributable to the oil sheiks) amid a generally favourable trend towards growth. Traditional 'stop-go' methods were therefore applied. Finance Minister Fourcade introduced a credit squeeze in June 1974 and also raised taxes on profits. The result was the first industrial recession in France since 1945, higher unemployment but no compensating downturn in the rate of inflation. Chirac therefore insisted on a return to expansionism, and in September 1975 introduced reflationary measures, including tax incentives to private industry, lower interest rates, an increase in public spending, and higher welfare benefits. Consequently, the revival of production was accompanied by a huge budget deficit, a weakening of the franc, and even higher inflation.

The replacement of Chirac with the trained economist Raymond Barre in August 1976 was a sign that Giscard had at last woken up to the gravity of the economic situation. Attaching top priority to the battle against inflation, Barre put forward a Plan to combine economic stability with inflation-free growth. In September 1976 he raised taxes and introduced a freeze on wages and prices, while at the same time providing incentives for the creation of new jobs. Prices were not easily held down, however, and controls provoked opposition from many quarters, including the bakers, who succeeded, after their 'croissant war' of 1977–8, in having bread prices deregulated for the first time since the days of the French Revolution. Regulation was in any case only a temporary expedient for Barre who, from 1978, in accordance with neo-liberal orthodoxies, favoured the progressive liberalization of prices as the soundest counter-inflationary strategy. On the other hand, Barre succeeded in encouraging the development of technologically-based industries, notably electronics, communications and nuclear energy. The nuclear programme was particularly effective in reducing French dependence on outside energy supplies, which by 1981 was down to 50 per cent, with a projected further fall to 40 per cent. Imaginative tax concessions and loans to investors were important governmental contributions to industrial expansion and a significant rise in French exports. The result was that the economy continued to grow at a rate of around 3 per cent a year, the trade deficit was wiped out and the balance of payments, in deficit between 1973 and 1977, was converted into a surplus of $4 billion by 1978.

Barre's achievements were considerable, but partial. Inflation remained in double figures, averaging over 11 per cent between 1974 and 1981 (not bad, perhaps, by the abysmal standards of Britain, but not so impressive by comparison with more serious industrial competitors such as the USA, Japan and West Germany). Profits, too, were squeezed, dropping by an average 7 per cent by 1981. Unemployment rose to 1.7 million, women and young people being its principal victims. Certainly, Giscard and Barre were unlucky in having to cope with a second oil shock in 1979–80, which undermined a good deal of their work. Nevertheless, for largely political reasons, the president and his prime minister refused to risk the unpopularity that more radical economic surgery would have incurred with the electorate. The hard economic decisions that a conservative administration might have been expected to take – a decisive shift of emphasis towards boosting industry and profits at the expense of wages, an end to the overvaluation of the franc, which allowed Barre to doctor the figures of the trade balance while harming exports, and cuts in the social services, the costs of which outstripped the rate of growth and added to the tax burdens of already hard-pressed employers – were shelved in the run-up to the presidential elections of 1981. Many of the problems that plagued the Left after the victory of Mitterrand can be attributed to the failure of Giscard administration to confront the harsh economic realities of the late 1970s.

The Giscard Presidency 1974–1981

The sudden death of Pompidou was a shock, especially to the Gaullists and their allies. In a reversal of the 1969 situation, the Left immediately united around the candidature of the socialist leader François Mitterrand, while the parties of the Right squabbled among themselves. First into the race (with a haste that some thought unseemly) was the former premier, Jacques Chaban-Delmas. He, however, could not count on the support of all elements in the Gaullist movement: hence the entry of Jean Royer, who claimed to speak for the interests of small businesses. But other Gaullists still (most notably the Minister of the Interior, Jacques Chirac) preferred the still youthful but experienced Finance Minister and Independent Republican, Valéry Giscard d'Estaing, who could count also on support from Centrists like Jean Lecanuet and Servan-Schreiber. Jean-Marie Le Pen, a former *poujadiste*, and Bertrand Renouvin of *Action Française* represented the far Right. At the other end of the spectrum, the Trotskyites were split between Alain Krivine and Arlette Laguiller, while René Dumont ran as a Green candidate.

The chances of a left-wing victory looked good. On the first ballot, Mitterrand topped the poll with 43.2 per cent of the vote. Giscard was his nearest rival with 32.6 per cent, and he in turn was well ahead of Chaban, with 15.1 per cent. In the second ballot, however, the Right closed ranks behind Giscard and after a keenly contested campaign (the culmination of which was a televised debate between Mitterrand and Giscard on 10 May), it just managed to cling on to power. In a very high turnout (87 per cent) Giscard obtained 13.4 million votes (50.8 percent) and Mitterrand 13 million (49.2 per cent). The 'Majority', as it liked to call itself, continued to rule, though for the first time it was headed by a non-Gaullist, and one who was deeply distrusted by the most faithful disciples of the General.

Valéry Giscard d'Estaing was born in 1926 into a wealthy Catholic and conservative family. His father, an *inspecteur des finances* and member of the Institut, was also a militant in the *Action Française*. Having grown up in the smart sixteenth arrondissement of Paris, the youthful Giscard just managed to see war service in 1944–5. After brilliant studies at the École Polytechnique and ENA, he followed his father into the Ministry of Finance and married a daughter of the plutocratic Schneider family. As early as 1953 Finance Minister Edgar Faure brought him into his private office. Then, having succeeded his grandfather as deputy for the Puy de Dôme in 1956, Giscard went on to serve as a junior minister at Finance between 1959 and 1962, before becoming Minister of Finance himself between 1962 and 1966. Rankled by his dismissal, he deliberately distanced himself and his party of Independent Republicans from de Gaulle, describing their attitude to the government on 10 January 1967 as '*oui-mais*' – that is, support, but only on conditions. He also castigated 'the solitary exercise of power', and in April 1969 refused to support the referendum. The reservations of orthodox Gaullists regarding him are not difficult to comprehend.

Giscard presented himself as a proponent of 'an advanced liberal society', one that reconciled individual freedom with social justice through the elimination of poverty, discrimination and privilege. Like Pompidou, he held that a key function of the state was to promote economic progress and the generalization of prosperity, but he also argued that a certain degree of social engineering was required to allow individuals to develop their potential to the full. Outlined in his book *Démocratie française* (1976), these unoriginal ideas allowed Giscard to appear before the French public as a champion of reform. *Giscardisme*, however, was as much a matter of style as of political ideas, and in the early days of his *septennat* he cultivated a youthful, Kennedyesque image, striving to appear dynamic yet relaxed, a superior mind, yet in touch with ordinary people. His first days at the Elysée were notable for publicity stunts such as entertaining road-sweepers at the palace and having himself invited to the homes of humble peasants and artisans. He also toured two Parisian *bidonvilles* (shanty towns), shook hands with prisoners in the Lyon jail, and even allowed himself to be photographed wearing only his swimming trunks. The sham egalitarianism did not last long, however, and soon he was more famous for his arrogant and monarchical style (as in his insistence on being served first at table) and general extravagance, evident in his fondness for lavish safaris in Africa. In many respects, Giscard was a latter-day Orleanist.

Yet his initial commitment to reform was genuine enough. His ministerial team included only five Gaullists, though he shrewdly appointed the ambitious Jacques Chirac as his prime minister. Three posts went to colleagues in his own Independent Republican party and four to the *Mouvement Réformateur* (though Jean-Jacques Servan-Schreiber, having spoken out against French nuclear testing in the South Pacific, lasted a mere 10 days). Another novelty was the inclusion of two women: the popular Simone Veil as Health Minister, and the journalist Françoise Giroud as Secretary of State for the Condition of Women. A whole series of reformist measures followed. The voting age was reduced to 18. A law of 7 August 1974 aimed at the liberalization of broadcasting by breaking up the monopoly of the ORTF and replacing it with seven separate agencies (the chief executives of which, however, continued to be appointed by the government, so that in practice the State retained its control of television and radio). In recognition of the advent of the 'permissive society', a law of December 1974 facilitated the sale of contraceptives and made them available to teenagers without the consent of their parents. More specifically addressed to the rights of women were the Veil Law of 17 January 1975, which allowed abortions within the first 10 weeks of pregnancy, and the law of 11 July 1975 which legalized divorce by mutual consent. Although in the eyes of many feminists the abortion law was not considered radical enough (it was provisional for five years, had a conscience clause which allowed many doctors in public hospitals to opt out and was modest by comparison with the British law which allowed pregnancies to be terminated up to the twenty-eighth week), it aroused bitter opposition among many Gaullists and the Catholic Right, and had to be passed with the help of socialist votes. Other legislation in 1975 favoured the introduction of equal pay and equal employment opportunities for women.

Education was another of Giscard's main concerns and the law of 1975, sponsored by his Education Minister René Haby, was a landmark in the evolution of the French educational system, in that it introduced comprehensive schools at the secondary level. Nevertheless, it failed to remove the inequalities by which the children of workers ended up being prepared for some form of manual employment, while the offspring of the bourgeoisie took the *baccalauréat* in preparation for university and a career (the brightest pupils now choosing to specialize in mathematics as the avenue to the most prestigious and well paid professions). Giscard claimed to be keen to see the status of manual workers upgraded and launched a media campaign to try to change their image in the eyes of the public. More tangibly, he introduced legislation to assist workers to save and to have more leisure time, while a law of 29 December 1975 envisaged a gradual reduction of the retirement age to 60. It is doubtful, however, if any of these measures had the desired effect of reconciling manual workers to their lot and making them more productive, because more contented, members of the work force. If anything, Giscard may have contributed to a hardening of the lines of social division.

As regards Paris, Giscard ended the anomalous municipal status which had pertained since 1900. A law of 31 December 1975 gave the capital the same rights as the other communes of France, and above all the right to elect its own mayor. Political regionalism, however, was never on his agenda, though he wished to encourage economic development in the regions. His concern for the environment, on the other hand, has already been mentioned: another of Pompidou's schemes to be squashed was the *plan neige*, a project that would have defaced beautiful mountain scenery with hideous ski resorts. But not all of Giscard's planned reforms came to fruition. A projected capital-gains tax provoked a rebellion in the ranks of parliamentary Gaullists in April 1976 and only reached the statute book in emasculated form. Other areas where legislation was necessary to tackle serious problems, such as health and immigration, were ignored. Nor was he willing to abolish the death penalty. Indeed, as his presidency wore on, Giscard appeared to prefer to talk about reform rather than to act. His record as a reforming president, therefore, remains somewhat mixed.

Giscard's difficulty was that, while he wished to govern France from the centre, he lacked a strong power base of his own. In addition to his Indpendent Republicans, he could count on the support of radicals and other centrists such as Jean Lecanuet's *Centre des Démocrates Sociaux*, all of whom were combined in his *Union pour la Démocratie Française* (UDF) as an electoral coalition for fighting the legislative elections of 1978. But relations with his Gaullist allies were always strained, and became increasingly fractious as mounting personal antagonism between the president and his premier made a bad situation worse. In August 1976 Chirac resigned, barely troubling to conceal his rancour. In December he then relaunched the Gaullist party as the *Rassemblement pour la République* (RPR) as a springboard from which to mount his own eventual presidential challenge to Giscard. The feud carried on into 1977, when Chirac succeeded in being elected mayor of Paris, despite presidential pressure exercised on behalf of Giscard's close friend Michel d'Ornano.

Chirac was not Giscard's only problem. More serious were the economic difficulties which persisted despite the best endeavours of new premier, Raymond Barre, and which were increasingly exploited by the Left to attack the president. The rise in the popularity of the rejuvenated socialist party had continued since the presidential elections of 1974. Not only had it been strengthened by the adhesion of most of Michel Rocard's PSU but, more significantly, it had won the approval of the CFDT, thereby signifying the end of the historic antagonism between Catholics and a socialism that had been most often anti-clerical. Good showings in local elections and by-elections seemed to augur well for the success of the Left in the legislative elections scheduled for March 1978. Some two-thirds of the larger cities of France now had left-wing municipalities, even in towns in the traditionally Catholic and conservative West (for example, Nantes, Rennes and Angers). Symptomatic of Giscard's concern was the cabinet reshuffle carried out at the end of March 1977, where centrists such as Lecanuet and Poniatowski were dropped in favour of committed Gaullists, the most notable of whom, Alain Peyrefitte, went to the Ministry of the Interior to mastermind the electoral campaign of 1978.

What saved the 'Majority', however, was less the tactics of Peyrefitte than the spectacular own goal scored by the parties of the Left themselves in abandoning the unity achieved in the common programme of 1972. Chief culprits here were the communists, who insisting on the need to revise and extend the programme, proposed further nationalizations and trade union (ie

CGT) controls to be exercised over nationalized enterprises. These and other differences, including the matter of the nuclear programme, supported by the communists but resisted by elements in the PS, led to the acrimonious breakdown of talks in September 1977. In reality, the PCF had been uneasy about the apparent gains of unity for some time. In 1972 its chiefs had anticipated that the Left would be united under PCF leadership. By 1974, however, it was clear that the main beneficiaries of unity were the socialists, and fierce internal wrangles took place between the communist old guard, led by Roland Leroy, and the Marchais wing. While the Stalinists launched open attacks on Mitterrand and the PS in the pages of *L'Humanité*, the reformists went so far as to propose deleting the goal of the 'dictatorship of the proletariat' from the party's constitution. A fragile unity with the socialists survived through the cantonal elections of 1976 and the municipal elections of March 1977, but in the run-up to the legislative elections of 1978 it was clear that the PCF had to choose between its own survival as a distinctive entity or marginalization as the junior partner in a wider left-wing coalition. In breaking with the PS over the common programme, the party was fighting to preserve its separate identity and its traditional bastions of support, even at the expense of a victory of the Right.

Giscard and Barre were not slow to seize on the disarray in the camp of their enemies. Marchais was given unaccustomed time on television to vilify the socialist party's right-wing deviationism and betrayal of the common programme. To embarrass Mitterrand in a televised debate with Barre on 12 May 1978, *L'Humanité* published its own vastly inflated estimates for the cost of implementing the common programme: Mitterrand was thrown on the defensive, and repeatedly forced to deny the figures. So serious was the deterioration in relations between the PS and the PCF that not even the traditional arrangements for the second ballot could be negotiated. It is a measure of the disillusionment with the government that, despite their serious split, the parties of the Left still managed to win over 45 per cent of the vote, with the socialists winning 22.6 per cent and the PCF 20.6. Disunity was a serious handicap in the second ballot, however, whereas the Right was able to move up from 48.8 to 50.5. The outcome was that the RPR took 154 seats, the UDF 124, the PS 113 and the PCF 86. The communists tried to heap the blame for the Left's defeat on Mitterrand, but few doubted where it really lay. A number of the party's own intellectual luminaries, such as Louis Althusser and Jean Ellenstein, articulated their dismay at its spoiling tactics.

Giscard had good reason to be satisfied with the results of the 1978 elections, but those of the first elections to the European Parliament, held in June 1979 were somewhat more ambiguous. Organized on a national PR system, these were widely regarded as a dress rehearsal for the presidential elections of 1981. Giscard could not run himself, but in his place he fielded the ever-popular Simone Veil at the head of the UDF list, while the other parties put up their leaders as their principal candidates. Raymond Barre did not scruple to use his position as prime minister to campaign actively for the UDF, making virtual party political broadcasts on television and manipulating state patronage against candidates on other lists, notably that of RPR candidate Jacques Chirac, who was constantly represented in the media as rash and irresponsible. In a 61 per cent poll (low by French standards, if high by British), the UDF won 27.5 per cent of the vote, the RPR 16.2, the PS and the MRG combined 23.6 and the PCF 20.6. Overall, the Left polled fewer votes (47.3 per cent to the Right's 48.3) but because of the way seats were distributed it got 41 seats to the Right's 40. (UDF, 25: RPR, 15: PS/MRG, 22: PCF, 19.) Giscard was able to enjoy the spectacle of the recrimination which Chirac had to face within the ranks of the RPR, though he was less happy with François Mitterrand's claim to have led the Left to a victory in terms of seats. Indeed, so incensed was he that he set up a Verification Commission which in due course found that there were 'irregularities' in the allocation of seats to the Left. Giscard was revealed as a bad loser, and a man more than a little infatuated with the power and prestige of his presidential office.

For it was no longer as a domestic reformer but as a world statesman that Giscard increasingly wished to be recognized. Gaullist grievances against him included the charge that he was unfaithful to the legacy of the General, and, despite his protestations of fidelity to the ideal of 'independence', it was not entirely without foundation. Giscard proved himself to be much more of an 'Atlanticist' than either of his predecessors. Not only was he ready to involve France in the defence of an 'enlarged strategic space' (meaning Western Europe) but he also indicated his willingness to move towards the tactical deployment of nuclear weapons, which in effect was to embrace the NATO doctrine of 'flexible response' rather than the all-out retaliation envisaged by the Gaullist ultras. At the same time, Giscard was keen to divert a bigger share of the defence budget to conventional weapons, and ordered a halt to the sixth nuclear submarine which had been commissioned under Pompidou. In defence policy, if the rhetoric remained Gaullian, the Gaullist critics were right to detect a certain shift away from the strategy devised by their master.

On the other hand, the elements of continuity in foreign and defence policies were strong. The state maintained its close co-operation with the armaments industry, which government viewed as both a symbol of prestige and a source of wealth. A ban on further sales of arms to South Africa in 1975 was based less on idealism than on a hard-headed calculation that the market there was already sated and that better deals were to be had with other countries. It was no accident that arms sales were largest with countries like Iraq and Saudi Arabia which could repay France with oil. In 1978 arms sales were worth some 25 billion francs, representing a fivefold increase since 1970. And, if Giscard devoted more attention to France's conventional defences, setting up a new mobile special unit, he also continued to develop and deploy nuclear weapons, despite the fearful financial costs and the dubious military advantages. The plans to abandon the construction of a sixth nuclear submarine were revised in the face of Gaullist protests. Under Giscard, France remained outside the command structure of NATO. Nevertheless, he improved relations considerably, having been convinced of the need for closer co-operation with his European allies by the twin threat of the Soviet Union's overwhelming superiority in the field of conventional weapons and its SS 20 missiles.

In foreign policy, whereas de Gaulle had talked of '*grandeur*', Giscard coined the term '*mondialisme*' to imply the same kind of world role for France. Like his predecessors, he developed a penchant for 'summit' diplomacy and, the better to maintain his control over policy, appointed career diplomats rather than senior politicians as foreign minister. In keeping with

Gaullist antipathy to bi-polarism, he cultivated the 'non-aligned' powers such as India, which he visited in 1980 and identified, along with Yugoslavia and Algeria, as a key partner in the creation of a 'Third World' grouping of associated countries. Like Pompidou, he had high hopes of the Chinese, entertaining their leaders in Paris before travelling to China himself in 1981. In the Middle East, Giscard's main concern was to cement French friendship with oil-producing countries such as Iran, Iraq and Saudi Arabia through the export of arms and high technology. At the same time, he was keen to present France as a potential peacemaker in the dispute between Israel and the Arab states. Although apparently more accommodating to Israel (he lifted de Gaulle's embargo on arms sales imposed after the Six Day War), he maintained a basically pro-Palestinian line. In 1974 France supported a place at the United Nations for the Palestinian Liberation Organization (PLO), which, after a meeting between Foreign Minister Sauvagnargues and its leader Yasser Arafat, was allowed to open an office in Paris in 1975. In 1977 the French rejected West German and Israeli demands for the extradition of the terrorist Abu Daoud. In 1980 Giscard toured the Gulf states putting forward proposals for a comprehensive settlement of the Arab–Israeli conflict which would, while guaranteeing the survival of Israel, oblige the Israelis to give up the occupied territories and establish a Palestinian state. The pursuit of stability in the highly volatile region of the Middle East was one of the principal manifestations of Giscard's *mondialisme* – though hardly one that was notable for its success. On the contrary, French policy in the Middle East, in addition to antagonizing the Jewish community in France, contributed significantly to the confusion in the region. The downfall of the Shah in Iran (previously the recipient of French support) owed not a little to the asylum accorded by France to his fundamentalist opponent Ayatollah Khomeni. The ensuing chaos in Iran and the further embroilment of France in the affairs of the Lebanon were not strong advertisements for Giscard's diplomatic skills.

Francophone Africa was another area which loomed large in his plans. The former colonies were seen not only as providers of vital raw materials but also as important centres of the French language and French culture. Giscard, in the tradition established by de Gaulle, made African policy very much his own, establishing ties with African leaders and promising them French *coopération*, which meant financial, technological and, where appropriate, military aid. As some former colonies readily appreciated (none more than Algeria), French *coopération* was essentially a form of neo-colonialism. Only with difficulty did Giscard begin to improve relations with Algeria after 1978, the problem of the racism experienced by the 800,000 Algerians resident in France doing nothing to ease a delicate situation. With other African states, such as the Ivory Coast and Gabon, *coopération* worked smoothly enough. On the other hand, a state troubled by internal rebellions, such as Chad, could rely on French military intervention aimed at maintaining order and stability. It was French paratroopers, too, who in May 1978 crushed the rebels occupying the town of Kolwezi in Zaire (the former Belgian Congo, ruled by the corrupt and despotic General Mobutu). The most notorious case of direct intervention was in the Central African Republic in September 1979, when Giscard launched 'Operation Barracuda' to depose the 'Emperor' Bokassa after atrocity stories about him had been confirmed. Bokassa's downfall may have been well merited, but the manner of it disturbed observers both at home and abroad by its echoes of gung-ho nineteenth-century imperialism. And, while in the short term any successful feat performed by the French military would not lack for chauvinistic admirers, the wisdom of backing oppressive reactionary African regimes with the force of French arms was open to doubt. In 1981 sections of the French electorate remembered that, before overthrowing Bokassa, Giscard had not only sent him military support, but had even received gifts of diamonds from him.

Mondialisme did not signify any diminished preoccupation with the affairs of Europe. Rather, these afforded opportunities for new French initiatives. At the core of French policy was a close partnership with Germany, which Giscard consolidated through his personal friendship with the German Chancellor Helmut Schmidt. Giscard wanted France to be seen as the leading country in the powerful EEC bloc and to that end invented the idea of a 'European Council' to bring together the heads of government of EEC member states in regular 'summit' meetings. Giscard was also the prime mover in the establishment of the European Monetary System (EMS) in 1979, an arrangement which limited the possibilities for fluctuations in the value of national currencies and linked these also to a European Currency Unit (the ECU). 'Europe', however, remained for Giscard what it had been for de Gaulle – a platform for the promotion of French interests. In the course of setting up the EMS, Giscard wrung important concessions out of the Germans, while in individual clashes with other member states he showed himself to be more of a nationalist than a model of Community solidarity. Thus in 1975 his government, at the behest of the powerful French wine-growing lobby, acted illegally to stop imports of Italian wine into France. In 1979 the French took similar steps against imports of British lamb and Giscard, indifferent to the wrath of Mrs Thatcher, invariably showed himself hostile to British protests about the size of its contributions to the Community budget.

Giscard also pursued the old Gaullist goal of *détente*. The cruder anti-Americanism of the Pompidou era may have disappeared, but Giscard was faithful to the General's notion that the Soviet Union could be wooed and won. Even the Soviet invasion of Afghanistan in 1979 was not allowed to stand in the way of attempts to improve relations with Moscow. France remained impervious to Washington's call for the imposition of economic sanctions and a boycott of the Moscow Olympic Games in 1980. Giscard's hope was that France could make the running for a new European approach to the complicated question of disarmament, which would let the issue be decided neither by direct bilateral negotiations between the Americans and the Soviets nor by the endless general talks in Geneva. In 1978 France broached the subject at the UN, proposing that a conference be staged by European powers 'from the Atlantic to the Urals' (a phrase rightly associated with, though not actually used by, General de Gaulle).

If it was Giscard's intention that his wide-ranging activities in the sphere of foreign policy would confer on him the image of global statesman, far removed from the petty preoccupations of French party politics, he was cruelly deceived. To the extent that the French public took any interest in his diplomacy, it seemed to heed not so much his achievements as his increasingly remote and regal style. His indifference to the Soviet invasion of Afghanistan alienated at least some of the better-educated sections of the population, while the whiff of scandal could not entirely be blown away by his repeated denials of wrongdoing in the affair of the Bokassa diamonds. The Jewish community was offended by his pro-Palestinian stance and by his silence following a terrorist attack on a Jewish synagogue in Paris (though prime minister Barre compounded the offence by remarking that 'innocent people', as well as Jews, had been the victims of the attack). What mattered most to the electorate, however, was its perception of his handling of the economy. Whether fairly or not, he was held to be found wanting, since the year preceding the election coincided with an economic downturn which, if not worse than in most other European countries, was sufficiently serious to alarm voters long accustomed to a growth rate much higher than the 1 per cent achieved. As both prices and unemployment continued to rise, Giscard came under fire from the Left for his apparent complacency in the face of the human suffering engendered by the recession. And, as the elections drew closer, the Left once again succeeded in re-creating the unity which had been lost with such disastrous consequences in 1978.

The recovery of the Left vindicated François Mitterrand's conviction that the only alternative to the perennial dominance of the Right–Centre was an administration of the Left under PS leadership. Wedded to its Stalinist past, the PCF had proved time and again that it was ill-equipped to transcend its sectarianism and to adjust to the presidential politics of the Fifth Republic. True, even within the PS itself there were those like Michel Rocard who considered that Mitterrand likewise was too much a figure of the past and insufficiently dynamic and modern. At the party congress held at Metz in 1979 Mitterrand needed all his political skills and some help from the CERES (*Centre d'études, de recherches et d'éducation socialiste*) wing to see off a leadership challenge from Rocard. In 1980 Rocard indicated his willingness to run as a presidential candidate but stood down once Mitterrand entered the race. The PCF fielded Marchais, and their machine ran a strong anti-Mitterrand campaign, but opinion polls and the actual election results demonstrated that many ordinary communist voters (as many as 25 per cent) preferred to vote for Mitterrand even on the first ballot rather than see victory go to the Right. Mitterrand's patience and persistence were about to pay off.

The Right in the meantime experienced some of the discord that had been the bane of the Left. Michel Debré, representing *le gaullisme gaullien*, was first to declare his candidacy, though the principal Gaullist challenger was, inevitably, RPR leader Jacques Chirac. Such was the enmity between him and Giscard that a good number of his supporters went to the polls prepared to vote for Mitterrand rather than Giscard at the second ballot. Even so, in the early stages of the campaign few opinion polls believed that Mitterrand could defeat Giscard. The latter's friend Michel Poniatowski dubbed Mitterrand 'the eternal loser'. But the polls also showed that Giscard had become deeply unpopular and was blamed for the country's economic malaise. A mood favourable to change had begun to emerge – among businessmen, professional people and farmers as well as among workers and the young. Skilfully, Mitterrand played on the widespread desire for a better future. Whereas in 1974 Giscard had been seen as the best hope for reform and a fresh start, in 1981 it was Mitterrand who embodied such aspirations. His was a highly personal campaign: the programme he presented was his own, not that of the United Left or of the PS, from which he resigned as First Secretary (though, of course, he continued to benefit both from the popularity of the party and from the strenuous activity of its militants).

The tide began to turn in January 1981, and after the first ballot, held on 29 April, Mitterrand, with 25.84 per cent of the vote, came second to Giscard (on 28.31 per cent), forcing Chirac (18 per cent) into third place and out of the race. Marchais could muster only 15.34 per cent – the PCF's lowest share of the vote since the Popular Front elections of 1936. In the run-off of 10 May, in a high (85.85 per cent) turnout and amidst great excitement, Mitterrand defeated Giscard by a margin of 3.51 per cent (51.75 per cent to 48.24). It was a famous victory, as sensational as that of the Popular Front, and the celebrations on the Left continued far into the night. But could Mitterrand, any more than Blum, deliver all that was expected of him? The precedent of 1936, after all, was not entirely a happy one.

20
France Under Mitterrand 1981–1991

The election of François Mitterrand to the presidency of the Fifth Republic was a remarkable achievement for a man whom many had written off as *l'éternel perdant* of French politics. The ironies contained in his victory were not lost on commentators who remembered how, formerly, the new president had been not merely the bitter adversary of General de Gaulle but an opponent of the establishment of the Fifth Republic in 1958 and then of its transformation in 1962 into a presidential regime based on universal suffrage. Gaullist fears that 'their' institutions might not be in safe hands appeared to have some foundation.

Though prominent in national politics since the time of the Liberation, Mitterrand remained something of a mystery man. No one could be entirely sure what he stood for, especially if one biographer is right in his claim that Mitterrand never does what he says and never says what he does. Born in 1916 in Jarnac, a small town in the South-West, he grew up in a provincial bourgeois and devoutly Catholic family, cultivating a strong literary bent while a student of political science and law in Paris during the turbulent years of the mid 1930s. Wounded in the battle of France, he was taken prisoner by the Germans and made two unsuccessful efforts to escape before succeeding at the third attempt. Back in France, he became an active Resistance leader, though for cover he worked in a department of the Vichy civil service and even accepted a decoration from the regime. Disagreeing with de Gaulle even in wartime, he emerged from the Occupation period as a hero and a man of the non-communist Left, his leftward leanings perhaps reinforced by marriage in 1944 to Danielle Gouze, a Resistance comrade from a militant socialist family. Elected deputy of the Nièvre in 1946, he was rapidly promoted to a ministerial post and remained a stalwart of many of the Fourth Republic's cabinets. The advent of the Fifth Republic consigned him to 23 long years in opposition, but throughout that time he remained in the public eye, especially as the architect of the socialist revival (though some also remembered more dubious incidents, such as the alleged attempt on his life in October 1959, which his enemies always represented as a publicity stunt). By 1981, however, he had forged for himself a new identity as an elder statesman more in tune with the needs and aspirations of the French people than the cold and distant Giscard. He was the *force tranquille*, the strong yet calm leader who promised change and reform appropriate to the 1980s.

The Socialist Experiment 1981–1986

First, Mitterrand wished the electorate to confirm its mandate for change by giving him a parliamentary majority which would support presidential policy. Having assumed office on 21 May, he appointed an interim socialist government under the veteran socialist politician Pierre Mauroy, dissolved parliament and called fresh elections for June. The Right, realizing that the quarrel between Giscard and Chirac had been at least partly responsible for Mitterrand's triumph, made haste to patch up an electoral alliance, in the UNM (Union for a New Majority). But all the energy expended by Chirac in the campaign proved powerless in the face of the voters' determination to reconfirm their choice of 10 May. In the first ballot the PS/MRG polled 37.5 per cent of the vote and the PCF 16.1, which put the combined Left well ahead of the Right (Gaullists 20.8 per cent, Giscardians 19.2). Once again, it was clear that the socialists had made inroads into the support of the communists as well as of the Right, since in 1978 the PCF had still been able to muster over 20 per cent of the vote on the first ballot. In the second round, the socialists swept to a convincing victory, winning 55 per cent of the vote and 270 seats – enough to give them an absolute majority. The MRG brought another 15 seats, while the PCF, with 9 per cent of the vote, had only 44. The Gaullists had 84, and the Giscardians 62. What made the margin of victory so convincing was the decision by many right-wing voters to abstain on the second ballot. The turn-out was low (70.4 per cent as against 82.8 in 1978): but it could scarcely be doubted that the electorate had given Mitterrand the mandate he sought. Inevitably, the PS was seen as the party of government and for the first time under the Fifth Republic the Left was called upon to assume power, its task being understood as the implementation of the 110 propositions which had formed Mitterrand's own electoral manifesto.

The government team continued to be headed by Mauroy, a former schoolteacher and longtime militant in the traditional socialist bastion of the Nord. Another battle-scarred veteran, Gaston Defferre, became Minister of the Interior, while Jean-Pierre Chevènement, representing the far Left (CERES) faction, was rewarded with Research and Industry. Mitterrand's friend Robert Badinter was made Minister of Justice and another ally, the career diplomat Claude Cheysson, was appointed Foreign Minister. Jacques Delors, once an adviser to Chaban-Delmas, was a force for moderation at Finance, but what gave rise to most comment was Mitterrand's decision to include four communists in his governmental team (the most prominent being Fiterman at Transport). It was a master stroke on the part of the new president, vindicating his long-term strategy of bringing the Left to power on his terms rather than on those of the PCF, and all the more effective in that it bound the communists to support the new government in its socialist experiment.

The shape the experiment would take was by no means clearcut, since the PS was far from united. Several *courants*, or tendencies, could be discerned, each associated with a particular personality. *Mitterrandistes* (such as Pierre Joxe, Lionel Jospin and Laurent Fabius) were themselves quite a diverse collection of individuals, united mainly in seeing Mitterrand as the man for the times and perhaps by a desire to maintain some of the secularist faith to which both Radicals and Socialists had been attached in the past. The Mauroy faction, on the other hand, was devoted to preserving the social democratic and pragmatic traditions of the old SFIO, and had its roots in the well-established socialist territories of the North and the Mediterranean South. By contrast, the Rocardians, grouped around Michel Rocard, the former leader of the PSU, rejected what they considered to be the outmoded doctrines associated with state socialism, secularism and alliance with the PCF, in favour of a new-style socialism committed to decentralization, *autogestion* and European unity – a new brand of socialism which had been largely responsible for winning over significant numbers of Catholic voters. Marxism, however, was by no means totally absent from the PS, but lived on in the CERES faction headed by Chevènement (though the group had its internal splits on this and on other issues, being united principally by a strongly patriotic outlook on defence). Such diversity of opinion within the party offered advantages as well as disadvantages, of course, since it meant that the PS could appeal to a wide spectrum of opinion, but it meant that there was considerable disagreement as to what the creation of a socialist society entailed.

Nevertheless, the general orientation of the PS was unambiguous. Conscious of its indebtedness to the broad republican tradition, it was happy to underline its commitment to democracy and the liberty of the individual. One of Mitterrand's first acts as president was to make a symbolic visit to the Pantheon to pay his respects to heroic figures such as Victor Schoelcher, the liberator of the slaves, Jean Jaurès, greatest of French socialists, and Jean Moulin, martyr of the Resistance. Moreover, as a party in which many militants came from the ranks of the teaching profession (so much so that the Fifth Republic under Mitterrand could, like the Third, be fairly dubbed the *République des professeurs*), an attachment to the *idée laïque* remained strong. Most of all, however, the party's socialism implied an aspiration to break with the capitalist system and to construct a new social and economic order in accord with its 1972 slogan of '*changer la vie*'. The way forward, it was thought, was not to establish a siege economy but rather to dismantle and to decentralize the power of the State in line with the doctrine of *autogestion*. At the same time, however, most elements in the party believed that nationalization should be extended and that economic growth could best be achieved through expansion of the public sector. The socialism of 1981 was to be a blend of the old and the new, in keeping with the party's diverse electoral bases.

Mauroy had written that he would *gouverner autrement*, and he kept his promise. On 8 July 1981 he announced a massive programme of reforms intended to bring about 'a new kind of citizenship'. In the sphere of justice and the law, the death penalty was abolished in September 1981 and the powers of examining magistrates reduced. Special state security courts and military tribunals also disappeared. On 20 October legislation was passed to free the media from state control. Local radio stations now had the right to start broadcasting (and did so in vast numbers). 'Audio-visual communication' was also the subject of another law in July 1982 which reorganized public broadcasting and set up an *Haute Autorité de l'Audio-Visuel*. The Authority was intended to introduce a real measure of independence into broadcasting services in France, but, since it also appointed the heads of the different sections, it could be said that the state still retained much of its power and influence.

The showpiece of the *septennat* was supposed to be political and adminis-

trative decentralization. From the early 1970s socialists had made decentralization one of the key themes in their programme and it was therefore hardly
surprising that as early as July 1981 Gaston Defferre, at the renamed Ministry
of the Interior and of Decentralization, introduced an enabling bill as a prelude to a spate of legislation and decrees to be enacted (frequently after
interminable debates and numerous amendments) over the next four years.
By the Defferre law of 2 March 1982 prefects were renamed *commissaires de
la République* and stripped of many of their former powers. Responsibility
for local affairs was to be assigned to elected presidents of new departmental
councils. Mayors had their powers enhanced, especially in the area of housing
and town planning, and communes were no longer liable to see their decisions
overturned by the prefect, even if the *commissaires*, as the executives of
Paris-based services, were not totally bereft of means of influence. Regionalism was to be strengthened by the creation of 22 new regional councils, whose
members were to be elected by universal suffrage and whose remit was to
encourage economic development. As a further sign of the socialists' attachment to regionalism, Corsica was granted 'special status' in March 1982, with
extra financial help and increased autonomy in education and the economic
sphere. The concessions, however, proved insufficient for separatists who
supported the Corsican National Liberation Movement (FLNC), which continued to perpetrate acts of terrorism.

If decentralization was, according to Mitterrand, *la grande affaire du septennat*, economic policy remained the decisive issue for signalling that the electoral victory of the Left implied a decisive break with the past. Harking back
to the Common Programme of the Left of 1972, Mitterrand's 110 propositions
affirmed a determination to carry out an assault against capitalism and to side
with the less well-off sections of French society. It was the socialists' conten-
tion that the crisis in the world economy since the mid 1970s had been exacerbated by the application of capitalist remedies. Barre's austerity programme
and his faith in market forces were therefore to be replaced by an expansion-
sary fiscal policy, increased expenditure on social welfare and efforts to redis-
tribute wealth. True, socialist measures would cost money, and swell the
budget deficit, but it was Mitterrand's and Mauroy's belief that the extra
finance could be found by soaking the rich. The essential thing was to go for
state-led growth, to curtail rising imports and to stimulate exports. At the
same time, the nationalization of a number of key enterprises was seen as an
integral part of the new interventionist strategy. Both Delors and Rocard
expressed the need to proceed with caution, but Mitterrand, determined to
affirm the left-wing orientation of his administration, insisted on pressing
ahead with what has been aptly called 'Keynesianism in one country'.

Encouraged by expert forecasts that 1982 would see an upturn in the world
economy, the socialists proceeded to implement an ambitious social and economic programme. The minimum wage (the SMIC) was increased by 10.6 per
cent in 1981–2, while family allowances and housing subsidy were raised by
some 50 per cent. Old-age pensions went up by 62 per cent. The working
week was lowered by one hour to 39 hours, without loss of pay, and workers
were also given a fifth week of paid holidays. Workers' rights were also
promoted by the Auroux Laws of 1982, which obliged firms to negotiate
annually on pay, to accord greater recognition to trade-union representatives,
to improve their standards of health and safety in the workplace and to release

more information about profits and general policy. At the same time, some 140,000 new jobs were created in the public sector. To finance these welfare and redistributive measures, the public-sector deficit was allowed to increase, higher taxes were imposed on employers, and, symbolically, a wealth tax was introduced to squeeze the 'super-rich'.

The most obvious sign of the socialists' anti-capitalist thrust, however, was their programme of nationalizations enshrined in the law of 13 February 1982, justified on the grounds that the state could overcome the economic crisis only if it had the power to channel investment and to generate employment opportunities, since neither the banks nor industry could be trusted. The state took 100 per cent of the shares in the parent companies specified in Mitterrand's election manifesto – Thomson (electronics and communications), Péchiney (chemicals), Compagnie Générale d'Electricité (CGE), Saint-Gobain (glass, paper and textiles), and Rhône-Poulenc (textiles and chemicals). Additionally, the state acquired a 51 per cent share in a number of other companies, namely the arms manufacturers Matra and Dassault, along with CGCT (the French subsidiary of the telecommunications multinational, ITT), Roussel-Uclaf (pharmaceuticals) and CII-Honeywell Bull (computers). At the same time, private banks, including the investment companies Paribas and Suez, were also nationalized. A judicious blend of *dirigisme* and pump-priming, it was anticipated, would soon steer the French economy back on to the road to recovery and expansion. Whereas Giscard had opted for a *politique de créneaux* (concentrating support on French market leaders and allowing 'lame ducks' to go to the wall), the socialists intended to give assistance to all sectors in a *politique de filières*, aimed at producing 100 per cent French products.

Unfortunately for Mitterrand and the socialists, the time for such a bold economic experiment could hardly have been less propitious. The world recession, which had done so much to damage perceptions of the Giscard presidency, was, if anything, deepening. Other Western governments had decided that the only solution was to cut public expenditure and to raise interest rates, rather than commit themselves to further expansionist goals. The rocketing cost of oil imports, which had to be paid for in dollars, inevitably damaged the French balance of payments as the dollar, protected by high interest rates, rose steeply in value (in three years the franc depreciated 60 per cent against the dollar). French socialist attempts to go it alone were also inevitably hampered by Giscard's and Barre's acceptance of a fixed exchange rate for the franc through the EMS, so that, with inflation much higher in France than in Germany, French industry was rendered uncompetitive by an overvalued currency. As in 1936, the socialists considered devaluation, only to reject it as unacceptable to the electorate. Yet without a devaluation their plans for reflation were unlikely to work. Nor was the French trade balance helped by the fact that French consumers elected to apply their new purchasing power to foreign rather than to domestic goods. Moreover, inflation remained high, and, more galling still, so did unemployment, which passed the 2 million mark in November 1981 (though it was stablized at around that figure and began to fall at the end of 1982). In the circumstances, it was hardly surprising that the franc came under intense pressure and that, resist though it might, the government was forced to carry out a 3 per cent devaluation within the EMS on 4 October 1981. Even more significantly, at the end of November Finance Minister Delors announced the need for a 'pause' in the reflation programme – a term which conjured up memories of the unhappy fate of the Blum government in 1937. After a mere five months, the socialist experiment appeared to be foundering and the Mauroy government was confronted with unenviable economic choices.

One option, which appealed to the communists and to certain elements in the socialist party (notably the CERES faction), was to quit the EEC, and to retreat into a command economy, protected by tariffs against foreign competition. Another was to stay in the EEC, but leave the EMS, so as to allow more effective devaluations. A third choice was to remain committed to an open economy and to resort to classic deflationary measures. That was the option which Mitterrand and Mauroy decided to adopt. In June 1982 the government introduced a five-month freeze on prices and wages and announced cuts in public expenditure of 20 billion francs for 1982. At the same time, the business community began to be represented in a more favourable light and benefited from a series of measures designed to reduce the share of the welfare budget borne by employers. In confirmation of its new austerity policy, a second dose of deflation was administered by a package announced on 25 March 1983. Health-service charges were raised, along with those in other public services. Wages and prices were to be increased by a maximum of 8 per cent in 1983–4. Draconian exchange controls were introduced, limiting tourists to a mere £200 for foreign travel. Taxes were raised by 1 per cent across the board, though, in an effort to sweeten the bitter pill of *rigueur* for its left-wing supporters, the government ordained also that those in the highest income bracket should contribute a compulsory loan to the state. Earlier, on 12 June 1982 and 21 March 1983, two further devaluations of the franc were carried out within the mechanism of the EMS (the second precipitated by an international financial crisis resulting from Mexico's inability to pay its debts).

The logic of new measures might have implied new men, but, despite the U-turn, Mitterrand retained Mauroy as prime minister. Minor cabinet reshuffles were carried out in mid 1982 and then again in March 1983, the main casualties being the CERES-backed Nicole Questiaux, replaced at Social Affairs by Mitterrand's close ally Pierre Bérégovoy, Jean-Pierre Chevènement, whose place at the Ministry of Industry was taken by the rising young technocrat Laurent Fabius, and Michel Jobert, formerly Pompidou's foreign minister who relinquished the Ministry of Overseas Trade to Edith Cresson. It was still a Mauroy government, therefore, that confronted another set of problems that, in the end, proved to be at least as difficult as, and ultimately more damaging than, the problems associated with handling the economy.

This was the question of educational reform. Alain Savary, Minister of Education, was given the unenviable task of framing legislation which would, on the one hand, encourage the further democratization of the higher-education system (in line with Edgar Faure's *loi d'orientation* of 1969) and, on the other hand, find a solution to the high drop-out rate among students. In December 1981 he tried to broaden access to the élite *grandes écoles* by recognizing the *baccalauréat* in general sciences, and not just that in mathematics, as an entrance qualification. As regards the universities, he appointed an advisory commission which sat for 18 months before Savary made its report the basis of a parliamentary bill in April 1983. In proposing to introduce a modest degree of selectivity and in attempting to make higher education more vocationally orientated, it could not fail to stir up controversy and when, with modifications, it became law on 27 January 1984, it was greeted with a barrage of criticism, not least from academics outraged by its decision to phase out the punishing, but prestigious, *doctorat d'État*. Once again student protesters spilled onto the streets of Paris demonstrating against the notion of a *numerus clausus*.

These protests, however, were as nothing beside the outrage that greeted the hapless minister's plans to reform private (that is, mainly Catholic) secondary education. Mitterrand's manifesto had included a pledge to establish 'a united and laic public service of national education', which seemed to imply the abolition of state subsidies to Catholic schools. In power, however, neither the president nor his minister was keen to embark on any full-scale battle with the Catholic hierarchy. Instead, Savary was charged with reorganizing private schools so that in size and in the length of the school year they conformed to the norms of state schools. Contacts with the bishops revealed that Church leaders had few reservations, except to further proposals which would have given Catholic teachers the option of becoming civil servants (and thus made them subject to the control of the state rather than of the Church). Made public at the end of 1982, Savary's proposals generated a good deal of debate. On one side, supporters of Catholic schools were suspicious of any state interference, and made their feelings known in an impressive demonstration held at Versailles on 4 March 1984 which brought some three-quarters of a million demonstrators onto the streets. On the other side, many supporters of the *idée laïque* (including prime minister Mauroy) considered that Savary's bill of March 1984 contained too many concessions to Catholic opinion and insisted on amendments with the result that, by the time the bill was passed as a confidence motion by the National Assembly on 24 June 1984, it had been transformed into a more secularist measure than originally intended. But the champions of the *idée laïque* had badly underestimated the lengths to which defenders of the private schools were prepared to go. Many parents who sent their children to Catholic schools did so less for religious reasons than for academic and social ones: private education, as in Britain, might cater better for the particular needs of the individual pupil and also had a certain snob value, appreciated by many sections of the bourgeoisie keen to reinforce rather than to erode social distinctions. Moreover, led by Jacques Chirac, right-wing politicians of the RPR and the UDF had been quick to spot the political mileage to be derived from attacking Savary's bill in the name of upholding Catholic freedom of education. As the culmination to the series of rallies which they had organized against the bill, to coincide with the Assembly debate of 24 June, they staged the largest ever street demonstration in Paris, in which some one million protesters took part. Mitterrand, who had approved Savary's bill, considered that he had no option but to yield. Without consulting his minister he withdrew the measure on 12 July and substituted a much diluted text which eventually became law on 20 December 1984 and merely restored the state's right to a say in the appointment of staff to positions in private schools (that is, to the status quo that had obtained after 1959 and before the Guermeur law of 1977). In the meantime, Savary had been obliged to resign, and in his train came the resignation of the Mauroy government itself. In July 1984 the Mitterrand presidency had reached a crucial turning point.

The defeat of the Savary bill was not the only reason why Mitterrand decided that it was time to change his governmental team. Since 1981 election results had consistently revealed that the voters were dissatisfied with the performance of the Mauroy government. As early as the cantonal elections of 1982, the socialist share of the vote dropped to 31.6 per cent as against the 37.8 per cent polled in the legislative elections of 1981. More significantly, in the municipal elections of 1983 (the first to be held under a new electoral system introduced along with the decentralization law and combining elements of the majority system and that of proportionality) the Union of the Left suffered disastrous reverses. Sixteen communist-controlled councils (including some in the Paris red belt) and 15 socialist-controlled councils (including Roubaix, Tourcoing and Grenoble) were lost, while in Paris itself, the decentralization of municipal power intended to break the stranglehold of Chirac on City Hall backfired completely, as the joint RPR and UDF list won power in each of the 20 arrondissements. The elections to the European parliament held on 17 June 1984 confirmed the trend against the Left. Though public interest in the EEC was limited, these elections were seen nevertheless as an important test of parties and political leaders on the domestic front. Held under a proportional-representation system, they again advertised the decline of the PS, which took only 21 per cent of the vote. The PCF slumped to a mere 11 per cent. The RPR/UDF list headed by the formidable Simone Veil won 42.7 per cent. Furthermore, the right-wing vote was reinforced by the rise to national prominence of the racist *Front National*, presided by Jean-Marie Le Pen, which took 11 per cent of the vote – the same share as that of the PCF – after polling particularly strongly in regions with a high immigrant population such as the Mediterranean coast, the Alpes-Maritimes, the Var and the Bouches-du-Rhône. As electoral defeat in the forthcoming legislative elections of 1986 began to look ever more likely, Mitterrand needed only the fiasco of the Savary bill to prompt him into the major cabinet reshuffle which many considered to be long overdue.

In place of the jovial party hack Mauroy, Mitterrand entrusted the premiership to his protégé Laurent Fabius, the Minister of Industry. A youthful 37, son of a wealthy antique dealer and a product of ENA, Fabius looked like a socialist version of Giscard, even to the point of sharing a premature baldness. Evidently, his brief was to intensify the austerity measures of 1982–3 with a view to curbing inflation in time for the elections of March 1986. The communists, already embarrassed at being associated with deflationary policies and alarmed by their continuing electoral decline, returned to opposition. The 'unity of the Left' was shattered. Mitterrand, Fabius and Finance Minister Bérégovoy now turned their backs on old-style socialism and set about 'relaunching' the economy in accordance with neo-liberal orthodoxies. Instead of the original emphasis on stimulating growth through investment in the public sector and the nationalized industries, the Fabius government sought to restore the initiative to the private sector by means of tax incentives, public spending cuts and the imposition of pay restraint. The budgets of 1985 and 1986 envisaged substantial job losses in the public sector. In industry, Fabius likewise ruthlessly pursued profitability at the expense of jobs, abandoning the *politique de filières* and allowing the 'unfit' to go to the wall. Heavy industry was particularly hard hit, suffering massive redundancies which included those caused by the closure of the Le Creusot steel works. Even Renault, hitherto regarded as a shining example of a successful nationalized industry, was obliged to shed labour and saw its director sacked for inefficiency. Altogether, the policies of Fabius were intended to appeal especially to the professional and managerial classes, in the hope that the loss of traditional socialist voters could be made good by capturing some of the centre ground. Cynically, he hoped even to reconcile the wealthy who had been forced to pay the compulsory loan to the state by reimbursing them with interest just before the elections. Whatever his government stood for, it was not something instantly recognizable as socialism.

If, on the other hand, making capitalism function more efficiently can be counted as a success for the PS, the Fabius government was not without achievements. By 1986 the country was in better shape economically in a number of important respects. Inflation, which had peaked at 15 per cent in 1982, was down below 5 per cent. A *de facto* incomes policy terminated the perennial wages–prices spiral. Economic growth was real, if small, amounting to 1.3 per cent in 1985. Rising exports restored the balance of trade and the balance of payments to a surplus position. In the nationalized industries, the granting of greater autonomy to the heads of enterprise was rewarded with a general return to profitability. Unemployment was tempered both by the creation of new jobs and by the introduction of early-retirement schemes. Remarkably, the government appeared to have achieved a high degree of consensus for the 'social market economy' in which market forces were the principal determinants of economic activity but in which the plight of those adversely affected by economic change was alleviated by welfare benefits. Nevertheless, there could be no disguising the retreat from the socialist ideals of 1981. Unemployment, though lower than that in most EEC countries, remained stubbornly high at over 10 per cent of the workforce. Even if it can be argued that the French socialist administrations tackled the problems of the recession more effectively than many other governments, it was inevitable that their abandonment of a truly socialist economic policy would breed disillusionment and discontent in some quarters, and incur the charge of incompetence from friend and foe alike – especially as the impression of opportunism and inconsistency was replicated in other spheres, and notably in the conduct of foreign policy.

In opposition, the socialists had talked of the need for a radical reorientation of French foreign policy. In Europe, Giscard was accused of being insufficiently attentive to French interests, whether through too accommodating an attitude to Germany, concessions to British claims for refunds from the EEC budget or his readiness to embrace enlargement of the Community to include Greece, Portugal and Spain. In the Middle East, on the other hand, he was criticized for being too machiavellian, and appearing to care only about guaranteeing oil supplies through the sale of arms. Likewise, his attempts to maintain good relations with Moscow after the Soviet invasion of Afghanistan at the end of 1979 came in for heavy criticism, as did his tight-fisted and neo-colonial policy towards African countries and the Third World generally. The socialists promised a fresh start and, symbolically, renamed the Ministry of Foreign Affairs the Ministry of External Relations. Deliberately underplaying the importance of Europe, and fusing socialist anti-capitalist discourse with Gaullist rhetoric of non-alignment, Mitterrand represented himself as a friend of the Third World and the author of a new policy which would show greater sensitivity to the issue of human rights. Régis Debray, one-time guerrilla alongside Che Guevarra and well-known leftist intellectual, was appointed special adviser on Latin American affairs. Jean-Pierre Cot, Minister for Co-operation and Development, was committed to increasing aid to the Third World, to be channelled through international agencies and without the strings usually attached by previous French governments. Mitterrand himself signalled that he was keen to forge new relations with countries such as Mexico, Algeria and India. The first he visited personally in October 1981 and, to the ire of Washington, supported in its stance in favour of the guerrillas of El Salvador. Likewise, he sent aircraft to Nicaragua to help in the fight against the American-backed Contra rebels. To improve relations with Algeria, France agreed to buy Algerian natural gas at above the market price, while in India, already cultivated by Giscard, Mitterrand continued to negotiate commercial deals which allowed France to export Mirage jets, telephones and, more controversially (since India refused to sign nuclear non-proliferation agreements), enriched uranium for use in nuclear power stations.

Third World-ism soon proved to have its limits, however. True, French aid did increase significantly from 0.36 per cent of GNP in 1980 to 0.5 per cent in 1985, but French generosity in subsidizing Algerian gas was balanced by cutting aid to other countries. In Latin America, the 'revolutionary' policy was dropped before it became too offensive to the US. Nor did it take long for more traditional lines of policy to re-emerge in Africa. The replacement of Cot with Christian Nucci in December 1982 confirmed a return to neo-colonial ways, already heralded by Cheysson's presence at the 1982 Kinshasa Summit, despite Zaire's notorious disregard for human rights. As was to be revealed in a scandal that broke in 1986, Nucci operated a slush fund that contributed largely to propping up shaky African regimes and to the minister's own electoral coffers. In 1983, at Nucci's strong insistence, France once again intervened militarily in the civil war in Chad, ostensibly to counter interference by Libya. An agreement of 10 November 1984, by which both the French and Libyan troops were to be withdrawn, was disregarded by the Libyans, who, after a face-to-face encounter between Mitterrand and Ghadaffi in Crete, effectively obtained a French endorsement of their intransigence. Not even Mitterrand's rhetorical skills could conceal that a French military victory had been followed by a diplomatic defeat.

In the Middle East, Mitterrand at first tried to temper Giscard's pro-Arab policy by cultivating better relations with Israel, in the hope that France might be recognized as a possible honest broker in the Arab–Israeli quarrel. Thus France withheld official recognition of the PLO (though Cheysson met a PLO delegation 'unofficially' in August 1981) and Mitterrand visited Israel in March 1982. The uncompromising attitude of the Begin government, however, was not susceptible to French influence, as the invasion of Lebanon and the massacre of Palestinians in the camps of Sabra and Shatila demonstrated in the summer of 1982. Regarding Lebanon as an area of special French influence, the French government had aspired to play a decisive role. A 'peacekeeping' force was sent in 1982, but after a terrorist bomb attack in October 1983 which killed 241 American and 58 French troops, ambitions were scaled down to trying to secure the return of French nationals held hostage by Islamic fundamentalists. In the Middle East generally, France continued to figure primarily as an arms merchant, especially as the supplier of the Iraqis in the Iran–Iraq war.

As regards relations with the United States and the Soviet Union, Mitterrand initially hoped for closer co-operation with the Americans at a moment when East–West tensions had increased dramatically, in large measure because of the Soviet invasion of Afghanistan, its threat to intervene in the Polish crisis of 1981 and above all its decision to deploy SS20 intermediate-range missiles against Western Europe, which Washington proposed to counter with European-based Cruise and Pershing II missiles. Protest against the proliferation of nuclear weapons in Europe was especially strong in Germany, not just among Greens but in the ranks of the SPD. But whereas Giscard had been equivocal about the deployment of Cruise and Pershing II, and had tried to keep lines open to Moscow, Mitterrand was solidly in favour of US and NATO policy. Invited to address the Bundestag to celebrate the twentieth anniversary of the Franco–German Treaty in 1983, Mitterrand seized the opportunity to put the case for a European Intermediate Nuclear Force, thereby implicitly counselling German voters to support Kohl's Christian Democrats rather than the SPD.

But the new Atlanticism proved to be as short-lived as the new Third World-ism. Constant American rebuffs to French overtures for reductions in American interest rates and the exchange rate led to an open breach at the Economic Summit held at Versailles in 1982. Nor was France ready to comply with an American embargo on firms involved in the construction of a gas pipeline in Siberia. Most serious of all was the rift that followed the US announcement in 1983 of its so-called 'Star Wars' programme, the Strategic Defence Initiative (SDI), intended to be the last word in nuclear defence through its development of new missiles, satellite stations and lasers. Such a massive escalation of the arms race threatened to destroy France's credibility as a nuclear power, since it could ill afford the expenditure involved in keeping abreast of American technology. Mitterrand responded in 1985 with Eureka (the European Research Co-ordination Agency) which aimed to promote 'star peace' around the creation of more advanced European technology. He also adopted a less cool attitude towards Moscow and the countries of the Eastern bloc. As early as July 1982 he visited Hungary and in June 1984 he went to Moscow, where he risked offending his hosts by raising the case of the dissident scientist Andrei Sakharov and the war in Afghanistan, while reaffirming French concerns about nuclear parity in Europe. (France had consistently refused to concede that the French independent deterrent should be included in the Geneva negotiations on arms reduction.) When Mikhail Gorbachev took over as Soviet leader in March 1985, France was chosen as the destination for his first foreign trip. At the end of the same year, to the surprise of prime minister Fabius and the horror of many of the PS faithful, Mitterrand also welcomed General Jaruzelski, the man who had subjected Poland to martial law in 1981. By 1986 the *volte-face* in foreign policy seemed to be as complete as the U-turn in economic policy.

The return to Gaullist *realpolitik* was nowhere more apparent than in the incident of the *Rainbow Warrior*, a vessel (belonging to the international environmentalist group Greenpeace) that was blown up in Auckland harbour on 10 July 1985 by French secret agents. One member of the crew was killed. The background to the affair was the socialist government's determination to maintain the nuclear testing programme in the South Pacific, itself based on the Gaullist idea that France must play a leading role in world politics. Reports of radioactive leaks from the Muroroa atoll testing site caused deep resentment in Australia and New Zealand and also helped to fuel an anti-French independence movement on the island of New Caledonia. Confronted with evidence from the New Zealand police that the perpetrators of the *Rainbow Warrior* crime were members of the DGSE (the General Directorate for External Security) the French government reacted first with complacency and then with a cover-up, the exposure of which by *Le Monde* obliged the Minister of Defence, Charles Hernu – one of Mitterrand's closest allies – to resign on 20 September. The head of the DGSE went down with him, clearing the way for Fabius to admit the role of the French security services but to deny that it had been authorized by the government. Not everyone believed him, since there were those who alleged that Hernu had been sacrificed to save the reputation of his old friend and master in the Elysée. Nor was this the end of the affair. On 22 November the two agents responsible for the sabotage were given a 10-year jail sentence in New Zealand. Nationalist sentiment in France was outraged and the French government reacted by conducting a commercial boycott of New Zealand products, notably butter. It took another year for a deal to be struck whereby the French apologized and agreed to pay compensation in return for the transfer of the guilty agents to a French military base in the Pacific. The whole sordid episode proved that, in matters of defence, socialist policy was indistinguishable from that of the Right. Significantly, at the 1985 party congress held at Toulouse in October 1985, the loudest ovation was accorded to Hernu.

The retreat from socialism both at home and abroad allowed the Right to claim that the policies of the Right were best implemented by a government of the Right. As the legislative elections of 1986 loomed up, the defeat of the PS appeared to be inevitable. Mitterrand, not relishing the prospect of having to 'cohabit' with a right-wing premier, did what he could to salvage the situation for the socialists. Hoping to have sections of the media on his side, in November 1985, for a bargain price, he turned over the new Channel Five TV to a consortium of cronies who included Berlusconi, the Italian magnate whose private TV empire had been built on the popularizing of the worst features of American commercial television. Earlier, a law of 1984 had attempted to strike at the power of the press baron Robert Hersant, only to be declared illegal by the Constitutional Council. More effectively, Mitterrand resorted to a time-honoured remedy for minimizing losses at the polls, namely changing the rules of the electoral game. While it was true that in the past the PS had committed itself to proportional representation, the decision to introduce it in April 1985 was rightly seen as a blatant piece of electoral engineering. The new system was a modified version of that of the 1946 list system by departments, which had been designed to favour larger parties, and was reinforced in this direction by a rule requiring a party to obtain at least 5 per cent of the departmental vote to qualify for seats. One obvious consequence of the change was the lack of any need to form electoral alliances (which, for the Left, would have been particularly difficult after the experience of 1981–4). Nevertheless, remembering the self-inflicted damage of

1981, the RPR and the UDF did join forces, issuing a joint manifesto and presenting joint lists in some two-thirds of the departments.

The campaign itself was muted in comparison with that of 1981 (not least because the party leaders also had an eye on the presidential elections of 1988 and wished to appear in a statesman-like guise). Most of the comment centred on what would happen if, as expected, the Right were to win. Could the constitution work if President and premier were at odds? Should Mitterrand resign in such a situation? Raymond Barre said no to the first question and yes to the second, whereas both Chirac and Giscard d'Estaing made it known that they would be willing to form governments of 'cohabitation'. In the absence of other major issues, the electorate showed itself less polarized and more indifferent than in 1981. Turn-out dropped to 78.5 per cent. The anticipated victory of the Right was reflected in the 43.1 per cent score of the combined RPR and UDF lists, as against 32.1 per cent for the socialists and a mere 9.7 per cent for the communists. The latter were the principal losers, having seen their electorate shrink by more than 50 per cent between 1978 and 1986. It was the PCF's worst result since 1932 and left them with just 35 seats. Their decline was evident everywhere, both in former strongholds in the north and along the southern coast. Ironically, the self-styled party of the workers now polled best in rural areas like the Auvergne, the Limousin and the Cher. The socialist vote, on the other hand, had held up reasonably well, confirming the emergence of the PS as a national party capable of polling over 30 per cent of the vote in almost every area, including the Catholic West. With 210 seats (plus 6 for the MRG) the party still formed the single largest parliamentary group.

On the other hand, if the RPR/UDF were clear victors with 281 seats, they had failed to improve significantly on their score of 1981. Moreover, they now also had to reckon with a new force on the Right – the National Front. With 9.8 per cent of the vote and 35 seats, Jean-Marie Le Pen's party had made the biggest gains for the extreme Right since the *poujadist* successes of 1956. Its message of 'France for the French' and the deportation of immigrants (blamed for rising crime rates, the increase in unemployment and the soaring cost of welfare) had a strong impact on the south coast and its hinterland. In the cities of Marseille and Perpignan the party took around 25 per cent of the vote. Likewise, it polled well in the older industrial regions of the North and East. Under the two-ballot system, the Front would have done much less well, and Mitterrand was frequently reproached for unleashing this racist and xenophobic party onto the French parliamentary scene. On the other hand, true machiavellian that he was, the president appreciated how the presence of a racist Right might serve to embarrass the constitutional and centre Right. A deal with the Front would be unacceptable to the more liberal elements of the RPR and UDF, while the process of distancing themselves from the FN would inevitably push them towards socialist positions. Mitterrand, therefore, could be reasonably pleased with the outcome of the 1986 elections. His party had been defeated, but less disastrously than it might have been, and he in any case had been careful to appear to remain above the fight during the campaign, thereby underlining his presidential role. He now had to work with a new right-wing majority, but his personal prestige and the powers invested in his office ensured that he would be anything but an honorary president of the Third or Fourth Republic type. Arguably, the real victor in the 1986 legislative elections was François Mitterrand.

The Cohabitation Interlude 1986–1988

In confirmation of his willingness to accept the verdict of the electorate, Mitterrand called on Jacques Chirac to form a government. The premier was left to put together a ministerial team reflecting the balance of the new majority, though, wherever possible, he promoted his own friends and colleagues of the RPR. His close associate Edouard Balladur took charge of Economy; Alain Juppé went to Budget: and the tough Charles Pasqua was appointed to the Ministry of the Interior. Non-Gaullists in the government included the free-marketeer Madelin at Industry, centrists Pierre Méhaignerie (Environment) and Monory (Education), and the Republican Party's secretary-general François Léotard at Culture and Communication. In the two key areas of Foreign Affairs and Defence, however, the president refused to accept Chiracian nominees (Jean Lecanuet and François Léotard respectively) who might have posed a challenge to his personal authority, but insisted instead on the appointment of 'technicians'.

As a boost to the new government, the swing to the Right was underlined by the results of the contests held on 21 March for the presidencies of the regional councils. The Left was routed, ending up with control in only two regions (the Nord and the Limousin), while RPR or UDF presidents were elected in the other twenty regions (in several cases only with the votes of the FN, which once again scored around 10 per cent of the poll). At all levels of local government, the dominance of the Right was now overwhelming. The socialist experiment was definitely over, making way for a new hard-line, neo-liberal approach to politics that owed much to the models of Thatcherism and Reaganism.

The key theme was the economy. Just as the PS had sponsored nationalization, the Right would promote privatization. By a law of 2 July 1986, Balladur set out plans to privatize some 65 companies, starting with Saint-Gobain. In a highly successful sell-off later in the year (some 1.5 million people bought shares) the French were introduced to 'popular capitalism' on the British Thatcherite model. The sale of Paribas in 1987 was even more successful, attracting 3.8 million new investors. The stock market crash of October 1987 temporarily interrupted the privatization programme, but early in 1988 it resumed with the sale of Matra, Suez and the Crédit Agricole. Altogether, some 6.5 million French men and women were turned into shareholders in under two years. Mitterrand publicly expressed his personal disapproval of privatization on 14 July 1986, but failed to make good his threat to refuse his signature for ordinances decreeing the denationalization of enterprises that had been nationalized before 1981. The wily president had no intention of provoking a constitutional crisis, and knew when to give Chirac his head. For the time being, he preferred to take a back seat, thus allowing his prime minister greater initiative than had been enjoyed by any of his predecessors under the Fifth Republic.

Chirac, with one eye always on the presidential elections of 1988, was keen to impress. First of all, he wasted no time in rewarding his own supporters. Thus he immediately announced his intention of repealing the anti-Hersant press law and, in the hope of making new friends in the media, privatized the public TV channel TFI and awarded the franchises of the fifth and sixth channels to sympathizers in the business community (Hersant got Channel 5, while a group headed by Monod, a former Secretary-General of the RPR, obtained Channel 6). To favour property owners rather than tenants, the government repealed the Quilliot housing law of 1982, which had given security of tenure to those in rented accommodation. The wealth tax was abolished, and an amnesty accorded to investors who had defied socialist regulations regarding the export of capital. Balladur's autumn budget also reduced taxation and imposed further public spending cuts. Self-interest similarly dictated changing the electoral system back to a majority system. Once again Mitterrand registered his disapproval and refused to allow the change to proceed by decree, thereby necessitating parliamentary legislation which was passed in October 1986.

Aware that in order to become president he needed to broaden his electoral base beyond the confines of the RPR, Chirac tried to make inroads into the National Front's vote by appearing tough on law and order issues. Pasqua and Justice Minister Chalandon promised more strenuous policing and heftier prison sentences, notwithstanding the existing overpopulation of the prisons. In 1987 Chalandon struck at the powers of examining magistrates, whom the Right regarded as over-sympathetic to the criminals they were supposed to bring to justice. A new wave of terrorist attacks also gave the government an opportunity to show its resolve. In September 1986 a series of bombs were set off in Paris by the Abdallah clan, a Paris-based Lebanese Christian group. An explosion in the rue de Rennes on 17 September left 6 dead and 60 injured. The government, already responding to FN pressure for tighter identity checks, introduced visa requirements for all foreign visitors except those from the EEC and Switzerland. At the same time, the police were given greater powers: to hold terrorist suspects for up to four days and to move their trials to Paris. Georges Ibrahim Abdallah was given a life sentence for conspiracy to murder in March 1987. The Chirac government also succeeded in cracking down on domestic terrorism, securing the arrest of leading members of the neo-anarchist group *Action Directe* in February 1987, though not before they had assassinated the director of the Régie Renault, Georges Besse, in November 1986.

Nevertheless, outside of France at least, the suspicion lingered that the French were not as tough on foreign terrorists as they might have been, and were willing to strike deals with them in return for the release of hostages. In November 1987 there was considerable indignation among other western governments when the return of two hostages from Beirut was seen to be part of an elaborate exchange involving the expulsion of an Iranian diplomat who had carried out terrorist attacks in Paris and also the ending of the house arrest under which a French diplomat had been detained in Teheran.

In the eyes of the extreme Right, terrorism and the increase in crime were intimately connected with the presence of immigrants. More rigorous identity checks and tighter immigration controls were another feature of the government's 'get tough' policy. Its single most important item of legislation was the law of 9 September 1986, which aimed at curbing illegal immigration by introducing more stringent conditions for foreigners who wished to enter or to reside in France. Chirac also considered revising the nationality code so as to remove the automatic right to French citizenship of persons born in France to non-French parents. The apparent adoption of FN postures, however, aroused disquiet among some of the government's own supporters on the Centre–Right, as well as the hostility of the entire Left (not excluding Mitterrand). Baulking at the prospect of unseemly internal divisions in the run-up to the presidential elections, Chirac decided not to press ahead with new legislation and to temporize by setting up a commission on nationality which would take evidence and then make recommendations. Playing the anti-immigrant card also backfired in December 1987, when Chirac deported a number of Iranians and Kurds. After a public outcry (to which Mitterrand again showed himself sympathetic) some of the deportees had to be readmitted. The prime minister's handling of law and order and immigration issues did little to win him new friends on the extreme Right while being sufficiently illiberal to alarm some of the more moderate elements in the government coalition.

Nor was his reputation for statesmanship helped by the government's performance in the area of education reform. In line with the ambitions of unreconstructed conservatives in the educational establishment who aspired to undo all the post-1968 changes in higher education, the government attempted to frame legislation that would suppress the law of 1983 on the universities. The proposals were greeted with massive student protests, both in Paris and in the provinces, in November 1986, since once again it was suspected that the real purpose of the bill was to introduce the principle of selectivity. As the government hesitated in the face of the unexpected scale of opposition to its plans, students all over France held a day of demonstrations on 4 December. In Paris the protests ended with violent clashes between the students and the police, as a result of which an Arab student was beaten to death. Badly shaken, Chirac withdrew the bill and sacked his luckless minister of education, Devaquet, who had only nominally been in charge of the measure.

In one area, however, cohabitation worked much better than had been generally anticipated. In foreign policy, the possibility of an embarrassing conflict over who really spoke for France was averted, partly because neither Mitterrand nor Chirac wanted to expose the country to ridicule in the eyes of other states and partly because neither man wished to weaken the powers and the prestige of the presidency – the office for which both men were expected to be contenders in 1988. In addition, Chirac inevitably had to defer to Mitterrand's greater experience in this area, though he was adamant about his right to co-direct. Not only did he attend summit meetings alongside Mitterrand (thus creating headaches for the personnel in charge of protocol) but he packed the ministries of foreign affairs and defence with as many of his own nominees as possible, and set up his own team of expert advisers, who included de Gaulle's shadowy *homme d'Afrique*, Jacques Foccart.

In any case, what really counted was that in most respects the president and his premier appeared to be in broad agreement regarding the general lines of policy. After Giscard's drift towards Atlanticism, Mitterrand's 'Gaullist' image was reassuring even to RPR stalwarts. Like the General, Mitterrand knew the value of symbols of French 'independence': hence his steadfast adhesion to the doctrine of a full strategic response to any 'tactical' nuclear attack. Hence, too, the French denial of air space to the US to facilitate its attack on Libya in April 1986, over which president and premier were as one. The potential for disagreement over defence issues remained, however, since, ironically, Mitterrand had become more Gaullist than the Gaullists. Whereas Chirac and the Right found themselves moving towards a position whereby they could contemplate extending French nuclear cover to West Germany (and other European states), Mitterrand baulked at giving any such undertaking. While the president was keen to develop Franco-German relations in the interests of French and European security, he drew the line at pledging any automatic French nuclear response to an attack on the Federal Republic. He readily consented to joint military exercises in 1987 and to co-operation on the development of a new battlefield helicopter. Likewise, a new joint army brigade was announced for 1988. But the activation of the French nuclear deterrent on behalf of the Germans was another matter. While the Right, in effect, began to embrace a version of Atlanticism, Mitterrand remained true to the Gaullist heritage of an independent nuclear option as the ultimate guarantee of defence, whatever France might contribute to improved conventional defences in a European context.

The legacy of the General was much less apparent in the approach of both Mitterrand and the RPR to the issue of European integration. The most strident champion of a Gaullist *Europe des États* was no longer to be found in France but in Britain, in the person of prime minister Margaret Thatcher. Mitterrand and Chirac, by contrast, threw their weight behind the push towards European unity. Thus Mitterrand supported the introduction of the principle of majority voting in the Council of Ministers in place of the veto, over which de Gaulle had proved so intransigent back in 1966. In addition to envisaging an enlarged role for the Commission and the European Parliament, Mitterrand took a leading part in the drive towards the creation of a single market by 1992, and sanctioned moves to bring about a single currency thereafter. Chirac and Balladur likewise loudly affirmed their commitment to the Single European Act. On the political and economic relations which should exist between European states, Mitterrand in practice donned the mantle of Giscard. In the matter of the EC, all sides abandoned Gaullism and embraced a European-oreintated future, thereby opting for inter-dependence rather than independence.

If, in foreign and defence policy, the role of Mitterrand continued to be decisive, the fact remained that in the domestic field he was obliged to accept a diminution of his powers which he found distasteful, and possibly humiliating. The president continued to preside at the weekly meeting of the council of ministers, but the real decisions had already been taken at a previous gathering, chaired by Chirac. Mitterrand's displeasure with the new situation was apparent in his hints that, after all, he might prefer to withdraw from politics and refuse to run for re-election. Chirac, on the other hand, was preoccupied above all else by the forthcoming presidential elections. In 1987, though the privatization programme continued, there was a marked slowing down of the pace of his right-wing reforms. After the educational débâcle at the end of 1986 (which had been followed by a spate of industrial conflicts, and notably a strike of train drivers over the Christmas holiday period), Chirac preferred to shelve some of his more radical proposals (such as the privatization of prisons and a reorganization of the Renault plant) until the elections were safely over. The need for caution was also suggested by opinion polls published in the first half of 1987 which showed that Raymond Barre rather than Chirac would be the candidate of the Right best placed to oust Mitterrand (or any other socialist nominee). Even members of his own governmental team, like Léotard, hinted that Chirac might be lacking in presidential qualities. In the circumstances, it was hardly surprising that 1987 was a fairly quiet year on the political front, punctuated by news and speculation about the candidates in 1988.

Quick to announce his candidature (in April) was Jean-Marie Le Pen, leader of the FN, who made no secret of his racism and anti–Semitism. In September 1987 he publicly stated that the gas chambers were a mere 'point of detail' in the history of the Second World War. Coming closely in the wake of the trial of Nazi war criminal Klaus Barbie, 'the butcher of Lyon', his words gave widespread offence and stirred up considerable controversy (though they doubtless did him no harm among his own racist supporters). The disruptive antics of FN deputies in parliament likewise served to deepen the conviction of members of the moderate right such as Michel Noir that there could be no electoral pact with so despicable an organization – a position not altogether shared by Chirac, who knew he needed FN votes to be elected, and who therefore equivocated by talking about repudiating FN ideology, but not its electorate. The communists were also early into the fray, announcing in May 1987 that their presidential candidate would not be party leader Georges Marchais but André Lajoinie, who, however, remained firmly in the Marchais camp. Dissidents within the PCF, dismayed at the failure of their attempts to modernize the party, rallied to the *renovateur* Pierre Juquin, who also decided to run as a presidential candidate and was duly expelled from the official party in October. Raymond Barre entered the lists in June. Two Trotskyite candidates and an ecologist also put their hats in the ring. The biggest mystery surrounded Mitterrand, who continued to refuse to say whether or not he would be a candidate (which effectively scuppered the chances of Michel Rocard, who, as ever, was only too keen to replace him). Over the course of the year, the opinion polls showed a drop in support for both Rocard and Barre and a surge in support for Chirac. Only very late in the day, on 22 March 1988, did Mitterrand finally announce that he would put himself up for re-election. The real contest, as originally expected, was to be between the partners in 'cohabitation'.

The closing stages of the campaign generated little of the excitement and ideological conflict that had been features of the elections of 1981. Mitterrand deliberately distanced himself from the PS and presented himself as a seasoned elder statesman now interested primarily in *ouverture*, a new opening to the centre ground of French politics and to 'civil society'. In a personal statement to the electorate, his *Lettre à tous les Français*, the president avoided references to socialist party policy and confined himself to a handful of pledges, the most important of which were a restoration of the wealth tax and a guaranteed minimum income for the less well off. Chirac and Barre, by contrast, preferred to extol the virtues of the market and of competition. The first ballot was held on 24 April and put Mitterrand comfortably ahead, with 34.11 per cent of the poll. Chirac came second, with 19.96 per cent. Barre came a poor third, with 16.54 per cent, not too far in front of Le Pen, who created a sensation by taking 14.38 per cent of the vote. PCF candidate Lajoinie managed only a humiliating 6.76 per cent, while the *renovateur*

Juquin took 2.10 per cent – less than the Ecology candidate Antoine Waechter, who scored a respectable 3.78 per cent. The run-off of 8 May thus turned out to be the long awaited contest between Mitterrand and Chirac.

In theory, Chirac stood a good chance of winning. The first ballot, after all, gave an overall majority to the parties of the Right (50.88 to 45.34 per cent). Mitterrand, however, was assured of the votes of the entire Left and, unlike Giscard in 1981, had improved his score in the first ballot by comparison with that obtained in the previous presidential election. In other words, despite the setback of 1986, Mitterrand had convinced a substantial proportion of the electorate of his fitness for the office. Chirac, on the other hand, could by no means be sure of rallying the entire Right. He badly needed the support of the FN voters, but Barre warned him that to cultivate Le Pen would cost him the support of the UDF. In the end Chirac refused to play the racist card, though Pasqua came close to doing so, by stressing how the FN embraced values which were dear to other members of the Right. In desperation, Chirac resorted to a series of measures designed to advertise his patriotism and dynamism to the voters before they went to the polls again on 8 May. Another deal was struck with Middle Eastern terrorists to secure the release of three more French hostages. One of the agents responsible for the blowing up of the *Rainbow Warrior* was released from captivity in the Pacific. Most reckless of all, Chirac gave the order to French troops to free by force a number of hostages who were being held in a cave by separatist guerrillas in New Caledonia. The mission was accomplished, though at the cost of the lives of 19 separatist militants (some allegedly shot after they had surrendered) and two soldiers. The voters were left to decide whether Chirac was a tough statesman or an unscrupulous firebrand, and the result showed that the great majority preferred Mitterrand's dignity and responsibility to Chirac's impulsiveness. The president cruised comfortably to a second term, taking 54 per cent of the poll to Chirac's 46 per cent. The emphatic nature of his victory was evident in the results at the level of the *département*, where Mitterrand won 77 to Chirac's 19. At least a fifth of Barre's supporters and a third of Le Pen's refused to rally to Chirac, a majority of them choosing to vote directly for Mitterrand rather than to abstain. Mitterrand, in short, was perceived as a national statesman, while Chirac could not free himself from the image of a highly partisan professional politician and party leader.

Fortified by the electorate's confidence in him, Mitterrand immediately decided that the time had come to end the experiment in cohabitation. As in 1981, he argued that a president was entitled to a parliamentary majority that would execute his programme. His first act was therefore to dissolve the National Assembly and fix new parliamentary elections for 5 and 12 June 1988. As caretaker prime minister, he appointed his old rival Michel Rocard, with a brief to engage in *ouverture*. Two of Giscard's former ministers were brought into the governmental team, along with a number of well-known names from 'civil society', but all the senior posts went to leading lights of the PS: Bérégovoy returned to Finance, Roland Dumas went to the Quai d'Orsay, Lionel Jospin, the party's first secretary, to Education, Jean-Paul Chevènement to Defence. Centrists, especially the Christian Democrats of the CDS under Pierre Méhaignerie, were still reluctant to cast in their lot with the socialists, knowing that without proportional representation they had to rely on traditional deals with the Right to secure the return of their candidates under the two-ballot system. Nor, indeed, were all PS militants ready to march to the president's orders or conform to his new-found taste for centrism in the place of the union of the Left. On 11 May the party preferred the veteran Mauroy to Mitterrand's protégé Fabius as party leader in the place of Jospin. Mitterrand's remarks about the undesirability of rule by a single party also caused dismay in the ranks of PS militants, and may well have blunted their enthusiasm for reproducing a socialist victory on the scale of 1981.

In practice, therefore, the elections were fought along well-worn lines of Left and Right coalitions, particularly on the second ballot. A born-again Giscard d'Estaing set about creating the URC (*Union du rassemblement et du centre*) to prevent disastrous competition among the parliamentary Right and the Centre. After the first ballot, the PS discovered that it lacked the support enjoyed personally by the president. In a low turn-out (65.7 per cent) which indicated considerable voter fatigue, the PS easily outstripped its rivals with 34.77 per cent of the vote. The PCF recovered from the nadir of Lajoinie's defeat to take 11.32 per cent. The RPR fared best of the right-wing parties, with 19.19 per cent, just marginally ahead of the UDF on 18.5 per cent, while the FN took 9.66 per cent. The distribution of seats gave the PS/MRG 277: PCF 27: UDF 130: and RPR 129. The FN was crushed, and could return only a single deputy, though other Right groups accounted for another 13 seats. The socialists had won – just, and without obtaining an overall majority. The Left was back in power, but in very different circumstances from the euphoria of 1981.

The Return of the Left 1988–1991

To renew the socialist experiment, but this time in the direction of *ouverture*, Mitterrand reconfirmed Rocard as prime minister. The former *gauchiste* of May '68 had long renounced the politics of ideological confrontation in favour of a sober pragmatism and realism. Like the president himself, he no longer subscribed to the Leftist myth of total and immediate change. Gone, too, was any 'grand design' or sweeping programme. Instead, Rocard promised caution as well as competence in confronting continuing economic problems. His consensual approach was not to the liking of all members of his own party (where, additionally, the *Mitterrandiste* wing neither forgot nor forgave his challenges to their chief) but it won him considerable sympathy in the country at large. Rocard, with his rhetoric of conciliation and *ouverture*, was a good choice of premier for the mood of the late 1980s.

Ouverture, however, continued to have its limits. The Centre, as a bloc, did not side with the government, though it was represented in power by individuals such as Jean-Marie Rausch, the CDS senator–mayor of Metz (Minister of Foreign Trade) and by Jean-Pierre Soisson, a prominent figure in the UDF (Minister of Labour). There were, too, further openings to 'civil society' (a favourite Rocardian phrase) in the enlistment of non-professional politicians. One such, the cancer specialist Léon Schwartzenberg, soon proved to be an embarrassment by advocating compulsory testing for AIDS and had to be sacked. Also, if roughly half of the (unusually large) governmental team consisted of non-socialists, all the high-ranking PS luminaries of the Rocard I administration remained in their key posts. Above all, the

Rocard government represented a reversion to presidentialism. The prime minister made it plain that his task was to shape policy in line with the ideas contained in Mitterrand's *Lettre à tous les Français* (which pledged to restore the wealth tax, legislate for a guaranteed minimum income, give tenants a better deal in housing and allocate additional resources for the expansion of higher education). Mitterrand was once again back in the driving seat.

One immediate problem for the government was how to defuse the tensions in New Caledonia, recently exacerbated by Chirac's precipitate action. For some years there had been growing conflict between the Melanesian population (the *Canaques*) and the Europeans (the *Caldoches*). In 1984 the socialist government had sympathized with the claims of the *Canaques*, and had agreed to the creation of regional assemblies on the island, to be followed by a referendum on self-determination. The Chirac government adopted a much harder stance towards the grievances of the native population and cancelled the projected referendum, thereby provoking the FLNKS (*Front de Libération Nationale Kanak et Socialiste*) to extremist measures that in turn led to Chirac's heavy-handed response during the election campaign. Rocard abandoned force for conciliation, and in June 1988 worked out a power-sharing agreement, which was to be put to the electorate by referendum in November 1988. The new arrangements were duly approved, despite a boycott by RPR supporters, and were intended to last for a 10-year period, at the end of which there would be a further referendum. It was a statesmanlike solution to a problem in an area deemed crucial to French ambition to remain a major nuclear power.

On the economy, Rocard persisted with a policy of *rigueur*. The budget of December 1988 was geared towards reducing the deficit, and also lowered corporation tax and VAT. In March 1989, by way of preparation for the single financial market, more restrictions on exchange controls were removed. The announcement of the Tenth National Plan in January 1989 also stressed the importance of the European dimension. Inflation was kept down to 3.4 per cent, though the fall in unemployment was slight (from 10.1 to 9.5 per cent) over the course of 1989. Nor did Rocard flinch from maintaining his austerity measures by force, when necessary. In the autumn of 1988 the government was confronted by a crop of public-sector strikes (involving groups such as transport workers, prison officers and nurses), which were organized mainly at grass-roots level but were strongly backed by the leaders of the CGT, who called for a general strike on 18 October. Yet Rocard refused to listen to the pleas from Mauroy urging special consideration for workers who often constituted an important part of the socialist electorate. Instead, he and Transport Minister Delebarre called in the army to bus Parisians to work. In this situation, he could count on centrist support in parliament, whereas in other circumstances he succeeded in mobilizing the support of the PCF, as when he made the reform of the Renault plant the subject of a confidence vote in April 1990. (The plan was to fix the state's share in the company at 75 per cent.) Altogether, despite his lack of a majority and his cool relations with Mitterrand, Rocard exercised considerable political skill in appearing to give the French what they had voted for – moderate, left-of-centre policies that addressed the economic and social problems attendant on modernization and the move towards the single European market.

The municipal elections held on 12 and 19 March 1989 provided an important test of the government's record (local elections in France under the Fifth Republic have increasingly assumed national significance). Local factors, of course, continued to be important, and rendered the task of interpreting the results far from easy. Nevertheless, a number of conclusions could be drawn. One was that voter fatigue persisted: over 27 per cent of the electorate did not bother to vote. Overall, no party was in a position to say that it had won, though the combined vote for the parties of the Right (50.34 per cent) outstripped that for those of the Left (48.2 per cent), with other groups accounting for only 1.63 per cent. Yet the Right also suffered setbacks. Despite Chirac's triumph in Paris and Michel Noir's in Lyon, the RPR lost control in a number of major cities and the UDF sustained defeats in traditional strongholds such as Mulhouse, Strasbourg, Orleans and Aix-en-Provence. Once again the FN proved a thorn in the flesh of the 'classic' Right, refusing to withdraw its candidates at the second ballot and therefore allowing socialists to win against split right-wing electorates. On the Left, where unity for the duration of the campaign was established, the PCF managed to hold onto its power bases in the Parisian suburbs, but lost control in a number of provincial cities, such as Le Mans and Amiens. The PS recovered much of the ground lost in 1983, scoring well in many of the cities of western and eastern France and making new gains in parts of the centre-west, as at Orleans, Blois and Châteauroux. The ecology candidates also did surprisingly well, polling an average of 9 per cent in 94 of the country's largest towns.

The European elections of 18 June 1989 gave the voters a further opportunity to pass their verdict on the Rocard government. The combined list of the RPR and the UDF, headed by the rejuvenated Giscard d'Estaing, came first, with 28.86 per cent of the vote and 26 seats. Once again, however, the FN polled well, with 11.73 per cent and 10 seats. The centrists of the CDS ran an autonomous campaign under Simone Veil and Pierre Méhaignerie and ended up with 8.41 per cent and 7 seats. All these divisions on the right were obviously advantageous to the PS, which scored 23.6 per cent and won 22 seats. The 'greens' maintained their challenge with an impressive 10.5 per cent – well ahead of the terminally languishing PCF, which managed only 7.72 per cent and 7 seats. Rocard, therefore, was entitled to think that his low-key, non-ideological and pragmatic approach to government, eschewing excessive legislation and encouraging wider consultation, was what a majority of the electorate wanted. Indeed, by May 1990, opinion polls revealed that Rocard had become more popular than the president – a fact many commentators seized on to predict his imminent demise.

In fact, he was to last another year, during which time France became embroiled, with important consequences, in the conflict in the Persian Gulf precipitated by the Iraqi invasion of Kuwait on 2 August 1990. The Gulf crisis was an important test of Mitterrand's statesmanship (which had not been seen to best effect in his ungracious reaction to the reunification of Germany, accomplished in the wake of the extraordinary series of revolutions and changes in Eastern Europe in 1989 and early 1990). Traditionally pro-Arab (as recently as 4 April 1990 Yasser Arafat had been officially received at the Elysée and a few days later both Mitterrand and Foreign Minister Dumas went out of their way to thank Libyan leader Colonel Ghadaffi for his help in securing the release of another French hostage), French policy-makers were more reluctant than their American or British counterparts to contemplate the use of force against Saddam Hussein. Defence Minister Jean-Pierre Chevènement, in particular, made known his opposition to the massive build-up of troops in the Gulf region in an anti-Saddam coalition formed under the auspices of the United Nations, but in reality dominated by the Americans. Chevènement spoke for many in denouncing American imperialism and in cautioning against antagonizing Arab allies whom France had long cultivated, not least as suppliers of oil and purchasers of French military hardware. Mitterrand, too, was sensitive to such considerations, and steered a hazardous course between backing the United Nations resolutions calling for the Iraqis to withdraw from Kuwait, and being seen not simply to be following the lead of Washington. As war loomed nearer, he produced a last-minute plan for peace, which in Britain and the United States was widely interpreted as an example of French duplicity, but which in France and in Arab countries was more correctly understood as signalling both France's 'difference' from other Western countries, and its claims to a say in the peace settlement that would inevitably follow a war. In reality, almost from the beginning of the crisis, Mitterrand accepted the logic of war should Saddam prove intransigent, and his fundamental alignment with the UN and the US was plain from his acceptance of Chevènement's resignation and his replacement of him with a trusted personal friend, Pierre Joxe, formerly a tough Minister of the Interior. Twelve thousand French troops were sent to the Gulf, and when hostilities broke out on 16 January 1991, they conducted themselves with distinction in the rout of the Iraqis in the ground war that followed the devastating bombing campaign carried out by allied aircraft.

From the point of view of Mitterrand's personal prestige, the Gulf War was a triumph, and added significantly to the deluge of praise heaped on him in May 1991 to commemorate his completion of a decade in power. Success for the flag stifled the clamour of opposition from opponents of the war – PS left-wingers, committed to the ideal of neutrality and viscerally hostile to the US: the PCF, enemies of capitalism and colonialism: and the FN, distrustful of any kind of foreign adventure. Likewise the war raised the standing of all the mainstream parties (PS, UDF, RPR) and their leaders, who had insisted on the necessity and the importance of a French presence in the Gulf. As regards French defence policy, the war produced some immediate re-thinking, evident in plans to equip France with a professional army and vastly improved conventional forces more appropriate to the post Cold War world. It is likely that the need to adjust to the collapse of Soviet power in Eastern Europe and the reunification of Germany would in time have required such a readjustment, but the fact remains that it was the Gulf War that brought home to French policy-makers how outdated, not to say redundant, their nuclear strategy had become. As the Americans (and to a lesser extent the British) demonstrated, to rank as a military power it was necessary to be able to put troops into battle. Since the French public would not countenance the dispatch of conscripts, but, according to opinion polls, would accept the deployment of a rapid action force of professionals, the creation of a professional army became a priority almost as soon as hostilities ceased.

In foreign policy, the war was less of a landmark. True, in making war alongside the Americans against Iraq (which had the strong backing of Arafat and the Palestinians), Mitterrand broke with the pro-Arab policy that had been one of the cornerstones of French foreign policy since the time of de Gaulle. Likewise, he could be seen as having taken a step towards improved Franco-American relations, if not towards 'Atlanticism'. Yet differences and suspicions persisted between Paris and Washington on the subject of European security, as was evident at the meeting of NATO foreign ministers in Copenhagen in early June 1991. France remained committed to the pursuit of a common defence policy for the countries of the European Community, despite, or perhaps because of, the disarray among the EC states over the conduct of the Gulf War (the Italians and the Dutch having been particularly outspoken about the bombing of Baghdad). The Americans continued to suspect the French of seeking to destabilize the NATO alliance, with the long-term objective of removing the United States from the European scene. In some areas, at least, Mitterrand was rightly perceived, both at home and abroad, as the true heir of his old rival, de Gaulle.

Whether or not Rocard would have been maintained as prime minister through 1990 without the Gulf War it is impossible to say. What is true is that the war inevitably acted as a distraction from the ordinary mundane business of domestic politics, which gave the government temporary respite from the mounting criticism levelled at it by the opposition parties and the right-wing press. In particular, the Right had been denouncing the 'slush funds' allegedly operated by the PS through the 1970s and 1980s, money from which was said to have contributed significantly to the financing of Mitterrand's electoral campaign in 1988. To protect PS politicians and militants from prosecution, the government twice – in 1988 and 1990 – prevailed on the National Assembly to pass amnesties on behalf of individuals who might have been found guilty of contravening the laws on the financing of political parties. The scandal refused to die away, however, since the Marseille policeman who had led the corruption enquiry (and been dismissed from the force for his pains) told his story in a book published just at the moment (April 1991) when the man who had headed Mitterrand's re-election campaign, Henri Nallet, was appointed Minister of Justice. Here were all the makings of a classic French 'affair'. With the Gulf war over, Rocard found himself increasingly under fire from the opposition and discovered that even his gifts for parliamentary manipulation were insufficient to pilot proposed measures through the Assembly. Thus he was obliged to tell Mitterrand that he could not risk a confidence vote over the issue of reform of the electoral system for the regional elections due to be held in March 1992 – 'reform' aimed at putting the socialists in with a chance of averting the disaster they had experienced in 1986.

In the circumstances, Rocard was probably not unhappy to be relieved of his responsibilities when Mitterrand eventually did ask for his resignation in May 1991. He had acquitted himself well in his three-year premiership, and still had four years left to prepare his campaign for the Elysée in 1995. At the same time, if the PS were to do badly in the regional elections of 1992 and the legislative elections of 1993, he would not have to take the blame. Mitterrand, on the other hand, clearly believed that he had to regain the political initiative. In Rocard's place, he caused a sensation by appointing Edith Cresson as France's first female prime minister. A 'Chanel' Socialist, daughter of an *inspecteur des finances* and married to a top Peugeot executive, she seemed a shrewd choice. As a woman, she added novelty and an air of radicalism to the government, which could well enhance the image of the PS with the electorate. Yet she remained very much a *mitterrandiste* (Mitterrand called her his '*petit soldat*' for the toughness and combativeness she had shown in the defence of her left-wing convictions), which suggested that the president was primarily concerned with tightening his own grip on policy. An economist by training, a former Minister of Agriculture and of Trade and European Affairs, and with high-level business experience, Cresson announced that her priority was to prepare French industry for the challenges of 1992 and the single European market. On her success or failure depends whether or not the Fifth Republic re-experiments with 'cohabitation' – which Mitterrand is known to be anxious to avoid – after the legislative elections of 1993. So far (October 1991) the omens for both Cresson and Mitterrand are not good. The prime minister's abrasive personality and her tendency to commit *gaffes* (she has described the Japanese as 'ants' and Englishmen as singularly prone to homosexuality) have produced a sharp fall in both her own standing and that of Mitterrand in the opinion polls. The president may be obliged to replace her sooner rather than later. The runes are difficult to read. But, whatever happens, the 1990's show every sign of proving as interesting a decade as the 1890's. Whether they will turn out to be a new – and genuine – *belle époque* remains to be seen.

Afterword

Anything as definite as a conclusion to a volume that has tried to outline mainstream developments in France over the course of a century seems altogether inappropriate. Yet it may be useful to reflect on some of the more important themes in the story, so as to help place the developments in the perspective of the longer term. As the French face a new *fin de siècle*, it is worth recalling how much their country has changed since the previous one.

As regards the economy and society, the years after the Second World War stand out as marking a decisive break with the past. The long post-war boom of the *trente glorieuses* was the main agent of change. The economy, traditionally protected by high tariffs, was opened up to the rigours of international competition. The end of expansion and the onset of recession in the mid 70s served only to accelerate the trend towards integration into a wider European and world economy. As François Mitterrand put it in his New Year's Eve address of 1988, 'France is our homeland, but Europe is our future.' The government of Edith Cresson has been charged with ensuring that France is ready for the challenge of the single European market, so that, with its European partners, it can compete successfully against Japan and the United States. French political leaders no longer preach the peculiarity of France but loudly proclaim their acceptance of economic interdependence. In that sense, France has become less French and more open and outward-looking.

Whereas the France of Daladier retained many of the characteristics of the France of Dreyfus, the France of Mitterrand is a recognizably different world from that of Méline, or even of Léon Blum. The 30 years of unprecedented economic growth after 1945 transformed a country of peasant farmers and small proprietors into a nation of employees and wage-earners. As late as 1945 agriculture still accounted for one-third of the entire work force. By 1990 the proportion was around a twentieth. The Frenchman in a beret has all but disappeared, whereas the manager or technician or salaried female office worker would be a more representative figure. Women, indeed, constitute an increasingly important element in the expansion of the tertiary sector of the economy, with some 2.5 million swelling the number of employees between 1968 and 1982. Huge, if unevenly distributed, rises in living standards have accompanied the growth in the economy: real wages tripled in the years since 1945 and the universal access to all kinds of consumer durables is testimony to the generalization of prosperity. It is no exaggeration to speak of a social revolution when describing the changes that have taken place in the post-war world, and more particularly from the mid 1960s.

Revolutions, of course, have losers as well as winners. Among the principal victims of the 'second French Revolution' were those thrown out of work. At present, there are 2.6 million unemployed, many of them young people. The persistence of high unemployment from the late 1970s is a novel and painful experience for France and a serious blot on the record of its socialist president and of successive socialist governments. Nor should the appointment of a female prime minister distract attention from the continuing inequalities endured by women, notably in the work place. The Ministry of Women's Rights, set up by the socialists in 1981 and run by the dynamic Yvette Roudy, was abolished by Chirac in 1986, not entirely to the dissatisfaction of many male leaders of the PS, who harboured a deep-seated distrust of feminism comparable to that of their predecessors in the old SFIO. (On their behalf, it could, however, be said that the violence, sectarianism and internecine quarrelling of post-1968 French feminists did little to commend their cause to a wider public.) The emergence of a Green Party is a reminder that the whole ideology of growth is itself contested, at least by a minority more concerned with preserving the environment than with unlimited economic expansion.

The xenophobia directed at the immigrant population, most vociferously but by no means exclusively by the FN, is yet another necessary qualification to any tendency to portray the history of the recent past as an unalloyed success story. Earlier in the century, Italians, Spaniards, Portuguese and Poles were often extended a less than cordial welcome in their adopted country, but the hostility towards the mainly Arab and Islamic immigrants who have settled in France in the last 30 years has been fuelled by a more overtly racist hatred. The strongly assimilationist and laic traditions of the PS do not necessarily predispose their leaders towards sensitive handling of the problems inherent in the creation of a multi-cultural society, as was illustrated by the episode of the *affaire du foulard* in 1989, when three young Muslim girls were excluded from a state school in the Parisian *banlieue* for wearing Islamic headscarves. Education Minister Lionel Jospin was heavily criticized for suggesting that the girls should be allowed to wear the scarves, on the grounds that he thereby endorsed Islam's oppression of women (whereas his real objective was to expose them to secular influence). Toleration for what is now the second largest religion in France is not widespread.

On the political front, the crucial turning point was reached with the creation of the Fifth Republic in 1958. Under the Third Republic, the regime was not particularly unstable (it did, after all, last for 70 years and would have continued longer still but for the consequences of a catastrophic military defeat) but governments, on the whole, were weak. The Fourth Republic, even if its problems were not entirely of its own making (one needs to recall the onset of the Cold War, the problems inherent in decolonization and the intransigence shown towards the regime by both Communists and Gaullists), produced another succession of mainly weak governments. De Gaulle's introduction of a political system weighted more heavily in favour of executive power gave France the kind of strong government it had not had on any consistent basis since the days of the Second Empire. The new political system was more of a hybrid than de Gaulle would ideally have liked but, by comparison with the Third and Fourth Republics, it was evidently much more presidential than parliamentary. The actual experience of rule by de Gaulle and his successors (with the exception of the 'cohabitation' interlude of 1986–

8) served to enhance presidentialism, while the stability of the regime was underlined by the *alternance* of 1981, when power passed to the socialists, and again in 1986 and 1988, when further changes of government were brought about as a result of changed preferences on the part of the electorate. Mitterrand, the bitter enemy of de Gaulle and his Constitution, has proved to be a devoted custodian of the General's institutions.

Some analysts consider that France has finally, in the late twentieth century, arrived at 'the politics of consensus', with the result that French politics, like the French economy and French society, are now less different from those of other countries. This view is only partially correct. 'Consensus' was not lacking in the past – the Third Republic was based on it. Nor is the concept of 'normalization' a particularly helpful one: who or what, after all, should be regarded as 'normal'? What is true, however, is that the parameters of politics have been redefined by the three main political parties of the Fifth Republic – the PS, the RPR and the UDF. The emergence of a rejuvenated socialist party and the spectacular decline of the PCF have led the Left to abandon the politics of utopia in favour of a new pragmatism, symbolized by the leadership of Mitterrand and Rocard. The old reactionary Right of the pre-war period, discredited by the experience of Vichy and the Occupation, has given way to the more forward-looking, neo-liberal, technocratic and nationalistic Gaullists and Giscardians. In consequence, true Centrists like the Christian Democrats and conservative Radicals have had difficulty in carving out a space for themselves, though the rise of the FN suggests that there is a *'poujadiste'* Right which will not easily be reconciled to any putative consensus. Certainly, the ideological divisions that derived from the French Revolution and that fuelled the politics of the nineteenth and early twentieth centuries are largely a thing of the past. In the Bicentennial celebrations of 1989 Mitterrand endeavoured to focus on the earlier, less controversial, stages of the Revolution, which were represented as proclaiming universal human rights. There was no harking back to the old Radical discourse of 1889, by which the Revolution was deemed to be a 'bloc', to be accepted as a totality, Terror and all. Even Chirac can now join in lusty renderings of the *Marseillaise*. The religious issue is no longer central to politics (notwithstanding the clash over the Savary bill in 1984) and even class has lost its power to determine political allegiance. But the difference between Left and Right will continue to be important, as long as debate on subjects such as the rights of the individual, private property and social justice remains part of the agenda of French politics.

As a final theme for reflection, one can hardly ignore the dramatic change that has taken place in the status of France as a world power over the course of the twentieth century. Before the First World War France was universally acknowledged as one of the principal Great Powers. Victory in 1918, purchased at an enormous price, prolonged the illusion that France could retain its position in the front rank. As late as 1930 France was still regarded as the leading (and possibly the most belligerent) military power in Europe. When war broke out again in 1939 few people either at home or abroad anticipated the collapse of 1940, which made its impact all the more shattering. French pretensions (the source of much of the confused diplomacy of the inter-war years) were cruelly exposed. The post-war world order, dominated by the two superpowers of the United States and the Soviet Union, inevitably demoted France to the second-class status where (with Britain) it had long properly belonged. Coming to terms with this reduced rank, after centuries as a leading world power, was no easier for the French than for the British. Hence the resistance, vain though it proved, to the loss of Empire in the Far East and in North Africa. Hence, too, the refusal of de Gaulle to accept bi-polarity and his search for a *politique de grandeur* in conformity with that 'exalted and exceptional destiny' which, in his memoirs and elsewhere, he stipulated as essential for France. As an old-fashioned apologist for the nation-state and a strident nationalist who peddled chauvinistic fantasies about an imaginary France ('the princess in the fairy stories or the Madonna in the frescoes'), entitled to conduct a world policy by dint of being France, he successfully massaged the *amour-propre* of his electorate and turned both his own personality and his *politique de grandeur* into part of the French national myth. But, as regards French relations with the outside world, his impact on geo-political realities was minimal. In some ways, the General was a relic from the nineteenth (if not the seventeenth) century.

Yet de Gaulle was more than a 'noble anachronism'. Apart from being an outstandingly gifted politician, well aware of the need for economic moderniz-ation and prepared to extricate his country from the Algerian morass, he appreciated that, if France were to regain its rank in the first division of international power politics, it had to be in association with other European states. In proposing a 'Europe from the Atlantic to the Urals', or a 'European Europe', he signalled his opposition to an 'Atlantic' Europe subject to Ameri-can influence exercised through NATO, and at the same time implied the possibility of a rapprochement with the Soviet Union (which he always referred to as 'Russia') should it divest itself of its empire east of the Urals and turn back to where it belonged, among the European family of nations. In the longer term, he seems to have envisaged the resurrection of a latter-day version of the old concert of Europe, which had assigned itself the role of maintaining world order. In the shorter term, in practice, he was realistic enough to accept the need to operate in a world polarized between the super-powers, but manoeuvred so that, where the overall balance of power between the Americans and the Soviets was not affected, France and other medium powers might be free to pursue their own goals. As the ultimate guarantee that France would count in the world, he championed the idea of an indepen-dent French nuclear deterrent.

None of de Gaulle's successors dared openly to repudiate the General's legacy in foreign and defence policy. In the event, however, as has been related, the European future that France has pursued, particularly under Giscard and Mitterrand, has involved not only ever closer economic union with its EC partners (in line with the vision of Jean Monnet and Jacques Delors rather than with that of de Gaulle) but also a 'Europeanization' of French foreign policy. French policy-makers continue to aspire to a world role for their country, but recognize that this is incompatible with Gaullist notions of sovereignty and the primacy of the nation-state. 'Integration' has rapidly overtaken 'independence' as the *leitmotif* of Mitterrand's France. De Gaulle's ideal of a '*Europe des patries*' has been quietly buried under the new Euro-rhetoric. On the other hand, having always refused to treat the Yalta settlement as definitive, de Gaulle would hardly have been surprised by the end of the Cold War and by the collapse of communism in Eastern Europe.

Whether the new European order will eventually approximate to his dream of a Europe from the Atlantic to the Urals is another matter. What is clear is that in the post-Cold War and post-Gulf War world, where warmer relations exist between Paris and Washington and between Paris and Moscow, France will make its voice heard in the international community because of its renunciation of independence and its commitment to interdependence. Having spent much of the twentieth century coping with the inheritance of the nineteenth century, the French have demonstrated that, in their approach to external relations, as in the modernization of their economy and their political system, they have already moved into the twenty-first century.

Select Bibliography

The following is intended essentially as a guide to further reading. It does not represent all the books and periodicals from which material has been drawn. Generally speaking, it concentrates on the most recent or definitive studies, the bibliographies of which can in turn provide references to sources and earlier contributions to the literature. Unless otherwise stated, place of publication of works in English is London, and of works in French Paris. Periodicals are abbreviated thus:

AHR	*American Historical Review*
CHIMT	*Cahiers d'Histoire de l'Institut Maurice Thorez*
EHQ	*European History Quarterly*
ESR	*European Studies Review*
FH	*French History*
FHS	*French Historical Studies*
H	*History*
HJ	*The Historical Journal*
HR	*Historical Reflections*
JCH	*Journal of Contemporary History*
JMH	*Journal of Modern History*
JSH	*Journal of Social History*
MCF	*Modern and Contemporary France*
MS	*Le Mouvement Social*
RH	*Revue Historique*
RHMC	*Revue d'Histoire Moderne et Contemporaine*
RHDGM	*Revue d'Histoire de la Deuxième Guerre Mondiale*
TRHS	*Transactions of the Royal Historical Society*
VS	*Vingtième Siècle*

I 1898–1914

The most wide-ranging and stimulating of recent contributions is T. Zeldin's *France 1848–1945* (2 vols., Oxford, 1973–7). More helpful for beginners is R.D. Anderson's well-organized and readable *France 1870–1914: Politics and Society* (1977). R. Magraw offers a Marxist perspective in *France 1815–1914: The Bourgeois Century* (1983). No serious student of French politics can ignore D. Brogan's evergreen *The Development of Modern France 1870–1939* (n.e. 1967), while D. Thomson, *Democracy in France* (5th edn., 1969) is still worth reading. S. Hoffmann's contribution to the collection of essays he edited under the title *France: Change and Tradition* (1963) is a penetrating analysis of the political and social structures of the Third Republic. The *Nouvelle histoire de la France contemporaine (NHFC)* published by Editions du Seuil contains many fine volumes, among them vol. 11, M. Rébérioux, *La République radicale? (1898–1914)* (1975). This, with its predecessor, has been translated and published as volume 4 of the *Cambridge History of Modern France*: J.-M. Mayeur and M. Rébérioux, *The Third Republic from its Origins to the Great War, 1871–1914* (1984). J.-M. Mayeur's *La vie politique sous la Troisième République* (1984) is an excellent guide to the high politics of the period. J.-B. Duroselle, *La France et les Français 1900–1914* (1972) is a masterly survey, while J. Estèbe, *Les ministres de la République 1871–1914* (1982) throws much light on the personal wealth of the regime's rulers. Two useful works of reference are P.M. Hutton, ed, *Historical Dictionary of the French Third Republic, 1870–1940*, 2 vols, (1986) and D. Bell, D. Johnson and P. Morris, eds, *A Biographical Dictionary of French Political Leaders Since 1870* (Hemel Hempstead, 1990). The most recent reinterpretation of the Third Republic is by P. Miquel, *La Troisième République* (1989). E. Weber's *France, Fin de Siècle* (1986) is replete with anecdotes and stresses 'progress' and 'modernization' in the *Belle Epoque*.

1 France and the Dreyfus Affair

The most up-to-date account is now J.D. Bredin, *The Affair: the Case of Alfred Dreyfus* (New York, 1986), a work first published in French in 1983. Still worth reading are D. Johnson, *France and the Dreyfus Affair* (1966) and H.R. Kedward, *The Dreyfus Affair: Catalyst for Tensions in French Society* (1965), which provides documentary illustration of the divisions engendered by the Affair. Also valuable is N.L. Kleenblatt, ed., *The Dreyfus Affair: Art, Truth and Justice* (Berkeley, 1987). A local perspective is provided by M. Burns, *Rural Society and French Politics: Boulangism and the Dreyfus Affair 1886–1900* (Princeton, 1984) and in *HR* (1978). The army's role is dealt with in D. Ralston, *The Army of the Republic* (1967) and reassessed by D. Porch, *The March to the Marne* (1981). The xenophobia and paranoia rife in French military circles are set out in an article by A. Mitchell in *JMH* (1980). The situation of the French Jewish community is well described by M. Marrus, *The Politics of Assimilation: A Study of the French Jewish Community at the Time of the Dreyfus Affair* (1971) and V. Caron, *Between France and Germany: the Jews of Alsace-Lorraine 1871–1918* (Stanford, 1988). There are also good essays in the collection edited by F. Malino and B. Wasserstein, *The Jews in Modern France* (1985). Stephen Wilson's *Ideology and Experience: Antisemitism in France at the Time of the Dreyfus Affair* (1982) provides massive evidence for the existence of anti-Semitic attitudes throughout French society. Other valuable contributions to this subject are N. Wilson, *Bernard-Lazare: Antisemitism and the Problem of Jewish Identity in Late-Nineteenth-Century France* (1978) and M. Winock's collection of essays, *Edouard Drumond et compagnie. Antisémitisme et fascisme en France* (1982). A. Silvera, *Daniel Halévy and His Times: A Gentleman Commoner in the Third Republic* (Ithaca, N.Y., 1966) is illuminating on the attitudes of intellectuals. Press coverage of the Affair may be studied in J. Ponty's article in *RHMC* (1974).

2 The Republic of the Radicals

The short volume in the admirable *Archives* series by J.T. Nordmann, *La France Radicale* (1977) is a good introduction. The connections between Radicalism and anti-clericalism may be explored in R. Rémond, *L'anticléricisme en France de 1815 à nos jours* (1976). J. Faury, *Cléricalisme et anticléricalisme dans le Tarn 1848–1900* (Toulouse, 1980) is an interesting case study. Good accounts of the clash between Church and State may be found in J. McManners, *Church and State in France 1870–1914* (1972) and M. Larkin, *Church and State after the Dreyfus Affair: The Separation Issue in France* (1974). J.-M. Mayeur's *La séparation de l'Église et de l'État* (1966) is another distinguished contribution to the *Archives* series. Three important biographies are P. Sorlin, *Waldeck-Rousseau* (1966); D.R. Watson, *Georges Clemenceau: A Political Biography* (1974); and J.C. Allain, *Caillaux* (2 vols., 1978–81). J.D. Ellis, *The Physician-Legislators of France: Medicine and Politics in the Early Third Republic 1870–1914* (Cambridge, 1990) analyses the political contribution of doctors, many of whom were Radicals.

3 The Challenge of the Left

The formation of the SFIO is explained in A. Noland, *The Founding of the French Socialist Party* (1956). L. Derfler, *Alexandre Millerand: the Socialist Years* (The Hague, 1977) examines the man at the centre of the crisis over 'ministerialism'. H. Goldberg, *The Life of Jean Jaurès* (1962) does justice to its illustrious subject. The Guesdist tendency is analysed by C. Willard, *Le Mouvement socialiste en France (1893–1905): les guesdistes* (1965). See also J. Howorth, *Edouard Vaillant* (1982). The appeal of socialism to skilled artisans is set out in B.H. Moss, *The Origins of the French Labor Movement, 1830–1914: The Socialism of Skilled Workers* (Berkeley, 1976), and to peasants in T. Judt, *Socialism in Provence 1871–1914* (1979). T. Judt offers further insights in *Marxism and the French Left: Studies in Labour and Politics in France 1830–1981* (Oxford, 1986). The changing fortunes of anarchism are related by J. Maitron, *Histoire du mouvement anarchiste en France (1880–1914)* (2 vols., 1951), while there are some new perspectives in R.D. Sonn, *Anarchism and Cultural Politics in Fin-de-Siècle France* (Lincoln, Nebraska, 1989). M. Fleming, *The Anarchist Way to Socialism* (1979) is a study of Elisée Reclus. Revolutionary syndicalism may be approached through H. Dubief, *Le syndicalisme révolutionnaire* (1969) and F.F. Ridley, *Revolutionary Syndicalism in France* (1970). P. Stearns, *Revolutionary Syndicalism and French Labor* (1971) minimizes the influence of the syndicalists, but E. Shorter and C. Tilly, *Strikes in France 1830–1968* (1974) argues the political implications of strike waves. J. Julliard, *Fernand Pelloutier et les origines du syndicalisme d'action directe* (1971) is the definitive study of the *bourses du travail*. G. Lefranc, *Le mouvement syndical sous la Troisième République* (1967) is a good general study. J. Jennings, *Syndicalism in France: A Study of Ideas* (1990) concentrates on ideology without investigating its diffusion. There is a two-volume biography of the leading figure in the French trade-union movement for four decades by B. Georges and D. Tintant, *Léon Jouhaux* (1962–79). Short biographies of other militants may be obtained from J. Maitron, ed., *Dictionnaire biographique du mouvement ouvrier français* (1964–   ). The repressive and provocative actions of the French State with regard to labour militancy are amply demonstrated in J. Julliard, *Clemenceau, briseur de grèves* (1965). The difficulties of co-ordinating international action among workers is stressed by J. Howorth in *EHQ* (1985). Longer-term perspectives are furnished by C. Tilly, *The Contentious French* (1986).

4 The Right and Nationalism

The starting point for any investigation of the French Right remains R. Rémond, *The Right Wing in France from 1815 to De Gaulle* (2nd American edn, Philadelphia, 1969). A revised French edition was published in 1982. The 'revolutionary' Right is best approached through Z. Sternhell, *La droite révolutionnaire* (1978). See also his *Maurice Barrès et le nationalisme français* (1972) and R. Soucy, *Fascism in France: The Case of Maurice Barrès* (1972). E. Weber, *Action Française: Royalism and Reaction in Twentieth-Century France* (1962) is a full treatment of its subject. The peculiar links between extreme Right and extreme Left are explored by P. Mazgaj, *The Action Française and Revolutionary Syndicalism* (1979). The same author has a useful historiographical essay on the origins of the Radical Right in *FHS* 15 (1987). The situation of French Catholics may be approached via R. Gibson, *A Social History of French Catholicism 1789–1914* (1989) and volume 2 of G. Cholvy and Y.M. Hilaire, *Histoire religieuse de la France contemporaine* (1986), which covers the period 1880–1930. F. Lebrun, ed., *Histoire des catholiques en France* (1980) remains useful on popular religion and 'dechristianization'. The history of Christian democracy is traced by J.M. Mayeur, *Des partis catholiques à démocratie chrétienne, xixe-xxe siècles* (1980). B. Martin, *Count Albert de Mun, Paladin of the Third Republic* (Chapel Hill, 1978) needs to be supplemented by P. Levillain, *Albert de Mun, catholicisme français et catholicisme romain du Syllabus au Ralliement* (Rome, 1983) and, for the history of 'social' Catholicism more generally, H. Rollet, *L'Action sociale des catholiques en France 1871–1914* (2 vols, 1947–58). J.F. McMillan discusses the role of women in social Catholicism in *Studies in Church History* 27, ed. W.J. Sheils and D. Wood (Oxford, 1990).

On nationalism generally, there is now an ambitious and stimulating interpretation from B. Jenkins, *Nationalism in France: Class and Nation Since 1789* (1990). For the argument that a *réveil national* took place in the years immediately before the First World War, see E. Weber, *The Nationalist Revival in France 1905–1914* (1968). The standard biography of its leading figure is P. Miquel, *Poincaré* (1961); but see also G. Wright, *Raymond Poincaré and the French Presidency* (1967). David E. Sumler, in *FHS* 6 (1969–70), expresses scepticism about the nationalist revival and stresses the importance of domestic rather than international politics.

5 The Road to War

The motivation behind French colonial expansion has generated considerable historical debate. Among those who argue that nationalism and 'prestige' were more important than financial or economic factors are H. Brunschwig, *French Colonialism, 1871–1914: Myths and Realities* (1966); R. Girardet, *L'idée coloniale en France de 1871 à 1962* (1972); and C. Andrew and A.S. Kanya-Forstner in *HJ* (1971) and *HJ* (1976). The economic case is put with considerable subtlety by J. Thobie, *La France impériale 1880–1914* (1982) and in the essays edited by J. Bouvier and R. Girault, *L'impérialisme français d'avant 1914* (1976). L. Abrams and D.J. Miller challenge the assessment of the 'Colonial Party' by Andrew and Kanya-Forstner in *HJ* (1976). The weight of financial considerations in French diplomacy can be guaged from R. Girault, *Emprunts russes et investissements français en Russie 1887–1914* (1973) and R. Poidevin, *Les relations économiques et financières entre la France et l'Allemagne de 1898–1914* (1969). J.F.V. Keiger reassesses French foreign policy in general and the role of Poincaré in particular in *France and the Origins of the First World War* (1983). An excellent survey of Franco-German relations is R. Poidevin and J. Bariéty, *Les relations franco-allemandes 1815–1975* (1977). A massive study of Franco-Italian relations, which goes far beyond the bounds of diplomatic history, is P. Milza, *Français et Italiens à la fin du xixe siècle: aux origines du rapprochement franco-italien de 1900–1902* (2 vols., Rome, 1981). Also important is C. Andrew, *Théophile Delcassé and the Making of the Entente Cordiale: A Reappraisal of French Foreign Policy 1898–1905* (1968). French, as well as German, aggression in the Agadir crisis is apparent in J.C. Allain, *Agadir 1911, une crise impérialiste en Europe pour la conquête du Maroc* (1976) and G. Barraclough, *From Agadir to Armageddon: Anatomy of a Crisis* (1982). For pre-war military planning see P.M. Kennedy, ed., *The War Plans of the Great Powers 1880–1914* (1979) and S.R. Williamson, *The Politics of Grand Strategy: Britain and France Prepare for War 1904–1914* (1969). A reassessment of the debate on the Three Year Law on military service has been made by G. Krumeich, *Armaments and politics in France on the Eve of the First World War: the Introduction of Three Year Conscription 1913–1914* (Leamington Spa, 1984), translated from the German edition of 1980. There is a characteristically suggestive piece on France by R.C. Cobb in R.J.W. Evans and H. Pogge von Strandemann, *The Coming of the First World War* (Oxford, 1988). The reactions of French public opinion to the July crisis are documented by J.J. Becker, *1914: Comment les Français sont entrés dans la guerre* (1977).

6   *A Belle Époque?*

The best introduction to French economic history is now F. Caron, *An Economic History of Modern France* (1979). J.J. Carré *et al.*, *French Economic Growth* (Stanford, 1976) is highly technical. J.M. Laux, *In First Gear: The French Automobile Industry to 1914* (Liverpool, 1976) stresses the dynamism of this sector, while P. Fridenson, *Histoire des usines Renault*: vol. I *Naissance de la grande entreprise 1898–1939* (1973) provides a case study. Broad demographic trends are outlined by C. Dyer, *Population and Society in Twentieth-Century France* (1978). An essential reference work is F. Braudel and E. Labrousse, eds., *Histoire économique et sociale de la France:* vol. IV *1880 à nos jours* (1976), which has not been superseded by the glossy Y. Lequin, ed., *Histoire des Français xixe-xxe siècles* (3 vols., 1983–4). In English, an overview of social and economic developments is available in R. Price, *A Social History of Nineteenth-Century France* (1987). M. Perrot has edited vol. 4 of *A History of Private Life* (General Editors P. Ariès and G. Duby), the English translation of which has been published by Harvard University Press: see *From the Fires of Revolution to the Great War* (1990). P. Sorlin, *La société française* (2 vols., 1969–71) is more ambitious and original than G. Dupeux, *French Society 1789–1970* (English edn. 1976), but the latter's *Aspects de l'histoire sociale et politique du Loir-et-Cher 1848–1914* (1962) is a model regional study. G. Duby and A. Wallon, eds., *Histoire de la France rurale*:

vol. III *1789–1914* (1976) is fundamental, but E. Weber, *Peasants into Frenchmen: The Modernization of Rural France 1870–1914* (Stanford, 1976) is more exciting. Weber answers some of his critics in *AHR* (1982). For the aristocracy, one should turn to R. Gibson's excellent contribution to J. Howorth and P. Cerny, eds., *Élites in France: Origins, Reproduction and Power* (1981). The attitude of employers to labour militancy is studied by P.N. Stearns in *JMH* (1968). Their outlook on economic growth and rationalization are discussed by M. Lévy-Leboyer in *MS* (1974), and by A. Moutet, *MS* (1975). P. Nord, *MS* (1981), studies the political outlook of small businessmen. See also his monograph *Paris Shopkeepers and the Politics of Resentment* (Princeton, 1986). S. Barrows, *Distorting Mirrors: Visions of the Crowd in Late-Nineteenth-Century France* (New Haven, 1981) and R. Nye, *The Origins of Crowd Psychology: Gustave Le Bon and the Crisis of Mass Democracy in the Third Republic* (1975) throw light on bourgeois perceptions and fears of the masses, as does D. Pick, *Faces of Degeneration: a European Disorder, c. 1848–1918* (Cambridge, 1989).

A useful collection of essays on the development of urbanization in nineteenth-century France is J. Merriman, ed., *Cities in Nineteenth-Century France* (1981). A case study is provided by J. Merriman in *The Red City: Limoges and the French Nineteenth Century* (Oxford, 1985). Another important collective work is G. Duby, ed., *Histoire de la France urbaine*: vol. IV *La ville de l'âge industriel* (1983). Class is discussed in J. Merriman, ed., *Consciousness and Class Experience in Nineteenth-Century Europe* (1979). Parisian workers are studied by L.R. Berlanstein, *The Working People of Paris 1871–1914* (1984), and their housing conditions in A.L. Shapiro, *Housing the Poor of Paris 1850–1902* (Madison, 1985). On the emergence of the proletarian 'red belt' around Paris, Bobigny is the focus of T. Stovall, *The Rise of the Paris Red Belt* (Berkeley, 1990) and Saint-Denis that of J.-P. Brunet, *Saint-Denis, La ville rouge: socialisme et communisme en banlieue ouvrière 1890–1939* (1980). A necessary point of departure for any study of industrial militancy is M. Perrot, *Workers on Strike, 1871–1890* (Leamington, 1987): original French edition 1984). Useful monographs are M. Hanagan, *The Logic of Solidarity* (1980); J.W. Scott, *The Glassworkers of Carmaux* (Cambridge, Mass., 1974); R. Cazals, *Avec les ouvriers de Mazamet* (1980); and R. Trempé, *Les mineurs de Carmaux 1848–1914* (2 vols., 1971). Y. Lequin, *Les ouvriers de la région lyonnaise (1848–1914)* (2 vols., Lyon, 1977) is a fine thesis.

For the situation of women in urban society, see J.F. McMillan, *Housewife or Harlot: the Place of Women in French Society 1870–1940* (Brighton, 1981), and for peasant women, M. Segalen, *Love and Power in the Peasant Family* (1983). There are good essays on France in S. Reynolds, ed., *Women, State and Revolution* (Brighton, 1986). J. Scott and L. Tilly, *Women, Work and Family* (1978) is fundamental for an appreciation of the sexual division of labour. *MS* 105 (1978) devotes the whole issue to the theme of women's work. The best treatment of women and trade unionism remains M. Guilbert, *La femme et l'organisation syndicale* (1966), though C. Sowerwine has an excellent article on the Couriau affair in *JMH* (1983). The situation of women textile workers in the Nord is depicted in P. Hilden, *Working Women and Socialist Politics in France 1880–1914: a Regional Study* (Oxford, 1986). For socialist women generally, see C. Sowerwine, *Sisters or Citizens? Women and*

Socialism in France since 1876 (1982). On the suffrage movement, there is S.C. Hause (with A. Kenney), *Women's Suffrage and Socialist Politics in the French Third Republic* (Princeton, 1984). Individual militants are studied in S.C. Hause, *Hubertine Auclert, the French Suffragette* (1987) and F. Gordon, *The Integral Feminist: Madeleine Pelletier 1874–1939* (Oxford 1990). L. Tilly examines women's collective action and feminism in L. and C. Tilly, eds., *Class Conflict and Collective Action* (Beverly Hills, 1981). M.L. Stewart sees 'protective' legislation as oppressive in *Women, Work and the French State: Labour Protection and Social Patriarchy 1879–1919* (Kingston, Montreal, 1989). On prostitution, there is now an English translation of A. Corbin's massive French work: *Women For Hire: Prostitution and Sexuality in France After 1850* (Cambridge, Mass., 1990). For a cause which engaged many feminists, see P.E. Prestwich, *Drink and the Politics of Social Reform: Anti-alcoholism in France Since 1870* (Palo Ato, 1988). Gender issues are also raised in A. Copley, *Sexual Moralities in France 1780–1980: New Ideas on the Family, Divorce and Homosexuality* (1989); R. Harris, *Murders and Madness: Medicine, Law and Society in the Fin-de-Siècle* (Oxford, 1989); and E. Berenson, 'The politics of divorce in France of the Belle Epoque: the case of Joseph and Henriette Caillaux', *AHR*, 93/1 (1988), 31–55. The lighter side of the era can be approached via C. Rearick, *Pleasures of the Belle Epoque: Entertainment and Festivity in Turn-of-the-Century France* (New Haven, 1985). See also J. Seigel, *Bohemian Paris: Culture, Politics and the Boundaries of Bourgeois Life, 1850–1930* (1986).

II   1914–1918

In the NHFC series, there are two recent replacements for the unsatisfactory earlier volumes: J.-J. Becker and S. Berstein, *Victoire et frustrations 1914–1929* (1990) and D. Borne and H. Dubief, *La crise des années 30, 1929–1938* (1989). In the same series, J.-P. Azéma, *From Munich to the Liberation (1938–1944)* (Cambridge, 1984) is outstanding. The 1930s are also covered by S. Berstein in *La France des années 30* (1988). A large-scale synthesis of political history can be found in R. Rémond, *Notre Siècle 1918–1988* (1988). For the intellectual trajectories and political involvement of intellectuals, see J.F. Sirinelli, *Génération intellectuelle: Khâgneux et Normaliens dans l'entre-deux-guerres* (1988). Sharp contemporary observations by the *Manchester Guardian* correspondent can be read in A. Werth, *The Destiny of France* (1937). Interesting anecdotal evidence is recalled in B.G. Smith, *Confessions of a Concierge. Madame Lucie's History of Twentieth Century France* (New Haven, 1985) and R.C. Cobb, *People and Places* (Oxford, 1985).

7   A Nation at War

An excellent overview is provided by J.B. Duroselle, *La France et les Français 1914–1920* (1972). The question of what the French were fighting for is discussed by D. Stevenson, *French War Aims against Germany 1914–1919* (1982) and by D. Johnson in B. Hunt and A. Preston, eds., *War Aims and Strategic Policy in the Great War* (1977). A recent contribution on 'French military war aims, 1914–1916' by R.A. Prete is in *HJ* 28 (1985). The international context is supplied by D. Stevenson, *The First World War and International Politics* (Oxford, 1988). Economic warfare is the subject of M.M. Farrar, *Conflict and Compromise: The Strategy, Politics and Diplomacy of the French Block-ade* (The Hague, 1974). M.J. Carley reassesses French intervention in the Russian Civil War in *JMH* (1976); while G. Soutou examines French ambitions in the Rhinelands in *RH* (1978). *Les carnets de guerre de Louis Barthas, tonnelier 1914–1918*, ed. Remy Cazals (1978) is a moving account of the war as seen by an ordinary *poilu*. The definitive study of the mutinies in the French army in 1917 is G. Pedroncini, *Les mutineries de 1917* (1967). Morale at the Front is dealt with by D. Englander in *FH* (1987) and by S. Audoin-Rouzeau, *14–18. Les Combattants des tranchées* (1988). Also valuable are the recollections of Marc Bloch, *Memoirs of War, 1914–1915* (Cambridge, 1988) edited by C. Fink.

J.J. Becker, *The Great War and the French People* (Leamington Spa, 1986) studies French morale on the home front. P.J. Flood, *France 1914–1918: Public Opinion and the War Effort* (1990) is a case study of the Isère. There are important essays in P. Fridenson, ed., *1914–1918: L'autre front* (1977). M. Gallo analyses the attitudes of workers on the war factories in *MS* (1966). A highly partisan, but absorbing account of revolutionary syndicalist opposition to the war is A. Rosmer, *Le mouvement ouvrier pendant la première guerre mondiale* (2 vols., 1936–59). J.-L. Robert comments perceptively on labour militancy during the war in *CHIMT* (1977). The latest work is J.N. Horne, *Labour at War: France and Britain 1914–1918* (Oxford, 1991).

8   The Aftermath of War

A good introduction to the complexities of devising a durable peace settlement is S. Marks, *The Illusion of Peace: International Relations in Europe 1919–1933* (1976). Financial aspects of the problem are stressed by D.P. Silverman, *Reconstructing Europe after the Great War* (Cambridge, Mass., 1982) and by M. Trachtenberg, *Reparation in World Politics: France and European Economic Diplomacy 1916–1923* (New York, 1980). B. Kent, *The Spoils of War: the Politics, Economics and Diplomacy of Reparations 1918–1932* (Oxford, 1989) takes a more traditional line. Strategic considerations are discussed by D. Watson in N. Waites, ed., *Troubled Neighbours: Franco-British Relations in the Twentieth Century* (1971); see also W.A. McDougall, *France's Rhineland Diplomacy 1914–1924: The Last Bid for a Balance of Power in Europe* (Princeton, 1978). J.C. King highlights the clash of views between military leaders and politicians in *Foch versus Clemenceau: France and German Dismemberment 1918–1919* (1960). The reactions of French public opinion as revealed in the press are documented in P. Miquel, *La paix de Versailles et l'opinion publique française* (1972). The post-war situation of the French empire is set out in C.M. Andrew and A.S. Kanya-Forstner, *France Overseas: The Great War and the Climax of French Imperial Expansion* (1981).

The fullest discussion of the economic impact of the war is still A. Fontaine, *French Industry during the War* (1926), the most remarkable volume in the marvellous series of studies commissioned after the war by the Carnegie Series for International Peace. G. Hatry, *Renault, usine de guerre 1914–1918* (1978) is a particularly illuminating case study. The expansion of the role of the state in economic affairs is the theme of R.F. Kuisel, *Capitalism and the State in Modern France: Renovation and Economic Management in the Twentieth Century* (1981). There are useful essays on post-war economic rationalization in *Recherches* (1978). For the effects of the war in the French countryside, see M. Gervais, M. Jollivet, and Y. Tavernier, eds., *Histoire de la France rurale:* vol. IV *De 1914 á nos jours* (1976). How the war affected women in urban France is discussed in part II of J.F. McMillan, *Housewife or Harlot*. See also J.L. Robert in *MS* (1981) for how the CGT viewed the working-class family. E.J. Lead, *No Man's Land: Combat and Identity in World War I* (1979) uses anthropological techniques and concepts to try to discover what the war did to the minds of the men who fought it, but the essential work on this subject is A. Prost's magnificent *Les anciens combattants et la société française 1914–1939* (3 vols., 1977), perhaps best approached after reading his shorter *Les anciens combattants* (1977) prepared for the *Archives* series. F. Field, *Three French Writers and the Great War* (1975) is suggestive about possible intellectual repercussions of the war. A more recent contribution by the same author is F. Field, *British and French Writers of the First World War: Comparative Studies in Cultural History* (Cambridge, 1991).

The fundamental study of the labour unrest which generated fears of the red menace and brought the French Communist party into being remains A. Kriegel, *Aux origines du communisme français (1914–1920)* (2 vols., 1964). R. Wohl, *French Communism in the Making* (1966) is also useful. The interpretation of the strike by metallurgical workers in 1919 by N. Papayanis in *MS* (1975) should be contrasted with that of J.-P. Brunet in *Saint-Denis: La ville rouge*. The aspirations of the revolutionary syndicalists can be appreciated from C. Gras, *Alfred Rosmer (1877–1964) et le mouvement révolutionnaire international* (1971) and J. Maitron and C. Chambelland, *Syndicalisme révolutionnaire et communisme. Les archives de Pierre Monatte 1914–1924* (1968). George Dumoulin's evolution from revolutionary to reformist is traced by P.M. Arum in *MS* (1974). The Editions Sociales have published the definitive texts of the debates at the Congress of Tours which split the SFIO: *Le Congrès de Tours (18e congrès national du parti socialiste). Texte intégrale*, ed. J. Charles *et al.* (1980). J.-L. Robert reassesses the schism in the CGT in *La scission de 1921: essai de reconnaissance de formes* (1980). See also J. Charles in CHIMT (1976). Also valuable is K. Amdur, *Syndicalist Legacy: Trade Unions and Politics in Two French Cities in the Era of World War I* (Urbana, 1987). There is a good essay on French workers by R. Magraw in S. Salter and J. Stevenson, eds., *The Working Class and Politics in Europe and America 1929–1945* (1990). J. Girault, *Benoît Frachon: communiste et syndicaliste* (1989) is the biography of an important militant.

9   The Game of Politics in Post-War France

For the general context of the recovery of political stability after the upheavals of war and its aftermath see C.S. Maier, *Recasting Bourgeois Europe: Stabilisation in France, Germany and Italy after World War I* (Princeton, 1975). J.-N. Jeanneney throws much new light on the relationship between wealth and political power in his thesis *François de Wendel en République: L'argent et le pouvoir 1914–1940* (1976) and in his collection of essays *L'argent caché. Milieux d'affaires et pouvoir politique dans la France du XXe siècle* (1980). Other useful studies on the same theme are J. Néré, *Le problème du mur d'argent. Les crises du franc (1924–1926)* (1985) and H. Bonin, *L'Argent en France depuis 1880. Banquiers, financiers, épargnants* (1989). An old, but invaluable guide to the political realities behind ideological shibboleths in

France is A. Siegfried, *France, a Study in Nationality* (1930). P. Warwick is discriminating on the subject of political 'gamesmanship' in *JMH* (1978). Biographies of the leading politicians of the inter-war years are scarce. Among the few are J. Sherwood, *George Mandel and the Third Republic* (Stanford, 1970) and for Tardieu the study by R. Binion, *Defeated Leaders: The Political Fate of Caillaux, Jouvenel and Tardieu* (1960). The essential work on the French Radical party is now S. Berstein, *Histoire du parti radical 1919–1939* (2 vols., 1980–2). T. Judt, *La reconstruction du parti socialiste 1921–1926* (1976) charts the revival in the fortunes of the SFIO after the split at Tours. See also G. Ziebura, *Léon Blum et le parti socialiste (1872–1934)* (1967). The shortcomings of the *Cartel des Gauches* government of Herriot are trenchantly exposed by J.-N. Jeanneney, *Leçons d'histoire pour une gauche au pouvoir. La faillite du Cartel 1924–1926* (1977). T. Judt explains socialist misgivings about joining with the Radicals in *JCH* (1976). The partial abatement of the old clerical-anti-clerical antagonisms is studied by H.S. Paul, *The Second Ralliement: the Rapprochement between Church and State in the Twentieth Century* (Washington, 1967) and should be supplemented with R. Rémond, *Les catholiques dans la France des années 30* (1979) and P. Christophe, *Les catholiques et le Front populaire* (1979). The right-wing bias of Catholics is emphasised by O. Arnal, *Ambivalent Alliance: the Catholic Church and the Action Française 1899–1939* (1985). On the temptations of fascism, see the essay by R.O. Paxton in R.J. Wolff and J.K. Hoensch, eds., *Catholics, the State and the European Radical Right 1919–1945* (Highland Lakes, New Jersey, 1987). M. Winock, *Histoire politique de la revue Esprit 1930–1950* (1975) shows how the doctrines of Emmanuel Mounier could reinforce the anti-parliamentary current of opinion. For contrasting views of Mounier, see R.W. Rauch, *Politics and Belief in Contemporary France: Emmanuel Mounier and Christian Democracy (1932–1950)* (The Hague, 1972) and J. Hellman, *Emmanuel Mounier and the New Catholic Left 1930–1950* (1981).

On the international position of France in the 1920s, J. Bariéty, *Les relations franco-allemandes après la première guerre mondiale* (1977) studies the German problem. The Ruhr occupation is re-examined by P. Guinn, *EHQ* 18 (1988). The French search for allies in eastern Europe is well studied by P.S. Wandycz, *France and Her Eastern Allies 1919–1925: French-Czechoslovak Relations from the Paris Peace Conference to Locarno* (Minneapolis, 1962). A. Hogenhuis-Seliverstoff, *Les relations franco-soviétiques 1917–1924* (1981) covers relations with the Soviet Union. The constraints imposed on French foreign policy by the state of national finances is spelled out by S.A. Schuker, *The End of French Predominance in Europe: The Financial Crisis of 1924 and the Adoption of the Dawes Plan* (Chapel Hill, 1976). For the hopes and illusions of the Locarno era see J. Jacobsen, *Locarno Diplomacy: Germany and the West 1925–1929* (Princeton, 1972). The debt problem is dealt with in D. Artaud, *La question des dettes interalliés et la reconstruction de l'Europe 1917–1929* (Lille, 1976) and the thorny question of disarmament by M. Vaïsse, *Sécurité d'abord: la politique française en matière de désarmement 9 décembre 1930–17 avril 1934* (1981).

10   The Depression and its Consequences
The basic reference work is A. Sauvy, *Histoire économique de la France entre les deux guerres* (3 vols., 1965–72). Volume III has a useful collection of

articles. A brief summary of Sauvy's views can be found in *JCH* (1969). T. Kemp, *The French Economy 1913–1939* (1972) gives a brief outline. Martin Wolfe reconsiders French interwar stagnation in C.K. Warner, ed., *From the Ancien Regime to the Popular Front* (1969). J. Jackson, *The Politics of Depression in France 1932–1936* (Cambridge, 1985) outlines the different policy options. The themes of economic rationalization and modernization are dealt with in a number of articles: see H.D. Peiter, *JSH* (1976); C. Maier, *JCH* (1970); Y. Lequin, *CHIMT* (1973); P. Fridenson, *MS* (1972); J.M. Sherwood, *JCH* (1980). R.F. Kuisel has written the biography of *Ernest Mercier, French Technocrat* (Berkeley, 1967). Gary S. Cross has examined the state's recourse to immigrant labour in *Immigrant Workers in Industrial France: The Making of a New Laboring Class* (Philadelphia, 1983). Polish immigrants are the subject of J. Ponty, *Polonnais méconnus. Histoire des travailleurs immigrés en France dans l'entre-deux guerres* (1988).

The political crisis is evoked in S. Berstein's *Archives* volume, *Le 6 février 1934* (1975). Still useful are the essays in J. Joll, ed., *The Decline of the Third Republic* (1959). N. Greene has studied the impact of the Depression on rural politics in *FHS* (1976). A nuanced perspective on French fascism may be found in P. Machefer, *Ligues et fascismes en France 1918–1939* (1974). Z. Sternhell has completed an impressive but controversial trilogy with *Ni droite ni gauche. L'Idéologie fasciste en France* (1983). S. Berstein assesses the fascist threat in *VS* (1984), as does R. Austin in M. Blinkhorn, ed., *Fascists and Conservatives: the Radical Right and the Establishment in Twentieth Century Europe* (1990). R. Soucy, *French Fascism: the First Wave 1924–1933* (New Haven, 1986) is the first volume of an archival-based history. P. Burrin, *La Dérive fasciste: Doriot, Déat, Bergery 1933–45* (1986) explores the move from Left to Right in three notable cases. Déat gives his own account in M. Déat, *Memoires politiques* (1989), now a major primary source for the period. W.R. Tucker, *The Fascist Ego: a Political Biography of Robert Brasillach* (Berkeley, 1975) studies a prominent fascist intellectual. W.D. Irvine, *French Conservatism in Crisis: the Republican Federation of France in the 1930s* (Baton Rouge, 1979) examines the parliamentary Right. For the SFIO, the starting point should be T. Judt's essay in *Marxism and the French Left*, but see also the older J.T. Marcus, *French Socialism in the Crisis Years 1933–1936* (New York, 1958). On the PCF, there are surveys by E. Mortimer, *The Rise of the French Communist Party 1920–1947* (1984) and R. Tiersky, *The French Communist Party 1920–1970* (1974), both of which concentrate on the leadership rather than the grass roots. P. Robrieux, *Histoire intérieure du Parti Communiste (1920–1945)* (1980) gives an inside view. A team of party historians have produced their own version of the story in R. Bourderon *et al.*, *Le PCF: étapes et problèmes 1920–1972* (1981). J. Girault *et al.* assess the progress of communism in *Sur l'implantation du PCF dans l'entre-deux guerres* (1972). A. Kriegel, *The French Communists: Profile of a People* (1972) advances the thesis of the party as 'counter-society'. P. Robrieux, *Maurice Thorez, vie sècrete et vie publique* (1975) explodes many of the legends to be found in the leader's own unreliable memoirs. The Popular Front strategy is discussed by D. Tartakovsky in *MS* 135 (1986). J. Haslam investigates the role of the Comintern in *HJ* (1979). T. Judt explains many of the difficulties which confront the historian of the PCF in his trenchant review article in *ESR* (1982). J.-J. Becker and S. Berstein develop an important theme in *Histoire de l'anticommunisme en France* vol. I: *1917–1940* (1987). The election results of 1936 are analysed by G. Dupeux, *Le Front populaire et les élections de 1936* (1959).

11 The Popular Front Era

J. Jackson, *The Popular Front in France: Defending Democracy 1934–1938* (Cambridge, 1988) is the best survey to date. There are valuable essays in M.S. Alexander and H. Graham, *The French and Spanish Popular Fronts: Comparative Perspectives* (Cambridge, 1989). For atmosphere, consult G. Lefranc, *Juin '36, l'explosion sociale* (1973) in the *Archives* series and L. Bodin and J. Touchard, *Front populaire* (1961), which presents extracts from the contemporary press. Two good biographies of Léon Blum are J. Colton, *Léon Blum: Humanist in Politics* (New York, 1966) and J. Lacouture, *Léon Blum* (1977). There are many illuminating contributions in R. Rémond and P. Renouvin, eds., *Léon Blum chef du gouvernement 1936–1937* (1967: n.e. 1982), the proceedings of a conference held in 1965. P. Warwick studies voting patterns in *The French Popular Front: A Legislative Analysis* (1977). The gradual disenchantment of the French working classes with the Blum government is the theme of an essay by A. Mitzman in J.C. Cairns, ed., *Contemporary France: Illusion, Conflict and Regeneration* (New York, 1978). A. Sauvy has frequently commented on what he regarded at the time as errors in the Popular Front's economic policies: see, for instance, *De Paul Reynaud à Charles de Gaulle* (1972). M. Margairaz in *MS* (1975) offers an alternative view. R. Frankenstein's thesis *Le Prix du réarmement français 1935–1939* (1982) spells out the dilemma which faced Blum in having to choose between guns and butter. The pressures on the government from its own left wing are discussed by D.N. Baker in *JMH* (1971) and by I.M. Wall *JMH* (1970). The *gauchistes* are studied in more detail by J.-P. Rioux, *Révolutionnaires du Front populaire: choix de documents 1935–1938* (1973) and by J. Rabaut, *Tout est possible: les gauchistes français 1929–1944* (1974). D. Guérin, *Front populaire, révolution manquée* (1970) sees 1936 as another missed opportunity for revolution. A. Prost studies the effects of the Popular Front experience on the CGT in *La CGT à l'époque du Front populaire 1934–1939* (1964). The PCF's strategy is discussed by D. Brower, *The New Jacobins: The French Communist Party and the Popular Front* (1968). D. Johnson, in *H* (1970), refuses to see the Popular Front as a complete failure. M. Seidmann advances the thesis that workers wanted leisure-time rather than revolution in *FHS* 13 (1982). G. Cross explores the same theme in *A Quest for Time: the Reduction of Work in Britain and France 1840–1940* (Berkeley, 1989). An excellent introduction to the Daladier ministry may be found in Azéma, *From Munich . . .*, which should be followed by the many original contributions to a colloquium on the Daladier regime, the proceedings of which have been edited in two volumes by R. Rémond and J. Bourdin as: vol. I *Édouard Daladier chef de gouvernement avril 1938–septembre 1939* (1977) and vol. II *La France et les Français en 1938–1939* (1978). G. Bourdé, *La défaite du Front populaire* (1977) analyses the systematic attempt to dismantle the Popular Front's social legislation.

The fundamental study of French foreign policy in the period is now J.-B. Duroselle, *La décadence (1932–1939)* (1979), which is based on all the available archival sources. The impact of the Depression on French foreign policy is the subject of H. Shami, *Economic Crisis and French Foreign Policy 1930–1936* (Leiden, 1989). The fate of the Little Entente is discussed by P. Wandycz, *Twilight of France's Eastern Alliances* (Princeton, 1988). The abortive Franco-Soviet alliance is studied by W.E. Scott, *Alliance against Hitler: the Origins of the Franco-Soviet Pact* (1962). On German reoccupation of the Rhineland, see J.T. Emmerson, *The Rhineland Crisis* (1977). The foreign policy of the Popular Front government is examined by J.E. Dreifort, *Yvon Delbos at the Quai d'Orsay* (1973). M.D. Gallagher discusses Léon Blum's attitude to the Spanish Civil War in *JCHC 1971)*. See also D. Wingeate Pike, *Les Français et la guerre d'Espagne* (1975). The evolution of French right-wing opinion on Nazi Germany is documented in C.A. Micaud, *The French Right and Nazi Germany 1933–1939: A Study of Public Opinion* (New York, 1972). The theme of appeasement in France may be approached through A. Adamthwaite, *France and the Coming of the Second World War 1936–1939* (1977) and the contributions to W.J. Mommsen and L. Kettenacher, eds., *The Fascist Challenge and the Policy of Appeasement* (1983). Strategic and financial considerations that affected French policy are developed by R.J. Young, *In Command of France: French Policy and Military Planning 1933–1940* (Cambridge, Mass., 1978) and Frankenstein, *Le prix du réarmement*. Aspects of Anglo-French relations are covered in the proceedings of two conferences published as *Les relations franco-britanniques de 1935 à 1939* (1975). For the renunciation of French ambitions in eastern Europe see D.E. Kaiser, *Economic Diplomacy and the Origins of the Second World War: Germany, Britain, France and Eastern Europe 1930–1939* (1980).

12   The Strange Defeat

W.L. Shirer, *The Collapse of the Third Republic: An Enquiry into the Fall of France 1940* (1970) illustrates the pitfalls of reading history backwards. Far more searching is J.-L. Crémieux-Brilhac, *Les Français de l'an 40*, 2 vols.: I *La Guerre oui ou non?* II *Ouvriers et soldats* (1990). Essential is J.-B. Duroselle's sequel to *La décadence*, entitled *L'Abîme 1939–1945* (1982). There is a growing literature on the period of the 'phoney war'. To G. Rossi-Landi, *La drôle de guerre. La vie politique en France, 2 Septembre 1939–10 mai 1940* (1971) can be added *Français et Britanniques dans la drôle de guerre* (1979), a collection of conference papers, and F. Bédarida's study of Anglo-French *mésentente*, *La stratégie secrète de la drôle de guerre: le Conseil Suprême Interallié, septembre 1939–avril 1940* (1979). A personal, but perceptive, viewpoint is F. Fonvieille-Alquier, *The French and the Phoney War 1939–1940* (1973). The influence of pacifist organizations is assessed by N. Ingram, *The Politics of Dissent: Pacifism in France 1919–1939* (Oxford, 1991).

The problems with different interpretations of the military defeat are discussed by John C. Cairns in *AHR* 64 (1959) and *JMH* 46 (1974). R.H.S. Stolfi, *H* (1970), shows that the French were not notably deficient in military equipment, apart from planes. Another survey is B.A. Lee, 'Strategy, arms and the collapse of France', in R. Langhorne, ed., *Diplomacy and Intelligence During the Second World War* (Cambridge, 1985). The adoption of the Maginot Line strategy is studied by J. Hughes, *To the Maginot Line: The Politics of French Military Preparations in the 1920s* (1971). See also A. Kemp, *The Maginot Line: Myth and Reality* (1981). A readable account of the military disaster is A. Horne, *To Lose a Battle: France 1940* (1969). Marc Bloch's impressions of extensive pessimism and defeatism in high military circles are recorded in his posthumously published *L'etrange défaite* (1946). The British attitude to possible French defeat is the theme of P.M.H. Bell, *A Certain Eventuality: Britain and the Fall of France* (1974). On the demise of the regime, see P.C. Bankwitz, *Maxime Weygand and Civil-Military Relations in Modern France* (Cambridge, Mass., 1967) and G. Warner, *Pierre Laval and the Eclipse of France* (1968). F. Pottecher, *Le procès de la défaite. Riom février–avril 1942* (1989) reveals how the political leaders of the Third Republic defended themselves against the accusations of Vichy. In the same vein, see Léon Blum's eloquent *For All Mankind* (1946).

III   1940–1991

In English, there is now M. Larkin, *France Since the Popular Front: Government and People 1936–1986* (Oxford, 1988), and in French the later chapters of Rémond, *Notre siècle*. The relevant volumes of the NHFC series are excellent: Azéma, followed by J.-P. Rioux, *The Fourth Republic 1914–1958* (Cambridge, 1987) and S. Berstein, *La France de l'expansion. I: La République gaullienne 1958–1969* (1989). G. Dupeux, *La France de 1945 à 1965* (1969) cites some useful texts. D.L. Hanley, A.P. Kerr and N.H. Waites, *Contemporary France: Politics and Society Since 1945* (1979 and later edns) is informative on many aspects of French life and has a good bibliography.

13   The Vichy Regime 1940–1944

The best account remains R.O. Paxton, *The Vichy Regime: Old Guard and New Order* (1972), but it should be supplemented by J.F. Sweets, *Choices in Vichy France. The French Under Nazi Occupation* (New York, 1986). Important collective works are *Le Gouvernement de Vichy 1940–42* (1972); H.R. Kedward and R. Austin, eds., *Vichy France and the Resistance: Ideology and Culture* (New York, 1985); and G. Hirschfeld and P. Marsh, eds., *Collaboration in France: Politics and Culture during the Nazi Occupation 1940–1944* (1989). Biographies of Pétain include R. Griffiths, *Marshal Pétain* (1970) and M. Ferro, *Pétain* (1987). On Laval, there is F. Kupferman, *Laval* (1987). H.R. Kedward suggests reasons for the widespread support for the Marshal in 1940 in *TRHS* (1982). See also H. Michel, *Vichy, année 40* (1966). R. Austin considers propaganda and public opinion in the Hérault in *ESR* (1983). Fuller studies of the same subject are P. Laborie's penetrating *L'Opinion française sous Vichy* (1990) and L. Gerverau and D. Peschanski, eds., *La Propagande sous Vichy* (1990). An interesting personal view is P. Jardin, *Vichy Boyhood: An Inside View of the Pétain Regime.* (1975) M.R. Marrus and R.O. Paxton, *Vichy France and the Jews* (New York, 1981) stress the indigenous nature of the regime's anti-Semitism. W.D. Halls, *The Youth of Vichy France* (Oxford, 1981) details the regime's youth policies. A local study of these (in Languedoc) is made by R. Austin in *FHS* 13 (1983). For the position of French Catholics, see J. Duquesne, *Les Catholiques français sous l'Occupation* (1966) and X. de Montclos, M. Luirard, F. Delpech and P. Bolle, *Eglises et Chrétiens dans la IIe guerre mondiale* (Lyon, 1981). Duroselle's *L'Abîme* supersedes all previous work on Vichy's foreign policy. A. Milward, *The New Order and the French Economy* (1970) documents the impressive extent of economic collaboration. The starting point for the study of collaborationism is S. Hoffmans characteristically brilliant essay 'Collaborationism in France during World War II' in his collection of essays *Decline or Renewal? France Since the 1930s* (New York, 1974). It can be followed by B.M. Gordon, *Collaborationism in France During the Second World War* (Ithaca, N.Y., 1980) and P. Ory, *Les collaborateurs 1940–1945* (1976). For the case of Doriot, see J.P. Brunet, *Jacques Doriot: Du communisme au fascisme* (1986) and D. Wolf, *Doriot du communisme à la collaboration* (1969). P. Jankowski, *Communism and Collaboration: Simon Sabiani and Politics in Marseille 1919–1944* (New Haven, 1989) evokes the *doriotiste* milieu in Marseille. Richard Cobb's *French and Germans, Germans and French: A Personal Interpretation of France Under Two Occupations 1914–1918/1940–1944* (Hanover, New England, 1983) is sensitive and thought-provoking. There are many important articles in *RHDGM*, *passim*.

14   Resistance and Liberation

M.R.D. Foot, *Resistance* (1976) provides the European context. There are useful essays on France in S. Hawes and R. White, *Resistance in Europe: 1939–1945* (1976). Easily the best study to date is H.R. Kedward, *Resistance in Vichy France* (Oxford, 1978). H. Michel points to directions that further research might take in *Bibliographie critique de la Resistance* (1964). For an overview, see his *Les courants de pensée de la Résistance* (1962) or the shorter *Histoire de la Résistance en France* (1972). C. de Gaulle, *Mémoires de guerre*, 3 vols. (1954–9) are essential reading, though his true role is better described by J. Lacouture, *De Gaulle*, 3 vols. (1984–6), vol. I *Le Rebelle 1890–1944*. The Free French episode is also covered by M. and J.-P. Cointet, *La France à Londres 1940–43* (Brussels, 1990). Much controversy surrounds the role of the PCF. The fullest study is now S. Courtois, *Le PCF dans la guerre* (1980). See also J.C. Simmonds in *ESR* (1981) and A.J. Rieber, *Stalin and the French Communist Party 1941–1947* (1962). Important additions to the literature on the PCF are J.-P. Azéma, A. Prost and J.-P. Rioux, eds., *Le PCF des années sombres 1939–1941* (1986) and J.-P. Rioux, A. Prost and J.-P. Azéma, eds., *Les communistes français de Munich à Châteaubruant (1938–1941)* (1987). C. Tillon, *On chantait rouge* (1977) are revealing memoirs. M. Sadoun, *Les Socialistes sous l'Occupation* (1982) is best on the SFIO. H. Footitt and J. Simmonds, *The Politics of Liberation: France 1943–1945* (Leicester, 1988) relates the story of the Liberation. The debate over how best to refashion the State is analysed by A. Shennan, *Rethinking France: Plans for Renewal 1940–1946* (Oxford, 1989). A succinct account of the liberation of Paris is H. Michel, *La libération de Paris* (1980). For a much more detailed picture of the Liberation experience as a whole see *La libération de la France* (1976), the proceedings of a colloquium held in 1974, and C.-L. Foulon, *Le pouvoir en province à la Liberation* (1975). P. Novick, *The Resistance versus Vichy: The Purge of Collaborators in Liberated France* (1968) is a good study of the *épuration*, though his figures for the number of executions need to be revised in the light of the calculations of Rioux, *La France* I. Again, see *RHDGM passim*.

15   The Fourth Republic

Easily the best work is that of Rioux, already cited. A recent chronicle by the former *Times* man in Paris is F. Giles, *The Locust Years: the Story of the*

Fourth French Republic 1946–1958 (1991), though a still more racy, if partisan, journalistic account is A. Werth, *France 1940–1955* (1956). G. Elgey,
La République des illusions (1945–1951) (1965) and *La République des contradictions (1951–1954)* (1965) also convey the flavour of the period. V. Auriol,
Journal du septennat, 1947–1954 (7 vols, 1970–1) is a valuable source. So too
are the *Mémoires* (1976) of Jean Monnet. P. Williams, *Crisis and Compromise: Politics in the Fourth Republic* (1964) is the basic reference work. See
also his stimulating collection of essays: *Wars, Plots and Scandals in Post-War
France* (1970) and *French Politicians and Elections 1951–1969* (1970). An
entertaining indictment of the 'gamesmanship' element in the politics of the
Fourth Republic is N. Leites, *On the Game of Politics in France* (Stanford,
1959). The regime's early years are examined by G. Wright, *The Reshaping
of French Democracy* (1950) and B.D. Graham, *The French Socialists and
Tripartism 1944–1947* (1965). A. Lacroix-Riz, *La CGT de la Libération à la
scission de 1944 à 1947* (1983) studies the labour movement and its struggles
in the post-Liberation period. R.E.M. Irving, *Christian Democracy in France*
(1973) looks at the MRP. French communists are compared unfavourably
with their Italian counterparts in D.L.M. Blackmer and S. Tarrow, *Communism in Italy and France* (1975). P. Robrieux, *Histoire intérieure du parti
communiste*, vol. II *1945–1972, de la Libération à l'avènement de Georges
Marchais* (1981) is full of interesting detail, while J.-P. Brunet, *Histoire du
PCF (Que sais-je?)* (1982) is a trenchant survey. In English one can turn to
I. Wall, *French Communism in the Era of Stalin: The Quest For Unity and
Integration 1945–1962* (Westport, Conn., 1983). *Mendésisme* has been studied
in the collection edited by F. Bédarida and J.-P. Rioux, *Pierre Mendès-France
et le mendésisme* (1985). Still worth reading is A. Werth, *The Strange History
of Pierre Mendès-France* (1957), though the best biography is now J. Lacout-
ure, *Pierre Mendès-France* (1981). On the SFIO, see the contributions to B.
Ménager, ed., *Guy Mollet: un camarade en République* (Lille, 1987) and
H.G. Simmons, *French Socialists in Search of a Role 1956–1967* (Ithaca,
1967). S. Hoffmann, *Le Mouvement Poujade* (1956) remains the essential
study of *poujadisme*. For religion and politics, the starting point is now G.
Cholvy and Y.M. Hilaire, *Histoire religieuse de la France contemporaine* (vol.
III *1930–1988*) (Toulouse, 1988), but still worth consulting are the older W.
Bosworth, *Catholicism and Crisis in Modern France: French Catholic Groups
at the Threshold of the Fifth Republic* (1962) and A. Coutrot and F.-G. Dreyfus, *Les forces religieuses dans la société française* (1965). On the role of
intellectuals see A. Chebel d'Appollonia, *Histoire politique des intellectuels
en France (1944–1954)* (2 vols., Brussels, 1991) as well as H.R. Lottman, *The
Left Bank, Writers in Paris* (1982). The Fourth Republic's foreign policy is
outlined by A. Grosser, *La Quatrième République et sa politique extérieure*
(1967). See also J.W. Young, *France, the Cold War and the Western Alliance
1944–1949* (1990) and F.R. Willis, *France, Germany and the New Europe
1945–1963* (Stanford, 1965). On the war in Indo-China, R.E.M. Irving's *The
First Indo-China War* (1975) can be followed with J. Dalloz, *The War in
Indo-China 1945–1954)* (Dublin, 1990). On Algeria, the best study is B. Droz
and E. Lever, *Histoire de la guerre d'Algérie (1954–1962)* (1982), though
Anglophone readers can enjoy A. Horne, *A Savage War of Peace: Algeria
1954–1962* (1977). Attitudes to the war are considered by J. Hamon and P.
Rotman, *Les porteurs de valises. La résistance française à la guerre d'Algérie*

(1979) and J.-P. Rioux, ed., *La guerre d'Algérie et les Français* (1990). The impact of the war on the army is analysed by J.S. Ambler, *The French Army in Politics 1945–1962* (Ohio, 1966) and G. Kelly, *Lost Soldiers: the French Army and Empire in Crisis 1947–62* (Boston, 1965).

16   De Gaulle's Republic

Biographies of de Gaulle abound. Perhaps the best in English is B. Ledwidge, *De Gaulle* (1982), but that of J. Lacouture, already cited, is being translated. C. de Gaulle, *Discours et Messages*, vols. iii–v (1970) are a vital source, as are the General's *Mémoires d'espoir*, vol. i, *Le Renouveau (1958–1962)* (1970) and the unfinished *L'Effort, 1962* (1971). On the advent to power there are O. Rudelle, *Mai 1958, de Gaulle et la République* (1988) and R. Rémond, *Le Retour de de Gaulle* (1985). For an introduction to the regime see P.M. Williams and M. Harrison, *Politics and Society in de Gaulle's Republic* (New York, 1973). Fuller is P. Viansson-Ponté, *Histoire de la République gaullienne 1958–1969* (2 vols., 1970–1). The evolution of the regime is also covered by H. Portelli, *La politique en France sous la Ve République* (1987). V. Wright, *The Government and the Politics of France* (1978 and subsequent editions) analyses presidential power. J. Charlot, *The Gaullist Phenomenon* (1971) is perceptive on the appeal of Gaullism. J. Touchard, *Le gaullisme 1940–1969* (1978) explores its ideological content and evolution. E. Jouve, *Le Général de Gaulle et la construction de l'Europe 1940–1966* (1967) is thorough on de Gaulle's vision of a 'Europe from the Atlantic to the Urals'. P. Cerny, *The Politics of Grandeur: Ideological Aspects of de Gaulle's Foreign Policy* (1980) relates the objectives of foreign policy to those of domestic policy. See also Hoffmann's reflections on Gaullist notions of grandeur in *Decline or Renewal?* G. Pompidou's posthumous memoirs, *Pour rétablir une vérité* (1982) claim that de Gaulle cracked during the May events. J. Massu's version of events can be read in *Baden 68* (1983).

17   Economic and Social Change 1945–1969

An introduction to the economic transformations which took place during the *trente glorieuses* is J.F. Eck, *Histoire de l'économie française depuis 1945* (1988). J.-J. Carré, P. Dubois and E. Malinvaud, *French Economic Growth* (1976) is the basic work of reference. For comparisons, see A. Boltho, ed., *The European Economy: Growth and Crisis* (Oxford, 1982) and S, Lieberman, *The Growth of European Mixed Economies, 1945–1970* (New York, 1977). Also valuable is H.D. Clout, *The Geography of Post-War France: a Social and Economic Approach* (Oxford, 1972). R.F. Kuisel, *Capitalism and the State in Modern France* is also useful on economic planning, as also is J. and A.M. Hackett, *Economic Planning in France* (1965). J. Ardagh, *The New France* (1969 and subsequent edns) is a readable and impressionistic survey. T. Zeldin, *The French* (1983) is erudite and entertaining as well as whimsical. M. Parodi, *L'Economie et la société française de 1945 à 1970* (1971) is more useful than the sketchy G. Vincent, *Les Français 1945–1975: chroniques et structures d'une société* (1977). G. Wright, *Rural Revolution in France* (1964) is good on the 'vanishing peasant', while P. Barral, *Les Agrariens français de Méline à Pisani* (1968) is standard. More personal accounts of agrarian change can be found in L. Wylie, *Village in the Vaucluse* (1957) and E. Grenadou, *Grenadou, paysan français* (1966). Workers are studied by G.

Noiriel, *Les Ouvriers dans la société française, xixe–xxe siècles* (1988) and G. Ross, *Workers and Communists in France: From the Popular Front to Eurocommunism* (Berkeley, 1982). S. Mallet describes the characteristics of *La nouvelle classe ouvrière* (4th edn, 1969). H. Hamon and P. Rotman, *La Deuxième gauche: histoire intellectuelle et politique de la CFDT* (1982) treats an important subject. H. Ehrmann, *Organised Business in France* (1957) studies the *patronat* as a pressure group. On élites more generally, see E. Suleiman, *Elites in French Society: the Politics of Survival* (1978) and J. Howorth and P.G. Cerny, eds., *Elites in France: Origins, Reproduction and Power* (1981). On inequalities, P. Morris, ed., *Equality and Inequalities in France* (Nottingham, 1984) contains valuable essays. See also J. Marceau, *Class and Status in France* (1977). On the position of women, there are insights in M. Grégoire, *Le Métier de femme* (1965) and H. Bouchardeau, *Pas d'histoire les femmes* (1977). The women's liberation movement is the subject of C. Duchen, ed., *French Connections* (1987), an anthology of texts, and *Feminism in France from May '68 to Mitterrand* (1986). Barriers to social change are analysed by M. Crozier, *La société bloquée* (1970). On education, consult W.D. Halls, *Education, Culture and Politics in Modern France* (Oxford, 1976) and for the role of education in the maintenance of class barriers P. Bourdieu and J.-C. Passeron, *Reproduction in Education, Society and Culture* (1977). On the growth of social services, there are W.C. Peterson, *The Welfare State in France* (1960) and W. Friedlander, *Individualism and Social Welfare: an Analysis of the System of Social Security and Social Welfare in France* (East Lansing, 1962). For private life, vol. 5 of the indispensable *Histoire de la vie privée* (1987) has been edited by G. Vincent and A. Prost.

18 May 1968

The May events generated many instant histories. One of the best was P. Seale and M. McConville, *French Revolution 1968* (1968). Others include J. Gretton, *Students and Workers* (1969) and D. Singer, *Prelude to Revolution* (1970). B.E. Brown, *Protest in Paris: The Anatomy of a Revolt* (1974) is a balanced survey. On the PCF line in the crisis, see R. Johnson, *The French Communist Party Versus the Students* (New Haven, 1972). An attempt to understand the significance of the events can be found in the collection of essays edited by C. Posner, *Reflections on the Revolution in France: 1968* (1970). A. Dansette, *Mai 68* (1971) is balanced. Recent assessments, combined with attempts to discover what became of the protagonists and what traces remained after the abortive revolution, include E. Morin, C. Lefort and C. Castoriadis, *Mai 68: la brèche, suivi de vingt ans après* (Brussels, 1988); H. Hamon and P. Moran, *Génération*, vol. I *Les années de rêve* and vol. II *Les années de poudre (1987–8)*; and H. Weber, *Vingt ans après. Que rest-t-il de 68?* (1988).

19 After de Gaulle: The Presidencies of Pompidou and Giscard 1969–1981

There is no biography of Pompidou in English. In French, there is E. Roussel, *Georges Pompidou* (1984). A number of studies throw light on his ideas and policies: S. Rials, *Les Idées politiques de Georges Pompidou* (1977); F. Decaumont, *La Presidence de Georges Pompidou* (1979); and especially the collective FNSP volume *La Présidence de la République de Georges Pompi-*

dou: Exercice du pouvoir et pratique des institutions (1983). Giscard has been studied by J. Frears, *France in the Giscard Presidency* (1981). His political credo has been translated as V. Giscard d'Estaing, *Towards a New Democracy* (1977). His foreign policy is the subject of S. Cohen and M.-C. Smouts, *La Politique extérieure de Valéry Giscard d'Estaing* (1985). On defence issues, see J. Howorth, *France: the Politics of Peace* (1984) and J. Howorth and P. Chilton, eds., *Defence and Dissent in Contemporary France* (1984). The Left has not lacked attention. Valuable guides are R.W. Johnson, *The Long March of the French Left* (1981) and D.S. Bell and B. Criddle, *The French Socialist Party: the Emergence of a Party of Government* (Oxford, 2nd edn, 1988). J. Gaffney, *The French Left in the Fifth Republic* (1989) analyses socialist and communist discourse. The influence of the Ceres faction is assessed by D. Hanley, *Keeping Left: Ceres and the French Socialist Party* (1986). V. Wright, ed., *Continuity and Change in France* (1985) is a valuable collection of essays, particularly good on the reasons for Giscard's defeat in 1981. On this see also T. Judt's analysis in *Marxism and the French Left*. For the themes of expansion and recession, consult H. Mendras, *La Seconde révolution française 1965–1984* (1988) and J. Tuppen, *France Under Recession 1981–1986* (1988). Immigration, perhaps the most important social issue of recent years, has begun to receive considerable scholarly attention. See in particular, O. Milza, *Les Français devant l'immigration* (Brussels, 1988).

20　France under Mitterrand 1981–1991

Commentators on the Mitterrand presidency are legion. Essential biographical data can be obtained from D. MacShane, *François Mitterrand: a Political Odyssey* (1982). Among the many French biographies, one might single out C. Nay, *Les Sept Mitterrand* (1988). Assessments of the socialist experiment include G. Ross, S. Hoffmann and S. Malzacher, eds., *The Mitterrand Experiment* (Oxford, 1987); S. Mazey and M. Newman, eds., *Mitterrand's France* (1987); and P. Cerny and M. Schain, eds., *Socialism, the State and Public Policy in France* (1983). The most recent French verdict is in P. Favier and M. Martin-Rolland, *La Décennie Mitterrand. i: Les Ruptures (1981–1984)* (1990). Disillusionment is evident in D. Singer, *Is Socialism Doomed? The Meaning of Mitterrand* (Oxford, 1988) and T. Pfister, *Lettre ouverte à la génération Mitterrand qui marche à côte de ses pompes* (1988). H. Penniman, ed., *France at the Polls, 1981 and 1986: Three National Elections* (1988) is good on the changing electoral fortunes of the PS. The politics and Parisian power base of Chirac can be appreciated in F.P. Giesbert, *Jacques Chirac* (1987); H. Liffran, *Les Paris de Chirac* (1988); and M. Ambroise-Rendu, *Paris–Chirac* (1987). On Le Pen, consult E. Plenel and A. Rollat, *L'Effet Le Pen* (1984) and N. Mayer and P. Perrinau, *Le Front National à découvert* (1983). The most recent events are best followed in *Modern and Contemporary France*, but valuable also are P. Hall *et al.*, *Developments in French Politics* (1989) and A. Cole, ed., *French Political Parties in Transition* (Dartmouth, 1990). Rocard's style is analysed by H. Hamon and P. Rotman, *L'Effet Rocard* (1980), while there is a biography by R. Schneider, *Michel Rocard* (1987). R. Aldrich and J. Connell, *France in World Politics* (1989) cover foreign policy.

Index